Authors & Artists for Young Adults

ISSN 1040-5682

Authors & Artists for Young Adults

VOLUME 2

**Agnes Garrett and Helga P. McCue,
Editors**

Gale Research Inc. • Book Tower • Detroit, Michigan 48226

Managing Editor: Anne Commire

Editors: Agnes Garrett, Helga P. McCue

Senior Assistant Editor: Dianne H. Anderson

Assistant Editors: Elisa Ann Ferraro,
Eunice L. Petrini, Linda Shedd

Sketchwriters: Catherine Coray, Catherine Courtney,
Johanna Cypis, Marguerite Feitlowitz, Deborah Klezmer,
Dieter Miller, Beatrice Smedley, Karen Walker

Researcher: Catherine Ruello

Permissions Assistant: Susan Pfanner

Production Manager: Mary Beth Trimper
External Production Assistant: Dorothy Maki

Art Director: Arthur Chartow
Graphic Designer: Cynthia D. Baldwin

Internal Production Supervisor: Laura Bryant
Internal Production Associate: Louise Gagné
Internal Production Assistants: Shelly Andrews, Sharana Wier

Library of Congress Catalog Card Number
ISBN 0-8103-5051-3
ISSN 1040-5682

Printed in the United States of America

Contents

Introduction vii

Acknowledgments xi

John Carpenter 1

Bret Easton Ellis......................17

E. M. Forster 25

Cathy Guisewite..................... 43

Virginia Hamilton..................... 53

S. E. Hinton.............................65

Chuck Jones 77

June Jordan.......................... 95

Garrison Keillor........................ 109

M. E. Kerr 123

Norma Klein.......................... 139

Milan Kundera..................... 151

Gary Paulsen....................... 165

Marilyn Sachs 175

Carl Sagan 187

J. D. Salinger 201

Todd Strasser..................... 211

Theodore Taylor............... 223

Barbara Wersba 235

Paul Zindel 245

Author/Artist Index.......................265

Introduction

"[Today's youth] is a generation whose grade-school years were informed and enlivened by Betsy Byars, who teaches the basic lesson to the next generation of book buyers: that a novel must entertain first before it can do anything else. But I don't get these readers until they hit puberty. They haven't even budded, and already the Blume is off. I don't get them till puberty, and it's the darkest moment of life. For while puberty is the death of childhood, it isn't the birth of reason.

"Puberty is the same gulag we all once did time in, robbed of the certainties of grade school and still years away from a driver's license. Puberty is waking up every morning wondering which sex you are, if any. Puberty is the practice of strict sexual segregation with all the girls on one side of an invisible line and all the boys on the other: big women, little men. Like a Shaker meeting but without the hope of eternal life. Puberty is no fun, and changing the name of the junior high to the middle school has fooled nobody. In America puberty is deciding at the age of twelve or so to divorce your own parents, charging irreconcilable differences. The children of the underclass hit the streets then and are thereafter out of reach of home and school and books. The children of the middle class recede to their rooms and lock themselves into elaborate sound systems, paid for by parents, that eliminate the possibility of a parental voice. They are free of us at twelve.

"I write for these people whose own parents haven't seen them for days. In our impotence we've reasoned that children must be given freedoms in order to learn how to handle them. But it doesn't work that way. The prematurely emancipated young transfer all their need for a dominating, problem-solving authority from weak adults at home and school to the peer group. The only government they recognize is the vengeful law-giving of each other.

"That's what I write: counterculture literature of individuality to a conformist readership. I write books for the knapsacks of young soldiers of both sexes going forth every school day hoping to survive the 'Chocolate War.' I write for the inmates of schools where you cannot win a letter sweater for literacy. You can win a letter sweater only for mindless conformity, for listening to language from the coach that would get the librarian into big trouble. I write for a generation of young people who don't have to drop by the library, even on the way to the Gifted Program. They don't have to drop by anywhere except, perhaps, the shopping mall."

—Richard Peck

"The time of adolescence is in itself a wonderful age to write about. It combines an idealism and honesty and a wily sophistication that no other time of life enjoys. The teenager has vitality and enjoys life although he sees the ugliness and absurdities as well as the joys.

"Adolescents are also engaged in some of the most important 'work' they will ever do. It is the time when one establishes one's identity and comes of age in a number of critical areas—social, political, cultural, sexual. Conflict prevails during these years with one's parents, teachers, peers and, most painfully, with oneself."

—Hila Colman

Authors and Artists for Young Adults is a new reference series designed to bridge the gap between Gale's *Something about the Author*, designed for children, and *Contemporary Authors*, intended for adults. This new series is aimed entirely at the needs and interests of the often overlooked young adults. We share the concerns of librarians who must send young readers to the adult reference shelves for which they may not be ready. *Authors and Artists for Young Adults* will give high school and junior high school students information about the life and work of their favorite creative artists—the people behind the books, movies, television programs, plays, lyrics, cartoon and animated features that they most enjoy. Although most of these will be present-day artists, the series is open to people of all time periods and all countries whose work has a special appeal to young adults today. Some of these artists may also be profiled in *Something about the Author* or *Contemporary Authors*, but their entries in *Authors and Artists for Young Adults* are completely updated and tailored to the information needs of the young adult user.

Entry Format

Authors and Artists for Young Adults will be published in two volumes each year. Each volume in the series will furnish in-depth coverage of about twenty authors and artists. The typical entry consists of:

—A personal section that includes date and place of birth, marriage, children, and education.

—A comprehensive bibliography or film-ography including publishers, producers, and years.

—Adaptations into other media forms.

—Works in progress.

—A distinctive sidelights section where secondary sources and exclusive interviews concentrate on an artist's craft, artistic intentions, career, world views, thematic discussions, and controversies.

—A "For More Information See" section arranged in chronological order to increase the scope of this reference work.

While the textual information in *Authors and Artists for Young Adults* is its primary reason for existing, entries are complemented by illustrations, photographs, movie stills, manuscript samples, dust jackets, book covers, and other relevant visual material.

A cumulative Author/Artist Index appears at the back of this volume.

Highlights of This Volume

A sampling of the variety of creative artists featured in this volume includes:

E. M. FORSTER . . . . . . British author who wrote when he finished his novel, *A Passage to India*: "I feel—or shall feel when the typing's over—great relief. I am so weary, not of working but of not working; of thinking the book bad and so not working, and of not working and so thinking it bad: that vicious circle. Now it is done and I think it good."

GARRISON KEILLOR . . . . . . American radio announcer, producer and author, defines writing as: "Very small parts pieced together into a whole, and if the parts are defective, the whole won't work. But that's a mechanical view. What really comes first is feeling and passion and curiosity. If the writer is true to personal experience, the reader is offered something recognizable. It's only as you are faithful to the peculiarities and the exact description of personal experience that you create something that other people will be able to take as their own."

GARY PAULSEN . . . . . . Prolific writer of young adult and adult fiction, as well as nonfiction stories on hunting, trapping, farming, animals, medicine and outdoor life, admits that: "I write because it's all I can do. Every time I've tried to do something else I cannot, and have to come back to writing, though often I hate it—hate it and love it. It's very much like being a slave, I suppose, and in slavery there is a kind of freedom that I find in writing: a perverse thing. I'm not 'motivated.' Nor am I particularly driven. I write because it's all there is."

J. D. SALINGER . . . . . . Author of the classic novel about adolescence, *The Catcher in the Rye*, describes the life of a writer as: "A hard life. But it's brought me enough happiness that I don't think I'd ever deliberately dissuade anybody (if he had talent) from taking it up. The compensations are few, but when they come, if they come, they're very beautiful."

PAUL ZINDEL . . . . . . American screenwriter, playwright, and novelist for young adults and children, believes that: "Teenagers have to rebel. It's part of the growing process. In effect, I try to show them they aren't alone in condemning parents and teachers as enemies or ciphers. I believe I must convince my readers that I am on their side; I know it's a continuing battle to get through the years between twelve and twenty—an abrasive time. And I write always from their point of view."

Forthcoming Volumes

Among the artists planned for future volumes are:

Arnold Adoff	Jim Davis	David Mamet
V. C. Andrews	Annie Dillard	Gary Marshall
Maya Angelou	Bob Dylan	Norma Fox Mazer
Jean Auel	Loren Eiseley	Robin McKinley
Avi	William Faulkner	Joan Lowry Nixon
Richard Bach	Jules Feiffer	Gene Roddenberry
James Baldwin	Bette Greene	Ntozake Shange
Toni Cade Bambara	Judith Guest	Stephen Sondheim
Judy Blume	Ann Head	Steven Spielberg
John Boorman	Hermann Hesse	Mary Stolz
Bianca Bradbury	Marjorie Holmes	Mildred D. Taylor
Robin Brancato	John Hughes	Julian Thompson
Sue Ellen Bridgers	Victor Hugo	J. R. R. Tolkien
Edgar Rice Burroughs	Bel Kaufman	Garry Trudeau
Agatha Christie	E. L. Konigsburg	Cynthia Voigt
Arthur Clarke	C. S. Lewis	Alice Walker
Robert Cormier	Barry Lopez	
Paula Danziger	Arnost Lustig	

The editors of *Authors and Artists for Young Adults* welcome any suggestions for additional biographees to be included in this series. Please write and give us your opinions and suggestions for making our series more helpful to you.

Acknowledgments

Grateful acknowledgment is made to the following
publishers, authors, and artists for their kind permission to reproduce copyrighted material.

ATHENEUM PUBLISHERS. Jacket illustration by Jerry Pinkney from *The Country of the Heart* by Barbara Wersba. Copyright © 1975 by Barbara Wersba./ Sidelight excerpts from the introduction to *Happy to Be Here* by Garrison Keillor. Copyright © 1982 by Garrison Keillor. Both reprinted by permission of Atheneum Publishers, an imprint of Macmillan Publishing Co.

AVON BOOKS. Illustration from *The Maldonado Miracle* by Theodore Taylor. Copyright © 1962 by McCall Corp. Copyright © 1973 by Theodore Taylor./ Cover illustration from *Mom, the Wolfman and Me* by Norma Klein. Copyright © 1972 by Norma Klein. Both reprinted by permission of Avon Books.

BALLANTINE/DEL REY/FAWCETT BOOKS. Cover illustration from *Older Men* by Norma Klein. Copyright © 1987 by Norma Klein./ Cover illustration from *Give and Take* by Norma Klein. Copyright © 1985 by Norma Klein. Both reprinted by permission of Ballantine/Del Rey/Fawcett Books.

BANTAM BOOKS. Cover illustration by John Thompson from *My Darling, My Hamburger* by Paul Zindel. Copyright © 1969 by Paul Zindel. Cover illustration copyright © 1984 by John Thompson. Reprinted by permission of Bantam Books.

BRADBURY PRESS. Jacket illustration by Jon Weiman from *Tracker* by Gary Paulsen. Copyright © 1984 by Gary Paulsen./ Jacket illustration by Neil Waldman from *Hatchet* by Gary Paulsen. Copyright © 1987 by Gary Paulsen and Bradbury Press./ Jacket illustration by Jon Weiman from *Dancing Carl* by Gary Paulsen. Text copyright © 1983 by Gary Paulsen. Jacket illustration copyright © 1983 by Bradbury Press. All reprinted by permission of Bradbury Press, an affiliate of Macmillan, Inc.

COWARD, McCANN & GEOGHEGAN, INC. Jacket illustration by Judy Clifford from *Angel Dust Blues* by Todd Strasser. Copyright © 1979 by Todd Strasser. Reprinted by permission of Coward, McCann & Geoghegan, Inc.

T. Y. CROWELL, INC. Jacket photo by June Jordan from *His Own Where* by June Jordan. Copyright © 1971 by June Jordan. Reprinted by permission of T. Y. Crowell, Inc., a subsidiary of Harper & Row, Publishers, Inc.

DELACORTE PRESS. Jacket illustration by Darrell Sweet from *Walking Up a Rainbow* by Theodore Taylor. Text copyright © 1986 by Theodore Taylor. Jacket illustration copyright © 1986 by Darrell Sweet./ Jacket illustration from *Friends Till the End* by Todd Strasser. Copyright © 1981 by Todd Strasser./ Jacket illustration by Charles Tang from *The Accident* by Todd Strasser. Text copyright © 1988 by Todd Strasser. Jacket illustration copyright © 1988 by Charles Tang. All reprinted by permission of Delacorte Press.

DELL PUBLISHING CO. Illustration from *A Very Touchy Subject* by Todd Strasser. Copyright © 1985 by Todd Strasser./ Cover illustration from *If I Love You, Am I Trapped Forever?* by M. E. Kerr. Copyright © 1973 by M. E. Kerr. Both reprinted by permission of Dell Publishing Co.

DIAL BOOKS FOR YOUNG READERS. Jacket illustration by Ed Martinez from *Family Secrets* by Norma Klein. Text copyright © 1985 by Norma Klein. Jacket illustration copyright © 1985 by Ed Martinez. Reprinted by permission of Dial Books for Young Readers.

DOUBLEDAY & CO. Jacket illustration by Milton Glaser from *The Cay* by Theodore Taylor. Copyright © 1969 by Theodore Taylor./ Jacket illustration by Richard Cuffari from *Teetoncey* by Theodore Taylor. Text copyright © 1974 by Theodore Taylor. Jacket illustration copyright © 1974 by Richard Cuffari./ Jacket illustration by Richard Cuffari from *The Odyssey of Ben O'Neal* by Theodore Taylor. Copyright © 1977 by Theodore Taylor./ Jacket illustration by Louis Glanzman from *Marv* by Marilyn Sachs. Copyright © 1970 by Marilyn Sachs. All reprinted by permission of Doubleday & Co.

E. P. DUTTON. Jacket illustration by Jim Spence from *Fourteen* by Marilyn Sachs. Copyright © 1983 by Marilyn Sachs./ Jacket illustration by Jim Spence from *Thunderbird* by Marilyn Sachs. Text copyright © 1985 by Marilyn Sachs. Jacket illustration copyright © 1985 by Jim Spence. Both reprinted by permission of E. P. Dutton.

GALLIMARD. Sidelight excerpts from the translation of *L'Art du roman* by Milan Kundera. Reprinted by permission of Gallimard.

GROVE PRESS INC. Jacket illustration by Milan Kundera from *The Art of the Novel* by Milan Kundera. Translated from the French by Linda Asher. Copyright © 1986 by Milan Kundera. English translation copyright © 1988 by Grove Press, Inc./

Guisewite. Copyright © 1984 by Universal Press Syndicate./ Illustration by Cathy Guisewite from *May I Borrow Your Husband and Baby?* by Cathy Guisewite. Copyright © 1987 by Universal Press Syndicate./ Illustrations by Cathy Guisewite from *Two Pies. One Fork* by Cathy Guisewite. Copyright © 1985 by Universal Press Syndicate. All reprinted with permission. All rights reserved.

VIKING PENGUIN, INC. Jacket illustration by Michael Tedesco from *The Outsiders* by S. E. Hinton. Copyright © 1967 by S. E. Hinton. Copyright © 1988 by Viking Penguin, Inc./ Jacket illustration by Peter Thorpe from *Leaving Home* by Garrison Keillor. Copyright © 1987 by Garrison Keillor./ Sidelight excerpts from the introduction to *Leaving Home.* Copyright © 1987 by Garrison Keillor. All reprinted by permission of Viking Penguin, Inc.

Sidelight excerpts from an article "Carpenter Builds Directing Dynasty on Past Successes," by Scott Cain, July 13, 1986 in *Atlanta Journal and Constitution.* Reprinted by permission of *Atlanta Journal and Constitution./* Cover photo by Sara Miles from *Passion: New Poems, 1977-1980* by June Jordan. Published by Beacon Press./ Sidelight excerpts from an article " 'Little China' Kicks Out Gloom," by Lloyd Sachs, July 6, 1986 in *Chicago Sun-Times.* Reprinted by permission of *Chicago Sun-Times./* Sidelight excerpts from an article "A Conversation with Virginia Hamilton," winter, 1983 in *Children's Literature in Education.* Copyright © 1983 by Agathon Press, Inc. Reprinted by permission of *Children's Literature in Education./* Sidelight excerpts from an article "In Praise of Teenage Outcasts," by Carol Wallace, September 26, 1982 in *Daily News.* Copyright © 1982 by New York News, Inc. Reprinted by permission of *Daily News./* Cover portrait of S. E. Hinton by Curt Doty in *School Library Journal,* June/July, 1988. Reprinted by permission of Curt Doty./ Illustration by James McMullan in *Esquire,* 1981. Reprinted by permission of *Esquire./* Sidelight excerpts from an article "Landis, Cronenberg, Carpenter: Fear on Film Continues!" by Mick Garris, July, 1982 in *Fangoria,* number 20. Reprinted by permission of *Fangoria./* Sidelight excerpts from an article "From Cult Homage to Creative Control," by Ralph Applebaum, June, 1979 in *Films & Filming.* Reprinted by permission of *Films & Filming./* Sidelight excerpts from *Civil Wars* by June Jordan. Reprinted by permission of June Jordan.

Sidelight excerpts from *On Call: Political Essays* by June Jordan. Reprinted by permission of June Jordan./ Sidelight excerpts from an article "Garrison Keillor: Beyond Lake Wobegon," National Public Radio, 1987. Reprinted by permission of Garrison Keillor./ Sidelight excerpts from the translation by Alain Finkielkraut of "Kundera: l'exode de la culture," June 21, 1980 in *L'Express.* Reprinted by permission of *L'Express./* Sidelight excerpts from the translation by Michel Contat of "Milan Kundera, La Musique e'est finiaujourd'hui," October, 1980 in *Le Monde de la musique.* Reprinted by permission of *Le Monde de la musique./* Sidelight excerpts from the translation by Yannick Pelletier of "Un passe a visage humain, entretien auec Milan Kundera," April 26, 1979 in *Les Nouvelles Litteraires.* Reprinted by permission of *Les Nouvelles Litteraires./* Sidelight excerpts from the translation by Christian Salmon of "Milan Kundera et la piege du paradoxe terminal," December 5-6, 1981 in *Liberation.* Reprinted by permission of *Liberation./* Sidelight excerpts from an article "The Search for the Mysterious J. D. Salinger," by Ernest Haveman in *Life,* November, 1969. Reprinted by permission of *Life./* Sidelight excerpts from an article "Trick or Treat," by Todd McCarthy, January/February, 1980 in *Film Comment.* Copyright © by Todd McCarthy. Reprinted by permission of Todd McCarthy.

Sidelight excerpts from an article "Interview: Budget-Conscious Director, John Carpenter," by Richard Meyers, April, 1980 in *Millimeter.* Reprinted by permission of *Millimeter./* Sidelight excerpts from an article "The Plowboy Interview," by Peter Hemingston, May/June, 1985 in *Mother Earth News.* Reprinted by permission of *Mother Earth News./* Jacket illustration by Richard Cuffari from *The Foxman* by Gary Paulsen. Copyright © 1977 by Gary Paulsen. Published by Thomas Nelson, Inc./ Sidelight excerpts from an article "Teen Agers Are for Real," by Susan Hinton, August 27, 1967 in *New York Times Book Review.* Copyright © 1967 by The New York Times Co. Reprinted by permission of The New York Times Co./ Sidelight excerpts from an article "Directors Join the S. E. Hinton Fan Club," by Stephen Farber, March 20, 1983 in *New York Times.* Copyright © 1983 by The New York Times Co. Reprinted by permission of The New York Times Co./ Sidelight excerpts from an article "Growing Up with Science Fiction," by Carl Sagan, May 28, 1978 in *New York Times Magazine.* Reprinted by permission of The New York Times Co./ Sidelight excerpts from an article "Carl Sagan: Oliged to Explain," by Boyce Rensberger, May 29, 1977 in *New York Times Book Review.* Reprinted by permission of The New York Times Co./ Sidelight excerpts from an article "Profiles: People Start Running," by James Stevenson, January 28, 1980 in *New Yorker.* Reprinted by permission of *New Yorker./* Sidelight excerpts from an article "The Art of Fiction," by Milan Kundera, summer, 1984 in *Paris Review.* Reprinted by permission of *Paris Review./* Sidelight excerpts from an article "PW Interviews: Garrison Keillor," by Diane Roback in *Publishers Weekly.* Reprinted by permission of *Publishers Weekly./* Sidelight excerpts from an article "June Jordan," by Pamela Bragg, February 21, 1972 in *Publishers Weekly.* Copyright © 1972 by Xerox Corp. Reprinted by permission of *Publishers Weekly.*

Sidelight excerpts from an article "The Cosmos," by Jonathan Cott, December 25, 1980 in *Rolling Stone.* Copyright © 1980 by Straight Arrow Publisher, Inc. Reprinted by permission of *Rolling Stone./* Sidelight excerpts from an article "Down and Out," by Bret Easton Ellis, September 26, 1985 in *Rolling Stone.* Reprinted by permission of *Rolling Stone./* Sidelight excerpts from an article "Cathy and 'Cathy': A Lot in Common," by Judy J. Newark in *St. Louis Post-Dispatch,* September 5, 1982. Copyright © 1982 by *St. Louis Post-Dispatch.* Reprinted by permission of *St. Louis Post-Dispatch./* Sidelight excerpts from an article "Face to Face with a Teenage Novelist," October, 1967 in *Seventeen.* Reprinted by permission of *Seventeen./* Sidelight excerpts from an article "How Cartoonist Cathy Guisewite Makes Us Laugh at Life's Little Frustrations," by Cork Miller in *Seventeen,* May, 1983. Reprinted by permission of *Seventeen./* Sidelight excerpts from *Selected Letter of E. M. Forster,* Volumes I and II, edited by Mary Largo and P. N. Furbank. Reprinted by permission of Society of Authors./ Sidelight excerpts from an article "High Adventure in the Future," by Steve Swires, December, 1980 in *Starlog.* Reprinted by permission of *Starlog./* Sidelight excerpts from the translation of "Kruta heros positif!," by Milan Kundera, April, 1974 in *Supplement a tepactualite.* Reprinted by permission of *Supplement a tepactualite./* Illustration by Albert Handell from *Who Look at Me* by June Jordan. Courtesy of Syracuse University Art Collection. Reprinted by permission of Syracuse University Art Collection.

Sidelight excerpts from an article "Lonesome Whistle Blowing," by John Skow, November 4, 1985 in *Time.* Copyright © 1985 by Time, Inc. Reprinted by permission of Time, Inc./ Illustration of "Horror Boys": Leatherface, Freddy, Jason, and Michael Myers in *People Weekly*, November 7, 1988. Mark Sennet/People Weekly/© 1988 by Time, Inc. Reprinted by permission of Time, Inc./ Sidelight excerpts from an article "To the Editor: Top of the News," by Theodore Taylor in *Top of the News*, April, 1975. Reprinted by permission of *Top of the News.*/ Jacket photo by UPI from *Dry Victories* by June Jordan. Text copyright © 1972 by June Jordan. Reprinted by permission of UPI/Bettmann Newsphotos./ Sidelight excerpts from an article "Beyond Viking: Where Missions to Mars Could Lead," August 30, 1976 in *U.S. News & World Report.* Copyright © 1976 by *U.S. News & World Report.* Reprinted by permission of *U.S. News & World Report.*/ Sidelight excerpts from an article "In Defense of Intimacy, Milan Kundera's Private Lives," by Philip Roth, June 26, 1984 in *Village Voice.* Reprinted by permission of *Village Voice.*

Appreciation also to the Performing Arts Research Center of the New York Public Library at Lincoln Center for permission to reprint the theater stills from "The Secret Affairs of Mildred Wild," "Ladies at the Alamo," "And Miss Reardon Drinks a Little," and "The Effect of Gamma Rays on Man-in-the-Moon Marigolds."

Photo Credits

John Carpenter: John Shannon; Brett Easton Ellis: Ian Gittler; Virginia Hamilton: Cox Studios; S. E. Hinton: David Inhofe; Chuck Jones: Copyright © 1983 by Karsh/Ottawa; June Jordan: © 1982 by Nancy Crampton; Garrison Keillor: Rob Levine, (at Radio City Music Hall) Henry Grossman, (at the lake) Kevin Horna/*People Weekly*/© 1987 by Time, Inc.; Norma Klein: Thomas Victor; Milan Kundera: Aaron Manheimer, 1987; Marijane Meaker: Zoe Kamitses; Gary Palsen: Tom Norgel, (numbered-up) *The Duluth (Minn.) News Tribune and Herald*; Marilyn Sachs: Morris Sachs; Carl Sagan (with wife): John Crispin/NYT Pictures; J. D. Salinger: Maurey Garber; Theodore Taylor: John Graves; Barbara Wersba: Charles Caron; Paul Zindel: Deforest.

Authors & Artists for Young Adults

John Carpenter

Born January 16, 1948, in Carthage, N.Y.; son of Howard Ralph (a musician) and Milton Jean (a housewife; maiden name, Carter) Carpenter; married Adrienne Barbeau (an actress), January 1, 1979 (divorced); children: John Cody. *Education:* University of Southern California, 1968-72; attended Western Kentucky University, 1966-68. *Agent:* Jim Wyatt, ICM 8899 Beverly Blvd., Los Angeles, Calif. 90048. *Office:* c/o Jim Jennings, Levy & Co., 8383 Wilshire Blvd.; Suite 840, Beverly Hills, Calif. 90212.

■ Career

Director, screenwriter, composer. Began making short films in 1962; published *Fantastic Films Illustrated* (magazine), 1965; with Tommy Wallace, formed the band "The Coupe de Villes," in the mid-seventies. *Member:* Directors Guild of America West, Writers Guild of America West. *Awards, honors:* Academy Award from the Academy of Motion Picture Arts and Sciences for "Best Live-action Short," 1970, for "The Resurrection of Bronco Billy."

■ Writings

Screenplays:

(With Dan O'Bannon; and director) "Dark Star," Jack H. Harris, 1974.
(With Debra Hill; and director) "Halloween," Falcon/Compass, 1978.
(With David Zelag Goodman) "The Eyes of Laura Mars," Columbia, 1978.
(With D. Hill; and director and composer) "The Fog," Avco-Embassy, 1979.
(With Nick Castle; and director and co-producer) "Escape from New York," Avco-Embassy, 1981.
(And co-producer) "Halloween II," Universal, 1981.
(With Desmond Nakano and William Gray) "Black Moon Rising," New World, 1986.

Editor and Composer:

"The Resurrection of Bronco Billy," John Longenecker, 1970.

Director:

"Assault on Precinct 13," Turtle Releasing, 1976.
"Someone's Watching Me" (television movie), Warner Bros./NBC, 1978.
"Halloween," Compass International, 1978.
"Elvis" (television movie), ABC-TV, 1979.
"The Fog," Avco-Embassy, 1980.
"Escape from New York, Avco-Embassy, 1981.
"The Thing," Universal, 1982.
"Christine," Columbia, 1983.
"Starman," Columbia, 1984.

"Big Trouble in Little China," 20th Century-
   Fox, 1986.
"Prince of Darkness," Universal, 1987.
"They Live," Universal, 1988.

Co-producer:

"Halloween II," Universal, 1981.
"Halloween III," Universal, 1983.

■ Sidelights

January 16, 1948. "I was raised in Bowling Green,
Kentucky. My father taught music history and
theory at Western Kentucky University there. We
lived in a log cabin on the grounds of the university
museum. The cabin was rented out to faculty
members for fifty dollars a month. It had a rail
fence, a garden, a man-made pond; there was a
creek, an open field, and woods. The university
had planted samples of every kind of tree, bush,
and flower that grew in Kentucky. I was an only
child, somewhat lonely, and I grew up in the wilds
of this extremely secluded, extremely beautiful
fantasy land.

"My father is a violinist, and I heard classical music
constantly—wall-to-wall string quartets. I learned
violin, piano, and guitar. My mother worked in a
bookstore. My parents were very encouraging
about creative endeavors. We had no TV until I
was twelve, and there were always a lot of books
and paper and pens around—even a typewriter I
could use. I remember once my father gave me a
blank sheet of music paper, and I sat down and
filled it in with little notes. Then he played it on
the piano. It was really atonal! Their attitude was
always 'Try your hand.'

"The first movie they ever took me to was 'The
African Queen,' and what I remember most is
Humphrey Bogart coming out of the water covered
with leeches. But my monumental experience with
films was in 1953, when I was five. My parents
took me to 'It Came from Outer Space,' in 3-D.
You had to wear special glasses. The first shot was
of this meteor—it came right off the screen and
exploded in my face. I couldn't believe it! It was
everything I'd ever wanted! After that, I was
addicted to films. I made movies in my head. The
cabin and the museum grounds became my movie
set, my back lot. I made up little stories.

"When I was eight, my dad gave me an 8-mm.
movie camera—a Eumig, with stop motion, so you
could shoot one frame at a time for 'animation.' It
was a terrific camera. I still have it....I got my
friends from school together, and we made a movie

called 'Gorgon the Space Monster.' It had a lot of
special effects—toy tanks running in animation,
things like that—and I put classical music (the
'1812 Overture' and 'Night on Bald Mountain') on
a tape, along with me doing different voices, for a
soundtrack. I remember a moment during the
shooting when I suddenly understood the process
of editing. I was shooting two actions at once: a
friend would run up, stop, and react to something;
then I'd turn around and shoot what he was
watching. I was editing in the camera. But suddenly I realized I could shoot the first kid all at once
and then, another day, shoot what he was reacting
to, and then I could splice them together. It was
like a thunderbolt! I remember thinking, How
clever!

"In another scene, I had a friend running down a
railroad track, and I ran after him with the camera.
The scene was very jerky, and my father said, 'You
should use a tripod.' But I said it looked exciting. A
titling kit came with the camera: you stuck little
letters on a board and shot the titles. When any of
my friends came over, they'd have to sit down and
watch 'Gorgon.' I kept telling my parents that I was
going to go to Hollywood and be a film director.
My friends quickly got tired of making movies, so I
did them myself in a vacuum. I felt I was quite a bit
the outsider, a little weird. I was pretty single-
minded. As a matter of fact, my movies now are
pretty single-minded movies. I'm a little obsessive.

"Bowling Green was very Southern—a small farm
town in the Bible Belt, truly Middle America and
nonsophisticated. I had an image of myself as a
lonely, isolated person—not ostracized but a loner.
In 1964, when the Beatles came along, I grew long
hair. It was risky, and I got a lot of flak. Still, it
fitted right in; maybe I was perpetuating my own
isolation, even though I was always lamenting that
I had no friends who were interested in movies.
But by the time I was in high school I'd lost touch
with making movies. I'd got interested in girls. I
would borrow my father's Cutlass and take a girl
driving up and down the bypass, or go to the Lost
River Drive-In (they showed second-run movies)
and neck, then stop at the Dairy Dip or Jerry's. The
big thing in those days was drinking beer. I thought
it tasted *so* bad, but I did it. Suddenly, one day, my
high school class voted me president. I wondered
why for days. It was an indication that I was
misjudging myself, and I realized I must be reaching out to people in some way—I must have
wanted their acceptance, and to be loved by
them."[1]

From the movie "Big Trouble in Little China," starring Kurt Russell. Copyright © 1986 by Twentieth Century-Fox Film Corp.

1968. Completed undergraduate studies at Western Kentucky University. "In my senior year, I did a little acting. We did 'Queens of France,' by Thornton Wilder. My technique was totally mechanical—nothing to do with real emotion—but I began to know what actors were going through. I started getting interested in making films again, and I started researching film schools. The best seemed to be U.S.C. [University of Southern California], and I told my father I'd like to go there. He didn't say too much. He probably thought I was making a silly move, but he supported me. I wish I could describe the naive kid who got off the plane in L.A. I had two suitcases and a map. U.S.C. didn't look that far; I thought I could walk it. An hour later, I'd only moved a fraction of an inch on the map. U.S.C. was fifteen miles away."[1]

"U.S.C. was invaluable, but not in the traditional college experience where you go and train for a job and then you move into a job, because that's not how it is in film. I learned the technical aspects of film, and got to work in every area of directing—editing, camera, sound. And every day in the screening room they were showing movies. All we did was watch movies. I watched movies for four years. I saw retrospectives on every big director. I saw the directors come down. I saw a John Ford retrospective, and I'll never forget it because we started with his silent film and went all the way up to his last movie. You got to see the work of a man. I saw Howard Hawks's work, I saw Orson Welles's work. I saw Orson Welles in person. I saw John Ford in person. And these are cinematic giants. I saw Roman Polanski, and there's nothing like it. It was very exciting. It was also very unrealistic in terms of what movies were like. But that wasn't important then."[2]

"...I remember there came this big moment of truth. They encourage socially-conscious films and they wanted them to be personal, and I finally said, 'What I care about is escapist entertainment. Those are the kind of movies I grew up on and I want to do for audiences the things those movies did for me.'"[3]

1970. Carpenter assisted director Jim Rokos, co-wrote the screenplay, wrote the music and edited "The Resurrection of Bronco Bill." The film won an Academy Award for "Best Live-Action Short Subject."

1974. Carpenter's first feature, "Dark Star," was released. The film is a black satire on spacemen and science-fiction films. The primary plot involves the crew of an interstellar space ship on a mission to destroy stars about to become super-novas. "...It began on the sound stage at U.S.C. and ended on a sound stage in Hollywood four years later."[1]

"I teamed up with Dan O'Bannon, who's a schoolmate of mine and we basically made 'Dark Star' ourselves. Building sets and putting it all together. It took a lot of hard work and a lot of love. We raised money as we went along, and we finally teamed up with Jack Harris, who provided the finishing money to make it into a feature. We had shot a feature on 16mm and we didn't have enough money to finish it, so he helped us out. And basically it was the will to do it, no more than that. And I think both Dan and I were young and naive enough not to realize that we were attempting the impossible."[2]

"'Dark Star'...was not successful. It was a weird little science-fiction movie, with a lot of imagination and energy but a cardboard spaceship. I wanted it to be slick and professional, with suspense and a sense of humor; it was youthful, naive, and innocent. It was exactly what I was—it reflected my cares and concerns. People said, 'What is this?' It was a tremendous disappointment, and a kind of hinge in my life: from 'Dark Star' on is a saga of getting into the film industry. I've blocked out a lot of the details, because it was so painful. I had so much faith in what I had done. Now I know the truth. I didn't listen to people; I didn't believe them.

"For a year and a half, I was so depressed. I got an agent, but nothing happened. When you're looking for work, your agent will tell you to 'take a meeting and pitch an idea.' I went to a lot of meetings, and it was like being on Mars. The fringes of Hollywood: hustlers who had a project but no money; gamblers. It was puzzling and frightening. They'd be very hostile. 'Why are you here?' they'd say, 'I'd like to make a movie with you,' but the undercurrent was 'You'll never make it, because you're not good enough or big enough.' I'd get anxiety when an agent told me to 'take a meeting.' It all comes down to selling, and I'm the worst salesman in the world. It was my first encounter with the realities. I thought, I have created this work—don't I have some credibility? I had *no* credibility. I never got a job. Most people treated me in a straight and businesslike way, but to me it was cold and brutal. I was living in an apartment off Beachwood Drive, in central Hollywood. No money. My father was sending checks; he came right through. 'Dark Star' was the end of youth for me. It

Ad for the first "Halloween" movie.

didn't work. I had to find some way to cope with reality and do what I wanted to do."[1]

"I figured the only way into the business was to write my way in, so I wrote a couple of screenplays and one of them was 'Eyes.' I wanted to do it as a low budget film and through Jack Harris, who knew Jon Peters, they made me an offer to do that for Barbra Streisand—as a big budget film. It ended up as 'The Eyes of Laura Mars,' which is not one of my favorite movies."[4]

"An investor from Philadelphia approached me and basically gave me carte blanche to make a film. I'd always wanted to do an old-fashioned Howard Hawks's type of western, but that was out of the question unless you had a big star. I thought I would do a western in disguise, a modern day western. I thought I'd use youth gangs as Indians and really stylize it and go from there. It was the good versus the bad guys. I had no intention of making a political or social statement. If I ever do make a political or social statement in a film, I'll either do it unconsciously or else I'll have to be

taken away, because I don't believe in that sort of thing."[2] "Assault on Precinct 13" was born.

"When I started 'Assault' I thought, well, here's another chance to direct my own films. It was the first film where I had to meet a schedule and shoot in 35mm and Panavision and Metrocolor and stuff like that. It was basically a TV schedule—I think we had 25 days. After we wrapped, I cut the film together myself in three months, and did the sound effects, then released it. Bascially the same thing happened—it came out and no one really paid any attention to it. It was considered an exploitation picture, period. It was sold as a black violence film."[4]

"'Assault' didn't do a thing. The majors weren't interested in it; it was a strange movie, and they didn't know how to sell it. It was the second time I'd had a film make no money. I tried not to get too upset or take it too personally, but no one wanted me as a director....A year later, I was in the commissary at Warner Brothers, where I'd just finished directing my first TV movie, when a stranger came up and told me that 'Assault' was breaking attendance records in England. The news and reviews filtered back, and there began to be interest in me as a director. But it all came so long after I'd made the picture; I'd got used to the idea the film was going to fail. There's a disconnection between what you've put in creatively and the final response of the audience. Very strange."[1]

1979. Carpenter met his future wife, Adrienne Barbeau during the filming of "Someone's Watching Me."

Carpenter's next project was "Halloween," a horror film which opens in a small Illinois town on Halloween night, 1963. A small boy, Michael, inexplicably murders his sister and is sent to an institution for the mentally insane. Exactly fifteen years later he escapes and returns to his home town where he terrorizes three teenage girls played by Jamie Lee Curtis, P. J. Soles and Nancy Loomis. Donald Pleasance plays the psychiatrist who has treated Michael for fifteen years without results. With total costs of approximately $300,000, "Halloween" grossed over $80,000,000, making it proportionally the most profitable film ever.

"...Around the time 'Assault' was shown at the London Film Festival, one of [producer Irwin Yablan's] contacts was around and I went to meet him. Through that he put up $300,000 to do a movie. Irwin had an idea to do 'the babysitter murders,' and I went along because I wanted to make movies. At one point Irwin called up and said, how about calling it Halloween and having it take place on Halloween night? At that point, this thing really took shape. What a great premise! Not making a movie about a babysitter killer, but make a movie about Halloween night."[4] "When I was a kid, I'd go to the Southern Kentucky Fair and pay twenty-five cents to go into the Haunted House. You'd walk down a dark hallway, and when you stepped on a certain place it would make things jump out at you—it scared the hell out of me! Your expectation built up and up. I went again, and again, to learn how it worked. 'Halloween' was maybe a way of being young again and scared, and innocent in that way."[1]

"'Halloween' was the first film where I didn't storyboard everything. I just went on the set and took what I had. It was the first film I've done entirely on location, and it worked out pretty well. I storyboarded everything from the time the boy and girl make love and he goes downstairs and he's stabbed. Then, the girl upstairs gets strangled with the 'phone wire, and Jamie walks across the street,

goes up the stairs, finds the bodies and runs out of the house. All that was storyboarded. What I did most of the time was figure out on paper the night before exactly what I was going to shoot. I've had a lot of editing experience at USC in addition to cutting several films, so I try now to shoot them to cut. The shooting ratio on 'Halloween' was very low."[2]

Wrote and directed "Elvis," a three-hour TV movie biography of Elvis Presley starring Kurt Russell. "Elvis" was enormously successful, earning higher ratings in its head-to-head telecast with "Gone with the Wind" and "One Flew Over the Cuckoo's Nest." "When I came in they were looking for a style, they didn't know what to do with it. Dick Clark was the producer and had a $3 million budget. They had Kurt Russell cast already. So off we went."[4]

"['Elvis' is a] period movie that takes place from 1945 through 1969. It's all period. We shot [it] in thirty days with 150 different locations. That means that some of the days we were moving to three and four different locations. When you have a big union crew with a lot of trucks and bullshit, you have to run very fast. You have to shoot something in the morning, shoot something in mid-afternoon, and shoot something right before you quit at night. That's what happened. We were just running. On the run.

"After it was over I was disappointed in some of my work, and I was disappointed that I didn't have more participation in the editing. The problem was; I didn't have any time. I had to run out of the country for a while, start up another film. I'm not going to do another one like that.

"Could I have [been more involved in the editing]? Again, it was a committee. It was a big network, and the producers, and I don't function very well that way. I was involved up to a point. I feel we had a pretty good film up to one point. My cut was a lot tougher than what was on television. It had a harder edge to it and it was a lot more driving; it blasted along. What they did was to bland it out, homogenize it, add some TV music to it. One of the things that can destroy a scene or ruin a mood is inappropriate music. There was a great deal of inappropriate music in 'Elvis.' There's one scene where Elvis comes to his mother and she's living in a trailer, she's sinking, she has something wrong with her. They have a big long conversation and there's this upbeat country music in the background. They turned this sad scene into 'The Beverly Hillbillies.'"[5]

Taking a break during the filming of "The Fog," Carpenter is surrounded by Adrienne Barbeau, Jamie Lee Curtis and Janet Leigh.

"There are basically two problems to television; one is the amount of time in which you have to do a project, and the second is censorship. You never have enough time to shoot a project. Neither in 'Highrise' nor 'Elvis' was there really the time required to get it perfect. I just had to storyboard as much as I could, get as prepared as I could, and do it within the time allowed. In 'Highrise' the time element wasn't too bad. But 'Elvis' is a different kind of film. We had a tremendous amount of locations, and trying to do them in a short amount of time was very difficult. The shooting schedule was eighteen days for 'Highrise' and thirty days for 'Elvis.' Secondly, there is the problem for censorship. You're constantly having to answer to Standards and Practices, which is the censoring body of the network itself—what they will and won't allow on television. There are certain things you can't get on the air. I just hate censorship in any form, especially in terms of a film. It's really aggravating. I must tell you, I've had very little problems with it. I've never shot a scene that I know of that had a censorship problem."[2]

1980. "The Fog," shot in 1979, was released. Carpenter directed, scored, and co-wrote the film with producer Debra Hill. It starred Adrienne Barbeau, Hal Holbrook, Janet Leigh, Jamie Lee Curtis, and John Houseman. "['The Fog' presented] immense challenges. All the big special effects shots; the fog rolling down the street, moving in from the sea, the driftwood changing, they all had to be done a certain way to look a certain way and they were very tough. It was a boring, time consuming process. Also the story was difficult to achieve. Like the fog itself, the concept wasn't very substantial. It was light. I needed to create an evil force from something that was very light and whispy, and that applies in a dramatic sense.

"I spent a whole year working on it, and we found some dramatic problems I wrote that didn't work on the screen. I had to go back and fiddle with them. It was the first time I ever did. There are so many options in directing. There are so many ways to film things. Getting just the right one that works can be a horror story in itself. You can move the camera from ten miles away up to their nose. Which certain camera spot is going to convey what

The spectral ship from the movie "The Fog." Directed by Carpenter, it was released in 1979.

I want to convey? That's the problem. I think that's the fear that afflicts directors on the floor. I think they say, what am I going to do? My God, I can shoot this from 25 angles and they would all be good. So that's what they do—shoot it from 25 angles then hope to cut it together. You've got to make a choice. It's all about making a choice: directing, writing, editing. You've got to make a choice, have a reason for it...and be right."[4]

1981. Shot on a budget of $7 million, "Escape from New York" was released, starring Ken Russell, Adrienne Barbeau, Lee Van Cleef, and Ernest Borgnine. "...I wrote 'Escape from New York' way back in 1974; I believe I was inspired by the movie 'Death Wish' (about a vigilante killer), that was very popular at the time. I didn't agree with the philosophy of it, taking the law into one's own hands, but the film came across with the sense of New York as a kind of jungle, and I wanted to make an SF film along those lines."[6]

"It was the first professional screenplay I ever wrote. It was always one of my favorite screenplays, and was always on a movie I wanted to make, but it was very big and I wasn't quite sure when the time would be to do it....Meanwhile, a commitment with Avco came up, and I was going to do a

picture for them. However, it wasn't working out, so I suggested we do 'Escape' instead.

"['Escape' is] a very tough and violent high adventure in the future. The year is 1997. The crime rate has increased enormously, resulting in a big war between the criminals and the United States Police Force, which is the size of the Army except it's all S.W.A.T. teams. The police win the war, but it is very costly and takes several cities with it. America becomes a police state, and Manhattan Island is evacuated and turned into a maximum-security prison that's walled off from the rest of the world. Every prisoner in the country is thrown in there and allowed to live the way they want, so it's basically hell on Earth. The government turns off the electricity, sterilizes the criminals and drops food into Central Park once a month, but otherwise leaves them on their own.

"The story concerns a rescue mission. A plane carrying the President is hijacked to New York, where it's crash landed inside the prison. The criminals hold him hostage, so the government has to send someone in to get him out. They send in the world's greatest criminal—Snake Plissken. The film is about what he runs into in Manhattan.

"When I first wrote the script, I set it in 1982, but I've since realized I was being premature, so I moved it ahead 17 years from today. Go back 17 years, to 1963, and think how the world has changed. It's been subtle but significant. I know, because I grew up during that time. That's the kind of perspective I want. Things aren't too different, but they *are* different. It's enough distance so that some of the outlandishly fantastic stuff I'll have happening *could* be possible, though it won't be a fantasy like 'Star Wars.'

"In realistic terms, in today's market, $7 million is considered to be a medium budget, but this could cost $30 million if I went all the way with it. Obviously, I'm cutting some corners in certain areas, and I have some tricks in mind, so I'm going to apply the same techniques I've used in low-budget filmmaking as much as I can. Unfortunately, all the money won't be going on the screen, because it's a union picture and I have to play by the rules. People know who I am now, so I can't shoot non-union anymore.

"What I usually did before was to say: I think I can make 'Halloween' for $300,000, and then wrote the script to fit that. This time I wrote the script first and budgeted it afterwards. I told Avco: 'If you want this film, you're not going to get me for just a certain amount of money. You'll have to do it for what it will cost.' And I must admit, they came through. This is the first time in years that they've invested this much money in a movie, so they have a lot of faith in it.

"'The Fog' was the hardest movie I've ever made, and it cost a million dollars. 'Escape' will be 10 times more difficult than 'The Fog,' and I have almost 10 times the budget, so I figure it will be just about as hard. However, I'm not worried and I don't feel I'm under tremendous pressure. What I *do* feel is a little surprised, because I didn't know I was going to do this one next. It's just sort of a happy accident.

"The requirements of the film are such that to do all of it in New York would be ridiculous. It all takes place at night, all the lights are out except for torches, the streets are deserted, the building windows are broken out and there are wrecked planes and burning cars. It would be absurd to try to stage that in Manhattan, because it would add months to the schedule."[7]

"Halloween II" was released with a script by Carpenter. "At first I was extremely reluctant because sequels are sometimes simply money-making devices, and inferior to the originals. But then I thought about Coppola's reasons for doing 'Godfather 2'—sequels are so bad so often, why not try to make a good one?

"Also there were certain things that happened in the first one that I wanted to 'clear up'; that was very attractive to me—and also kind of freeing thing. On the business aspect, it was a good move. Then there was the challenge of it—what could we do with a sequel to 'Halloween?' Could it be exciting and scary? And then the final thing; after thinking about it a long time, I thought that there really might be another story in it, and I thought it really might be a lot of fun. So I thought, let's try it.

"But my biggest problem was that I did not want to direct it—I had made that film once, and I really didn't want to do it again."[8] Rick Rosenthal was hired to direct.

Kurt Russell stars in the Avco-Embassy film "Escape from New York."

Carpenter's experiences with Rosenthal, were not positive, however. "The cut he delivered to me was one of the *worst* movies I've ever seen in my life. It was an amateurish mishmash, and was about as frightening as an episode of 'Quincy.' He didn't make the film, he didn't take responsibility for his movie, and he placed the blame on everybody else. He was a spoiled little child.

"We gave him another chance to make it work, but he didn't do it. Therefore I had to assume my contractual responsibility of sole creative control, because I wasn't going to release a piece of garbage. I came into the editing room for two weeks and cut the picture to compress his material and make it go at a decent pace. After cutting out 17 minutes of bad, sub-television moviemaking we had a 77 minute film. We needed a 90 minute movie, so I shot some connective material to fill it out."[9]

1982. Carpenter directed "The Thing," starring Kurt Russell, with a script by Bill Lancaster. It was the first Carpenter-directed feature he did not also write. "Universal wanted to do a remake of 'The Thing,' which was filmed in 1950-51, directed by Christian Nyby, codirected by Howard Hawks, based on a short story by John Campbell called 'Who Goes There?' And it was an excellent film, one of my favorite movies, with James Arness as a giant, blood-drinking carrot from outer space.

"It was a chair-lifter, for me. Popcorn flew. But I realized that I really couldn't remake 'The Thing' from the movie; it just wouldn't work out. So we went back to the short story, which was an entirely different thing. It's more about a creature that can become you, rather than [about its ability to] kill you. Imitate you perfectly, cell for cell. So that these men in this arctic camp suddenly realize that their friends may not be their friends. And that if they don't stop it, it can become the population of the world in about two weeks—if it gets any further than this arctic camp. When it's threatened, the thing goes through several incantations and does some strange things to the human body; that's what the movie is about.

"I'm really fond of it; and I'm really fond of the short story. I've always thought that it never got its due. Hawks and Nyby changed it so much from what the story was—a sort of Agatha Christie mystery up in the arctic, with people walking down dark corridors. . .I thought that might be interesting to do. It's a story more about people than it is about a monster."[10]

1983. "Christine" released. Directed by Carpenter, script by Bill Phillips, it is based on the novel by Stephen King. Christine is a 1958 Plymouth Fury born with a malevolent streak: her first murder is an assembly line worker who drops cigar ashes on her factory fresh upolstery. Teamed up with her eventual owner, Arnie Cunningham, a meek, repressed adolescent, she becomes an instrument of Arnie's rage against the world. Carpenter considers "Christine" as "just a job." "Everybody wants to get their hands on Stephen King. But they're so bad now, most of them, *so* bad. I don't think I'll do another right away. A few people are doing great horror films, like George Romero and David Cronenberg. Romero is supposed to do 'Pet Sematary,' which is the best but the most difficult of Stephen King's novels to adapt, I would think. . . .Spielberg is going to do 'The Talisman.' If he doesn't chicken out. For most of us, it's a chance to do a teenage movie, and that's not to put it down at all."[11]

Nonetheless, "Christine" received generally favorable notices including one from critic Richard Corliss: "Director John Carpenter and screenwriter Bill Phillips have compacted and customized Stephen King's screaming jalopy of a novel until it moves with sleek '50s lines and a sassy tail-fin flip at the end. Graceful tracking shots mime the killer car's gliding menace; the deserted nighttime streets are washed chrome-shiny by rain. The high-school scenes, which are neither coarse nor condescending, put every other current teen-pic to shame. Carpenter's cast mixes vigorous old pros with young comers; Keith Gordon is a hilariously intense Jekyll-and-Snide. The movie—Carpenter's best since 'Halloween'—is at heart a deadpan satire of the American male's love affair with his car. This 'Christine' is one lean mean funny machine."[12]

1984. Carpenter's "Starman" won an Academy Award nomination for lead actor Jeff Bridges. "I was offered the film in October of 1983 by the men in charge at Columbia pictures. I knew that it had been in development at the studio for quite a while. I also knew that Columbia had done market reasearch on the concepts of both 'E.T.' and 'Starman' and that 'Starman' came out ahead. And I'm aware that studios put great belief in that kind of data. With all that in mind, I went home, read the script and two days later, I knew it was going to be my next film. People seem to find this hard to believe, but it was that fast, and that simple."[13]

"Frank Prince, who was then a producer at Columbia presented 'Starman' as a love story. A friend

People magazine's November 7, 1988 issue featured "Horror Boys": Leatherface, Freddy, Jason, and Michael Myers (right), Carpenter's maniac of the "Halloween" series. Mark Sennet/*People Weekly* © 1988 by Time, Inc.

once told me about studios, 'find out what they want and if it's not too abhorent, give it to them.' I remembered that advice, so when I heard the cue love story, I mentioned 'It Happened One Night.' It didn't seem to bother them, so I thought we were in good shape."[11]

"At one point [Columbia Pictures executives] even scrapped the project because they felt it was too much like 'E.T.' I read the script and realized immediately what the similarities were. I felt there's no way you can compete with a movie like 'E.T.' It's so unique and special; the audience has taken it to heart. It would be like trying to remake 'The Wizard of Oz.' You just can't do it. But I felt that 'E.T.' had a relationship between a boy and a rubber puppet. And I felt that 'Starman' had a relationship between two people. So I saw it as an opportunity for me, as a director, to try my hand at a large-budget love story. I rarely get the chance to do that. People don't think of me in that vein."[14]

1986. "Big Trouble in Little China" released. The film stars Kurt Russell as a truck driver named Jack Burton, Dennis Dun as Burton's Chinese friend and a Chinese restaurateur. The trio sets out in search of the restaurateur's wife-to-be who has been kidnapped by the emissaries of Lo Pan, a 2,000 year-old dead (but active) Chinese ghost. "It's a mystical action-adventure-comedy-kung-fu-monster-ghost story. It's the first American film to involve all these elements. I've always wanted to make a kung fu movie and deal with Chinese mythology, the essence of Chinese tradition, by incorporating it into the melting-pot sensibility of American entertainment. It's very complicated and has a lot of twists, but also straightforward—almost like a 1940s adventure."[15]

"As a moviegoer I fell in love with kung fu movies in 1973. The first film that I saw that got me hooked was a picture called 'Five Fingers of Death.' It was pretty much the usual fare. However, it took place around the Boxer Rebellion. It

From the Warner Brothers movie "Someone Is Watching Me," starring Lauren Hutton.

was basically a costume picture, but it introduced me to the astonishing and balletic movement of kung fu. As I watched these films through the years, they had a wonderful, unsophisticated, uncynical view. They presented heroes and villains in situations without the kind of cynicism you see in American films. The heroes had an emormous macho quality to them untainted by the world, and this is true of a lot of the Chinese cinema that I researched for 'Big Trouble in Little China.'"[16]

With the birth of his son, Carpenter re-experienced the joys of being young again "...and coming into the world without too much knowledge of nuclear weapons and human rights violations and just the horrors of life. My son is unaware of that, so to him the world is this wondrous place. Simple things are wonderful. Communication is wonderful. Hugs are wonderful.

"...It's really down to an elemental level. And I started to really change my thinking. I thought, well, before I get too old here and too set, I better kick out the jams and do something that really sort of celebrates this point of view. And so 'Big Trouble in Little China' was just the perfect vehicle. When I read the script, it was impossible for me to get too moody about it because it's so outrageous."[17]

"As a movie maker, the appeal of 'Big Trouble in Little China,' is to incorporate the kung fu moves into an elaborate visual ballet. Because kung fu is about movement. It's about motion. If I were going to stage a dance scene like 'Singin' in the Rain,' I would approach it in the same way. You're dealing with rhythm. You're dealing with impact. I'm talking about that in a very cinematic way."[16]

"Big Trouble in Little China" cost $25 million and was produced by Twentieth Century-Fox. The film was not a commercial success and relations with Fox were troubled. By the time "Big Trouble" was released, Carpenter was re-evaluating his relationship to the studio system. "I think the studio wanted an Indiana Jones. I don't think they realized I was going to do a high-tech Chinese farcical. I think that's what threw them. The studio didn't understand the film until they showed it to an audience.

"To me it's like 'The Wizard of Oz.' You go over the hill and there's something else. You go over another hill and there's something else.

From the movie "The Thing," starring Kurt Russell. Copyright © 1982 by Universal City Studios, Inc.

"I'm very disenchanted with Hollywood. Hollywood has become a bad place for film directors. I'm exploring some options, new ways of making movies on my own terms."[18]

"One of the things I have been trying to come to grips with is that people in Hollywood are simply not the way that I always assume they are. I act like they are all from Kentucky and then, when they act differently, I feel betrayed. I have had to realize they are the way they are, not the way I wish they were. I must learn to adjust. They don't have to change. I do. I must learn to see them as they are."[19]

"I used to think when they told you how much they liked what you did, your style, your way of making a movie, that they really meant it—it was a compulsion in me to believe it. But they only like you if you make money. So I'm going to find a way to make low-budget movies, while still making films like 'Big Trouble.' I know there's a way to do it. And it should be interesting to find out exactly how."

"I've come full circle. 'Big Trouble' is much more like a (John Carpenter) film. And I'm recognizing that now. I think the next step is that I'm going to start writing my own movies again. And go right back to where I started, which is a really exciting idea. Because I've come to realize that I *like* John Carpenter movies. And they're fun to make. And they won't all be great, and they won't always make lots of money, but who cares?"[17]

"...This is my 11th movie as a director. I'm starting to creep toward 40 and starting to leave behind certain eras, and now I realize the most important thing is how I feel about a picture. I'm always anxious that people like my work and respond to it. You always want somebody to like you, but that's not the most important thing. If I'm happy with it, then I'm going to wish it the best of luck out there. You've got to love yourself."[18]

"...My whole philosophy of movies is that movies are not intellectual, they are not ideas, that is done in literature and all sorts of other forms. Movies are *emotional*, an audience should cry or laugh or get scared. I think the audience should project into the film, into a character, into a situation, and *react*. The great thing about some of the B movies or the *film noir*, say, is that the audience did just that. In 'The Big Sleep' they wanted to know what Hum-

Carpenter directed the Columbia Pictures film "Starman." Starring Karen Allen and Jeff Bridges, it was released in 1984.

phrey Bogart was going to do. These other directors don't do that. They take the superficial aspects of it but they don't get down to the real guts of the thing, which is that the audience has to care. I don't feel you can just sit and analyse the film intellectually, because then it has failed. So in terms of extending the genres, philosophical ideas, I'm not as interested in that as I am in getting the audience to react, really to project into the film, and come away having had an experience."[4]

Footnote Sources:

[1] James Stevenson, "Profiles: People Start Running," *New Yorker,* January 28, 1980.

[2] Ralph Applebaum, "From Cult Homage to Creative Control," *Films and Filming* (London), June, 1979.

[3] Anna Quindlen, *New York Times,* February 24, 1980 (section 2, p. 1).

[4] Richard Meyers, "Interview: Budget-Conscious Director, John Carpenter," *Millimeter,* April, 1980.

[5] Todd McCarthy, "Trick and Treat," *Film Comment,* January/Februry, 1980.

[6] Samuel J. Maronie, "On the Set with 'Escape from New York,'" *Starlog,* April, 1981.

[7] Steve Swires, "High Adventure in the Future," *Starlog,* December, 1980.

[8] Bob Martin, "John Carpenter: The Multi-Talented Filmmaker Discusses His Latest Projects: 'Halloween 2' and 'The Thing!,'" *Fangoria,* number 14, August, 1981.

[9] S. Swires, "John Carpenter: Directing 'The Thing,'" *Starlog,* July, 1982.

[10] Mick Garris, "Landis, Cronenberg, Carpenter: Fear on Film Continues!," *Fangoria,* number 20, July, 1982.

[11] Karen Jaehne, "The Man Behind 'Starman,'" *Films on Screen and Video,* May, 1985.

[12] Richard Corliss, "Season's Bleedings in Tinseltown," *Time,* December 19, 1983.

[13] Susan Stark, "Carpenter's New Tack: 'Starman' Shatters His Horror Mold," *Detroit News,* December 14, 1984.

[14] Tom Hinckley, "A Love Story from the Director of 'Halloween?,'" *Cable Guide,* January, 1986.

[15] Dan Yakir, "Director Carpenter Mixes His Genres," *Boston Globe,* June 25, 1986.

[16] Lawrence Van Gelder, "John Carpenter after 'Big Trouble,'" *New York Times,* June 27, 1986.

[17] Lloyd Sachs, "'Little China' Kicks Out Gloom," *Chicago Sun-Times,* July 6, 1986.

[18] Scott Cain, "Carpenter Builds Directing Dynasty on Past Successes," *Atlanta Journal and Constitution*, July 13, 1986.

[19] Julia Cameron, "'Trouble' Director Carpenter Sees New Route to Screen," *Chicago Tribune*, July 6, 1986.

■ For More Information See

Cinefantastique, winter, 1975 (p. 40), winter, 1979 (p. 39), summer, 1980 (p. 5).

Ecran (Paris), September, 1978.

Jeff Walker, "Man Who Eyed Laura Mars Has a Happy 'Halloween,'" *Feature*, January, 1979 (p. 12).

People Weekly, May 21, 1979 (p. 131), December 17, 1984, January 27, 1986 (p. 12), July 28, 1986.

Paul Scanlon, "'The Fog': A Spook Ride on Film," *Rolling Stone*, June 28, 1979 (p. 42).

New York Post, July 13, 1979 (p. 47), January 30, 1980 (p. 24), February 28, 1980 (p. 29), October 14, 1980 (p. 21), October 15, 1981.

Soho Weekly News, July 26, 1979 (p. 46), February 27, 1980 (p. 37).

Films and Filming, September, 1979.

Fangoria, number 5, 1980 (p. 11), number 19, May, 1982.

New Yorker, January 28, 1980, December 17, 1984, January 28, 1985 (p. 88).

New York, February 18, 1980 (p. 50), December 17, 1984.

Daily News (New York), February 24, 1980, June 20, 1982, December 23, 1984.

Alan Oddie, "An Interview with John Carpenter," *Filmmakers Monthly*, March, 1980 (p. 17).

David Sterritt, "His Low-Budget Films Have a Punch," *Christian Science Monitor*, March 13, 1980 (p. 18).

Jeffrey Wells, "New Fright Master: John Carpenter," *Films in Review*, April, 1980 (p. 218).

Tinkerbelle, "Suspense Builder John Carpenter," *Interview*, May, 1980.

Image et Son (Paris), May, 1981.

Steve Swires, "Starlog Interview: John Carpenter," *Starlog*, July 1981 (p. 73).

Judy Stone, "'Maude's' Barbeau Escapes Her Image," *San Francisco Chronicle*, July 8, 1981 (p. 47).

Todd McCarthy, "What Hawks Discarded (1951) Back in Carpenter 'Thing' Re-Do," *Variety*, July 29, 1981 (p. 28).

Contracamp (Madrid), October, 1981.

New York Times Biographical Service, November, 1981.

New York Times, November 24, 1981 (p. C-7), June 25, 1982 (p. C-10), December 7, 1984 (p. C-8), August 9, 1985 (p. C-16).

Jonathan Rosenbaum, "The Arts," *Omni*, July, 1982 (p. 26).

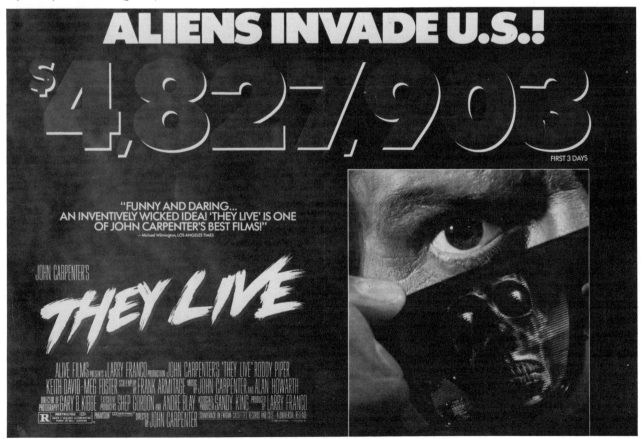

Ad from *Daily Variety*, November 9, 1988.

O. Assayas, S. Le Peron and S. Toubiana, "Entretien aven John Carpenter," *Cahiers du Cinema,* September, 1982 (p. 15).

David Quinlan, *The Illustrated Guide to Film Directors,* Barnes and Noble, 1983.

Maclean's, December 19, 1983 (p. 54), December 17, 1984 (p. 59), July 14, 1986 (p. 49).

Newsweek, December 19, 1983 (p. 66), December 17, 1984 (p. 80), July 14, 1986 (p. 69).

USA Today, March, 1984 (p. 96), March, 1985 (p. 95), September, 1986 (p. 94).

Time, December 24, 1984 (p. 65), July 14, 1986 (p. 62).

Commonweal, January 11, 1985 (p. 19).

Glenn Lovell, "'Starman' Stirs Up a Storm from Sci-Fi Fans and Experts," *Chicago Tribune,* January 18, 1985.

Andrew Kopkind, "The Cartoon Epic," *Nation,* January 26, 1985.

Saturday Review, January/February, 1985 (p. 80).

Glamour, February, 1985 (p. 134).

Mademoiselle, April, 1985 (p. 88).

Jack Sullivan, editor, *The Penguin Encyclopedia of Horror and the Supernatural,* Viking, 1986 (p. 70).

Bob Thomas, "Low-Budget Director Flies High Nowadays," *Detroit News,* July 26, 1986.

Bret Easton Ellis

Born March 7, 1964, in Los Angeles, Calif.; son of Robert Martin (a real estate investment analyst) and Dale (a housewife; maiden name, Dennis) Ellis. *Education:* Bennington College, B.A., 1986. *Residence:* Sherman Oaks, Calif. *Agent:* Amanda Urban, International Creative Management, 40 West 57th St., New York, N.Y. 10019.

■ Career

Writer, 1985—. *Member:* Authors Guild.

■ Writings

Less Than Zero (novel), Simon & Schuster, 1985.
The Rules of Attraction (novel), Simon & Schuster, 1987.

Contributor of articles to periodicals, including *Rolling Stone, Vogue, Vanity Fair, Wall Street Journal,* and *Interview.*

■ Adaptations

"Less Than Zero" (cassette) Simon & Schuster, 1986, (motion picture) starring Andrew McCarthy, Jami Gertz, and Robert Downey, Jr., Twentieth-Century-Fox, 1987.

■ Work In Progress

A third novel.

■ Sidelights

While still an undergraduate at Bennington College in Vermont, Ellis published his best-selling novel *Less Than Zero.* His books have endured literary criticism ranging from "infantile and sophomoric" to the "voice of a new generation."

Much like Clay, his protagonist, Ellis is the product of a well-to-do family from the hills above Los Angeles. Like Clay, he has two sisters, but he is quick to point out that his novels are not autobiographical. "It's sort of a hassle, all these assumptions that we're one and the same. The reaction is sort of insulting. But sometimes I take it as a compliment—that people were so persuaded by that voice that they thought it had to be real."[1]

Ellis' childhood was by his own account fairly benign. Born March 7, 1964, he grew up in Southern California where his father was in real estate and his mother was a housewife. His parents separated when Ellis was a teenager, a situation he regards as "typical of the era.

"A lot of people don't think that 'normal' and 'Southern California' go together, but my childhood was very normal and happy. Nothing marked it as different or strange."[2]

Attended a private school in the fourth grade and recalled that while his peers were painting and playing, he was frequenting libraries and reading voraciously. "*The Lorax* by Dr. Seuss was probably my favorite picture book when I was a kid. Dahl's *James and the Giant Peach* appealed to the very nasty side of a third and fourth grader. I liked Dahl a lot. I also went through the whole thing with the Judy Blume books, which must be sort of strange. I don't know if there are a lot of male readers for that. I read all of the typical seventies teen books, like S.E. Hinton. While other kids were bringing home paintings to their parents, I brought home short stories. There was no definite moment when this fourth grade kid reached an epiphany as to when he knew he wanted to be a writer. It was a very gradual awakening of a desire to express myself.

"I hate to sound goody-goody, but it was in high school when I became more interested in writing. For example, that's where I discovered Hemingway's *The Sun Also Rises*. After that, I read everything by Hemingway, which seems typical for adolescent writers. They find Hemingway and think that's how they have to write. I also sneaked peeks at a lot of pop fiction—Stephen King, science fiction, spy novels. Joan Didion, specifically, *Play It as It Lays* and her essay collections, *The White Album* and *Slouching Towards Bethlehem*, had a profound impact on me stylistically, as did short stories by Ann Beattie, Raymond Carver and various other practitioners of that particular craft.

"The marked difference between kids growing up in California and kids in New York is having a car. You become a legitimate semi-adult once you get the keys and learn how to drive. That has to do with geography. In New York or Chicago, a car isn't an important thing. The freedom of having a car really affected me—you can go out and experience a city's nightlife. The club scene in Los Angeles fascinated me. Movies also had a tremendous effect, as, I think they do on any writer coming of age in the last fifteen years. A lot of people I knew had parents involved in the film industry. So our lives revolved around movies and rock music.

"I was in a band, playing very straight-forward pop music. I came of age right at the point when 'new wave' and all these bands from England became fashionable—Soft Cell, Human League, Duran Duran. I like everything from Clash to Abba.

"The genesis of *Less Than Zero* started in my junior and senior years, not by observing my high school but by *observing* in general. I wrote a lot of pieces for writing courses I was taking. The book idea started with that."[2]

1982. Left the West Coast for exclusive Bennington College in Vermont. "I didn't understand why people went to college in Los Angeles. I had always made a correlation between college and the East. I guess I had a lot of those ideas that West Coast kids have of the East—ivy, brick walls, and maybe snow. Going to college in L.A. would have been an extension of high school. I wanted to get away from that."[2]

Bennington had a reputation as a haven for rich misfits. "It's too bad. A high percentage of the people were really quite into their art, whether it was writing, music, painting, drama, dancing, or whatever. Bennington, like a lot of art schools, seems to give off a negative impression. It's not wholly true. Alot of those wealthy misfits, I was amazed to find, were enormously talented. I think that there are cliques of wealthy misfits in most schools, that would include UCLA, Oakland, Columbia, NYU.

"Their writing program appealed to me, along with the fact that you could start taking writing courses very seriously as a freshman, without having to fulfill all these requirements. I liked the freedom that Bennington offered. Besides, I didn't think that I was going to get in anywhere else. My high school grades were terrible. My SAT scores weren't anything impressive. So I said okay to Bennington. The campus is extraordinarily beautiful."[2]

His teachers proved exceptionally helpful, especially Joe McGinniss, author of *Fatal Vision*. "Joe sort of discovered me, if you can use the term in the writing world. In one of my freshman writing classes, I gave him those pieces that I had written in high school. He actually sent them to editors at Simon & Schuster. They called me back and asked if I could write a novel based on those pieces. That was a real incentive for writing. I probably would have written it anyway, but this speeded up the process a little bit."[2]

Dedicated to McGinniss, "the first draft of *Less Than Zero* took eight weeks to write. But the overall writing process took two years. I went through four or five rewrites. Joe really took me under his wing. He influenced the shape and form of *Less Than Zero* and essentially edited the book.

"I don't know if I would have been introduced to the right sort of people without his help. *Less Than Zero* might have languished around for a long time and missed that moment when it was hot to pick up young writers."[2]

In 1985, *Less Than Zero*, the anthem of teenage boredom and apathy, was published. Ellis took its title from an Elvis Costello song that says "Everything is less than zero." Some lauded it as the voice of a new "lost generation"; some called it "the worst novel since the invention of movable type...."[3]

"This tale of privileged college students at their self-absorbed and childish worst," wrote reviewer Sybil Steinberg in *Publishers Weekly*, "is the very book that countless students have dreamed of writing at their most self-absorbed and childish moments. With one bestseller to his credit, *Less Than Zero* author and recent Bennington College graduate has had the unique opportunity of seeing his dream become a reality—and all those other once-and-future students can breathe a sigh of relief that it didn't happen to them. Through a series of brief first-person accounts, the novel chronicles one term at a fictional New England college, with particular emphasis on a decidedly contemporary love triangle (one woman and two men) in which all possible combinations have been explored, and each pines after the one who's pining after the other. Theirs is a world of physical, chemical and emotional excess—an adolescent fantasy of sex, drugs and *sturm and drang*—wherein characters are distinguished only by the respective means by which they squander their health, wealth and youth. Despite its contemporary feel and flashy structure—the book begins and ends midsentence—the narrative relies on the stalest staples of melodrama and manages to pack in a suicide, assorted suicide attempts, an abortion and the death of a parent without giving the impression that anything is happening—or that any of it matters."

"It has affected critics wholly and completely. I really think that *Less Than Zero* wouldn't have gotten that much attention if it had been written by someone in his thirties. The interest came because someone young wrote a book like that. It's rare. I don't pick up a review that doesn't start with, 'at age so and so...' It is the major thing on people's minds. They automatically assume that if you are that young and you are getting published, you must

Cover from the Penguin edition.

be the biggest, most precocious brat in the world. There is a lot of hostility, especially from the critical community. I don't pay attention to them anyway. There is really very little that a writer can learn from them. I thought that I was going to be a lot more excited by the critical reception when the novel came out than I was. Everyone has their own take on it, and it rarely connects with yours. The critical stuff hasn't really battered me. The good reviews don't particularly make me happy."[2]

Less Than Zero has been described as a "pruriently violent book" with a voice of "traumatized self-pity, passivity, and blind self-absorption...."[4] "I thought that it was a fairly accurate description of the book and of the narrator. I don't know why writers choose to write from a particular vantage point. I choose characters who are passive because it's easier to move them around. I give them such weak narratives for purely selfish reasons. I'm more interested in pushing a weak-willed character through any kind of scene I want and letting the scene go from there. I'd prefer that he just observe a scene rather than take immediate action in it. I have little desire to make characters likeable, or to go through major events to change their lives. Character and character development do not interest me. A character is a tool to express my ideas about something, whether about language, my feelings about this generation, or my ideas on life. I have a hard time picturing a lot of my characters."[2]

1986. Graduated from Bennington. "[Now] there is a computer room. There is a weight room. There is an aerobics instructor. The admissions office now asks for SAT scores; it never used to. The idea that SAT's were any indication of how dedicated one was to the artistic inclinations one pursued, it simply was never in the school's policy. But now it is. There is a girl studying a computer screen on one of the covers of an admissions pamphlet that was recently passed out to prospective college students in high schools around the nation. I think that there were no more than two students planning to go into med school when I arrived in the fall of 1982. Now there are about eighteen. . . .

"The strange thing is that everyone is starting to look slightly the same, monotonous, almost robotic. The same short haircut, the same skin and color tone, the same designer clothes. If this new generation has an identity, it's one of sameness. The familiar and easily identifiable and recognizable are what make them the most secure. For all their seriousness and tough posing about making money and their fear of failure and their desire to look perfect, they're really a fairly bland group, a group unaccustomed to experimentation or risk."[5]

1987. Motion picture *Less Than Zero* released, without Ellis' involvement. "I didn't think they would ever make it into a movie. Hundreds of books are optioned by studios. Maybe three or four of them eventually get made. So why do a screenplay, sign a contract, and waste time with a movie that was never going to be made? I was still in school. I had to do my thesis, plus I owed the company a new book. I just didn't have the time. So I said no. When they finally decided to do it and hired a screenwriter, I kicked myself and said, 'You idiot. Why the hell didn't you do it? Your screenplay might have been bad, but I don't think it could be any worse.' Then I realized, I couldn't have given a major company the sort of movie they wanted. The changes that would have made it a 'releasable' movie would have hurt too much."[2]

The final movie bore little resemblance to the book. "That didn't bother me as much as giving the characters last names. Like giving Clay the last name of Easton. That was such a low blow. I almost called the producer and complained. Some people think I have a blase' attitude toward Hollywood. It comes from growing up around the industry. I'd expected something more mangled and unrepresentative of the book than what actually appeared. So when I first saw the movie, I was relieved even though they hadn't used a single scene or line of dialogue from the book. Watching it was a confusing experience. I felt powerless. I could have refused the rights to the book, but I think that would have been foolish. The book will always be there. What usually happens is that people feel that the book was better anyway, so the book's reputation is raised. I'd feel like a baby to complain at this point."[2]

In that same year, *Rules of Attraction*, a rambling tale of obnoxious, promiscuous college students told through twelve first-person narrators, was published. "It started as a short story about a guy and a girl meeting each other at a party. It was only four pages long. The male perceptions and female perceptions were quite different. I actually started writing it a year and a half before *Less Than Zero*. One line in *Less Than Zero* kept coming back to me. Someone asks Clay at a party if he is going to go back to school, and he answers, 'I don't know. Things aren't that different there.' After I had rewritten that scene about twenty times, I wondered why I had written that line. It was a typical thing for Clay to say, but it was also a weird thing to come out while I was writing. I thought, *what* was going on back there?

"I took Clay back to school. Writing from his point of view seemed ridiculous. I realized that trying to do any kind of sequel to *Less Than Zero* was a dumb idea, because Clay in that atmosphere would be an object of ridicule. I went back to that short story and elongated it into Sean and Lauren. A lot of *The Rules of Attraction* was based on that clique of wealthy misfits from Bennington who really didn't go to class and were more concerned about vacationing and having sex. 'Why don't you just put all these characters together and see what happens?' I thought. Having separate narrators comment on the same scenes is not really the most original idea in the world, but it seemed like the right move to make with this book, to do a novel that was more playful and not as deadly depressing as *Less Than Zero*. And though it *is* depressing and serious, while writing it I kept saying to myself— it's also not as morbid and 'pruriently violent.' Why not be a little playful and make it funnier, even if it is mean-spirited and nasty? I did passages in

Robert Downey, Jr. starred in the film adaptation of "Less Than Zero."

French, left blank pages, started in mid-sentences, and did all the things that I probably will be embarrassed by fifteen years down the line, but still, for now, the book accurately reflects my feelings at the time it was written, and if it means anything to me its more about having fun with the structure of the novel rather than begging an audience to like these people."[2]

The critics responded with their usual division. Some praised this second effort, others have called it "a giant soiled revolving mattress for the young and the wasted."[6]

"In both books I guess I'm relentless in my desire to show how boring or wasted these lives are. The most interesting way to do this is to show it through action and scenes, rather than through internalized, subjective passages that describe Sean, Clay, and Lauren as bored young people who constantly hang out at restaurants and don't want to do anything with their lives. I'm interested in *showing* the reader how boring or wasted their lives are. This really rubs some readers the wrong way, and they can't deal with it because it doesn't conform to the traditional rules of literature. When you write that way, you always risk alienating

readers. I know. I've done it twice. Don't think I'm not going to do it a third time either.

"Both books are period pieces that accurately reflect a segment of the 1980's population. I suppose that's one goal, to get the period down right. But at the same time, I feel awkward in the role of sociologist and I really don't know where young people are heading, more than anyone else does.

"When I graduated from Bennington, I went back home to finish the final draft of *Rules of Attraction* and to work on a screenplay. Once that was out of the way, I immediately moved to New York. It wasn't really to be close to the publishing industry or anything like that. I like the idea that everything doesn't revolve around the film industry here, because that can become kind of grating. Besides, all my friends live here."[2]

These friends include Jay McInerney, *Bright Lights, Big City*, Jill Eisenstadt, *From Rockaway*, and Tama Janowitz, *Slaves of New York*. All are young authors who found early acclaim, but the critics have cooled. "I can only speak for myself. I guess critics didn't really expect it to become as big

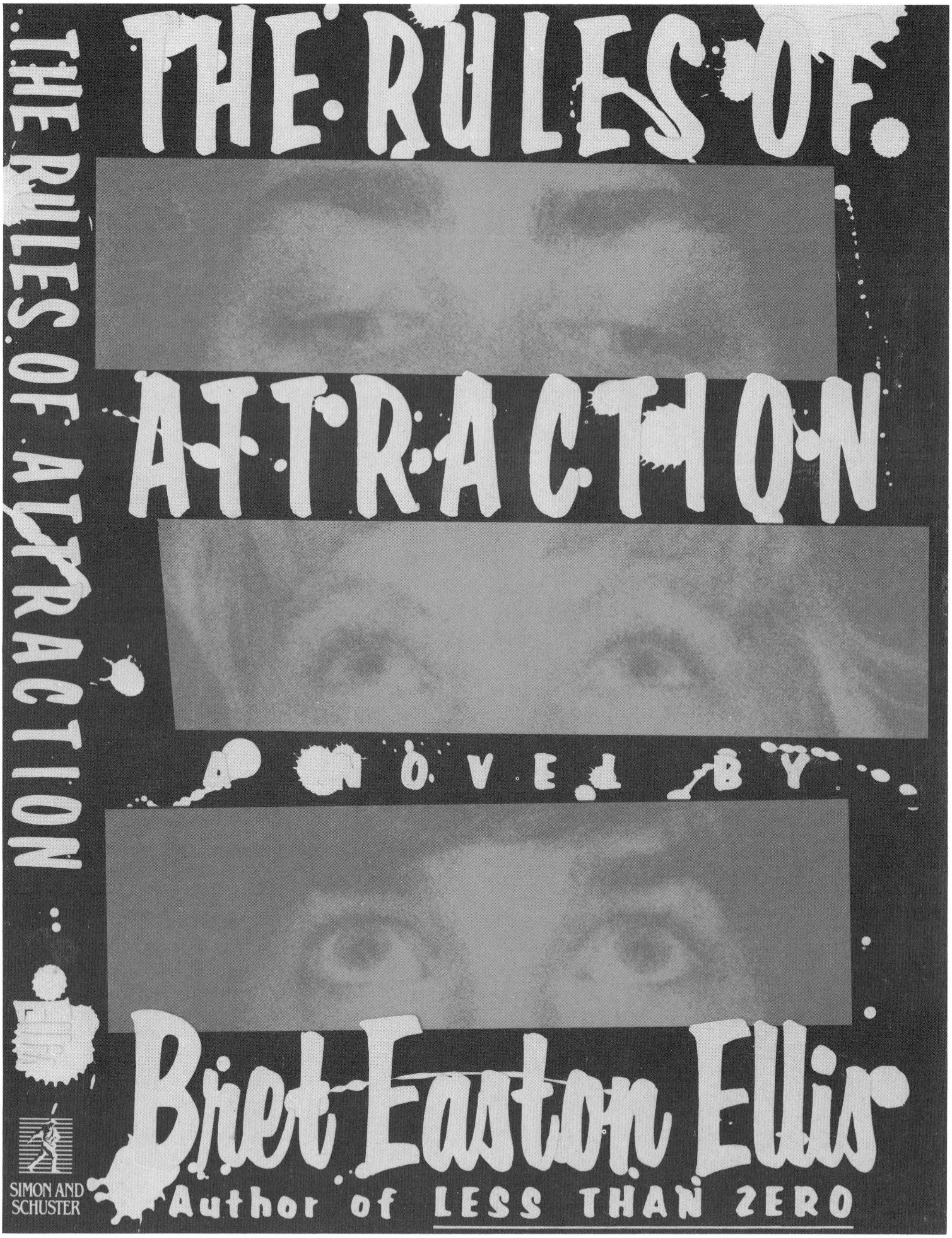

THE RULES OF ATTRACTION
THE RULES OF ATTRACTION
A NOVEL BY
Bret Easton Ellis
Author of LESS THAN ZERO
SIMON AND SCHUSTER

Cover of Ellis' second novel.

as it did, but they can really only blame themselves. Maybe they're kicking themselves for giving a group of writers so much press. And then, of course, when it becomes big, they think, 'What can we do now? It's not news anymore to say good things about them, so maybe it's news to trash them.' There is a fairly high level of skepticism about the entire new group of writers in the critical press: that the writing is shallow and only about club-crawling rich kids hanging out in the east village or in L.A. But it seems to me that the main thing the critics are really complaining about is the *culture* and the *times*, and a narcissistic era, rather than whether a book is poorly written or loses its appeal on page 120. All the books, no matter what you think about their literary quality, reflect the times we live in right now.

"Jay's book has much better humor and is definitely not as bleak as mine. It's a little more sophisticated in terms of it's writing style and doesn't have the harshness or violence of *Less Than Zero*. Both have flashy covers and the residue of cocaine. The reason these two books were lumped together was a marketing phenomena. They were released within five months of each other and found an untapped young readership. No one thought that young people would go out and buy books that were in big trade paperback. For some reason, they had lucky timing. But the books are very different. And the same for Tama. Her scene is as far away from Jay's as possible."[2]

Ellis is presently working on a third novel. "All I can say is that it continues whatever my concerns are over what is happening to this generation as it gets older, and it's set on Wall Street."[2]

Reflecting on the legacy of his work, Ellis believes that it has helped other young writers to become published. "I think it's definitely helping young writers. There's a serious backlash right now, but that was expected. Once that dies down, the vitriolic attacks on the young writing community about what a sham the critics think it is, (even though they thought it was a good thing two years ago), will blow away. It has already changed the industry for good. There won't be a period, like seven years ago, where publishing houses refused to look at unsolicited manuscripts from people under twenty five."[2]

Footnote Sources:

[1] Diana Maychick, "Bret Ellis Is Too Hip for Hype," *Mademoiselle,* June, 1986.
[2] Based on an interview by Karen Walker and Dieter Miller for *Authors and Artists for Young Adults.*
[3] George F. Will, "A Catcher for the '80s," *Washington Post*, February 27, 1986.
[4] *Contemporary Literary Criticism*, Volume 39, Gale, 1986.
[5] Bret Easton Ellis, "Down and Out," *Rolling Stone*, September 26, 1985.
[6] James Wolcott, "The Young and the Wasted," *Vanity Fair*, September 1987.

■ For More Information See

Voice Literary Supplement, May, 1985, September, 1987.
Elizabeth Mehren, "An Updated 'Catcher' in Lotusland," *Los Angeles Times*, May 22, 1985.
Los Angeles Times Book Review, May 26, 1985, September 13, 1987.
David Masello, "Bret Easton Ellis," *Interview*, June, 1985 (p. 71).
New York Times, June 8, 1985, August 30, 1987, November 18, 1987.
New Republic, June 10, 1985 (p. 42).
Time, June 10, 1985 (p. 80), October 19, 1987 (p. 77).
People Weekly, June 24, 1985 (p. 18), July 29, 1985 (p. 92), September 28, 1987.
Newsweek, July 8, 1985 (p. 70), September 7, 1987 (p. 72).
New Yorker, July 29, 1985, July 7, 1986 (p. 25).
Detroit News, August 11, 1985.
Detroit Free Press, August 18, 1985.
New York, September 9, 1985 (p. 34), November 23, 1987.
Joann Davis, "S & S's Newest Vice-President, Bob Asahina, Rides the Crest of a New Best Seller—*Less Than Zero*," *Publisher's Weekly*, September 13, 1985.
John Powers, "The MTV Novel Arrives," *Film Comment*, November/December 1985.
Terry Teachout, "Are These Your Children?," *National Review*, February 14, 1986 (p. 52).
Times Literary Supplement, February 28, 1986 (p. 216).
Candy Schulman, "Good News for Unpublished Novelists," *Writer's Digest*, December, 1986 (p. 21).
Chicago Tribune, September 13, 1987.
Mark Muro, "Bennington," *Boston Globe*, October 13, 1987 (p. 65).
Anka Radakovich, "Is Bret a Brat?," *Daily News*, November 8, 1987.

E. M. Forster

ber), Bavarian Academy of Fine Arts (honorary corresponding member), Cambridge Humanists (president), Reform Club.

Awards, Honors

Tukojirao Gold Medal, Dewas State Senior, India, 1921; James Tait Black Memorial Prize, and Prix Femina/Vie Heureuse, both 1925, both for *A Passage to India*; Fellow, King's College, Cambridge, England, 1927-1930; LL.D., University of Aberdeen, 1931; Benson Medal, Royal Society of Literature, 1937; honorary fellow, King's College, Cambridge, 1946-70; Litt.D., University of Liverpool, 1947, Hamilton College, 1949, Cambridge University, 1950, University of Nottingham, 1951, University of Manchester, 1954, Leyden University, 1954, University of Leicester, 1958; Tukojimo III Gold Medal; Companion of Honour, 1953; Companion of Royal Society of Literature, 1961; Order of Merit, 1969.

Writings

Where Angels Fear to Tread (novel), Blackwood, 1905, Knopf, 1920.
The Longest Journey (novel), Blackwood, 1907, Knopf, 1922, Holmes & Meier, 1984.
A Room with a View (novel), Edward Arnold, 1908, Putnam, 1911, new edition, Vintage Books, 1986.
Howards End (novel), Putnam, 1910, later edition, Buccaneer Books, 1984.
The Celestial Omnibus and Other Stories, Sidgwick & Jackson, 1911, Knopf, 1923.

B orn Edward Morgan Forster, January 1, 1879, in London, England; died of a stroke, June 7, 1970, in Coventry, England; son of Edward Morgan Llewellyn (an architect) and Alice Clara (Whichelo) Forster. *Education:* King's College, Cambridge, B.A. (second-class honors in classics), 1900, B.A. (second-class honors in history), 1901, M.A., 1910. *Home:* King's College, Cambridge University, Cambridge, England.

Career

Working Men's College, London, England, lecturer, for a period beginning in 1907; Red Cross volunteer in Alexandria, Egypt, 1915-19; literary editor for the *Daily Herald*, London, England; served as private secretary to the Maharajah of Dewas State Senior, India, 1921; writer and lecturer, 1921-70. Annual Clark Lecturer at Cambridge University, beginning, 1927, Rede Lecturer, Cambridge, 1941, W. P. Ker Lecturer, University of Glasgow, 1944; made a lecture tour of United States in 1947. Member of general advisory council, British Broadcasting Corp., and writer of numerous broadcasts; was a vice-president of the London Library. *Member:* American Academy of Arts and Letters (honorary corresponding mem-

The Story of the Siren (short story), Hogarth Press, 1920.

The Government of Egypt (history), Labour Research Department, 1921.

Alexandria: A History and a Guide, W. Morris, 1922, 3rd edition, Doubleday-Anchor, 1961.

Pharos and Pharillon (history), Knopf, 1923, 3rd edition, Hogarth Press, 1961.

A Passage to India (novel), Harcourt, 1924, new edition, Meier, 1978.

Anonymity: An Enquiry, Hogarth Press, 1925, Norwood, 1978.

Original Letters from India, edited by Eliza Fay, Hogarth Press, 1925, new edition, 1986.

Aspects of the Novel (Clark Lecture, 1927), Harcourt, 1927.

The Eternal Moment and Other Stories, Harcourt, 1928.

A Letter to Madan Blanchard (belles lettres), Hogarth Press, 1931, Harcourt, 1932.

Goldsworthy Lowes Dickinson (biography), Harcourt, 1934, new edition, Edward Arnold, 1945.

Abinger Harvest (essays), Harcourt, 1936.

What I Believe (political), Hogarth Press, 1939, Folcroft, 1970.

Reading as Usual (criticism), 1939, Folcroft, 1970.

Nordic Twilight (political), Macmillan (London), 1940, Norwood, 1978.

England's Pleasant Land (pageant play; first produced in Surrey, England, July 9, 1938), Hogarth Press, 1940.

Virginia Woolf (criticism; Rede Lecture, 1941), Harcourt, 1942.

The Development of English Prose between 1918 and 1939 (criticism; W. P. Ker Lecture, 1944), Jackson (Glasgow), 1945.

The Collected Tales of E. M. Forster (previously published as *The Celestial Omnibus* and *The Eternal Moment*), Knopf, 1947, new edition, Modern Library, 1968 (published in England as *Collected Short Stories of E. M. Forster,* Sidgwick & Jackson, 1948, new enlarged edition published as *The New Collected Short Stories* (large print), G. K. Hall, 1986.

(Author of libretto with Eric Crozier) *Billy Budd: An Opera in Four Acts* (based on the novel by Herman Melville; music by Benjamin Britten), Boosey & Hawkes, 1951, revised edition, 1961.

Two Cheers for Democracy (essays), Harcourt, 1951.

Desmond MacCarthy, Mill House Press, 1952.

The Hill of Devi, Harcourt, 1953, new edition, 1985 (published in England as *The Hill of Devi: Being Letters from Dewas State Senior,* Edward Arnold, 1953).

Battersea Rise (first chapter of *Marianne Thornton*), Harcourt, 1955.

Marianne Thornton: A Domestic Biography, 1797-1887, Harcourt, 1956.

E. M. Forster: Selected Writings, edited by G. B. Parker, Heinemann Educational, 1968.

Albergo Empedocle and Other Writings (previously unpublished material, written 1900-15), edited by George H. Thomson, Liveright, 1971.

Maurice (novel), Norton, 1971.

The Life to Come and Other Stories, Norton, 1972, republished as *The Life to Come and Other Short Stories,* 1972.

The Arbinger Edition of E. M. Forster, 13 volumes, edited by O. Stallybrass and E. Heine, E. Arnold, 1972-83, Holmes & Meier, 1973-84.

Aspects of the Novel and Related Writings, edited by O. Stallybrass, Holmes & Meier, 1974.

A View without a Room (essay), Albondocani Press, 1973.

The Lucy Novels: Early Sketches for "A Room with a View," edited by O. Stallybrass, Holmes & Meier, 1973.

The Manuscripts of "Howards End," edited by O. Stallybrass, Holmes & Meier, 1973.

Goldsworthy Lowes Dickinson and Related Writings, edited by O. Stallybrass, Holmes & Meier, 1973.

E. M. Forster's Letters to Donald Windham, privately printed, 1975.

A Commonplace Book, Scolar, 1978, new edition, edited by Philip Gardner, Stanford University Press, 1985.

The Machine Stops and Other Stories (illustrated by Alan Gilham), abridged by S. H. Burton, Longman, 197(?).

The Manuscripts of "A Passage to India," edited by O. Stallybrass, E. Arnold, 1978, Holmes & Meier, 1979.

Only Connect: Letters to Indian Friends, edited by Syed Hamid Husain, Arnold-Heinemann, 1979.

Arctic Summer and Other Fiction, E. Arnold, 1980, Holmes & Meier, 1981.

Selected Letters of E. M. Forster: Volume 1, 1879-1920, edited by Mary Lago and P. N. Furbank, Harvard University Press, 1983.

The Hill of Devi and Other Indian Writings,
    edited by E. Heine, Holmes & Meier, 1983.
Foster-Masood Letters, edited by Jalil Ahmad
    Kidwai, Ross Masood Education and Culture
    Society of Pakistan, 1984.
Selected Letters of E. M. Forster: Volume II,
    1921-1970, edited by M. Lago and P. N.
    Furbank, Harvard University Press, 1984.
Calendar of the Letters of E. M. Forster,
    compiled by M. Lago, Mansell, 1985.

Also author of plays, "The Heart of Bosnia," 1911,
and "The Abinger Pageant," 1934, and script for
film, "Diary for Timothy."

Contributor:

Arnold W. Lawrence, editor, *T. E. Lawrence by*
    His Friends, J. Cape, 1937.
Hermon Ould, editor, *Writers in Freedom,*
    Hutchinson, 1942.
George Orwell, editor, *Talking to India,* Allen
    & Unwin, 1943.
Peter Grimes: Essays, John Lane, for the
    governors of Sadler's Wells Foundation,
    1945.
H. Ould, editor, *Freedom of Expression: A*
    Symposium, Hutchinson, 1945.
S. Radhakrishnan, *Mahatma Gandhi: Essays and*
    Reflections on His Life and Work, 2nd
    edition, Allen & Unwin, 1949.
Hermon Ould: A Tribute, [London], 1952.
The Fearful Choice: A Debate on Nuclear Policy,
    conducted by Philip Toynbee, Wayne State
    University Press, 1959.

Also contributor to *Aspects of England,* 1935, and
Britain and the Beast, 1937.

Author of Introduction:

(And notes) Virgil, *The Aeneid,* 2 volumes,
    translated by E. Fairfax Taylor, Dent, 1906.
(And notes) Eliza Fay, *Original Letters from*
    India, 1799-1815, Harcourt, 1925.
Constance Sitwell, *Flowers and Elephants,* J.
    Cape, 1927.
George Crabbe, Jr., *The Life of George Crabbe,*
    Oxford University Press, 1932.
Maurice O'Sullivan, *Twenty Years A-Growing,*
    Chatto & Windus, 1933.
Mulk Raj Anand, *Untouchable,* Wishart, 1935.
Alec Craig, *The Banned Books of England,*
    Allen & Unwin, 1937.
K. R. Srinivasa Iyengar, *Literature and*
    Authorship in India, Allen & Unwin, 1943.

Goldsworthy Lowes Dickinson, *Letters from*
    John Chinaman, and Other Essays, Allen &
    Unwin, 1946.
Huthi Singh, *Maura,* Longmans, Green, 1951.
Zeenuth Futehally, *Zohra,* Hind Kitabs
    (Bombay), 1951.
Peter Townsend, editor, *Cambridge, Anthology,*
    Hogarth Press, 1952.
Forrest Reid, *Tom Barber,* Pantheon, 1955.
(And notes) William Golding, *Lord of the Flies,*
    Coward, 1955.
G. L. Dickinson, *The Greek View of Life,*
    University of Michigan Press, 1958.
D. Windham, *The Warm Country,* Hart-Davis,
    1960.
Guiseppe Tomasi di Lampedusa, *Two Stories*
    and a Memory, translated by A. Colquhoun,
    Pantheon, 1962.
Frank Sargeson, *Collected Stories,* MacGibbon &
    Kee, 1965.

Work is represented in collections, including *The*
Challenge of Our Time, Percival Marshall, 1948,
and *Fairy Tales for Computers,* Eakins Press, 1969.
Contributor to journals and periodicals, including
Listener, Independent Review, Observer, New
Statesman, Nation, Albany Review, Open Window,
Athenaeum, Egyptian Mail, and *Horizon.* Forster's
works have been translated into twenty-one lan-
guages.

■ Adaptations

A Room with a View (play; adapted by Stephen
    Tait and Kenneth Allott), produced in
    Cambridge, England, February, 1950, Edward
    Arnold, 1951; (television dramatization) BBC,
    April 15, 1973; (motion picture) Merchant
    Ivory, 1986.
A Passage to India (play; adapted by Santha
    Rama Rau), produced in London, England,
    1960, Ambassador Theatre (New York),
    January, 1962; (television; adapted by John
    Maynard), produced by BBC, broadcast by
    NET, 1968, (cassette), Newmann
    Communications, 1984; (movie) Columbia,
    1984.
Where Angels Fear to Tread (play; adapted by
    Elizabeth Hart), S. French, 1963.
Howards End (play; adapted by Lance
    Sieveking and Richard Cottrell), produced in
    London, 1967; (television; adapted by Pauline
    Macaulay; starring Glenda Jackson), BBC,
    April, 1970; (three-part radio drama), Radio-4
    (London), September 1985.

"A Passage to E. M. Forster" (play; based on his works; compiled by William Roerick and Thomas Coley), produced in New York, N.Y. at Theatre de Lys, October 26, 1970.

"The Longest Journey" (play), Lampa Theatre (London), August, 23, 1974.

"The Obelisk" (television), BBC, October 13, 1977.

Maggie Smith plays Charlotte Bartlett, spinster cousin and traveling chaperone in the 1986 film, "A Room with a View."

"The Celestial Omnibus" (recording), American Forces Radio and Television Service, 1978.

"Maurice" (motion picture), Merchant Ivory, 1987.

■ Sidelights

January 1, 1879. E. M. Forster was born in London, England, the only child of Alice Clara (Lily) Whichelo and Edward Morgan Llewellyn Forster, an architect. His name had been registered as Henri, but at his christening "the old verger asked my father what the baby was to be called, and he, distrait, gave his own name, Edward Morgan. This the verger wrote down on a piece of paper. My maternal grandmother held me at the font. When the clergyman asked her what I was to be called she became afraid of the sound of her voice in a sacred edifice, and indicated the piece of paper. My mother, in a distant pew, heard the announcement with horror. I had been registered one way and christened another. What on earth was to happen. It turned out after agitated research that the christening had it, so Edward I am."[1]

After his father died of tuberculosis, young Forster was brought up almost exclusively by the women in the family and various maids. His great Aunt Marianne was particularly intent on managing his and his mother's lives. "I realised without being told, that I was in the power of a failing old woman who wanted to be kind but she was old and each visit she was older. How old was she? Born in the reign of George the Fourth, my mother thought. 'More likely Edward the Fourth' cried I."[1]

"Those early years made a deep impression which no amount of suburbianism or travel has dispelled. When I think of England it is of the countryside, and I still think of her thus though so little of our countryside remains. And my patriotism, which is very steady, is loyalty to the place where I happen to belong. It doesn't go any further...."[2]

The family, considering him of delicate constitution, was over-protective, coddling him and dressing him in frilly outfits with his hair in long curls. His mother recalled: "We have rather a life of it if we do anything baby doesn't like....He calls us 'monstrous crows and rats,' and when his grandmother asked him 'not to do it' he said 'I shall, Mrs piece of suet.'

"...[He has]...such a stupid habit of throwing things for no reason in the world—he had just flung my prayer book and hymn book across the room and when we were with Laura he all but

Still from the movie "A Room with a View," starring Julian Sands and Helena Bonham Carter. Winner of three Academy Awards, it was produced by Merchant Ivory in 1986.

knocked down some valuable vases by throwing a sofa cushion at them...."[1]

Great Aunt Marianne died at the age of ninety-one and left Forster 8,000 pounds (approximately $2,000). The interest of this amount was to be used for his education and at the age of twenty-five he was to receive the capital. "I am grateful to Marianne Thornton; for she and no one else made my career as a writer possible, and her love in a most tangible sense followed me beyond the grave."[3]

1890. Sent to preparatory school, Kent House, in Eastbourne, he was bullied by the other boys, who called him "Mousie." Painfully homesick and "...I feel so very nervous somehow. I don't know why it is but perhaps it is excitement, but lately I have always been taking the dark side of things. I have never been like it before, but it is not at all nice. It is very much like despondency; I am afraid I shall miss the train in the morning...afraid I shall lose my tickets; those are instances of the kind of state of mind I am in; it is not so bad in the day-time as at night, then I cry a lot. I also have...a kind of forboding that something dreadful will happen before the holidays....The worst of school is that you have nothing and nobody to love, if I only had somebody; I shall be much happier."[4]

1892. Sent for the summer term to the "The Granger," a local school. "...Two of the boys in my dormitory last night kept on taking my pillow, and wetting my clothes; so I bore it for a long time and then when they began hitting me and hurting my face, I thought 'no more of this' and I slapped their faces. So they say they will take it out on me this evening. Let them do it!, but I shan't go at them with my fists closed till they do the same to me. And I believe the reason for this is that I did not bring back any grub on Sunday. I don't feel at all worried about it, but I am threatened with all the school setting on to me to morrow. I rather hope they do, and I don't intend to stand still and be bullied; and perhaps I shall get on better afterwards...."[1] His mother withdrew him and brought him home.

Moved to Tonbridge where he enrolled in Tonbridge School as a dayboy. Because those who attended as dayboys were branded as socially inferior by the boarders and staff, Forster was bullied more extensively than in previous school experiences. As a schoolmate recounted years later: "Forster? The writer? Yes, I remember him. A little cissy. We took it out on him, I can tell you...."[1]

1897. Entered King's College, Cambridge. "Body and spirit, reason and emotion, work and play, architecture and scenery, laughter and seriousness, life and art—these pairs which are elsewhere contrasted were there fused into one. People and books reinforced one another, intelligence joined hands with affection, speculation became a passion, and discussion was made profound by love."[5]

"The education I received in those far-off and fantastic days made me soft and I am very glad it did, for I have seen plenty of hardness since, and I know it does not even pay....But though the education was humane it was imperfect, inasmuch as we none of us realised our economic position. In came the nice fat dividends, up rose the lofty thoughts, and we did not realise that all the time we were exploiting the poor of our country and the backward races abroad, and getting bigger profits from our investments than we should. We refused to face this unpalatable truth. I remember being told as a small boy, 'Dear, don't talk about money, it's ugly'—a good example of Victorian defence mechanism."[6]

"...It was Cambridge that first set me off writing....At one time my tutor suggested to me that I might write. He did it in a very informal way. He said in a sort of drawling voice 'I don't see why you should not write,' and I being very diffident was delighted at this remark and thought, after all why shouldn't I write? And I did. It is really owing to Wedd and to that start at Cambridge that I have written. I might have started for some other reason.

"[Cambridge] is not a place in which a writer ought to remain. I am quite sure he ought to go out into the world and meet more types. I was going to say meet people of more classes, but of course in Cambridge you can now meet people of all classes, but mostly selected intellectuals. It is most necessary for the writer, and for everyone else, to go all over the place. That is my general feeling."[7]

October, 1901. Forster and his mother embarked on a one-year voyage to Italy, Sicily, and Austria. "I missed nothing—neither the campaniles, nor the crooked bridges over dry torrent beds, nor the uniformity of blue sky, nor the purple shadows of the mountains over the lake. But I knew that I must wait for many days before they meant any thing to me or gave me any pleasure. We—that is I—are never too tired or unhappy to record, and while we are young a little time purges away our frailties and leaves us with the pure gold. But I would rather have the pure gold at once."[1]

Their days were filled with museums, galleries and churches. His mother's concern was for Forster's health, impracticality, absent-mindedness and occasional clumsiness: first he sprained his ankle, then he broke his arm walking up the steps of St. Peter's.

In Florence, Forster began to work on a new novel. His early version called "Lucy" evolved into *A Room with a View*. "In a hotel lounge one day—at Siena or that sort of place—I overheard an English lady talking to another English lady about a third English lady who had married an Italian far beneath her socially and also much younger, and how most unfortunate it was. This sorry bit of twaddle stuck in my mind. I worked at it until it became alive and grew into a novel of contrasts."[2]

Back in London, mother and son took up residence at the Kingsley Hotel in Bloomsbury and Forster began giving weekly classes in Latin at the Working Men's College. He was to teach there for more than twenty years, developing friendships with students, participating in the college's social activities and writing for the college journal.

1904. Moved into a house in Weybridge which he shared with his mother and grandmother. "...I worry...about myself. I write so slowly, and I think not so well. It is impossible to work at Cambridge: here I'm dull and fairly bright.

"Is it impossible to live with old people without deteriorating?

"My life is now straightening into something rather sad & dull to be sure, & I want to set it & me down, as I see us now. Nothing more great will come out of me. I've made my two discoveries—the religious about 4 years ago, the other in the winter of 1902—and the reconstruction is practically over. If I'm wrecked now it will be on little things—idleness, irritability, & still more, shyness. Self-consciousness will do for me if I'm not careful—drive me into books, or the piano. The truth is I'm living a very difficult life: I never come into contact with any one's work, & that makes things difficult. I may sit year after year in my pretty sitting room, watching things grow more unreal, because I'm afraid of being remarked. . . .It begins to look that I'm not good enough to do without regular work. . . .A few people like my work, but most of them like me. As to lecturing. . .I'm not good at it. . . .I still want, in all moods, the greatest happiness but perhaps it is well it should be denied me. . . .Unimportant as my youth has been, it's been less unimportant than I expected & than other people think. And ardently as I desire beauty & strength & a truer outlook, I don't despise myself, or think life not worth while."[1]

1905. Went to Germany as a tutor. ". . .I wanted to learn some German and do some writing, and a Cambridge friend put me in touch with his aunt. She was English (born in Australia actually) and she had married an aristocratic Pomeranian landowner. She was, furthermore, a well-known and gifted authoress, who wrote under the name of Elizabeth. Her *Elizabeth and Her German Garden* was widely read, and her three eldest girls had become household words in many a British household. . . .I was one of a series of tutors. . .and I was to pick up in exchange what German I could. At first I feared I should not get the job, for I met none of her requirements: refused to come permanently, could not give all my time, could not teach mathematics or anything except English. But the more difficulties I raised the warmer grew Elizabeth's letters. She begged me to come when I liked and as I liked. She trusted I should not find Nassenheide dull, and she asked me to be so good as to bring her from London a packet of orris root.

"My arrival occurred on April 4, 1905. . . .[I] came to the long low building I was presently to know under sunlight. The bell pealed, a hound bayed, and a half-dressed underservant unlocked the hall door and asked me what I wanted. I replied, 'I want to live here'. . . .And presently I stood in the presence of the Countess herself. . . .

". . .The discomforts of my arrival seemed to have lowered me in her opinion: indeed I lost all the ground I had gained through refusing to come. Glancing up at my tired and peaked face, she said in her rather grating voice, 'How d'ye do, Mr. Forster. We confused you with the new housemaid. . . .Can you teach the children, do you think? They are very difficult. . .oh yes Mr. Forster, very difficult, they'll laugh at you, you know. You'll have to be stern or it'll end as it did with Mr. Stokoe.' I gave her the packet of orris root, which

she accepted as only her due, and the interview ended.

"Subsequently our relations became easy and she told me that she had nearly sent me straight back to England there and then, since I was wearing a particularly ugly tie. I do not believe her. I was not. She had no respect for what may be called the lower forms of truth. Then we spoke of some friends of hers whom I had met in Dresden. 'They don't like me,' she said. I replied: 'So I saw.' This gave her a jump.

"So my arrival was on the tough side. Still all went well, and all around us stretched the German countryside. . . .When I began to look about me I was filled with delight.

"It was the country, the flat agricultural surround, that so ravished me. . . .

". . .I had a little room which got the morning sun, so that I could sit in my bath and be shone upon. . . .

"My teaching duties were only an hour a day. I had abundant leisure for my German and my writing and was most considerately treated if I asked for leave. . .our pupils, delightful and original and easy. . .their mother, delightful and original and occasionally difficult.

"It is curious that Germany, a country which I do not know well or instinctively embrace, should twice have seduced me through her countryside. I have described the first occasion. The second was half a century later when I stayed in a remote hamlet in Franconia. . . .The two districts resembled each other in their vastness and openness and in their freedom from industrialism. They were free from smoke and wires, and masts and placards, and they were full of living air: they remind me of what our own countryside used to be before it was ruined.

"The tragedy of England is that she is too small to become a modern state and yet to retain her freshness. The freshness has to go. Even when there is a National Park it has to be mucked up. Germany is anyhow larger, and thanks to her superior size she may preserve the rural heritage that smaller national units have had to scrap—the heritage which I used to see from my own doorstep in Hertfordshire when I was a child, and which has failed to outlast me."[8]

1907. *The Longest Journey* published. "All I write is, to me, sentimental. A book which doesn't leave people either happier or better than it found them, which doesn't add some permanent treasure to the world, isn't worth doing. (A book *about* good and happy people may be still better but hasn't attracted me yet so much.) This is my 'theory,' and I maintain it's sentimental...."[2]

"...Though critics do not think highly of it. It is sometimes dismissed as a failure. Yet I like it most because it is so close to me...to what I am."[9]

October 14, 1908. *A Room with a View* released to warm reviews. "...It *is* gratifying when those who know the world and men at work can find a book by me not sloppy nor unconnected with life....I can't write down 'I care about love, beauty, liberty, affection, and truth,' though I should like to.

"I don't at all know about [*A Room with a View*]. It is slight, unambitious, and uninteresting, but—in rather an external way—the characters seem more alive to me than any others that I have put together. The publisher is much pleased—which is all to the bad, I admit—and I have got good terms. Have tried to get it taken in America, but that was no go. 'Not sufficiently compelling for a transatlantic audience.' Which, I admit, is all to the good....The thing comes out in October, and will probably gratify the home circle, but not those whose opinions I value most."[1] The book was not a commercial success.

October 18, 1910. *Howards End* was "...my best novel and approaching a good novel. Very elaborate and all pervading plot that is seldom tiresome or forced, range of characters, social sense, wit, wisdom, colour. Have only just discovered why I don't care for it: not a single character in it for whom I care....Perhaps the house in *H.E.*, for which I did once care, took the place of people and now that I no longer care for it, their barrenness has become evident. I feel pride in the achievement, but cannot love it, and occasionally the swish of the skirts and the non-sexual embraces irritate...."[1]

Began a deep friendship with Florence Barger with whom he could also discuss his homosexuality. She was to become one of his close female friends. "She loves me and I her, and reverence her without feeling ashamed of my uselessness....Very great happiness, and must try not to impose on her and tout for sympathy."[1]

October, 1912. Departed for India, leaving his mother in Italy for a vacation. The Rajah of Dewas was to have a great impact on Forster's life, and they met many times. "The Rajah has just been

The Lomas Rishi cave...model for the Marabar Caves in "A Passage to India."

From the 1984 Columbia Pictures' film "A Passage to India." Winner of two Academy Awards, it starred Judy Davis and Victor Banerjee.

talking to me, cross-legged and barefoot on a little cane chair. We had a long talk about religion. . . .Indians are so easy and communicative on this subject, whereas English people are mostly offended when it is introduced, or else shocked if there is a difference of opinion. His attitude was very difficult for a Westerner. He believes that we—men, birds, everything—are part of God, and that men have developed more than birds because they have come nearer to realising this....

"...He is really a remarkable man, for all this goes with much practical ability and a sense of humour. In the middle of a chat he will suddenly pray, tapping his forehead and bobbing on his knees, and then continuing the sentence where he left it off; 'On days when one feels gratitude, it is well to show it,' he said.

"...He was certainly a genius and possibly a saint, and he had to be a king."[10]

November, 1915. Left for Alexandria, Egypt. "I am liking my work out here. I am what is called a 'Red Cross Searcher':—that is to say I go round the Hospitals and question the wounded soldiers for news of their missing comrades. It is depressing in a way, for if one does get news about the missing it is generally bad news. But I am able to be of use to the wounded soldiers themselves in various unofficial ways....

"I live in a comfortable hotel here, and start out about 10.0., returning for lunch and finishing about 7.0. In the evening I write my reports which go—ultimately—to the relatives in England and to the War Office. The Red X is a semi-military organisation, so, though technically a civilian, I wear officer's uniform, and get various privileges and conveniences....I have one or two friends here, and the regular and definite work has stopped me thinking about the war, which is a mercy, for in England I very nearly went mad.

"...I do not like Egypt much—or rather, I do not see it, for Alexandria is cosmopolitan. But what I have seen seems vastly inferior to India, for which I am always longing in the most persistent way, and where I still hope to die. It is only at sunset that Egypt surpasses India—at all other hours it is flat, unromantic, unmysterious, and godless—the soil is mud, the inhabitants are of mud moving, and exasperating in the extreme: I feel as instinctively not at home among them as I feel instinctively at home among Indians....

"...It is useless to make plans when at any moment one may be submarined or conscripted....All that I cared for in civilisation has gone forever, and I am trying to live without either hopes or fears—not an easy job, but one keeps going some how."[4]

January, 1919. Returned to England. "...Isn't it awful how all the outward nonsense of England has been absolutely untouched by the war—still this unbroken front of dress-shirts and golf. I'm damned if I know what bucks one up...."[4]

In need of money, Forster began working in literary journalism. Wrote approximately a hundred articles and reviews for *Nation, Daily News, Herald* and *Athenaeum.* "...I am happiest when busy. How fatuous! I see my middle age as clearly as middle age can be seen. Always working, never creating. Pleasant to all, trusting no one. A mixture of cowardice and sympathy. Blaming civilization for my failure. At the end of these activities begins a great pain, after which death, but I cannot realize such things....I long for something of which youth was only a part. I don't see what it is clearly yet, but know what keeps me from it. I am not vain, but I am sensitive to praise and blame: this is bad. Is it just the aimiable [sic] journalist—who can't even write as soon as he looks into his own mind."[11]

1921. Returned to India to work as private secretary to the Rajah. "The day after my arrival we had a bewildering interview and [the Maharajah] assigned me my duties: gardens, tennis courts, motors, Guest House, Electric House. None of these had much to do with reading or writing, my supposed specialities. I had an office (hours 7-11 and 4-5). All the post was to pass through my hands. These were not the duties which I had expected or for which I was qualified, but this did not disturb us, and he spent most of the interview in writing me out lists of the dignitaries of state. They fell into four categories: the Ruling Family, the great Maratha nobles, the secondary nobles, and the lesser nobles, who bore the title of Mankari: 'in this last lot you will be the first.' Reverting to the ruling Family, he emphasized the names and titles of his brother, his son, his brother's wife, his aunt, and his own absent wife. These were the highest in the land: I was to salaam with two hands and the whole hand, and to extend similar courtesies to the Dewan, the A.G.G. and the P.A. These last two were British officials. I was to regard myself when meeting them as an Indian. But I began by this time to get a little mixed—far from clear for instance as to the composition of the all-powerful council of State. 'Wait a minute!' he cried. On he swept, descending to individual Mankaris and clerks and mysterious persons called 'Eighteen Offices' or 'Horse Doctor.'

"'I shall never get all this right,' I said.

"'Oh yes, you will. Besides it does not matter in the least, except in the case of Brother and those others whom I have specially mentioned.'...

"The suite he assigned me was on the first floor at the end of the drawing-room wing: bedroom, sitting room, anteroom, bathroom, all decently

From the movie "Maurice," starring Rupert Graves. Produced by Merchant Ivory, 1987.

furnished in the European style. It was reached either by a verandah along the inner side of the courtyard, or by a staircase that descended straight into the garden and was sometimes, though not often, locked at the bottom, or by an outside verandah which communicated with the bedroom. It was not very private, but what was? We all of us lived in a passage, the Ruler included. I usually slept on the roof, facing Devi...."[10]

He returned to Weybridge "...to come back to an ugly house a mile from the station, an old, fussy, exacting mother, to come back having lost your Rajah, without a novel, and with no power to write one—this is dismal, I expect, at the age of 43."[11]

He continued working on one of his unfinished novels. "I began this novel before my 1921 visit [to India], and took out the opening chapters with me, with the intention of continuing them. But as soon as they were confronted with the country they purported to describe, they seemed to wilt and go dead and I could do nothing with them. I used to look at them of an evening in my room at Dewas, and felt only distaste and despair. The gap between India remembered and India experienced was too wide. When I got back to England the gap narrowed, and I was able to resume. But I still thought the book bad, and probably should not have completed it without the encouragement of Leonard Woolf."[10]

"...[A Passage to India] is done at last and I feel—or shall feel when the typing's over—great relief. I am so weary, not of working but of not working; of thinking the book bad and so not working, and of not working and so thinking it bad: that vicious circle. Now it is done and I think it good. Publishers fall into ecstacies! But I know much about publishers...and sent them those chapters that are likely to make them ecstatic, concealing the residue in the W. C. until the contracts are signed. They unite, though, in restraining their joy until the autumn. I'm afraid it won't come out till then."[12]

"I shall never write another novel...—my patience with ordinary people has given out. But I shall go on writing. I don't feel any decline in my 'powers.'"[13]

"I have wondered—not whether I was getting down or up, which is too difficult, but whether I had moved at all since King's [College]. King's stands for personal relationships, and these still seem to me the most real things on the surface of the earth, but I have acquired a feeling that people must go away from each other (spiritually) every now and then, and improve themselves if the relationship is to develop or even endure. A Passage to India describes such a going away—preparatory to the next advance, which I am not capable of describing. It seems to me that individuals progress alternately by loneliness and intimacy...."[12]

There were some accusations from political and social circles that the book was not fair in dealing with it's subject. "Isn't 'fair-mindedness' dreary! A rare achievement, and a valuable one, you will tell me, but how sterile in one's own soul. I fall in love with Orientals, with Anglo-Indians—no: that is roughly my internal condition, and all the time I had to repress the consequences, or fail to hold the scales. Where is truth? It makes me so sad that I could not give the beloved a better show. One's deepest emotions count for so little as soon as one tries to describe external life honestly, or even readably....

"...As to what qualifies a man to write a novel dealing with India, to what extent blue-book accuracy is desirable, to what extent intensity of impression and sensitiveness, is a controversial question, and one on which gibes are apt to be exchanged. I have only been to the country twice (year & a half in all), and only been acquainted with Indians for eighteen years, yet I believe that I have seen certain important truths...."[11]

1925-1926. Moved into West Hackhurst with his mother, though she resisted. He described himself as: "...Famous, wealthy, miserable, physically ugly—red nose enormous, round patch in middle of scalp which I forget less than I did and which is brown when I don't wash my head and pink when I do. Face in the distance...is toad-like and pallid, with a tiny rim of hair along the top of the triangle. My stoop must be appalling yet I don't think much of it, indeed I still don't think often. Now I do, and am surprised I don't repel more generally: I can still get to know any one I want and have that illusion that I am charming and beautiful. Take no bother over nails or teeth but would powder my nose if I wasn't found out. Stomach increases, but not yet visible under waistcoat....Eyes & probably hearing weaker."[11]

Forster experienced emotional difficulty with his mother and was plagued with waves of melancholy. "...The fact that I don't create, or get idler, is depressing me, even to the point of making me self-conscious and disinclining me to see certain people....I don't know what to do with my existence, my memory's worse, my vitality probably less, and yet I am feeling perfectly well—unless the sense that I couldn't face anything except what I actually do face is a sign of morbidity. There is no doubt that work would put every thing right, but what work?

"I never felt work was a duty—indeed, the less one adds to civilisation the longer perhaps it will take to topple over. But not to feel intact, not to [be] able to expose oneself to certain contacts because of self-consciousness—that really is an aweful nuisance, and I spend a good deal of time now with people who are (vaguely speaking) my inferiors, and to whom I can very easily be kind."[12]

1930. "...I am now 51, and perhaps the fact that I'm awfully young in some ways make difficulties that wouldn't come to people who bow themselves down all of a piece."[12]

Struck up a close friendship with police officer Bob Buckingham. "...I'm quite sure that his feeling for me is something he has never had before. It's a spiritual feeling which has extended to my physique."[11]

Regularly reviewed books on BBC Radio. "It is nice getting all this money, as I have been losing investments like everyone else in the last few months. Now I shall be rich again, as I have not been for a long time, and I am not again making the mistake of investing, or even of letting it lie in the Bank. I shall bury it to be disinterred as wanted...."[12]

"The ugly habit has crept on me. I bring myself to the front by saying jokingly that I am rich, poor, have made good terms in America, paid a lot at a restaurant; and a man who has had real worries over money rebukes me. 'A thing to use if one's got it'—I have always preached that, yet I am letting it use me, and take hold of me where I feel safest, through my sense of humour."[11]

"...One of the evils of money is that it tempts us to look at it rather than at the things that it buys. They are dimmed because of the metal and the paper through which we receive them. That is the fundamental deceitfulness of riches, which kept worrying Christ. That is the treachery of the purse, the wallet and the bank-balance, even from the capitalist point of view. They were invented as a convenience to the flesh, they have become a chain for the spirit. Surely they can be cut out, like some sorts of pain. Though deprived of them in the human mind might surely still keep its delicacy unimpaired, and the human body eat, drink and make love."[6]

"Life is certainly odd," Forster wrote to a friend during World War II. "And what I resent is that it must be making me so odd, and people elsewhere...still odder. It does not seem natural that I should have interrupted this letter to call out to my mother (aged 88) to keep away from glass, that she should have transmitted the warning in calm tones while packing me up some margarine, and that I should have gone on with this letter equally calmly. One adapts oneself to conditions, and it is depressing that one should, for it means that one is failing to notice them."[11]

"I am tearing up papers and fill the wastepaper basket nightly, mostly with old letters. I don't know what to do with my unpublished stories, of which there are an untidy bunch. They are mostly frivolous, many would be repelled by them, and I don't really know whether they are any good."[12]

1945. "...Mother is dead. Peacefully, while I was spooning her some lunch on Sunday, and the famous death-rattle wasn't too bad. I said 'Can you hear me?' and she nodded. I think there was something deeper between us than I knew, for the shock is worse than I expected. I can't explain—or could explain all too well, being a writer—but it has to do with the greatness of love and one's own smallness...."[12] "...I partly died when [she] did, and must smell sometimes of the grave.—I have noticed and disliked that smell in others occasionally."[11]

Returned to India. "I feel like a sponge which has been dropped back into an ocean whose existence it had forgotten."[11]

1946. Upon his return home, King's College offered to make him an honorary fellow, giving him residence at the college. His first weeks were uncomfortable. "...There is no privacy, and people are always pestering one to be interesting."[11]

He soon acclimatized, however, reconnecting with the Apostles Society and mingling with undergraduates. "...I have no mystic faith in the people. I have in the individual. He seems to me a divine achievement and I mistrust any view which belittles him. If anyone calls you a wretched little individual—and I've been called that—don't you take it lying down. You are important because everyone else is an individual too—including the person who criticises you. In asserting your personality you are playing for your side."[6]

1947. Invited by Harvard University to give a lecture at their "Symposium on Music Criticism." "An extraordinary invitation, really. I'm to speak

"Rooksnest," the model for *Howards End.*

on 'The Raison d'Etre of Criticism in the Arts,' revealing whether or not criticism is any use....Actually, it was jolly smart of the Harvard people to find out that I'm fond of music. England hasn't got onto it yet. The Harvard people wrote that they liked something I said about Beethoven's Fifth in my novel *Howards End,* which came out in 1910. I was so grateful for their perspicacity that I accepted their invitation at once. Of course, I've always fancied that I am rather better than the average music listener in comprehension....

"America has been awfully kind to my books. But admiration can be a little frightening you know. I understand there are some very deep readers of mine at Harvard and I'm a bit uneasy about facing them. It's unsettling to have people going over your work with a magnifying glass and turning up hidden meanings.

"All I seem to write any more is little essays. But I must say I keep right on looking at things from a novelist's point of view.

"Perhaps an idea will come along."[14]

"I have refused $25,000 from Fox Films for the movie rights of *A Room with a View.* Stimulated by my refusal, they offer more....Nothing would have survived of the original except my name, and if I had tried to control the production I should have broken my heart at Hollywood...."[12]

"America is rather like life. You can usually find in it what you look for. If you look for skyscrapers or cowboys or cocktail parties or gangsters or business connections or political problems or women's clubs, they will certainly be there. You can be very hot there or very cold. You can explore the America of your choice by plane or train, by hitch-hike or on foot. It will probably be interesting, and it is sure to be large.

"I went there for the first time at the age of sixty-eight. By sixty-eight one is so to speak a pilgrim grandfather who knows very clearly what to look for when he disembarks. I had no doubt as to what I wanted to discover in America. It was to provide me with scenery and individuals. The scenery was to be of two sorts—gigantic and homely. The individuals were not to be representative—I never could get on with representative individuals—but people who existed on their own account and with whom it might therefore be possible to be friends. That is the America I looked for and was to find. My visit was a complete success from my own point of view."[6]

1953. Received the order of Companions of Honour to the Queen. "...All went well between myself and the queen yesterday. I was alone with her for about ten minutes—she was quite an ickle thing, very straight and charming, stood with her back to a huge fire, gave me a very handsome decoration in a case...and we talked about this and that very pleasantly. She shook hands to start and to finish, and I threw in some bows, and occasionally threw in Your Majesty or Ma'am. She was much better at the chat than I was. I liked her very much indeed. Finally she rang a buzzer in the mantel piece and I retired. It was a state dining room I

think, which was gold, and very long. She looked tiny at the end of it, dressed in blue. I drove up to the Palace in a taxi and departed from it on foot."[12]

1960-1963. Stage adaptation of *A Passage to India* by Santha Rama Rau premiered in London. "Though you might not think so, this is not the first time I have trodden the stage. On the previous occasion it was that of Covent Garden: then I only had to bow. Tonight's undertaking is more difficult....How good the actors were. And how pleased I was that there were so many of them. I am so used to seeing the sort of play which deals with one man and two women. They do not leave me with the feeling I have made a full theatrical meal. They are excellent in many ways, but they do not give me the impression of the multiplicity of life....As a member of the audience I have on occasion been thanked by the actors for being so good. It did not arouse in me any great emotion. All the same, it is a pretty thought, so I will give you my bow."[12]

Forster at King's College in the 1950's.

June 7, 1970. Died of a stroke. He had left instructions that he was to be "disposed of" wherever he was at the time of his death, without any religious observances. Forster was cremated and his ashes scattered on Buckingham's rose bed.

"I suppose such views and beliefs that I have, have come out incidentally in my books....Anyone who has cared to read my books will see what high value I attach to personal relationships and to tolerance and, I may add, to pleasure. Pleasure one is not supposed to talk about in public however such one enjoys it in private. But if I have had any influence I should be very glad that it had induced people to enjoy this wonderful world into which we are born, and of course to help others to enjoy it too."[7]

Footnote Sources:

[1] P. N. Furbank, *E. M. Forster: A Life, Volume I,* Harcourt, 1977.
[2] E. M. Forster, *The Hill of Devi,* E. Arnold, 1983.
[3] E. M. Forster, *Marianne Thornton: A Domestic Biography, 1797-1887,* Harcourt, 1956.
[4] Mary Lago and P. N. Furbank, editors, *Selected Letters of E. M. Forster, Volume I, 1879-1920,* Belknop Press, 1983.
[5] Francis King, *E. M. Forster and His World,* Thames & Hudson, 1978.
[6] E. M. Forster, *Two Cheers for Democracy,* Harcourt, 1951.
[7] David Jones, "E. M. Forster on His Life and His Books," *Listener,* January 1, 1959.
[8] E. M. Forster, "Recollections of Nassenheide," *Listener,* January 1, 1959.
[9] V. A. Shahane, "A Visit to Mr. E. M. Forster," *Quest* (Bombay), spring, 1967.
[10] E. M. Forster, *The Hill of Devi,* Harcourt, 1953.
[11] P. N. Furbank, *E. M. Forster: A Life, Volume II,* Harcourt, 1978.
[12] M. Lago and P. N. Furbank, editors, *Selected Letters of E. M. Forster, Volume II, 1921-1970,* Belknop Press, 1977.
[13] E. M. Forster, *The Life to Come and Other Stories,* Norton, 1972.
[14] "Tourist," *New Yorker,* May 3, 1947.

■ For More Information See

Books:

Frank Swinnerton, *The Georgian Literary Scene,* Dent, 1938, revised edition, 1951.
Rose Macaulay, *The Writings of E. M. Forster,* Harcourt, 1938, new edition, Barnes & Noble, 1970.
Lionel Trilling, *E. M. Forster,* New Directions, 1943, 2nd revised edition, 1965.
Austin Warren, *Rage for Order,* University of Chicago Press, 1948.
John K. Johnstone, *The Bloomsbury Group: A Study of E. M. Forster, Lytton Strachey, Virginia Woolf, and Their Circle,* Noonday, 1954.

Morton Dauwen Zabel, *Craft and Character,* Viking, 1957.
James McConkey, *The Novels of E. M. Forster,* Cornell University Press, 1957.
Malcolm Cowley, editor, *Writers at Work: The Paris Review Interviews,* first series, Viking, 1958.
H. J. Oliver, *The Art of E. M. Forster,* Cambridge University Press, 1960.
Karl Watts Gransden, *E. M. Forster,* Grove, 1962, revised edition, Oliver & Boyd, 1970.
F. C. Crews, *E. M. Forster: The Perils of Humanism,* Princeton University Press, 1962.
John Beer, *The Achievement of E. M. Forster,* Chatto, 1962, Barnes & Noble, 1963.
James Hall, *The Tragic Comedians: Seven Modern British Novelists,* Indiana University Press, 1963.
John Edward Hardy, *Man in the Modern Novel,* University of Washington Press, 1964.
Alan Wilde, *Art and Order: A Study of E. M. Forster,* New York University Press, 1964.
K. Natwar-Singh, editor, *E. M. Forster: A Tribute,* Harcourt, 1964.
David Shusterman, *The Quest for Certitude in E. M. Forster's Fiction,* Indiana University Press, 1965.
B. J. Kirkpatrick, *A Bibliography of E. M. Forster,* Hart-Davis, 1965, revised edition, 1968.
Wilfred Stone, *The Cave and the Mountain: A Study of E. M. Forster,* Stanford University Press, 1966.
Malcolm Bradbury, editor, *Forster: A Collection of Critical Essays,* Prentice-Hall, 1966.
George H. Thomson, *The Fiction of E. M. Forster,* Wayne State University Press, 1967.
Norman Kelvin, *E. M. Forster,* Southern Illinois University Press, 1967.
Vasant Anant Shahane, editor, *Perspectives on E. M. Forster's A Passage to India,* Barnes & Noble, 1968.
Laurence Brander, *E. M. Forster: A Critical Study,* Hart-Davis, 1968.
Denis Godfrey, *E. M. Forster's Other Kingdom,* Barnes & Noble, 1968.
Frederick P. W. McDowell, *E. M. Forster,* Twayne, 1969, revised edition, 1982.
H. H. Anniah Gowda, *A Garland for E. M. Forster,* Literary Half-Yearly (Mysore, India), 1969.
Oliver Stallybrass, editor, *Aspects of E. M. Forster: Essays and Recollections Written for His Ninetieth Birthday, January 1, 1969,* Harcourt, 1969.
Andrew Rutherford, *Twentieth Century Interpretations of A Passage to India,* Prentice-Hall, 1970.
June P. Levine, *Creation and Criticism: A Passage to India,* University of Nebraska Press, 1971.
Alfred Borrello, *An E. M. Forster Dictionary,* Scarecrow, 1971.
James McConkey, *The Novels of E. M. Forster,* Archon Books, 1971.
Martial Rose, *E. M. Forster,* Arco, 1971.
A. Borrello, *An E. M. Forster Glossary,* Scarecrow, 1972.
P. Gardner, editor, *E. M. Forster: The Critical Heritage,* Routledge & Kegan Paul, 1974.
John Colmer, *E. M. Forster: The Personal Voice,* Routledge & Kegan Paul, 1975.
John Sayre Martin, *E. M. Forster: The Endless Journey,* Cambridge University Press, 1976.

F. P. W. McDowell, editor, *E. M. Forster: An Annotated Bibliography of Writings about Him*, Northern Illinois University Press, 1977.

Jane Lagoudis Pinchin, *Alexandria Still: Forster, Durrell and Cavafy*, Princeton University Press, 1977.

G. K. Das, *Forster's India*, Macmillan (London), 1977, Rowman & Littlefield, 1978.

P. N. Furbank, *E. M. Forster: A Life*, Secker & Warburg, *Volume One: The Growth of a Novelist (1870-1914)*, 1977, *Volume Two: Polycrates' Ring (1914-1970)*, 1978, published in America in one volume as *E. M. Forster: A Life*, Harcourt, 1978.

Philip Gardner, *E. M. Forster*, Longman, 1978.

Francis E. King, *E. M. Forster and His World*, Scribner, 1978.

G. K. Das and J. Beer, editors, *E. M. Forster, a Human Exploration: Centenary Essays*, New York University Press, 1979.

Robin Jared Lewis, *E. M. Forster's Passages to India*, Columbia University Press, 1979.

V. A. Shahane, *Approaches to E. M. Forster: A Centenary Volume*, Arnold-Heinemann (New Delhi), 1981.

J. S. Herz and Robert K. Martin, editors, *E. M. Forster: Centenary Revaluations*, Macmillan (London), 1982.

Barbara Rosecrance, *Forster's Narrative Vision*, Cornell University Press, 1982.

British Writers, Volume 6, Scribner, 1983.

Christopher C. Brown and William B. Thesing, *English Prose and Criticism, 1900-1950*, Gale, 1983.

H. F. Oxbury, *Great Britons: Twentieth-Century Lives*, Oxford University Press, 1985.

David Dowling, *Bloomsbury Aesthetics and the Novels of Forster*, Macmillan (London), 1985.

J. Beer, *"A Passage to India": Essays in Interpretation*, Macmillan (England), 1986.

Graham Chainey, *A Literary History of Cambridge*, University of Michigan Press, 1986.

Judith Scherer Herz, *The Short Narratives of E. M. Forster*, Macmillan (England), 1987.

Periodicals:

Forum, December, 1927.

Atlantic Monthly, November, 1927 (p. 642), January, 1949 (p. 60).

E. M. Forster, "Breaking Up," *Spectator*, July 28, 1933.

Criterion, October, 1934.

Scrutiny, September, 1938.

Theology, April, 1940.

P. N. Furbank and F. J. H. Haskell, "The Art of Fiction I: E. M. Forster," *New Republic*, October 5, 1949 (biographical; p. 17), January 11, 1964 (biographical; p. 15), June 20, 1970 (p. 28).

Newsweek, October 26, 1953 (p. 119), January 13, 1969 (p. 52).

Angus Wilson, "A Conversation with E. M. Forster," *Encounter*, November, 1957.

Modern Fiction Studies, autumn, 1961 (p. 258), summer, 1967 (p. 195), winter, 1983 (p. 623).

Times Literary Supplement, June 22, 1962, November 14, 1975 (p. 1356), November, 1980 (p. 1294), November 18, 1983 (p. 1267).

Theoria, June 15, 1963 (p. 17).

Commonweal, February 21, 1964 (p. 635), September 21, 1973 (review; p. 506).

Mademoiselle, June, 1964 (biographical).

Vogue, January 1, 1965 (biographical; p. 12).

New York Public Library Bulletin, May, 1967 (p. 283).

Observer, June 14, 1970.

Christian Science Monitor, June 18, 1970.

Nation, June 29, 1970, November 11, 1978 (p. 500).

Listener, July 9, 1970.

Christian Century, July 22, 1970.

Books and Bookmen, August, 1970.

Journal of Aesthetics and Art Criticism, fall, 1971 (p. 101).

Extrapolation, May, 1976 (p. 172).

Time, November 6, 1978 (p. 113), December 31, 1984 (p. 57).

New Leader, November 20, 1978 (p. 14).

New Statesman, November 14, 1980 (p. 21).

International Fiction Review, winter, 1980 (p. 46).

Encounter, February, 1980 (p. 51), September/October, 1985 (p. 43).

Modern Language Quarterly, June, 1981 (p. 166).

London, July, 1981 (p. 94).

Modern Philology, August, 1981 (p. 45), August, 1982 (p. 61).

Prose Studies, December, 1982 (p. 326).

Journal of Modern Literature, March, 1983 (p. 109).

Twentieth Century Literature, summer/fall, 1985 (p. 170).

Commentary, September, 1985 (p. 48).

Variety, August 26, 1987 (review; p. 15).

Obituaries:

New York Times, June 8, 1970 (p. 1).

Times (London), June 8, 1970 (p. 8).

Washington Post, June 8, 1970.

New Statesman, June 12, 1970.

L'Express, June 15-21, 1970.

Antiquarian Bookman, June 22, 1970.

Time, June 22, 1970 (p. 72).

Newsweek, June 22, 1970 (p. 84).

Publishers Weekly, June 22, 1970 (p. 42).

Collections:

E. M. Forster Archive at King's College Library, King's College, Cambridge, England.

Humanities Research Center, University of Texas.

Cathy Guisewite

S urname rhymes with "rice-white"; born September 5, 1950, in Dayton, Ohio; daughter of William Lee (in advertising) and Anne (Duly) Guisewite. *Education:* University of Michigan, A.B., 1972. *Home:* Los Angeles, Calif. *Office:* c/o Universal Press Syndicate, 4900 Main St., Kansas City, Mo. 64112.

■ Career

Campbell-Ewald Advertising Agency, Detroit, Mich., writer, 1972-73; Norman Prady Ltd. (advertising agency), Detroit, writer, 1973-74; W. B. Doner & Co. (advertising agency), Southfield, Mich., writer, 1974-75, group supervisor, 1975-76, vice-president, 1976-77; Universal Press Syndicate, Mission, Kan., creator, author, and artist of "Cathy" comic strip, 1976—. Creator of "Cathy" novelty items.

■ Awards, Honors

L.H.D. from Rhode Island College, 1979, Eastern Michigan University, 1981, and Russell Sage College, 1986; Emmy Award from the Academy of Television Arts and Sciences, for best animated program, 1987, for "Cathy."

■ Writings

Collections:

The Cathy Chronicles, Andrews & McMeel, 1978.
What Do You Mean, I Still Don't Have Equal Rights?, Andrews & McMeel, 1980.
What's a Nice Single Girl Doing with a Double Bed?, Bantam, 1981.
I Think I'm Having a Relationship with a Blueberry Pie, Bantam, 1981.
It Must Be Love, My Face Is Breaking Out, Andrews & McMeel, 1982.
Another Saturday Night of Wild and Reckless Abandon, Andrews & McMeel, 1982.
A Mouthful of Breath Mints and No One to Kiss, Andrews & McMeel, 1983.
Climb Every Mountain, Bounce Every Check, Andrews & McMeel, 1983.
The Salesclerk Made Me Buy It, Fawcett, 1983.
Men Should Come with Instruction Booklets, Andrews & McMeel, 1984.
My Cologne Backfired, Fawcett, 1984.
I'll Pay $5,000 for a Swimsuit That Fits Me!!!, Fawcett, 1985.
A Hand to Hold, an Opinion to Reject, Andrews & McMeel, 1987.
Why Do the Right Words Always Come Out of the Wrong Mouth?, Andrews & McMeel, 1988.
Wake Me Up When I'm a Size Five, Andrews & McMeel, 1985.
Sorry I'm Late, My Hair Won't Start, Fawcett, 1986.

Stressed for Success, Fawcett, 1986.
Thin Thighs in Thirty Years, Andrews & McMeel, 1986.
Two Pies. One Fork, Fawcett, 1987.
It Must Be Something in the Ink, Fawcett, 1987.
It's More Than a Pregnancy. It's a Religion, Fawcett, 1986.

Other:

Cathy's Valentine Day Survival Kit: How to Live through Another February 14th, Andrews & McMeel, 1983.
How to Get Rich, Fall in Love, Lose Weight, and Solve All Your Problems by Saying "No," Andrews & McMeel, 1983.
Eat Your Way to a Better Relationship, Andrews & McMeel, 1983.

■ Adaptations

"Cathy" (animated television special), CBS-TV, May 15, 1987.
"Cathy's Last Resort" (animated television special), CBX-TV, fall, 1988.

■ Work In Progress

An animated television special for Valentine's Day, to be aired on CBS-TV, 1989.

■ Sidelights

Cathy Guisewite was born in Dayton, Ohio on September 5, 1950. "All my life my parents have been wildly enthusiastic about anything creative my sisters or I did. Every time we made a greeting card—and we almost always made our own—Mom would say, 'Oh, this is good enough to be published.' Most mothers tape their children's work to the refrigerator door. Mine would send them off to the Museum of Modern Art.

"When I was growing up, I resented my mom for not being the kind of mother who sat home baking all day. She didn't bake and she didn't knit, and I felt mothers should do those things. Mom tended to be more cosmopolitan than the other mothers I knew. She took us to art museums and foreign films, and I hated everything she dragged us to. I wanted a fat little mother baking cookies.

"But I have never doubted for a second that her children come first. She would stop anything and travel any distance if one of us needed her—and she has."[1]

1972. Received a B.A. in English from the University of Michigan.

1974. Began working as a writer at W. B. Doner and Co. (advertising agency), where by 1976 she had become vice-president. "My career was going great, but I was miserable about my love life. Balancing those two have always been a major conflict for me. . . .So there I was, sitting around my apartment, snacking, waiting for this guy to call, and writing a depressing letter to my mother. I drew a picture of how I looked and another of how I'd look if the phone would ring. It made me see the humorous side of my situation."[2]

"My mother had always taught me that the real strength of a person was her ability to move through a crisis—that every big crisis has a purpose and every little disappointment has a bright and wonderful side."[3]

"But actually, my dad is the central sense of humor in the family. Both my parents have sickeningly cheerful attitudes. They always forced us to look for the bright side in any disaster. And that's how I do the strip.

"You just recreate your worst moments and think of a twist to make them feel better. That's my favorite part of my job."[4]

"I spent a lot of evenings drawing out my frustrations and then I'd send the sketches home. They were simply a release. I didn't know I was creating a comic strip."[3]

"When I saw my situation in a cartoon it looked cute, not tragic. After that I would try to think of something funny to say to save me from being totally depressed.

"My mother went to the library and researched comic-strip syndicates. She put them in order and typed up a list. I didn't want the syndicates to get a cover letter from my mom, so when I thought she was getting serious, I sent a letter to the first one on the list."[5]

Universal Press Syndicate accepted what was to become the "Cathy" strip. "I've come to realize how amazing that day really was. I have talked to other cartoonists who've literally spent half their lives trying to get a syndicate to respond to their ideas and accept their comic strip for publication. . . .Yes, it was a remarkable day!"[3]

"It was totally stunning in every way. I was shocked! I'm just as incoherent about it today as I was then.

"I stayed [with W. B. Doner and Co.] for about nine months after I started the strip, so it was hardly a sudden transition. I really only quit the agency when I was just exhausted—you know, it was a lot of work to try to do both. But I think I stayed at the agency partly because of the security of the routine I was in there and partly because I was sure that somebody would call me up and tell me they were just kidding about the comic strip!

"It was about six months between the time that I first heard from them and when the strip really started appearing. In the first few months they had me prepare six weeks' worth of strips so that their sales people could take them out and sell 'Cathy' to the newspapers. So I had a few months to work on the drawing, and they gave me a lot of guidance in that."[6]

"I ran out and bought several books on how to draw cartoon characters. I took them home and studied and practiced. I felt that I already had a natural knack for showing emotion and character in my drawings. If a comic figure felt sheepish or wishy-washy, the lines I drew would be wiggly, if the person was mad, the lines would be straight and hard. If a character was happy, the lines became soft and pleasant. If you try to 'feel' what you're drawing, it will work its way out to your hand."[3]

"It used to take me an entire afternoon to get Cathy to walk across the room in one frame. Drawing anything was a totally new experience for me. It's gotten way, way easier.

"Mostly my art has been a result of personal trial and error. But I do look at other cartoonists' work and always have. For instance, if I have a scene with a lot of motion and a lot of commotion in it, I know that 'Beetle Bailey' often has strips like that where there's a big flurry of activity; I'll look back at those strips and see what the artist does that makes it look like that's happening. As far as people's expressions go, I think that I probably was most inspired by Charles Schulz and still am. He's wonderful at capturing great expressions with very few lines."[6]

With "Cathy" in syndication, readers came to know and sympathize with the young woman executive who works for a company called "Product Testing, Inc." "Cathy is a woman who does not have it under total control and tends to run back to horrible relationships. There's a vulnerability in her that some feminists may not like. I feel you can be a feminist and still keep your insurance policy stuffed in your sock drawer."[5]

"Cathy" vascillates between serious dieting, and serious food binging. Furthermore, she's usually in conflict trying to meet pressure from her boss and her chauvinistic boyfriend, Irving of whom Guisewite admits: "I wouldn't pin him on any one man—he is every negative trait rolled into one. I tried to reform him a couple of times, but it didn't work. Guys like that don't change."[4]

As for "Cathy's" best friend, an ardent feminist named Andrea: "...She's pretty much my conscience, saying, 'You know better.' In one of the best strips, Cathy says, 'I'll be fat for the rest of my life.' Andrea says, 'No, you don't have to be. You're the one in control.' 'I know,' Cathy says, 'That's why I'll always be fat.'

"It would be nice to see Andrea grappling with some problems of her own. But she'll always be the voice of authority."[4]

From *Two Pies. One Fork* by Cathy Guisewite. Illustrated by the author.

Of "Cathy's" sweet and slightly crazy cousin, Cellophane, Guisewite said: "My younger sister, Mickey, came to spend a couple of months with me a while ago, I was exposed to a whole new breed of music and clothes. Cellophane came from that. I did like her—I'm thinking of bringing her back."[4]

Readers frequently ask how much of Guisewite is in "Cathy." "I'm pretty much a combination of Andrea and Cathy in the strip, but I'm most like Cathy in that I see both sides of everything."[3]

"Cathy is my more emotional side. I think I'm a little more together than her. I think I'm a combination of great self-confidence and total insecurity sort of at once."[7]

"Periodically I'm better at everything than Cathy is, but when I'm not, I can be like she is or worse. I can be frantically organized, like I'll spend days working on an address book while the whole world around me is crumbling."[8]

"When the comic strip first began, I was horrified with the idea of calling it 'Cathy.'"[3]

"We had long discussions at first about what to call the character. The syndicate wanted me to stay with Cathy because they liked the idea that it was true to life. I thought it would be a good idea to call her something else. I went through all the name-your-baby books and tried everything."[5]

"Not only did the character resemble me a little physically, but what I was writing about was quite personal. I didn't want friends calling me up the next day, saying 'Idiot, why did you say that about yourself?'

"In the early days, she spent a lot of time getting dumped on. Cathy was a kind of doormat, because that's the way it was at that point in *my* life. Of course, Cathy will never have it all together. She has many weaknesses. Her character is built on them.

"I have an obsession with food—something anyone who's eaten a hot-fudge sundae while hiding in a closet will understand. I let my obsession rub off on Cathy."[3] "...A lot of my material is based on my neuroses. If all that vanished, it would be 'bye-bye career.'"[9]

"I have a way to use every disaster in my life now. That's one of the nicest things and probably one of the problems, too: I can't just wallow in my misery all the time; I have a responsibility to turn it into material. But it's a real blessing. The more chaotic and trauma-filled my life is, the better my work is!"[6]

Some think "Cathy" is Guisewite's way of commenting on a woman's role in today's society. "...But what I am really writing about is gum wrappers and why I dropped the hair dryer in the toilet on the day it was important for me to look nice at the office meeting. I don't write about the big picture and the emerging new woman. What Cathy is doing is floundering in the middle of her ideals or concepts: traditionalism and feminism. She likes what she sees in both areas so she is walking down the middle. Because many of us are walking the same line, it makes us laugh.

"For instance, Cathy is looking at an ad for 'Creamy-Dreamy Lipstick' and tells her feminist friend, Andrea, that she wants to get some. Andrea screams, 'That's chauvinistic capitalism at its worst.

From *Two Pies. One Fork* by Cathy Guisewite. Illustrated by the author.

From *A Hand to Hold, an Opinion to Reject* by Cathy Guisewite. Illustrated by the author.

All they are selling is sex, hope and dreams!' Cathy grins and says, 'I'll take it.'"[3]

"It's a confusing time....We're getting a lot of different signals. I was just getting used to the 'Me Decade,' starting to revel in putting other people's needs second, when suddenly they pulled the rug out from under me by proclaiming the '80s the 'We Decade,' with the family unit making a comeback."[9]

"The problem with the concept of the 'New Woman' is that she is too perfect....The women I read about in magazines and see on television are self-confident, self-assured, dynamic business people and they are also cheery homemakers and understanding nonsexist mothers.

"It's a wonderful idea, but most of us feel we are not living up to it. We feel frustrated with our little failures, and then we want to give up and say forget it. In a nice way, Cathy evokes a lot of empathy. She makes us feel we're not the only ones with problems."[3]

Guisewite believes much of her inspiration comes from her mother, and from their close, sometimes volatile relationship. "I'm more like her than my sisters are. Like her, I'm essentially quiet and private. I'm also strong in some ways because I've modeled myself after her.

"The only problem I've had with my mother is that I see myself in her so much that I tend to be crabbiest around her. I am truly even-tempered. I never yell or snap at anybody—except her. Since I see myself in her—and *I* want to be perfect—I want *her* to be perfect, and I can't stand it when she isn't. When I snap, it's almost like being impatient with myself.

"Fortunately, my mother is very down-to-earth and has a wonderful sense of humor. If she didn't, I couldn't do what I do with Cathy's mother! She's got an especially good sense of humor about the contradictions she lays out for me—cheering my career, yet waiting for the day when I get married, settle down and start my real life."[4]

She finds that women like her mother are some of her most avid readers. "I'd say the second biggest group of mail I get is from women the age of the mothers of women my age. Some are writing to say that the mother-daughter relationship in 'Cathy' has really meant a lot to them and their daughters and that the strip has really become like a sounding board for them with each other. And many mothers or women who are a little bit older than Cathy write to say that they are identifying not with the mother but with Cathy because she's a lot like them or a lot like they were. I also hear increasingly from men. Not that many men come right out and say that they are identifying with Irving, but a lot say they have a girlfriend just like Cathy; that Cathy has really helped them understand what's going on with women. Some write to say that they feel a lot like Cathy themselves; that her anxieties and frustrations are not all that different from men's.

"Specifically, people comment on the mother-daughter relationship a lot. Many letters come in on the food strips. It just depends on the person who's writing. If somebody happens to be in a relationship crisis around the time that Cathy is, then they're writing about that.

"I think people can interpret what's going on however they'd like. Once I had Cathy fly to St. Louis to spend the weekend with somebody she had met and I remember, after that, hearing from a mother and daughter. They both wrote to me at the same time. They had had a discussion about what had happened that weekend: The mother was sure that the boy had put Cathy up in a nice hotel somewhere and the daughter read...that she was going there to spend the weekend at his place. They both were equally convinced that the way they saw it was the way it happened, and that is fine with me."[6]

Besides the strip, Guisewite is also the creator of several specialty items, such as T-shirts, aprons, mugs, and iron-on transfers, all based on the "Cathy" characters. "...They take a lot of time, considering that it used to take me every waking minute of the day to get the strip done and now we're doing products for about thirty different companies. You know, it's the old business of it takes as long as you have to do it, I guess. I really like doing designs for the merchandise. I think that some of the things are very appropriate to the characters, and that has been an exciting area for me to get into. I know that some people just turn over the rights and don't get that involved. I've become obsessed with getting totally involved with every project, so I put a lot more time into it than is probably necessary. But I love it.

"I am always at the office by 8:30 or 9:00 and begin panicking immediately about what's most overdue on that particular day. Sometimes it's the comic strip. I usually send the strip...in groups of two weeks, so, as that deadline gets close, that's all I do. Some days that deadline is not so pressing but the deadlines for merchandise that we're doing are pressing, and I'll work on those, I work by myself in the mornings; in the afternoons a secretary and her baby come in, and also a graphic designer. He does mechanical work for the merchandise: He'll get type set or do coloring or stat things. He has taken a lot of the detail work off my hands for the licensed products we're doing."[6]

From *May I Borrow Your Husband and Baby?* by Cathy Guisewite. Illustrated by the author.

Even with help, deadlines can be a problem. "I haven't sent a piece of mail in the last five years that wasn't Federal Express."[9]

"Panic is just part of a cartoonist's life, though an idea always comes. Sometimes, I just have to force it a bit."[3]

SENSITIVE PEOPLE

Cathy Guisewite, cartoonist, creator of the comic strip *Cathy*: "People say, 'You know exactly how I feel; I'm so relieved that somebody else sits in the closet and eats a cheesecake after a bad date.' I think I verbalize for a lot of women the anxieties and insecurities we live out every day, like I'll buy anything that will promise me a miracle. But, I've bought the 25-step skin care and it's still in the bottom drawer, because I never have the energy even to get to Step Two. I always go back to Neutrogena Soap, because it's so simple. I mean, I stagger into the bathroom, I wash my face, and I can handle it. It's the one thing I don't have to torture myself about."

Neutrogena: The sensitive soap for sensitive people.

Neutrogena's spokeswoman.

1978. Guisewite published *The Cathy Chronicles,* the first of several collections of her comic strip. Other titles include: *It Must Be Love, My Face Is Breaking Out,* and *A Mouthful of Breath Mints and No One to Kiss.* "...I don't actually keep them in the theme of the title. We've gotten into a pattern now of doing a book a year, so I go through the strips, and pull out ones that I do not ever want to see in print again; but otherwise, in the books, I try to keep them in chronological order and from a certain period."[6]

1980. Moved from the Midwest to Santa Barbara, California, and lived by herself in a Victorian house where her mother would visit and make herself at home. "...She visits me in Santa Barbara and I don't think she ever leaves my house. She just works on projects—anything she thinks I need done: reorganizing my cupboards, cleaning my

From *My Cologne Backfired* by Cathy Guisewite. Illustrated by the author.

closets, taking care of paperwork. She makes the meals and packages any leftovers in individual servings to freeze for when she's gone. She also encloses any opened packages in my cupboard in plastic bags. After she's been here awhile, everything in the house is wrapped up.

"I'm touched by how much she wants to help."[1]

But Santa Barbara proved too small to provide anonymity: "...I need to be able to go to a bank and scream at the teller and not have them go, 'Oh, you're the one who does the comic strip.'"[8]

So she relocated to Los Angeles. "I wanted to expand my horizons. I'm still not going outside much, but at least sitting in my house, I get a feeling there's a lot going on out there.

"I still have my health club that I don't go to. I'm told that a supermarket on Ventura Boulevard is a great place on Thursday nights, but since you know that, who wants to go?

"I don't own a bathing suit. They make size 5 suits for babies; they're this big. Everybody in California is size 5. But you have to be a perfectly toned, perfectly tanned size 5. No normal person, would wear a bathing suit in California."[8]

The distance hasn't diminished her relationship with "Mom." "I still call Mom long distance and ask her what I should wear on a date. Then I get annoyed because she lives 2,500 miles away and isn't familiar with my clothes,...or I tell her about a guy I see only a few times and get angry because she asks me about him for the next five years."[2]

"It's a constant contradiction of loving and worshipping her, and being horrified as I see myself turning into her. Every week I say I'm nothing like her and that I'm going to lead my own life, and 15 minutes later I'm calling to ask what to wear....It's awful. I think a lot of people really relate to it, to that contradiction of dependence and independence. She still says I moved to California to put distance between us."[8]

"She's the greatest support system in the world. The sense of being loved, that no matter what I do, someone thinks I'm wonderful has made it possible for me to strive and succeed."[2]

Though being a famous cartoonist has its advantages, "this is probably the best of both worlds, because I get the recognition of people knowing my name, but nobody knows what I look like, so I can look like a pig when I go to the grocery store."[7]

Guisewite finds her old neuroses haven't disappeared—they've only become inspiration for her

From *A Hand to Hold, an Opinion to Reject* by Cathy Guisewite. Illustrated by the author.

strip. "I used to be heavier. And I still turn to food in times of crisis. But now I'll eat steamed vegetables for a week instead of a box of frozen doughnuts I haven't bothered to defrost!

"Oh, the food themes are near and dear to my heart. You can be pretty sure, if you see Cathy eating in a strip it's because I couldn't think of anything to write and consoled myself with food."[4]

"I got in the habit, when I was overweight, of always buying clothes at least one size smaller than I am, 'cause I thought then, 'I'm gonna lose weight; why waste the money on the correct size? I'll buy it one size smaller; it will motivate me.'...Now I'm my normal size, and I still buy clothes that are slightly too small for me."[7]

"I have every type of look in my closet. Every now and then I'll try the exotic, but then I'll stand there too humilitated to let anyone else see."[8]

"Definitely any insecurities that I have, have been wonderful for my career....So it puts me in the unfortunate position of never being able to just sit and wallow in misery, because some little part of me always has to be sort of entertained by it."[7]

"I've never gotten married. I think if I did, that would have to happen to Cathy, because I write the strip so much from my own point of view. The cartoon syndicate, in fact, is horrified by that possibility—it would destroy everything we've all worked for! So they manage to keep me busy enough to make sure it's not real likely."[4]

"As my friends have gotten married—and some of these were diehard singles—I've sensed my own feelings of desertion. I don't want Cathy to do that."[8]

"I like being single. It's given me a huge amount of freedom to really go for it in my career. I think that I have avoided relationships that threaten that."[7]

Even dating has its own set of pressures. "My mother, who is terribly supportive of my career and lifestyles, will talk to me about the virtues of independence and not having to depend on a man, and then she'll drag one of my sisters aside and say, 'Who is she going out with now? What does she think of him? Does he have possibilities?'"[10]

"This ticking biological clock business has taken the fun out of dating. Guys think, 'Oh, my God, she's 36. If I take her out to dinner, she'll probably want me to marry her.' I'm so paranoid about seeming to act that way that I'm barely friendly to guys I really like."[2]

1987. "Cathy" appeared in an animated television special, and was met with fine reviews. "...I find it so liberating to get to carry on a conversation longer than four boxes.

"I think that Cathy will continue to grow and change and be affected by things as I am. This year, for instance, I did a series that lasted about two weeks on the fact that half the women in her office suddenly were pregnant. That's not a subject I would have done a couple of years ago, but this year I found that every time I turned around another woman I knew (who swore she would never get married or pregnant) had transformed herself. When I was doing some promotions, I talked to some other women about it and found that, in fact, that was something a lot of single women were experiencing: Their single friends were dropping like flies and becoming married mothers. So I thought it was a very appropriate subject to address.

"I can't think of too many other jobs where total strangers write you or meet you and say, 'I love what you do for a living!' That's a great kind of support to get. It really is very reasuring for me, and it's just nice. If I weren't fairly insecure myself I would never write the things I do, and getting that sort of feedback from people is great for me."[6]

"I think this is the opportunity that writers dream about—to write from life. That's the richest material. One of my greatest pleasures is having someone write to me and say, 'Cathy, you said it just right!'"[3]

Footnote Sources:

[1] Mary James, "Cathy and Her Mom," *Woman's Day,* July 13, 1982.
[2] Lynn Emmerman, "Comic Relief from 'Cathy' and Her 'Mom,'" *Chicago Tribune,* May 10, 1987.
[3] Cork Miller, "How Cartoonist Cathy Guisewite Makes Us Laugh at Life's Little Frustrations," *Seventeen,* May, 1983.
[4] Judy J. Newmark, "Cathy and 'Cathy': A Lot in Common," *St. Louis Post-Dispatch,* September 5, 1982.
[5] Ann Japenga, "The Real-Life 'Cathy': A Cartoonist's Dream," *Los Angeles Times,* April 28, 1981.
[6] *Contemporary Authors,* Volume 113, Gale, 1985.
[7] Dan Sperling, "Cathy Guisewite: She Cashes in on Her Insecurities—Comically," *USA Today,* October 30, 1986.
[8] Millie Ball, "And Now, the Real Cathy," *New Orleans Times-Picayune,* June 8, 1986.
[9] Sally Koris, "Cartoons Are No Laughing Matter for Cathy Guisewite," *People,* July 5, 1982.
[10] Sylvia Rubin, "The Woman Behind 'Cathy,'" *San Francisco Chronicle,* November 29, 1982.

■ For More Information See

Glamour, July, 1978, August, 1982.
Laurence J. Peter, "Peter's People," *Human Behavior,* January, 1979 (p. 68).
Rosemarie Robotham, "Funny Females in the Funny Pages," *Life,* September, 1982 (p. 90).
Jonathan Friendly, "Women's New Roles in Comics," *New York Times,* February 28, 1983.
Detroit Free Press, February 27, 1984.
Jonathan Alter, Linda Tibbetts, Michael Reese, and Holly Morris, "Comics in Yuppiedom," *Newsweek,* October 1, 1984 (p. 76).
Lynn Emmerman, "Mom Makes Cathy Run in Comics and in Life," *St. Louis Post-Dispatch,* June 7, 1987.

Virginia Hamilton

Born March 12, 1936, in Yellow Springs, Ohio; daughter of Kenneth James (a musician) and Etta Belle (Perry) Hamilton; married Arnold Adoff (an anthologist and author), March 19, 1960; children: Leigh Hamilton (daughter), Jaime Levi (son). *Education:* Antioch College, B.A., 1955, attended Ohio State University, 1957-58, and New School for Social Research, 1959. *Address:* Box 293, Yellow Springs, Ohio 45387. *Agent:* Arnold Adoff, Arnold Adoff Agency, 1 Lincoln Plaza, 37U, 20 West 64th St., New York, N.Y. 10023.

■ Career

"Every source of occupation imaginable, from singer to bookkeeper"; author of books for young people. Whittall Lecturer, Library of Congress, Washington, D.C., 1975; visiting professor, Queens College, 1986-87.

■ Awards, Honors

Nancy Block Memorial Award from the Downtown (N.Y.) Community School Awards Committee, 1967, for *Zeely*; *The House of Dies Drear* was chosen one of Child Study Association of America's Children's Books of the Year, 1968, *The Time-Ago Tales of Jahdu*, 1969, *Time-Ago Lost: More Tales of Jahdu*, 1973, *Paul Robeson: The Life and Times of a Free Black Man* and *M.C. Higgins, the Great*, both 1974, *Arilla Sun Down*, 1976, and *Junius over Far*, and *The People Could Fly*, 1985; Edgar Allan Poe Award from the Mystery Writers of America for best juvenile mystery, and Ohioana Book Award from the Ohioana Library Association, both 1969, both for *The House of Dies Drear*.

The Planet of Junior Brown was chosen one of *School Library Journal*'s Best Books, 1971, and selected a Newbery Honor Book by the American Library Association, National Book Award finalist, and received the Lewis Carroll Shelf Award from the University of Wisconsin, all 1972; *Book World*'s Children's Spring Book Festival Honor Book, 1973, for *Time-Ago Lost: More Tales of Jahdu*; *Boston Globe-Horn Book* Award for Text, and chosen one of *New York Times* Outstanding Books of the Year and one of American Library Association's Best Young Adult Books, all 1974, National Book Award, and Newbery Medal, both 1975, Lewis Carroll Shelf Award, and International Board on Books for Young People (IBBY) Honor List for Text, both 1976, all for *M. C. Higgins, the Great*; *Arilla Sun Down* was chosen one of *School Library Journal*'s Best Books of the Year, 1976, and *The People Could Fly*, 1985.

The Gathering was chosen one of New York Public Library's Books for the Teen Age, 1982; *Sweet Whispers, Brother Rush* was chosen one of American Library Association's Best Young Adult Books, one of *New York Times* Outstanding Books of the

Year, and one of *School Library Journal*'s Best Children's Books, all 1982, received the Coretta Scott King Award from the American Library Association for outstanding inspirational and educational contributions to literature for children and young adults, *Boston Globe-Horn Book* Award for Fiction, Certificate of Honor from the International Board on Books for Young People for outstanding example of literature with international importance, American Book Award finalist, and Newbery Honor Book, all 1983; Parents' Choice Award for Literature from the Parents' Choice Foundation, one of American Library Association's Best Young Adult Books, one of *School Library Journal*'s Best Books for Spring, and one of New York Public Library's Children's Books, all 1983, and Coretta Scott King Award Honorable Mention, 1984, all for *The Magical Adventures of Pretty Pearl*; Ohioana Book Award, 1984, for her body of work; *A Little Love* was selected one of American Library Association's Best Books for Young Adults, 1984, and Coretta Scott King Award Honorable Mention, 1985; *Willie Bea and the Time the Martians Landed* was chosen one of New York Public Library's Children's Books, 1984; *The People Could Fly* was chosen one of *New York Times* Best Illustrated Children's Books, a *Booklist* Editors' Choice, and a Notable Childrens Trade Book in the Field of Social Studies from the National Council of Social Studies and the Children's Book Council, all 1985, and received the Coretta Scott King Award, 1986; Coretta Scott King Award Honorable Mention, 1986, for *Junius over Far*; Other Award (Great Britain), 1986, for *The People Could Fly*.

■ Writings

Novels:

Zeely (ALA Notable Book; illustrated by Symeon Shimin), Macmillan, 1967.
The House of Dies Drear (ALA Notable Book; illustrated by Eros Keith), Macmillan, 1968.
The Time-Ago Tales of Jahdu (ALA Notable Book; illustrated by Nonny Hogrogian), Macmillan, 1969.
The Planet of Junior Brown (ALA Notable Book), Macmillan, 1971.
Time-Ago Lost: More Tales of Jahdu (illustrated by Ray Prather), Macmillan, 1973.
M. C. Higgins, the Great (ALA Notable Book; *Horn Book* honor list; teacher's guide), Macmillan, 1974, large print edition, G. K. Hall, 1976.
Arilla Sun Down (ALA Notable Book; *Horn Book* honor list), Greenwillow, 1976.

Jahdu (illustrated by Jerry Pinkney), Greenwillow, 1980, large print edition, 1980.
Sweet Whispers, Brother Rush, Philomel, 1982.
The Magical Adventures of Pretty Pearl (ALA Notable Book), Harper, 1983.
Willie Bea and the Time the Martians Landed (ALA Notable Book), Greenwillow, 1983.
A Little Love, Philomel, 1984.
Junius over Far, Harper, 1985.
The People Could Fly: American Black Folktales (ALA Notable Book; *Horn Book* honor list; illustrated by Leo Dillon and Diane Dillon), Knopf, 1985.
The Mystery of Drear House: Book Two of Dies Drear, Greenwillow, 1987.
A White Romance, Philomel, 1987.

Justice Trilogy:

Justice and Her Brothers, Greenwillow, 1978.
Dustland, Greenwillow, 1980.
The Gathering, Greenwillow, 1981.

Other:

W. E. B. Du Bois: A Biography (ALA Notable Book), Crowell, 1972.
Paul Robeson: The Life and Times of a Free Black Man (ALA Notable Book), Harper, 1975.
(Editor) *The Writings of W. E. B. Du Bois*, Crowell, 1976.
(Contibutor) *Once upon a Time...Celebrating the Magic of Children's Books in Honor of the Twentieth Anniversary of Reading Is Fundamental*, Putnam, 1986.

Also author of introduction of the *Newbery Award Reader*, edited by Charles G. Waugh and Martin H. Greenberg, Harcourt, 1974, *Anthony Burns: The Defeat and Triumph of a Fugitive Slave*, Knopf, 1988, and *In the Beginning*, Harcourt, 1988.

■ Adaptations

"Virginia Hamilton Reads Zeely" (cassette), Caedmon, 1974.
"Sweet Whispers, Brother Rush" (listening cassette; filmstrip with cassette), Miller-Brody, 1974.
"M. C. Higgins, the Great" (listening record or cassette; filmstrip with cassette), Listening Post, 1975.
"The Planet of Junior Brown" (record or cassette; filmstrip with record or cassette), Miller-Brody, 1976.
"Time-Ago Lost" (cassette and book).
"The People Could Fly" (cassette).

Virginia Hamilton and Arnold Adoff with their children.

The House of Dies Drear, M. C. Higgins, the Great, Paul Robeson, The Time-Ago Tales of Jahdu, W. E. B. Du Bois, and *Zeely* have been adapted into talking books, and *The House of Dies Drear* has been adapted into Braille.

■ Work In Progress

"A collection of short stories tentatively titled *Choices, Changes, Gambles and Games*; a book about the life of a runaway slave; a book on creation myth."

■ Sidelights

Virginia Hamilton was the first Black writer to win the Newbery Medal in recognition of *M. C. Higgins, the Great*, a novel published in 1974. Considered challenging, literary and thematically complex, Hamilton's oeuvre is often credited by critics with having raised the standards of American literature for younger readers.

"What personal self I have is in my books. Everything that might become neurotic or personally problematic I put into a narrative. My stories are little pieces of me."[1]

"Most of my writing is flavored from my childhood experience; although I write about the rural present, there is much of the Depression thirties in everything I create. So when I write about the road, as I'm doing in a new book, I see what somebody might have seen when she traveled the road a long time ago. I see the empty spaces and billboards; I don't see the motels. I choose what I see, and what I see is another time. It's the same thing with my hometown. I write about the areas in and around Yellow Springs, Ohio, or southern Ohio, but since we've been there for generations, I see that locale through my eyes, my mother's eyes, and my grandmother's eyes. I can do that anytime I want to because I know the way they saw it, the way my mother still sees it, and she's 90: she has a very long vision. I can walk through the door of her house, and sometimes she sees me as an aunt. Well, that's all right—I'm my aunt, too. For me, it's all a continuum....I'm afraid I'm unable to deal with one time frame when I'm writing: I seem not to be able to create a character in one dimension of time....I think that living on the land that supported my ancestors has a lot to do with it."[2]

"I am a teller of tales, in part, because of the informal way I learned from Mother and her relatives of passing the time, which they also utilize for transmitting information, for entertainment, and for putting their own flesh and blood in the proper perspective. The Perrys are interesting talkers. They began as farmers who had been fugitives from injustice. Acquiring land and homes, place and time, was to them the final payment in the cause of freedom. After long days, a long history in the fields, they talked their way into new states of mind. They could appreciate a good story in the companionship of one another, not only as entertainment but as a way to mark their progress. Stories, talking, grew and changed into a kind of folk history of timely incidents. And these developed in lines of force that had beginnings, middles, and endings—a certain style. True memory might lapse, and creativity come into play. It was the same creativity and versatility that had helped the first African survive on the American continent. An uncle of mine told the most astonishing lies. An aunt whispered in perfect rememory the incident of Blind Martha and how she found her way down the dusty road to the spot where the log cabin had stood in which she was born. The day Uncle Saunders was killed, all of the ivy fell from the Pasony house. Pasonys were neighbors, quiet and shrewd. But they could not save the ivy.

"There's the story I remember always knowing about my Grandpaw Levi Perry and how his hand burned shut from a fire in the gunpowder mill where he worked. And from the time that his life and mine coincided, his hand was a fist with burn scars hidden in the tightly shut palm. I would lace my fingers over his closed fist when I was a child, and he would lift me up and up, swing me around and around—to my enormous delight. Ever after, the raised Black fist became for me both myth and history, and they were mine. Grandpaw Perry was John Henry and High John de Conquer. He was power—the fugitive, the self-made, the closed fist in which I knew was kept magic. . . .

"What is transformed from myth, history, and family narrative in my own fictions is not a play—pretty to be held in the hands of children. My fictions for young people derive from the progress of Black adults and their children across the American hopescape. Occasionally, they are lighthearted; often they are speculative, symbolic and dark, and brooding. The people are always uneasy because the ideological difference they feel from the majority is directly derived from heritage. In the background of much of my writing is the dream of freedom tantalizingly out of reach."[3]

"One of my uncles, on my mother's side, made an annual pilgrimage down to Ripley, Ohio to the John Rankin House. John Rankin and his nine sons were Presbyterian abolishionists, former southerners who hated slavery. Their house stood high on Liberty Hill with a light and a bell for slaves coming across to freedom. My Grandpaw Perry was brought north by his mother, who then promptly disappeared. She was believed to be a conductor in the Underground Railroad. They came up through Virginia to Ripley to Jamestown, Ohio, about ten miles from Yellow Springs. I believe she was caught on one of her many trips. She was never heard from again. . . .

"My grandpaw sat his children down once a year and told them the story. 'This was what slavery was like, and why I ran away. . .I am telling you so that it will never happen to you.' He made an enormous impression on my mother. I have asked her, 'What did he say?' And she never has told.

"I have done some digging into the history of the Underground Railroad and runaway slaves. The things I've discovered. . .the books I can write!. . ."[1]

"I've noticed lately that I have been speaking more about my mother and her family than early on when I spoke mostly about my father. I think that I'm beginning to come around. The males in my family were very dominant. I had two older brothers and my father, of course. The women were not as strong; it was a very traditional household. My father was the dominant one and also the very creative and sensitive one. He was the sun: we revolved around him."[2]

"He was a musician. He played in mandolin clubs all over the country in the early nineteen hundreds. The clubs were racially integrated and allowed females as well. I have wonderful old photographs of them, and still have my father's mandolin, a Gibson 1902, Patent Pending, all ivory and white. He was a fine classical mandolinist.

"He was also a very moody man. Mother was his third wife. His dream was to be the most famous mandolinist of his time. But he was barred from all the great concert halls because he could not belong to the musicians' union as a Black man. He never forgave the unions for that. He worked outside the system, creating his own musical groups, performing on radio and in dance halls in mining towns where you checked your guns at the door.

"Yes, without a doubt, I idolized him, not merely because he was a flamboyant figure, but because he was deeply sensitive, literate and politically committed. A strong childhood memory is of the men who passed through our town during the Depression—men completely broke, many for years without jobs, men who were hungry. 'Do you have work?' they would ask. My father would always find something for them to do. He would leave food by the side of the road for those passing by. 'If you give something to people who are hungry,' he'd say, 'they'll never steal anything from you.' We grew everything ourselves and had much more than we could eat.

"My father was also a great reader. He loved Wendell Wilkie, whose *One World* was one of his favorite books. He knew W. E. B. Du Bois, and subscribed to *Crisis* magazine, which Du Bois edited under the auspices of the NAACP. Du Bois and Franklin Delano Roosevelt were my father's heroes. He subscribed to *The New Yorker*, and talked about what he read. Books were an important part of our lives—Poe, de Maupassant, many of the classics. I didn't realize then how unusual it was for a man like my father to have such a library. It was an important factor in my education.

"I attended a small country school where we weren't taught much more than some English and history—no black history. As a matter of fact, I was the only black girl in my class until seventh grade or so. I did very well, but our curriculum was so limited it would be years before I felt reasonably well educated.

"Oh, how I wanted to leave the little town of Yellow Spring. Every night I lay in bed listening to the long, sad whistle of the train passing through from New York to Chicago. I wanted with all my soul to get to Manhattan, but it seemed I was trapped forever.

"My cousin Marleen and I were inseparable—we made stilts together, we roller skated, we explored, we picked berries. The day she got married, I remember saying to her, 'Let's go for a walk.' And she said, 'I can't leave my husband.' Those words marked an irreversible change in my life. I was just seventeen, and had the feeling my life was over. There was so much I wanted to do, but couldn't see my way clear.

"Well, that evening, after Marleen's wedding, the telephone rang and a high school teacher gave me the news that she had arranged for a five-year scholarship for college. A bolt from the blue. A dream I had thought beyond my grasp.

"I started off in my home town at Antioch College. Going away to school was out of my reach even with my tuition paid for. Antioch was one of the few schools then that had a major in writing. That was lucky for me, but still I was restless.

"One of my teachers told me that I really ought to leave school, go to New York and try to become published. I spent summers in New York, working as a bookkeeper. I could earn much more money there than in the Midwest. I often went back and forth between Ohio and New York, a semester on, a semester off. Finally, I took my teacher's advice and left before taking my degree.

"I don't have a clear recollection of the day I officially left home to go to New York. My plan was to find a cheap apartment, a part-time job, write, and have a good time. And it all came together. I took a place in the East Village, in what is today called Alphabet City. Mornings I was a cost accountant for an engineering firm; afternoons I wrote; and evenings I went out or read. I read

She didn't know she had begun to talk to herself. (From *Zeely* by Virginia Hamilton.)

everything I could get my hands on, tore through all the Modern Library classics. Mexican writers were very popular at the time and I steeped myself in that work, as well.

"New York was such a different scene in the fifties. The East Village was a mix of Polish and Ukrainian immigrants, young writers and artists. It was easy to meet people. The painters Raphael and Moses Soyer held a weekly salon, attended by everyone who was anyone. Today, I get the feeling that writers, artists and musicians operate pretty much in separate spheres. It wasn't like that then. We were all together. It was a completely integrated scene.

"I worked hard at my writing, but wasn't singularly fixed on it. The fact that it wasn't being published did not eat away at me. *The New Yorker* wrote me very encouraging letters and tried to help me. But I would never quite fit their mold. I was meeting all kinds of people and having a wonderful time. Seriousness came slowly.

"Still, I thought I should try to find out a little more about how publishing worked. When a friend told me she was going to be taking a writing course at The New School, I pricked up my ears. It sounded interesting, but only twelve students would be admitted on the basis of samples. I was intimidated. Well, my friend and I applied, and I got in and she didn't, which made me feel terrible. This class was taught by Hiram Hayden, a founder of Atheneum. Hiram loved my writing, and in a sense became my mentor. He was a terribly handsome, raw-boned man. All the women in class had a crush on him. For a farm girl from Ohio, class was quite a scene. At the time I was writing an adult novel, *Mayo*, which Hiram wanted very much to publish. Unfortunately, his partners didn't agree. If they had, I might never have become a writer of children's books.

"A few years later a college friend who was working at Macmillan asked, 'Whatever happened to that children's story you wrote at Antioch?' 'What children's story?' I asked. I honestly didn't remember. But she was right, I had written such a piece. I began working on it again and at her prodding, I sent it to Susan Hirschman, head of their children's book department. I didn't even know there was such a thing as children's book departments!

"That children's story became *Zeely*, my first book. I wrote what became the final manuscript when my daughter was very young. We were together the whole time I worked on that book. I'd show her the typed pages and tell her what it was. I'd explain how I was sending it off, and when the galleys came back, we would look at them together. And then I'd send back the galleys and the proofs would come. Then, one day the book arrived with my name on the cover. Suddenly it all came together for her—the look on her face was wonderful.

"*Zeely* looks to Africa. For years, I had kept a scrapbook on Africa, and a map that I was constantly revising as nations won their independence from European powers. A lot of the material became part of *Zeely*.

"The plot centers on Elizabeth, who fancies that Zeely, a beautiful six-foot Black woman who does tenant farming and raises pigs on Elizabeth's uncle's farm, is in reality an African princess. Elizabeth, the young protagonist who idolizes Zeely, is much like I was as a girl. Many of my characters are loners, unsure of who they are, and given to wild imaginings.

"Because it was my first book, I have a special fondness for it. That said, it is hard for me to read it today; there are many things I would do differently."[1]

Hamilton's reservations notwithstanding, *Zeely* garnered very good reviews. Critics praised the author's storytelling abilities, her apt descriptions and prepossessing characters. Elinore Standard's assessment, which appeared in *The Washington Post*, was typical: "*Zeely* is a fresh, sensitive story, with a lingering, serene, misty quality about it which the reader can save and savor."[4]

Hamilton's next book, *The House of Dies Drear*, was awarded the Edgar Allan Poe Award for the best juvenile mystery of 1968, and generally lauded in the popular and literary press. The novel abounds with elements of ghost stories and the gothic. Dorothy Sterling of the *The New York Times Book Review* wrote: "*The House of Dies Drear* is written with poetic precision. Miss Hamilton polishes her sentences with care, develops her characters with imagination and love....*The House of Dies Drear* is not an angry book—although there is a need for anger too. Instead, Miss Hamilton has found her own way of saying 'Black is beautiful.'"[5]

"There's nothing really you can do about being referred to as a 'minority' or 'black' writer. For a long time, I tried to fight it, saying I'm a writer, *period*. But in a country like ours, there really is a dominant culture. I prefer the term 'parallel culture.' If you look at things globally, blacks and latinos do not constitute a small minority.

Cover illustration by Jerry Pinkney for the paperback edition of *The Planet of Junior Brown* by Virginia Hamilton.

Cover illustration for the paperback edition.

"The sixties was a great time for children's books, and books in general. There was a lot of federal money around, and libraries and schools were able to acquire good-sized collections of so-called minority books. But it had its downside, too. There was a lot of infighting among people supposedly fighting for the same cause—namely, equality for *all*. Raising the consciousness about black heritage, black culture, black people was, and remains to be, of vital importance. But political work is very tricky for a writer. Writers need time alone. And the idea of a collective stance can be dangerous. There was a lot of violence during the sixties, not only in the streets, but in the rhetoric as well. Writers were called upon by the leaders of the movement to be violent in their poetry or prose. I had a lot of trouble with that. One of the best poems of the period has a line that goes, 'must I shoot the/white man dead/to free the nigger/in his head?' A very important point of view. Politically, I did what I could, but mostly, I just continued to write my books."[1]

"I attempt in each book to take hold of one single theme of the black experience and present it as clearly as I can. I don't mean to make the writing of fiction sound cold or calculating—it isn't at all. . . .The black experience in America is deep like the rivers of this country. At times through our history it became submerged only to emerge again and again. Each time it emerges, it seems strong, more explicit and insistent.

"There are themes in my writing that are strains through the whole of black history. The strain of the wanderer, like the theme of Jahdu; the strain of the fleeing slave or the persecuted moving and searching for a better place becomes the theme of the Night Traveller in *Zeely*. And the black man hiding his true self, ever acting so that those who betray him will never touch him....Perhaps some day when I've written my last book, there will stand the whole of the black experience in white America as I see it."[6]

"I have consistently written nonfiction, as well as fiction. The nonfiction not only provides a rest from novels and stories, but satisfies a need to do ongoing research and to tell the factual, historical stories of our people. It makes perfect sense, in view of the stature he had in the home I grew up in, that I would one day write a biography of W. E. B. Du Bois."[1]

Hamilton's 1972 biography of Du Bois received generally high praise, although a few critics had reservations about the author's overt didacticism. *Horn Book*'s, Sheryl B. Andrews, said, "William Edward Burghardt Du Bois struggled for ninety-five years as educator, writer, intellectual, and poet against prejudice and fear, so that black people throughout the world could claim their blackness with pride, their humanity with honor. There is no easy definition for such a man; perhaps the most honest approach is simply to chronicle his achievements and let them speak for themselves. The author has done just that....The book is an affirmation of Du Bois' life, and a fascinating historical document of the Black Movement in America. Comprehensive Notes, Bibliography, and Index complete a fine, scholarly work. Unfortunately, there are often more facts than characterization, and a young reader may find it, at times, a little dry and difficult. Still, this is unequivocally the best of all the biographies of Du Bois for young people—and clearly conveys the sense of his intellectual struggle, frustration, and search."[7]

Hamilton has also written a biography of Paul Robeson. "I had hoped, by writing the personal history of a real individual through a disciplined presentation of facts, to create the illusion of total reality; to give readers the feeling that they walked along with the subject in his life; and through the creative use of source material, to allow the subject to speak as closely as possible in his own voice.

"In this respect, of the two biographies, the Robeson biography is the more successful. The research and study of the Robeson material took a number of years. When that phase of the work was completed, I discovered it was possible during the day to evoke the Robeson spirit in my mind and to live with it as though the man were a guest in my house. I began to know Paul Robeson quite well, and slowly two aspects of him emerged to trouble

me and to pose definite problems in the actual writing.

"The first problem, and the one easiest to deal with, was the problem of Robeson emerging not as a man but as a symbol...In my Robeson research, it was almost impossible to find a single newspaper account that did not depict the man as somehow supernatural and larger than life....

"Hardly ever was Robeson described as a man. Rather, he was 'this giant,' 'that great, noble prince,' or 'the original stuff of the earth....' Eventually, I learned to use these overwrought passages to an advantage. But it became necessary for me to write in a very tight, simple style; to write close up to the individual in the hope that a concise and straightforward revelation of his life would finally produce a composite of the man.

"The second problem was more difficult and became clear to me only after I had written a first draft of the book. Then Robeson still seemed elusive...For the basic difficulty of writing about blacks in America was intensely a problem here: the origins of black American history is fundamentally different from that of traditional American history....

"In order to understand Paul Robeson or Dr. Du Bois, it is necessary that we understand that what the majority viewed as radical in their time was quite a normal point of view for these men whose lives were profoundly restricted by a whole system of established mores...Furthermore, it became necessary to go beyond the usual thorough and traditional histories having to do with political America, Europe, and the rest of the world, such as those written by Commager and Leuchtenburg, and to search for and find those revisionist historians, like Gabriel Kolko, whose historical truths emerge as radically different from what we have taken for granted as the truth....

"Paul Robeson's drift toward radicalism and the appeal radicalism had for him become understandable from the viewpoint of a colonized people. Robeson saw himself as a citizen of the world and identified himself, as did Du Bois, with the world's workers and colonized peoples, whom he deemed criminally exploited under capitalism....

"Curiously, my studies in radical history and research into black life and history have tended to radicalize me not so much in terms of world political views as in fictional terms. I would be a rather useless individual in any revolutionary situation. I hate violence and tend to view it as a human

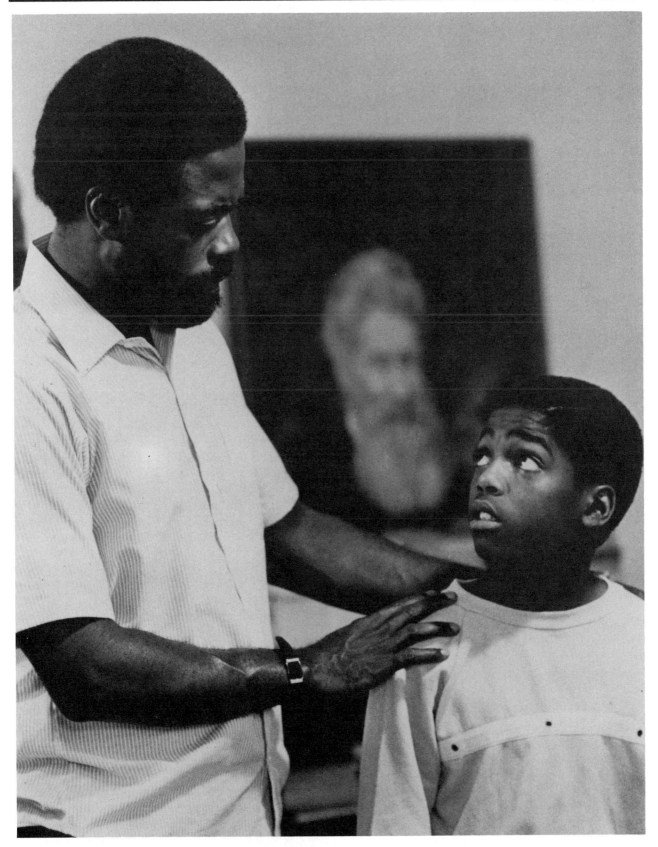

Howard Rollins (left) starred in "The House of Dies Drear." The film adaptation of Hamilton's novel appeared on PBS as part of the "Wonderworks" series in November, 1986.

aberration—certainly not a very radical point of view...In any case, for myself, I deliberately attempt a kind of literary radicalism in the hope of removing traditional prose restrictions and creating new ways to approach literary forms from a perspective other than that of the majority. It is a way of continuing to legitimize nonwhite literature, bringing it into full view to provoke curiosity and discussion."[8]

Hamilton's travails were rewarded with excellent reviews. Ethel L. Heins of *Horn Book* wrote, 'In her preface—as significant as the book itself—[Hamilton] explains how her father was responsible for her initial appreciation of the great black artist, who is still alive but almost unknown to young people. Drawing information from an impressive list of sources, she painstakingly tells the story of Robeson's life [dealing] objectively and skillfully with the tangled complexities of Robeson's beliefs and with the American political climate of the Cold War period....[This is an] important book for readers of all ages."[9]

Hamilton, who teaches as well as writes, has strong ideas concerning genre. "Traditionally, the young adult, or YA category of books has been maligned. I believe this is due more to the way the so-called movers and shakers of publishing houses think about YA, than to the qualities of the books themselves. Ask most editors, and they will talk about novels for young adults as 'problem books.' Supposedly, adolescents should be able to read them for the answers to the questions that typically plague them at that time of their life. Of course books can, and do, help us to live; and some may even change our lives, but it is not a good thing to put sociological/didactic considerations before literary ones. Besides, kids are very knowing. I tend to treat sexuality as a given, as something almost commonplace, in the lives of my characters. This leaves me—and my readers—free to concentrate on other things. I think about my story, characters, images, symbolism—the dynamics that hold those elements together in a pleasing sort of tension.

"There are certain technical advantages for writing for YA. You're allowed to linger over descriptions—words, rather than actions, may be in the forefront. I love setting up scenes, starting with a wide view and then gradually moving in for the close-up. You can develop characters in a more sophisticated way. I consider most of the novels I've written for adolescents to be classical romances. Certainly love figures prominently in romances, but there are other, equally important, themes. The protagonist is made to undertake a

journey—physical, psychic or both. As a result of that journey, she grows and changes, a complicated, usually painful, process.

"My last book, *A White Romance,* is about two central couples—one white girl and boy; one black girl and white boy. The setting for the black girl's epiphany is a heavy-metal rock concert. I learned fascinating things in the course of this book, including that I find myself more frequently on the same wavelength with people a generation or so younger; and 'out of sync' with readers and editors my own age. At least for this book.

"My son, a musician, was an invaluable help to me. He spent long hours talking with me into a tape recorder, giving me the lingo, the sounds, the scents, all the hidden things you have to be adept to know. He made sure I always placed the band members on the correct side of the stage—no drummers where the bass players should be—and called the instruments and the techniques used for playing them by their proper names. I must confess that this book grew partly out of my own anxiety about the heavy metal scene. Our son went often to these concerts, coming home with urine on his shoes and telling the most amazing stories. It frightened me. It went against the grain, however, to ask him to stop attending the concerts. So we struck a deal: he could continue to go, if he told me all about it. I was as much intrigued as I was scared by them.

"And so, because Jamie is such a marvellous storyteller and has such an extraordinary eye, place and milieu have a central role in *A White Romance.* Apparently these concerts are absolutely *packed.* Kids wait all night, sleeping outdoors, in order to get to the box office in time to buy a ticket. Far greater than the danger of drugs, apparently, is the danger of being trampled inside. People get so wound up in the hard-hitting music, that there's no way to say, 'Excuse me, I'd like to go to the rest room;' you would be crushed. Jaime says the only possible (not probable) way to get out of your row during the concert is if you yell that you are about to vomit. He told me something else that flabbergasted me. Heavy metal music attracts a lot of Vietnam veterans, many of whom are missing limbs. He says the weirdest thing is that after a concert there are all these crutches, canes and walkers just left lying. It makes you wonder: did people have mystical experiences in which they regained their ability to walk unaided? It sounds far-fetched, but....

"All in all, this seemed to me a perfect place for a crucial epiphany. A number of readers of my generation have told me they don't know what to make of the book. A reviewer from a prominent magazine even called me, saying she felt totally over her head. (Needless to say, this didn't prevent her from writing a review.) But young people love the book. And that matters most to me.

"I wanted to 'test limits' in *A White Romance*. I was thoroughly tired of YA books filled with tantalizingly suggestive sex scenes. As though adolescents don't know what the score is. I wrote some very graphic scenes. I did have to make some cuts. For example, in one scene, I had the girl wrap her legs around her boyfriend's behind. That detail, as they say, ended up on the cutting room floor. But my big rock concert scene stayed in pretty much as I wrote it."[1]

Hamilton feels that another of her YA works—the *Justice Cycle*, including *Justice and Her Brothers*, *Dustland* and *The Gathering*—has suffered somewhat because of generic confusion. Although the books have all received glowing reviews, they have often been referred to as 'science fiction.' "I don't think of those books as science fiction, at all. They fall into the category of fantasy, and have elements of the cautionary tale. Science fiction is based on scientific fact; fantasy need not be. Someone did say that these books start with reality, turn into fantasy and end in science fiction. This may be true. I certainly did a lot of research for the third book. The original idea for the book was The Great Snake Race, which as a child I misunderstood in the same way that Justice does. Twins and clairvoyance are themes that have long fascinated me. So, too, has the theme of the alien, and the possibility of global disaster. I feel less involved with my own heritage and more preoccupied with survivors of all kinds: Will the few who survive the cataclysm do so because they are genetically different? Is it possible that telepathy, prophecy, and genius are genetic mutations? Could the striking talents of a few be the means of survival for many? These are the questions I explore in *The Justice Cycle*."[1]

A book that means a great deal to Hamilton is *The People Could Fly*, a collection of American black folk tales with illustrations by Leo and Diane Dillon. "You see, the slaves—those former Africans— brought, chained, to this continent, had no power, no weapons to aid them in overcoming their oppressors. So it was that they used the folklore they created here to comment on their lives of servitude and to give themselves comfort and strength through endless hard times. Some of

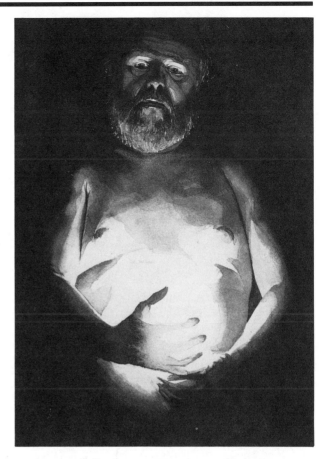

From "Prometheus the Creator" in *In the Beginning: Creation Stories from Around the World* by Virginia Hamilton.

these tales are absolutely unique in the folk-tale genre. But how were they told—and where—is the question I asked myself again and again.

"There could not have been an easy way for them to develop over time. There was no safe place where, and no condition under which, the slaves could sit down and simply tell stories, except in the safety of the forests. Most of the southern country was forest....Here they gathered under cover of darkness to pass gossip and to discuss what was beyond the forest....Their meetings were so secret they dared not use their own names for fear the names would somehow reach the ears of the overseer. They dared not touch one another, lest the mere touching give away an identity.

"I've not found the research in black heritage and culture a cause for despair, however sorrowful some of the areas might seem. One feels like an explorer many times, tracking along the 'hope-steps' of beings dead and gone. Following trails of dogged courage and will beyond imagining across dangerous entrapments.

"Black folk tales, I believe, allow us to share in the known, the remembered, and the imagined together as Americans sharing the same history....From teller to reader is the unbroken circle of communication. We all contribute to a construction of mere words. We are all together. That is what language does for us. That is what *The People Could Fly* may do for us. To say from one of us handed down to the other, you are not alone."[10]

Footnote Sources:

[1] Based on an interview by Marguerite Feitlowitz for *Authors and Artists for Young Adults.*
[2] Marilyn Apseloff, "A Conversation with Virginia Hamilton," *Children's Literature in Education*, winter, 1983.
[3] Virginia Hamilton, "Ah, Sweet Rememory!" *Horn Book*, December 1981.
[4] Elinor Standard, "Weaving Spells," *Book Week—The Washington Post*, June 25, 1967.
[5] Dorothy Sterling, "The House of Dies Drear," *New York Times Book Review*, October 13, 1968.
[6] V. Hamilton, "Portrait of the Author as a Working Writer," *Authors and Illustrators of Children's Books*, edited by Miriam Hoffman and Eva Samuels, 1972.
[7] Sheryl B. Andrews, "W. E. B. Du Bois: A Biography," *Horn Book*, October 1972.
[8] V. Hamilton, *Illusion and Reality*, Library of Congress, 1976.
[9] Ethel L. Heins, "Paul Robeson: The Life and Times of a Free Black Man," *Horn Book*, April 1975.
[10] V. Hamilton, "Coretta Scott King Award Acceptance," *Horn Book*, November/December 1986.

■ For More Information See

Top of the News, June, 1969, April, 1975.
Horn Book, February, 1970, February, 1972, December, 1972 (p. 563), June, 1973, December, 1974 (p. 671), April, 1975 (p. 113), August, 1975 (p. 337), December, 1978, October, 1982, June, 1983, February, 1984 (p. 24).
Elementary English, April, 1971.
Library Journal, September 15, 1971.
Christian Science Monitor, November 11, 1971, May 12, 1980, August 3, 1984.
Donnarae MacCann and Gloria Woodard, editors, *The Black American in Books for Children: Readings in Racism*, Scarecrow, 1972.
Washington Post Book World, November 10, 1974, November 11, 1979, September 14, 1980, November 7, 1982, November 10, 1985.
Lee Bennett Hopkins, *More Books by More People*, Citation Press, 1974.
Listener, November 6, 1975.
Francelia Butler, editor, *Children's Literature: Annual of the Modern Language Association Seminar on Children's Literature and the Children's Literature Association*, Volume IV, Temple University Press, 1975.
Lee Kingman, editor, *Newbery and Caldecott Medal Books: 1966-1975*, Horn Book, 1975.

Theressa Gunnels Rush and others, *Black American Writers Past and Present: A Biographical and Bibliographical Dictionary*, two volumes, Scarecrow, 1975.
Judith Wagner, "More Vivid than Daylight," *Cincinnati Enquirer* (Ohio), Januuary 5, 1975.
"Meet the Newbery Author: Virginia Hamilton," (filmstrip with record or cassette), Miller-Brody, 1976.
Barbara Nykoruk, editor, *Authors in the News*, Volume 1, Gale, 1976.
Doris de Montreville and Elizabeth D. Crawford, editors, *Fourth Book of Junior Authors and Illustrators*, H. W. Wilson, 1978.
Jacqueline S. Weiss, "Profiles in Literature" (videocassette), Temple University, 1978.
D. L. Kirkpatrick, editor, *Twentieth-Century Children's Writers*, St. Martin's, 1978, 2nd edition, 1983.
John Rowe Townsend, *A Sounding of Storytellers*, Lippincott, 1979.
Marilyn Apseloff, *Virginia Hamilton/Ohio Explorer in the World of Imagination*, State Library of Ohio, 1979.
Betsy Hearne, "Virginia Hamilton—An Eminent Writer for Children in the U.S.A.," *Bookbird*, number 2, 1980 (p. 22).
School Library Journal, February, 1980 (p. 21), May, 1980, April, 1983.
Lina Mainiero, editor, *American Women Writers*, Ungar, 1980.
Virginia Haviland, editor, *The Openhearted Audience: Ten Authors Talk about Writing for Children*, Library of Congress, 1980.
Mary Lystad, *From Dr. Mather to Dr. Seuss: 200 Years of American Books for Children*, Schenkman Books, 1980 (p. 179).
Betsy Hearne and Marilyn Kaye, editors, *Celebrating Children's Books: Essays on Children's Literature in Honor of Zena Sutherland*, Lothrop, 1981.
"Fanciful Words," *New York Times Book Review*, April 26, 1981.
Children's Literature Association Quarterly, fall, 1982 (p. 45), spring, 1983 (p. 17), winter, 1983 (p. 25).
Jim Roginski, compiler, *Newbery and Caldecott Medalists and Honor Book Winners*, Libraries Unlimited, 1982.
Publishers Weekly, July 6, 1983.
Donna Norton, editor, *Through the Eyes of a Child: Introduction to Children's Literature*, Merrill, 1983 (p. 500).
Seventeen, April, 1984.
Writer, August, 1984.
J. H. Dressel, "The Legacy of Ralph Ellison in Virginia Hamilton's 'Justice Trilogy,'" *English Journal*, November, 1984.
David Rees, *Painted Desert, Green Shade: Essays on Contemporary Writers of Fiction for Children and Young Adults*, Horn Book, 1984 (p. 168).
Dictionary of Literary Biography, Gale, Volume XXXIII, 1984, Volume LII, 1986.
Chicago Tribune Book World, November 10, 1985.
Anita Moss, "Mythical Narrative: Virginia Hamilton's *The Magical Adventures of Pretty Pearl*," *The Lion and the Unicorn*, Volume 9, 1985.

S. E. Hinton

Born Susan Eloise Hinton in 1950, in Tulsa, Okla.; married David E. Inhofe (a mail order businessman), September, 1970; children: Nicholas David. *Education:* University of Tulsa, B.S., 1970. *Residence:* Tulsa, Okla. *Agent:* c/o Delacorte Press, 1 Dag Hammarskjold Plaza, New York, N.Y. 10017.

■ Career

Author of young adult novels.

■ Awards, Honors

New York Herald Tribune's Children's Spring Book Festival Honor Book, 1967, *Media & Methods* Maxi Award, and one of the American Library Association's Best Young Adult Books, both 1975, and Massachusetts Children's Book Award from Salem State College, 1979, all for *The Outsiders*; *Book World*'s Children's Spring Book Festival Award Honor Book, and one of American Library Association's Best Books for Young Adults, both 1971, and Massachusetts Children's Book Award, 1978, all for *That Was Then, This Is Now; Rumble Fish* was named one of American Library Association's Best

Books for Young Adults, and one of *School Library Journal*'s Best Books of the Year, both 1975.

American Library Association Best Book for Young Adults, one of *School Library Journal*'s Best Books of the Year, and one of *Booklist*'s Reviewers' Choices, all 1979, American Book Award finalist for Children's Paperback Fiction from the Association of American Publishers, and one of New York Public Library's Books for the Teen Age, both 1980, Sue Hefly Award Honor Book from the Louisiana Association of School Libraries, California Young Reader Medal nominee from the California Reading Association, both 1982, and Sue Hefly Award 1983, all for *Tex*; Land of Enchantment Book Award from the New Mexico Library Association, 1982, for *Rumble Fish*.

■ Writings

Fiction:

The Outsiders, Viking, 1967.
That Was Then, This Is Now (ALA Notable Book; illustrated by Hal Siegel), Viking, 1971, new edition, 1985.
Rumble Fish, Delacorte, 1975.
Tex, Delacorte, 1979.
Taming the Star Runner, Delacorte, in press.

Teacher's guides are available for *The Outsiders, That Was Then, This Is Now, Rumble Fish,* and *Tex,* all written by Lou Willett Stanek, all published by Dell. Hinton's books have been published in England, Denmark, Finland and Germany.

■ Adaptations

"Rumble Fish" (record or cassette), Viking, 1977.

"The Outsiders" (filmstrip with cassette), Current Affairs and Mark Twain Media, 1978, (cassette), Random House.

"That Was Then, This Is Now" (filmstrip with cassette), Current Affairs and Mark Twain Media, 1978.

Films:

"Tex," starring Matt Dillon, Walt Disney Productions, 1982.

"The Outsiders," starring C. Thomas Howell and Matt Dillon, Warner Bros., 1983.

"Rumble Fish," starring Matt Dillon and Mickey Rourke, Universal, 1983.

"That Was Then, This Is Now," starring Emilio Estevez and Craig Sheffer, Paramount, 1985.

■ Sidelights

"I was born in Tulsa, Oklahoma [in 1950], where I have lived most of my life. There is nothing to do there, but it is a pleasant place to live if you don't want to do anything. . . .

"I started reading about the same time everyone else did, and began to write a short time later. The major influence on my writing has been my reading. I read everything, including Comet cans and coffee labels. Reading taught me sentence structure, paragraphing, how to build a chapter. Strangely enough, it never taught me spelling.

"I've always written about things that interest me, so my first years of writing (grade three through grade ten) I wrote about cowboys and horses. I wanted to be a cowboy and have a horse. I was strange for my era, but feel quite comfortable in this one, when everyone wants to be a cowboy and I have a horse."[1]

In 1967, while attending Tulsa's Will Rogers High School, Hinton revolutionized the genre of the young adult novel with the publication of *The Outsiders,* the story of a confrontation between a group of "greasers" and their more affluent high school peers, the "socs." Hinton began the first draft of her novel at the age of fifteen, and was published when she was seventeen. *"The Outsiders* took me a year and a half. During that time, I did four complete drafts. The first draft was forty pages; then I just kept rewriting and adding details."[2]

While Hinton's first book was acclaimed by book critics and applauded by teenagers, many parents objected to the characters' unruly and often violent nature. Some adults became concerned that the storyline might encourage teens to idolize a life of lawlessness and destruction, while others felt it was wrong for young people to be exposed to violence in literature under any circumstances. ". . .There was no realistic fiction being written for teenagers. It was all Mary Jane goes to the prom, that kind of stuff. I'd been to a few proms and they weren't anything like that. There weren't any books that dealt realistically with teenage life so I wrote *The Outsiders* to fill that gap."[3]

"I felt the greasers were getting knocked when they didn't deserve it. The custom, for instance, of driving by a shabby boy and screaming 'Greaser!' at him always made me boil. But it was the cold-blooded beating of a friend of mine that gave me the idea of writing a book; I wanted to do something that would change people's opinion of greasers. Some 'socs' (the abbreviation of socials) didn't like the way my friend was combing his hair, so they beat him up! Another friend of mine never got enough to eat and frequently slept in the bus station because his father was always beating him up. The socs teased *him* because of his grades. Grades!"[4]

"It always irritated me that people would make assumptions on the way other people dressed or their economic backgrounds that they didn't have feelings. It drove me nuts that people would set up social rules and social games and never ask where these rules came from or who was saying they *have* to do this or that.

"As a kid, everything is life and death. As you get older, it's harder to get suicidal about a bad haircut. But I have a real good memory for what it was like. And I can't stand it when adults say to teenagers, 'Why are you sulking around with that look on your face, you're in the best time of your life!' If it's the best time of my life, I may as well shoot myself."[5]

"*The Outsiders,* like most of the things I write, is written from a boy's point of view. That's why I'm listed as S. E. Hinton rather than Susan on the book; since my subject was gang fights I figured most boys would look at the book and think, 'What can a chick know about stuff like that?'"[4]

"I started writing before the women's movement was in full swing, and at the time, people wouldn't have believed that girls would do the things that I was writing about. I also felt more comfortable

Hinton's films have consistently launched the careers of young actors. In "The Outsiders," Emilio Estevez, Rob Lowe, Thomas Howell, Matt Dillon, Ralph Macchio, Patrick Swayze and Tom Cruise all went on to greater success.

with the male point of view—I had grown up around boys. . ."[2]

". . .Most of my close friends were boys. In those days, girls were mainly concerned about getting their hair done and lining their eyes. It was such a passive society. Girls got their status from their boyfriends. They weren't interested in doing anything on their own. I didn't understand what they were talking about."[6]

". . .I found nothing in the female culture to identify with. Sometimes, though, I feel like I spent the first part of my life wishing to be a teen-age boy, and the second part condemned to being one."[7]

"None of the events in the book [The Outsiders] are taken from life, but the rest—how kids think and live and feel—is for real. The characters—Dallas, who wasn't tough enough; Sodapop, the happy-go-lucky dropout; Bob, the rich kid whose arrogance cost him his life; Ponyboy, the sensitive, green-eyed greaser who didn't want to be a hood—they're all real to me, though I didn't put my friends into the book. The characters are mixtures of people I know, with a bit of myself thrown in."[4]

"The characters have to be part of yourself, you have to understand them. By the time they go through your head and work their way down on paper, they reflect some aspect of you. Ponyboy

Curtis probably comes closest to me—he's absent-minded and quiet and daydreams a lot."[2]

Although Hinton wrote *The Outsiders* about a gang, she was not a part of any group at the time. At the time of publication, seventeen-year-old Hinton remarked: "Many of my friends are greasers, but I'm not. I have friends who are rich too, but nobody will ever call me a soc—I've seen what money and too much idle time and parental approval can do to people. That's why I tried not to be too hard on the socs in the book. The thing is, they are *so* cool. Cool people mean nothing to me—they're living behind masks, and I'm always wondering, 'Is there a real person underneath?'

"It's great when people come up and say, 'I read your book and liked it.' But I've always been a quiet person, the kind who takes her time about things. Schedules and details are beyond me—I nearly flunked creative writing because I couldn't spell and couldn't write under pressure. And I'm shy around older people, which doesn't make publicizing the book much fun. I do the best I can but sometimes I wish I'd never written the thing. Then I remember why I wrote it and I don't mind so much.

"My younger sister hasn't once said she's sick of hearing about the book although I know she must be. My mother, after the first shock of reading it ('Susie, where *did* you pick up all of this?'), is selling it to everyone she meets. But it's the reaction of my greaser friends I'm happiest about. 'Did you put me in it?' is the question they ask most, not 'What could *you* know about the way we feel?' They have confidence in me.

"The gang that inspired my book is gone now, and I'm too old to go around in jeans and carry a knife. But I don't need to anymore; I can still be a friend in dresses and make-up. Maybe not a buddy, but a friend. And if I ever forget how it is to be a teenager in a savage social system, I've got it all written down."[4]

The Outsiders was a major success among teenagers, selling more than four million copies in the United States. The book's popularity enabled Hinton to attend the University of Tulsa, where in 1970 she earned an education degree and met her future husband David Inhofe. However, being catapulted into fame and fortune at eighteen was not without problems; Hinton had a writer's block for several years. "I couldn't even write a letter. All these people were going, 'Oh, look at this teenage writer' and you think, God, they're ex-

pecting a masterpiece and I haven't got a masterpiece."[5]

1971. Hinton's second book, *That Was Then, This is Now*, was written with the encouragement of her future husband. The writing was slow—two pages of manuscript a day over a period of three to four months—and deliberate. But the result was a book that Hinton considered better written than *The Outsiders*. "I have no idea why I write. The old standards are: I like to express my feelings, stretch my imagination, earn money. (One you don't usually see on the list is 'total incompetence at anything else,' which certainly applies in my case.) Writing is much easier to do than to talk about.

"I'm a character writer. Some writers are plot writers....I have to begin with people. I always know my characters, exactly what they look like, their birthdays, what they like for breakfast. It doesn't matter if these things appear in the book. I still have to know. My characters are fictional. I get ideas from real people, sometimes, but my characters always exist only in my head....Those characters are as real to me as anyone else in my life, so much so that if I ran into one of them at the laundry I wouldn't be all that surprised.

"There is an interesting transformation that takes place in the beginning of a book. I go straight from thinking about my narrator to being him. Like Lon Chaney becoming the werewolf. Only substitute typewriter for full moon. This can be fun...."[7]

1975. *Rumble Fish*, the story of a boy who struggles to acquire a tough reputation, continued the theme of delinquent youths. "When I was writing *Rumble Fish* I was reading a lot about color symbolism and mythology, and that came through without my realizing it. It was a hard book to write because Rusty-James is a simple person, yet the Motorcycle Boy is the most complex character I've ever created. And Rusty-James sees him one way, which is not right, and I had to make that clear.

"It's about over-identifying with something which you can never understand, which is what Rusty-James is doing. The Motorcycle Boy can't identify with anything. He's something other than what his neighborhood thinks, but he can't find anything he wants to be or do.

"The Motorcycle Boy's flaw is his inability to compromise, and that's why I made him colorblind. He interprets life 'in black and white,' and he has the ability to walk off and leave anything, which is what ultimately destroys him.

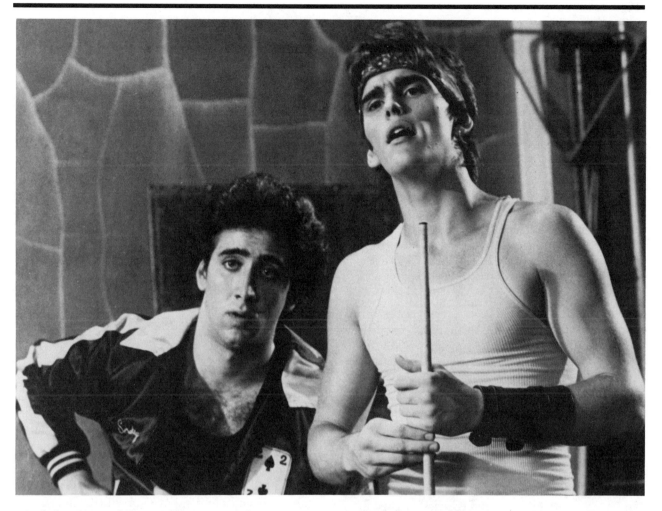

Nicholas Cage and Matt Dillon, stars of the movie "Rumble Fish." Copyright © 1983 Universal City Studios, Inc.

"I did not give the Motorcycle Boy a name because I wanted to emphasize his alienation. Actually, he did not give himself the title, others did. The neighborhood was so bad that the boys needed something to boast about.

"Every time I get a letter from a kid who says that *Rumble Fish* is his favourite book, he's usually in the reformatory. I write about kids who don't fit into the mold; I wouldn't make them up. But the book's readers don't identify with the Motorcycle Boy; they identify with Rusty-James."[8]

Hinton's next book, *Tex* (the story of two brothers left in each other's care by their rambling father) is also about deliquent youths trying to make it in a world shaped by protest, drugs, violence and family disruption. "I can't say that Tex is a lot like me. But he was the narrator I most enjoyed being. Capable of thinking, he has to be made to think: he relies on instinct instead of intellect. And basically his instincts are good. Capable of violence, but not malice, he has to learn things the hard way—a

basically happy person trying to deal with unhappiness. I envied his total lack of suspicion.

"His brother tells him, 'Tex, you are not stupid, and you're not all that ignorant. But how anybody as simpleminded as you are has managed to survive for fourteen years is beyond me.' A person of action, without much physical fear, Tex does manage to survive situations he brings on himself—but he also survives those he has no control of and can see no justice in. He does so by learning that every action has a reaction—but many times there is a *choice* of reactions.

"Tex McCormick will very likely grow up to be a horse-trainer and live in a rather narrow world. His brother, Mason, however, will go as far as brains and ambition will carry him. I don't think it's impossible these two kinds of people could respect and like each other, without wanting the other's life.

"In trying to say what Tex is about, the best I can come up with is: relationships, which are complicated even for simple people; and maybe love, which can't cure anything but sometimes makes the unbearable bearable; and being a teen-ager, which is problem enough for anybody. Mainly it's about Tex McCormick, perhaps the most childlike character I've ever done, but the one who makes the biggest strides toward maturity. I have to admit he's a favorite child."[7]

According to librarians, Hinton is one of the most popular authors of "reluctant readers," in the junior-high age group. Her books are read without having to be assigned. One high school teacher, deeply concerned about the drop in reading, pointed out: "The choice is not between an adolescent's reading *Tex* and reading [D. H. Lawrence's] *Sons and Lover*, but between reading *Tex* and reading nothing." "...My stories just pull young readers in.

"Teachers will read the first chapter of one of my books aloud to a class, then assign the rest for home reading. The kids find themselves finishing the volume in one or two sittings."[9]

"I think the readers identify with the characters so strongly. They either know somebody like that

Jacket illustration by Michael Tedesco from *The Outsiders*.

person or they feel they are just like that person. I get letters from kids saying, 'Those aren't my problems, but those are my feelings.' And I get the same kinds of letters today that I got 15 years ago. The problems are different but the feelings are the same."[5]

"The trouble is, grownups write about teen-agers from their own memories, or else write about teen-agers from a stand-off, I'm-a-little-scared-to-get-close-they're-hairy view. Teen-agers today want to read about teen-agers today. The world is changing, yet the authors of books for teen-agers are still fifteen years behind the times.

"In the fiction they write, romance is still the most popular theme, with a-horse-and-the-girl-who-loved-it coming in a close second. Nowhere is the drive-in social jungle mentioned, the behind-the-scenes politicking that goes on in big schools, the cruel social system in which, if you can afford to snub every fourth person you meet, you're popular. In short, where is reality? On the other side of the coin, there are the hair-raising accounts of gangs, motorcycle and otherwise; gangs hold a fatal fascination for adults. Adults who try to write realistically seem to mix up the real with the dirty.

"And speaking of realism, nothing makes a teen-ager blush more than a grown-up writer trying to use 'geer,' 'fab,' 'camp,' 'groovy' in dialogue. The rule is: If you don't say it yourself, don't say it. It comes out fake. And one of the more redeeming qualities of teen-agers is their loathing for anything fake.

"...We still get books on Mary Jane's big date with the football hero. Why not write it realistically? (I said real, not dirty.) Most kids nowadays date for status. There are cliques and classes and you date so you can say you had a date with so-and-so, the president of the student council. You may loathe him, but personal likes and dislikes don't matter anymore. And the higher up the social ladder you go, the cooler it gets. You say what everyone else says. You wear what everyone else wears. And you are so cool, so scared someone is going to think you're not 'In,' that you don't have time to think about another person. Your date is there to enhance your status. It's a role you're playing for a very cruel audience, and you don't make slips.

"That, friends, would make a realistic romance. Because in spite of everything, you may still make slips.

"Now let's take the business of cars. Teen-agers spend half their waking hours in cars, and yet they

The 1985 Paramount film "That Was Then, This Is Now," starred Emilio Estevez (above) who also wrote the screenplay.

are scarcely mentioned in teen-age literature. If they're mentioned at all, it's the story of how Tommy fixed up his jalopy and won the local drags, or lost them and enriched his character: either ending is satisfactory. Yet Tommy is more likely out dragging his SS397 up and down the local strip, impressing girls and risking his life and other people's lives, and if the cops chase him to give him a ticket he (1) stops because he lives on the very 'right' side of town and his parents or friends can fix the ticket; (2) stops because it's the local cop, who probably just wants to say, 'Why don't you take it out to the expressway tonight. I'll match you against my cousin's Vet'; or (3) runs.

"*That* would make a realistic story about cars.

"All we hear is how teen-agers are rebelling against authority, against lack of authority, against country, against parents. This is partly true. It is more true that all we are doing most of the time is asking, 'Why?' and getting as an answer, 'Because it's always been done this way.' If there were more stopping and explaining *why* it's always been done this way, there'd be more understanding. Understanding breeds communication. There we are back at the root of the matter.

"Books for teen-agers portray us as a carefree group, when all we hear is 'The future is in your hands!' Our parents didn't have to worry through their childhood about whose hands the future was in. And when responsibilities did come, they were ready for them. Now, from 13 on, you worry about the future. No wonder, then, by 17, some say, 'You made the world, you fix it,' and retreat into a hazy drug world where there are no responsibilities.

"People are always asking for teen-agers' opinions on things, and writing about them. You've heard of people reading the symptoms of a disease, and then suddenly developing the disease? Well, you can't pick up a magazine or a newspaper that doesn't declare that teen-agers are rebellious, over-worked, over-pampered, under-privileged, smart, stupid and sex-crazed. No wonder some develop the symptoms.

"Adults who let small children watch hours of violence, unfunny comedy, abnormal behavior and suggestive actions on TV, scream their heads off when a book written for children contains a fist fight. But violence too is a part of teen-agers' lives. If it's not on television or in the movies, it's a beating-up at a local drive-in. Things like this are

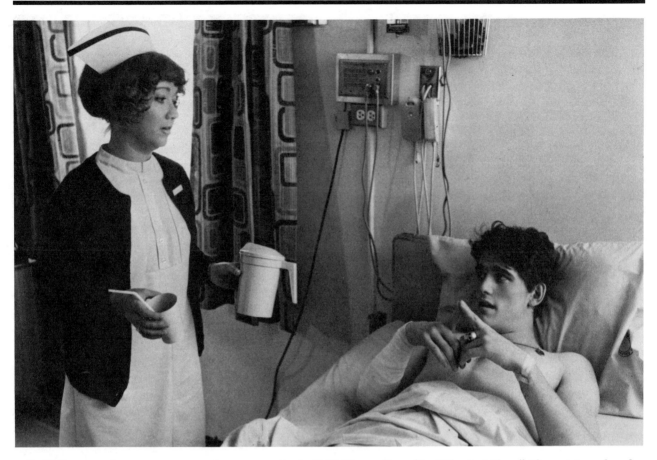

S. E. Hinton made a cameo appearance as a nurse in the 1983 Warner Bros. film "The Outsiders." The script was based on the novel Hinton wrote while still in high school.

going to take place as long as there are kids. Only when violence is for a sensational effect should it be objected to in books for teen-agers. Such books should not be blood and gore, but not a fairyland of proms and double-dates, either. Sometimes I wonder which extreme does the most harm.

"Teen-agers should not be written down to; anyone can tell when his intelligence is being underestimated. Those who are not ready for adult novels can easily have their love of reading killed by the inane junk lining the teen-age shelf in the library. Parents complain of their children's lack of enthusiasm for reading, but if they had to read a 'Jeri Doe, Girl Reporter' series, they'd turn off, too.

"Teen-agers know a lot today. Not just things out of a textbook, but about living. They know their parents aren't superhuman, they know that justice doesn't always win out, and that sometimes the bad guys win. They know that persons in high places aren't safe from corruption, that some men have their price, and that some people sell out. Writers needn't be afraid that they will shock their teen-age audience. But give them something to hang onto. Show that some people don't sell out, and

that everyone can't be bought. Do it realistically. Earn respect by giving it."[10]

Hinton continues to speak to teens. All four of her books have been made into major Hollywood feature films; "Tex," the first movie, released in 1982, was produced by Walt Disney. "At first I said, 'No, thank you, I'm not interested in doing a Disney movie.' I thought they'd really sugar it up, take out all the sex, drugs and violence and leave nothing but a story of a boy and his horse. Then Tom Wilhite, vice president at Disney, landed on my doorstep and convinced me that they wanted to broaden their audience and do a hard PG movie. I liked Tom Wilhite and agreed to sell on the condition that my horse got to play the lead horse. Those two deals happened within a week of each other."[6]

The shooting was done in Tulsa, and Hinton was involved in the casting, scriptwriting, and directing of her own work as a collaborator of director Tim Hunter. "Once I sold the books I expected to be asked to drop off the face of the earth. But that didn't happen. I know that I had extremely rare experiences for a writer. Usually the director does

JUNE/JULY 1988
A CAHNERS / R. R. BOWKER PUBLICATION

SCHOOL LIBRARY JOURNAL

S. E. Hinton-Winner
of the 1988 Young Adult Author Award
Sponsored by *School Library Journal*
Selected & Administered by
ALA's Young Adult Services Division

THE MAGAZINE OF CHILDREN'S, YOUNG ADULT & SCHOOL LIBRARIANS

Cover portrait by Curt Doty of S. E. Hinton who won an award for her body of work.

not say, 'Boys, these are important lines, so you've got to know them word for word....'"[6]

"I was just stunned that I liked all these movie people. I thought they'd all be money-grubbing, sex-crazed dope addicts, but they're not money-grubbing at all."[5]

"But, on the other hand, I'm well aware that the writer is usually not the most respected member of the crew."[11]

During the same period, a group of high school students from Lone Star, California sent a petition to Francis Coppola nominating him to make a movie of their favorite book, *The Outsiders.* Coppola's producer, Fred Roos recalled: "The jacket was so tacky. It looked like the book was privately printed by some religious organization. I carried it around with me for weeks, but I didn't open it. One day I found myself on an airplane, and I was tired of carrying it around. I said to myself that I'd give it 10 pages. I ended up reading it cover to cover and I agreed with the kids. I thought it was a movie."[12]

Roos highly recommended the project to Coppola who eventually contacted Hinton: "When I met Susie, it was confirmed to me that she was not just a young people's novelist, but a real American novelist. For me the primary thing about her books is that the characters come across as very real. Her dialogue is memorable, and her prose is striking. Often a paragraph of her descriptive prose sums up something essential and stays with you....'"[6]

Hinton, who had turned down previous offers for the movie rights to *The Outsiders,* accepted Coppola's offer after being impressed by his screen adaptation of "Black Stallion." As with "Tex," she was on the set as a creative consultant. "When Francis visited me in Tulsa, he showed me how he was writing the screenplay. He had literally taken the book apart, outlining in red the sections with action and the passages of introspection in blue.

"Working with that guy is so funny. He can go forever and thinks that everyone else can, too."[11]

"Halfway through 'The Outsiders,' Francis looked up at me one day and said, 'Susie, we get along great. Have you written anything else I can film?' I told him about *Rumble Fish*, and he read the book and loved it. He said, 'I know what we can do. On our Sundays off, let's write a screenplay, and then as soon as we can wrap 'The Outsiders,' we'll take a two-week break and start filming 'Rumble Fish.' I said, 'Sure, Francis, we're working 16 hours a day,

and you want to spend Sundays writing another screenplay?' But that's what we did."[6]

"...We were in his office for about 12 hours writing before I finally said, 'I can't go any further, I'm beat.' And he said, 'No, no, no! We'll put some more tapes on the machine. Here's another glass of wine. Stay, stay.'

"He put a tape of the Police on the machine and after a while he looked up and said, 'I really like that drummer. Get me that drummer!' And the next thing I knew Stewart Copeland was sitting in on the 'Rumble Fish' rehearsals playing the drums so we could rehearse to his beat."[11]

"It's the first time I've ever felt at home in a group situation. I've never been a joiner. In Tulsa I have a reputation for being slightly eccentric. Even my close friends think I'm a little nutty. But with the movie people I was accepted instantly.

"Also, when you're making a movie, you feel like an outlaw. Traffic stops for you, and you don't keep the same hours that anybody else keeps. I like that outlaw feeling. And there's one other nice thing about the movies. There's always somebody else to blame. With a novel, you have to take all the blame yourself."[6]

"I really have had a wonderful time and made some very good friends during the filming. Like a lot of authors, I'd heard the horror stories about how they buy the property and then want the author to disappear and not meddle around worrying about what they're doing to the book.

"But that didn't happen at all. They invited me in right from the start, and I helped with the screenplays. The scripts stick closely to the books, and so much of the dialogue is mine, so naturally I'm happy with them.

"...I guess I thought I'd collect some really funny, cynical Hollywood stories. And that's where I got disillusioned. The movies are damn near as good as my books."[13]

"Rumble Fish" and "The Outsiders" were both released in 1982 starring Matt Dillon, one of America's most successful teenage actors. "Matt identifies with Rusty-James [in *Rumble Fish*]. He told me a long time ago, when we were shooting 'Tex,' that *Rumble Fish* was his favourite book. He said '[We] gotta get somebody to make a movie of it so I can play the part.' And I said that by that time, he might be too old; I asked him if he'd play the Motorycyle Boy. He said, '[Y]eah, and if I'm really old, like 27, I'll direct.'

Matt Dillon, star of the movie "Tex."

"Matt is exactly the kind of kid I write about. Of course, he's a much more complex person than any of my characters, but he has facets of all of them. He has a sweet side, which was good for 'Tex,' and that street-wise thing that got him through Dallas in 'The Outsiders,' and a funny, charming cockiness that's perfect for Rusty-James.

"I love to see Matt walking around reading books. He had read all of mine before we ever met, and I feel I'm partly responsible for the fact that he likes to read now.

"I didn't know Mickey Rourke [Motorcycle Boy in 'Rumble Fish'], but after Francis told me who he was, I remembered seeing 'Body Heat' and thinking, when he came on the screen, 'I know that guy.' It was such a strong recognition factor, I wonder if it was a premonition."[8]

1985. Release of the movie 'That Was Then, This is Now." While Hinton enjoyed working for the movie industry, her primary involvement as a writer continued. "...I still think of myself as a novelist, and with the next book I'm writing, I'm doing everything I can to make it unfilmable."[6]

"I don't think I have a masterpiece in me, but I do know I'm writing well in the area I choose to write in. I understand kids and I really like them. And I have a very good memory. I remember exactly what it was like to be a teen-ager that nobody listened to or paid attention to or wanted around. I mean, it wasn't like that with my own family, but I knew a lot of kids like that and hung around with them. They were street kids, gang kids, sort of scrounging around, and somehow I always understood them. They were my type."[13]

Footnote Sources:

[1] Doris de Montreville and Elizabeth J. Crawford, editors, *Fourth Book of Junior Authors*, H. W. Wilson, 1978.
[2] Lisa Ehrichs, "Advice from a Penwoman," *Seventeen*, November, 1981.
[3] "Tex and Other Teen Tales," *Teen*, July, 1982.
[4] "Face to Face with a Teen-Age Novelist," *Seventeen*, October, 1967.
[5] Carol Wallace, "In Praise of Teenage Outcasts," *Daily News*, September 26, 1982.
[6] Stephen Farber, "Directors Join the S. E. Hinton Fan Club," *New York Times*, March 20, 1983.
[7] "Notes from Delacorte Press for Books for Young Readers," *Delacorte Press*, winter, 1979/spring, 1980.
[8] "Rumble Fish," *Production Notes*, No Weather Films, 1983.
[9] Lisa Robin, "The Young and the Restless," *Media and Methods*, May/June, 1982.
[10] Susan Hinton, "Teen Agers Are for Real," *New York Times Book Review*, August 27, 1967.
[11] Hal Hinton, "Writer of 'Tex' Is Comfortable Dealing with Disney and Coppola," *Chicago Tribune*, December 24, 1982.
[12] Aljean Harmetz, "Making 'The Outsiders,' a Librarian's Dream," *New York Times*, March 23, 1983.
[13] Dave Smith, "Hinton, What Boys Are Made Of," *Los Angles Times*, July 15, 1982.

■ For More Information See

School Library Journal, May, 1967 (p. 64), September, 1971 (p. 174), October, 1975 (p. 106).
Publishers Weekly, May 22, 1967 (p. 64).
Atlantic Monthly, December, 1967 (p. 401).
Zena Sutherland, "The Teen-Ager Speaks," *Saturday Review*, January 27, 1968.
English Journal, February, 1969 (p. 295).
Times Literary Supplement, October, 30, 1970 (p. 1258), April 2, 1976 (p. 388).
School Librarian, December, 1970 (p. 455), December, 1976 (p. 335), March, 1977 (p. 21).
Horn Book, August, 1971 (p. 389), December, 1975 (p. 601).
D. L. Kirkpatrick, editor, *Twentieth-Century Children's Writers*, St. Martin's, 1978, new edition, 1983.
Variety, May 12, 1982 (p. 445), October 6, 1982, October 6, 1983.
Richard Dodds, "Matt Dillon Shrugs, Mumbles While Novelist Takes up the Slack," *Times-Picayune* (New Orleans), July 25, 1982 (section 8, p. 4).
"On Tulsa's Mean Streets," *Newsweek*, October 11, 1982 (p. 105).
"Cinema," *Time*, October 11, 1982, April 4, 1983, October 24, 1983.
Bob Thomas, "Children's Author Hits Film Jackpot," *Detroit News*, October 15, 1982 (section D, p. 3).
David Sterritt, "Key to Filming the World of Young Adults: Credibility," *Christian Science Monitor*, November 4, 1982 (p. 19).
"Susie Loves Matt," *American Film*, April, 1983 (p. 34).
New York, April 4, 1983.
People, April 4, 1983.
Arthur Bell, "One from the Crotch," *Village Voice*, April 5, 1983 (p. 53).
Cynthia Rose, "The Fiction of S. E. Hinton," *Monthly Film Bulletin*, September, 1983 (p. 238).
David Rees, *Painted Desert, Green Shade*, Horn Book, 1984.
Patty Campbell, "The Young Adult Perplex," *Wilson Library Bulletin*, September, 1985 (p. 61).
Michael Malone, "Tough Puppies," *Nation*, March 8, 1986 (p. 276).
"Is the Young Adult Novel Dead?," *Society of Children's Book Writers*, November/December, 1987.

Chuck Jones

Born September 21, 1912, in Spokane, Wash.; son of Charles Adams and Mabel (Martin) Jones; married Dorothy Webster, January 31, 1935 (died, 1978); married Marian Dern (a writer), January 14, 1983; children: Linda Jones Clough. *Education:* Chouinard Art Institute (now California Institute of the Arts), diploma, 1931. *Politics:* Democrat. *Religion:* Unitarian. *Office:* 789 West 20th St., Costa Mesa, Calif. 92627.

■ Career

Began career working as a seaman and portrait painter, among other posts; worked as animator, director, and scenario writer for Ub Iwerks, Charles Mintz, and Walter Lantz, beginning in the early 1930s; Warner Bros., Inc., animator, 1933-38, director of numerous animated films featuring "Daffy Duck," "Bugs Bunny," "Sylvester," "Porky Pig," and others, 1938-63, co-creator of cartoon characters "Road Runner," "Wile E. Coyote," "Pepe le Pew," and "Snafu"; co-producer, writer, and director of "The Bugs Bunny Show," ABC-TV, 1960-62, and "The Bugs Bunny/Road Runner Hour," CBS-TV, 1968-71; writer, producer, and director of television specials, 1962—, including "How the Grinch Stole Christmas,"

1970, "The Cricket in Times Square," ABC-TV, 1973, "Rikki-Tikki-Tavi," CBS-TV, 1975, "Bugs Bunny in King Arthur's Court," CBS-TV, 1978, "Raggedy Ann and Andy in the Great Santa Claus Caper," CBS-TV, 1978, and "The Pumpkin Who Couldn't Smile," 1979; Metro-Goldwyn-Mayer, Inc., Hollywood, Calif., producer of "Tom and Jerry" cartoon series, beginning 1963, head of animation department, beginning 1966; founder, Tower Twelve Productions, 1965; American Broadcasting Companies, Inc., vice-president of children's programming, beginning 1970, creator of program "The Curiosity Shop," 1971-73; founder, Chuck Jones Enterprises (motion picture company); creator of syndicated comic strip "Crawford," beginning 1978. Teacher and lecturer at various colleges and universities in the United States and abroad.

Exhibitions:

Gallery Lainzberg, 1976; Circle Fine Art Galleries, 1984. Film retrospectives: Museum of Modern Art, New York; British Film Institute at National Film Theater, London; American Film Institute at Kennedy Center, Washington, D.C.; New York Cultural Center; Harvard University, Cambridge, Mass.; Ottawa Art Center; London Film School; Filmex Festival, Hollywood; Deauville Festival of American Films (France); Moscow Film Festival; Montreal Film Festival. *Wartime service:* Worked on training films for the U.S. Army during World War II. *Member:* Academy of Motion Picture Arts and Sciences, Screen Writers Guild, Academy of Television Arts and Sciences, National Council on Children and Television, Screen Actors Guild.

■ Awards, Honors

Newsreel Theatre Award for the Best Animated Cartoon of the Year, 1940, for "Old Glory"; Academy Award from the Academy of Motion Picture Arts and Sciences for Best Animated Cartoon, 1950, for "For Scenti-mental Reasons," and 1965, for "The Dot and the Line," and for Best Documentary Short Subject, 1950, for "So Much for So Little"; CINE (Council on International Nontheatrical Events) Eagle Certificates for animated films, 1966, for "The Dot and the Line," 1973, for "The Cricket in Times Square," 1976, for "Rikki-Tikki-Tavi," and "The White Seal," and 1977, for "Mowgli's Brothers"; Peabody Award for Television Programming Excellence, 1971, for "How the Grinch Stole Christmas" and "Horton Hears a Who"; American Film Institute Tribute, 1975, 1980; Best Educational Film Award from the Columbus (Ohio) Film Festival, 1976; first prize at the Tehran Festival of Films for Children, 1977; British Film Institute Tribute, 1979; New York Film Festival Tribute, 1979; Parents' Choice Award for videos from the Parents' Choice Foundation, 1985, for "Rikki-Tikki-Tavi" and "Mowgli's Brothers"; Great Director Award from the USA Film Festival, 1986.

■ Writings

Juvenile; All Self-Illustrated:

(Adapter) Rudyard Kipling, *Rikki-Tikki-Tavi* (based on feature film of same title), Ideals, 1982.
(Editor) R. Kipling, *The White Seal* (based on feature film of same title), Ideals, 1982.
(Adapter) George Selden, *A Cricket in Times Square* (based on feature film of same title), Ideals, 1984.
William the Backwards Skunk, Crown, 1987.

Also author of articles in the field of animation.

Director of cartoons; All Produced By Warner Bros.:

"Night Watchman," 1938.
"Dog Gone Modern," 1938.
"Robin Hood Makes Good," 1939.
"Presto Change-O," 1939.
"Daffy Duck and the Dinosaur," 1939.
"Naughty but Mice," 1939.
"Old Glory," 1939.
"Snowman's Land," 1939.
"Little Brother Rat," 1939.
"Little Lion Hunter," 1939.
"The Good Egg," 1939.

"Sniffles and the Bookworm," 1939.
"Curious Puppy," 1939.
"Mighty Hunters," 1940.
"Elmer's Candid Camera," 1940.
"Sniffles Takes a Trip," 1940.
"Tom Thumb in Trouble," 1940.
"The Egg Collector," 1940.
"Ghost Wanted," 1940.
"Good Night Elmer," 1940.
"Bedtime for Sniffles," 1940.
"Elmer's Pet Rabbit," 1940.
"Sniffles Bells the Cat," 1940.
"Toy Trouble," 1941.
"The Wacky Worm," 1941.
"Inki and the Lion," 1941.
"Snow Time for Comedy," 1941.
"Joe Glow the Firefly," 1941.
"Brave Little Bat," 1941.
"Saddle Silly," 1941.
"The Bird Came C.O.D.," 1941.
"Porky's Ant," 1941.
"Conrad the Sailor," 1941.
"Porky's Prize Pony," 1941.
"Dog Tired," 1941.
"The Draft Horse," 1941.
"Hold the Lion Please," 1941.
"Porky's Midnight Matinee," 1941.
"The Squawkin' Hawk," 1942.
"Fox Pop," 1942.
"My Favorite Duck," 1942.
"To Duck or Not to Duck," 1942.
"The Dover Boys," 1942.
"Case of the Missing Hare," 1942.
"Porky's Cafe," 1942.
"Flop Goes the Weasel," 1943.
"Super Rabbit," 1943.
"The Unbearable Bear," 1943.
"The Aristo Cat," 1943.
"Wackiki Wabbit," 1943.
"Fin 'n Catty," 1943.
"Inki and the Mynah Bird," 1943.
"Tom Turk and Daffy," 1944.
"Angel Puss," 1944.
"From Hand to Mouse," 1944.
"The Odor-able Kitty," 1944.
"Bugs Bunny and the Three Bears," 1944.
"The Weakly Reporter," 1944.
"Lost and Foundling," 1944.
"Trap Happy Porky," 1945.
"Hare Conditioned," 1945.
"Hare Tonic," 1945.
"Hush My Mouse," 1945.
"Fresh Airedale," 1945.
"Quentin Quail," 1945.
"Hair Raising Hare," 1945.

"The Eager Beaver," 1945.
"Roughly Squeaking," 1946.
"Scent-Imental Over You," 1946.
"Fair and Worm-er," 1946.
"A Feather in His Hare," 1946.
"Little Orphan Airedale," 1947.
"What's Brewin' Bruin," 1947.
"House Hunting Mice," 1947.
"Haredevil Hare," 1947.
"Inki at the Circus," 1947.
"A Pest in the House," 1947.
"Rabbit Punch," 1947.
"You Were Never Duckier," 1948.
"Mississippi Hare," 1948.
"Mouse Wreckers," 1948.
"Scaredy Cat," 1948.
"My Bunny Lies over the Sea," 1948.
"Awful Orphan," 1948.
"The Bee-Deviled Bruin," 1948.
"Daffy Dilly," 1948.
"Long-Haired Hare," 1948.
"Frigid Hare," 1949.
"Rabbit Hood," 1949.
"Often an Orphan," 1949.
"Fast and Furry-Outs," 1949.
"For Scenti-Mental Reasons," 1949.
"Bear Feat," 1949.
"Homeless Hare," 1949.
"So Much for So Little," 1949.
"The Hypochondri-Cat," 1950.
"Dog Gone South," 1950.
"The Scarlet Pumpernickel," 1950.
"Eight-Ball Bunny," 1950.
"The Ducksters," 1950.
"Rabbit of Seville," 1950.
"Caveman Inki," 1950.
"Two's a Crowd," 1951.
"A Hound for Trouble," 1951.
"Rabbit Fire," 1951.
"Chow Hound," 1951.
"The Wearing of the Grin," 1951.
"A Bear for Punishment," 1951.
"Bunny Hugged," 1951.
"Scent-imental Romeo," 1951.
"Cheese Chasers," 1951.
"Drip-Along Daffy," 1951.
"Operation: Rabbit," 1952.
"Water, Water Every Hare," 1952.
"The Hasty Hare," 1952.
"Mousewarming," 1952.
"Don't Give up the Sheep," 1952.
"Feed the Kitty," 1952.
"Little Beau Pepe," 1952.
"Beep Beep," 1952.
"Going! Going! Gosh!," 1952.

"Terrier Stricken," 1952.
"Rabbit Seasoning," 1952.
"Kiss Me Cat," 1952.
"Forward March Hare," 1953.
"Wild over You," 1953.
"Bully for Bugs," 1953.
"Duck Amuck," 1953.
"Much Ado about Nutting," 1953.
"Duck Dodgers in the 24 1/2 Century," 1953.
"Zipping Along," 1953.
"Feline Frame-Up," 1953.
"Punch Trunk," 1954.
"From A to ZZZZ," 1954.
"Bewitched Bunny," 1954.
"Duck! Rabbit! Duck!," 1954.
"No Barking," 1954.
"Stop, Look, and Hasten!," 1954.
"Sheep Ahoy," 1954.
"My Little Duckaroo," 1954.
"The Cat's Bah," 1955.
"Claws for Alarm," 1955.
"Lumberjack Rabbit" (3-D), 1955.
"Ready, Set, Zoom!," 1955.
"Rabbit Rampage," 1955.
"Double or Mutton," 1955.
"Baby Buggy Bunny," 1955.
"Beanstalk Bunny," 1955.
"Past Performance," 1955.
"Jumpin' Jupiter," 1955.
"Guided Muscle," 1955.
"Knight-Mare Hare," 1955.
"Two Scents' Worth," 1956.
"One Froggy Evening," 1956.
"Bugs' Bonnets," 1956.
"Rocket Squad," 1956.
"Heaven Scent," 1956.
"Rocket-Bye-Baby," 1956.
"Broomstick Bunny," 1956.
"Gee Whizzzz," 1956.
"Barbary Coast Bunny," 1956.
"Deduce, You Say," 1957.
"There They Go-Go-Go!," 1957.
"Scrambled Aches," 1957.
"Go Fly a Kit," 1957.
"Steal Wool," 1957.
"Zoom and Bored," 1957.
"To Hare Is Human," 1957.
"Ali Baba Bunny," 1957.
"Boyhood Daze," 1957.
"What's Opera, Doc?," 1957.
"Touche and Go," 1957.
"Hare-Way to the Stars," 1958.
"Hook, Line, and Stinker," 1958.
"Robin Hood Daffy," 1958.
"Whoa, Be Gone!," 1958.

"To Itch His Own," 1958.
"Baton Bunny," 1959.
"Hot Rod and Reel," 1959.
"Cat Feud," 1959.
"Hip Hip—Hurry!," 1959.
"Really Scent," 1959.
"Fastest with the Mostest," 1960.
"Who Scent You?," 1960.
"Rabbit's Feat," 1960.
"Wild about Hurry," 1960.
"Ready, Woolen and Able," 1960.
"High Note," 1961.
"Hopalong Casualty," 1961.
"The Abominable Snow Rabbit," 1961.
"A Scent of the Matterhorn," 1961.
"Lickety Splat," 1961.
"Zip 'n Snort," 1961.
"The Mouse on 57th Street," 1961.
"Compressed Hare," 1961.
"Louvre Come Back to Me," 1962.
"Beep Prepared," 1962.
"A Sheep in the Deep," 1962.
"Nelly's Folly," 1962.
"Zoom at the Top," 1962.
"Martian thru Georgia," 1963.
"Now Hear This," 1963.
"Hare-Breadth Hurry," 1963.
"I Was a Teenage Thumb," 1963.
"Woolen Under Where," 1963.
"War and Pieces," 1964.
"Translyvania 6-5000," 1964.
"Mad as a Mars Hare," 1964.
"To Beep or Not to Beep," 1964.

Director of cartoons; All Produced By Metro-Goldwyn-Mayer:

"Penthouse Mouse," 1963.
"The Cat above and the Mouse Below," 1964.
"Is There a Doctor in the Mouse," 1964.
"Much Ado about Mousing," 1964.
"Snowbody Loves Me," 1964.
"Unshrinkable Jerry Mouse," 1964.
"The Dot and the Line," 1965.
"Ah Sweet Mouse-Story of Life," 1965.
"Tom-ic Energy," 1965.
"Bad Day at Cat Rock," 1965.
"Brothers Carry Mouse Off," 1965.
"Haunted Mouse," 1965.
"I'm Just Wild about Jerry," 1965.
"Of Feline Bondage," 1965.
"Year of the Mouse," 1965.
"Cat's Me-Ouch," 1965.
"Duel Personality," 1966.
"Jerry Jerry Quite Contrary," 1966.

(With Ben Washam) "Love Me, Love My Mouse" 1966.
"The Bear That Wasn't," 1967.
"Cat and Duplicat," 1967.

Producer And Director Of Feature Films And Television Specials:

(Also author and scriptwriter) "Gay Purr-ee," UPA, 1962.
"How the Grinch Stole Christmas," 1970.
(Co-author of screenplay) "The Phantom Toll Booth," Metro-Goldyn-Mayer, 1971.
"Horton Hears a Who," 1971.
"The Pogo Special Birthday Special," 1971.
(Executive producer), "A Christmas Carol," 1973.
"The Cricket in Times Square," ABC-TV, 1973.
"A Very Merry Cricket," ABC-TV, 1973.
"Yankee Doodle Cricket," ABC-TV, 1974.
"The White Seal," CBS-TV, 1974.
"Rikki-Tikki-Tavi," CBS-TV, 1975.
"Carnival of the Animals," CBS-TV, 1976.
"Mowgli's Brothers," CBS-TV, 1976.
"Bugs Bunny in King Arthur's Court," CBS-TV, 1978.
"Raggedy Ann and Andy in the Great Santa Claus Caper," CBS-TV, 1978.
"The Bugs Bunny/Roadrunner Movie," 1979.
"Daffy Duck's Thanks for Giving Special," CBS-TV, 1979.
"Bugs Bunny's Looney Christmas Tales," 1979.
"The Pumpkin Who Couldn't Smile," CBS-TV, 1979.
"Bugs Bunny's Bustin' Out All Over," CBS-TV, 1980.
"Duck Dodgers and the Return of the 24 1/2 Century," CBS-TV, 1980.

Also director of "Hell Bent for Election," 1945, for Stephen Bosustow and co-creator of the "Private Snafu" series of cartoons for the U.S. Army.

■ Adaptations

"A Very Merry Cricket" (filmstrip with record or cassette), Miller-Brody, 1975.
"Rikki-Tikki-Tavi" (filmstrip with cassette), Xerox Films, 1976.
"The White Seal" (filmstrip with cassette), Xerox Films, 1976.
"The Cricket in Times Square" (motion picture), Xerox Films, 1976.
"Yankee Doodle Cricket," (motion picture; with teacher's guide), Xerox Films, 1976.

"Mowgli's Brothers" (filmstrip with cassette; with teacher's guide), 1977.

Videocassettes:

"Bugs Bunny's Wacky Adventures" (Beta, VHS; contains "Long-Haired Hare," "Bunny Hugged," "Bully for Bugs," "Ali Baba Bunny," and "Duck! Rabbit! Duck!"), Warner.

"Daffy Duck: The Nuttiness Continues" (Beta, VHS; contains "Duck Amuck," "Beanstalk Bunny," "Deduce You Say," "Rabbit Fire," "Dripalong Daffy," and "The Scarlet Pumpernickel"), Warner.

"Looney Toons Video Show #1-#7" (Beta, VHS; #1 contains "The Ducksters" and "Zipping Along," #2 contains "Two Scents Worth," #3 contains "Double or Mutton," "Feline Frameup," "Eight-Ball Bunny," "Scaredy Cat," and "Louvre Come Back to Me," #4 contains "Heaven Scent" and "Don't Give Up the Sheep," #5 contains "Fastest with the Mostest" and "Forward March Hare," #6 contains "Lickety Splat" and "Scent of the Matterhorn," and #7 contains "Beep Beep"), Warner.

"Porky Pig's Screwball Comedies" (Beta, VHS; contains "Often an Orphan" and "Wearing of the Grin"), Warner.

"Classic Chase" (Beta, VHS), Warner.

"A Salute to Chuck Jones" (Beta, VHS), Warner.

"The Bugs Bunny/Road Runner Show" (Beta, VHS).

"Warner Bros. Cartoons" (Beta, VHS; contains "Case of the Missing Hare" and "Daffy Duck and the Dinosaur"), Yesteryear.

"The Best of Bugs Bunny and Friends" (Beta, VHS; contains "Bedtime for Sniffles" and "The Little Lion Hunter"), MGM/UA.

"Looney Tunes and Merrie Melodies 3" (Beta, VHS; contains "To Duck or Not to Duck"), Yesteryear.

"A Cricket in Times Square" (Beta, VHS), Family.

"Horton Hears a Who" (Beta, VHS).

■ Sidelights

Chuck Jones is described by Steven Spielberg as "a comic genius, up there with Keaton and Mack Sennett...." In the following excerpts from his own biographical account of his career, "Diary of a Mad Cel Washer," Jones' sense of humor becomes evident.

"Chuck was born in Spokane, Washington, U.S.A. on September 21, 1912. He soon became bored and immigrated to Southern California at the age of six months. He was accompanied on this journey by two (2) parents and two (2) sisters. A brother, Richard Kent Jones, who joined the procession later, corraled a substantial and unfair portion of the cerebral matter allocated to the Jones Family.

"Mr. Jones (Chuck) received a sketchy but catholic (not Catholic) education in California and attended Chouinard Art Institute, now California Institute of the Arts, graduating without distinction or the ability to draw. After nearly ten years of night school with the help of a great teacher, Donald Graham, Mr. Jones still could not draw but he could now fake it quite well.

"While his education was continuing Mr. Jones found work in a commercial art studio and also found that bad drawing was no particular advantage in the field of commercial art. However he soon found that it was ideal for cel(uloid) washing. As a cel-washer Mr. Jones was discovered by Ub Iwerks, who had just started his own studio after leaving Walt Disney. Mr. Jones washed 'Flip the Frog' with distinction and alacrity and began his long climb to mediocrity by becoming successively a painter, an inker, and eventually an inbetweener, from which lofty post he was immediately fired; Mr. Iwerks recognizing the Peter Principle even then: that a good cel-washer could become a singularly incapable inbetweener.

"After brief sorties with Charles Mintz and Walt Lantz, neither of whom wanted cel-washers inbetweening, Mr. Jones returned to the Iwerks studio where he was unrecognized, but his work unfortunately was, and he was fired again this time by Dorothy Webster, a sociologist from Portland, Oregon who later became his wife, probably with her wan supposition that a good cel-washer might be also a good dish-washer.

"Mr. Jones, carrying his credentials under his arm, shipped out before the mast hoping to find a cel-washing factory in Central America, but the large schooner which carried him promptly caught fire and burned to the waterline, leaving Mr. Jones with a suit of long red underwear and one tennis shoe to face the world.

"Feeling rightly that his haberdashery fitted him for the life of a Bohemian (Hippy) he moved into the artist's section of Olvera Street in Los Angeles working as a maladroit puppeteer and sketch artist ($1.00 a throw—a grotesque overcharge).

Cover duck of the year.

"After a year of this and having had to refund ninety cents on the dollar of about 85% of his portraits, Mr. Jones felt the need for greater security and married Dorothy Webster who was still working steadily and had saved up $3.00 for the marriage license. Then Mrs. Jones proved herself perfidious by obtaining a job for Mr. Jones with Leon Schlesinger who had just split off from Harman/Ising to form his own studio.

"Since Leon Schlesinger did not draw, he didn't know the difference between a cel-washer and an inbetweener and Mr. Jones, knowing a good thing when he saw it, remained in those cloistered halls most of his adult life. By the time Mr. Edward Selzer took over command when Leon Schlesinger sold out to Warner Bros., Mr. Jones was directing. The first time a cel-washer had accomplished this without detection. Mr. Selzer, who did not know a director from a hole-in-the-ground, supposed Mr. Jones to be a hole and treated him accordingly.

"As an animator Mr. Jones worked (if the term can be used this loosely) for directors Jack King, Earl Herd and Friz Freleng, and as inbetweener to Ham Hamilton, who then forced him into animation to get him off inbetweening. This was on the 'Buddy'

series and fortunately nothing in the way of bad animation could make Buddy worse than he was anyway.

"Messers. King, Herd and Freleng put up no resistance whatsoever when Mr. Jones and Bob Clampett were assigned to the newly formed Tex Avery unit, known accurately if not affectionately as 'Termite Terrace.' The prime product of Termite Terrace beside termites, was 'Porky Pig' and the beginnings of the wildly insane version of 'Daffy Duck.'

"Mr. Jones' admiration for Friz Freleng and Tex Avery was and is boundless. Both were masters of great timing, faultless gag structure and a kind of nutty believability. Being exposed over a long period of time to genius was bound to have its effect—even on an accomplished cel-washer.

"Poor Ub Iwerks! Mr. Schlesinger came to his financial aid about then but as a penalty sent Mr. Jones and Mr. Clampett to Ub's studio to act as co-directors on a series called 'Gabby Goat.' By some peculiar alchemy not yet understood by Mr. Jones the co-directorship disappeared and Mr. Jones found himself animating for Bob Clampett.

"Henry Binder, business manager for Leon Schlesinger, a man who could not bear to see dumb animals suffer, rescued Mr. Jones and put him in as a director of the Frank Tashlin unit, Mr. Tashlin having lost interest in animation. (He was to go on and become a very successful live-action writer, director, producer.)

"During the war years Mr. Jones collaborated (there must be a better word) with Theodore Geisel (Dr. Seuss) on a goof-up soldier named 'Private Snafu.' Almost twenty-five years later this writer/director team would produce 'How the Grinch Stole Christmas' and 'Horton Hears a Who.'

"In 1941 Mr. Jones directed 'The Dover Boys,' considered by many animators, including John Hubley, to have helped set the method and timing for much of the stylized animation to follow. Along with John McGrew, Bernyce Polifka and Eugene Fleury, he was also experimenting with stylized and formalized backgrounds in such films as 'Fox Pop' 'Bugs Bunny and the Three Bears' and the 'Aristo-Cat.' That's right, 'The Aristo-Cat,' in 1943. The Walt Disney studio used the same title twenty years later—but deftly added an *s*; this is what is known as retroactive plagiarism.

"After the war Mr. Jones began his long association with Mike Maltese, writer; Maurice Noble and Phil DeGuard, layout and background; and, among others, animators Ken Harris, Ben Waham, Phil Monroe, Abe Levitow, Lloyd Vaughan and Dick Thompson. Mr. Jones graciously, and in order to avoid confusion, took credit for everything happening in the unit for the next twenty-five years, including the discovery of the Road Runner and Coyote, Pepe le Pew, Michigan J. Frog, The Three Bears, Hubie and Bertie, etc., and the character and drawing development of Bugs Bunny, Daffy Duck, Elmer Fudd, Porky Pig and company.

"In 1955 Mr. Jones had a brief four-month stint at Disney when Mr. Jack Warner, responding to the obvious logic that all films would soon be 3-D and that all babies would be soon born with one green and one red retina, closed the Warner Cartoon plant.

"Mr. Warner's insight fortunately proved to be slightly flawed in logic and the Warner Cartoon plant inhaled and exhaled again only to go permanently rigor as well as mortis in 1962.

"MGM at this time wanted some more 'Tom 'n' Jerrys' and couldn't afford Hanna and Barbera, who had originated the series. So Mr. Jones rallied his old crew around him and made some. . . .

"Subsequently, Mr. Jones established his own independent production company, Chuck Jones Enterprises [which] has produced nine half-hour prime time television specials.

"Mr. Jones' dotage has been enlivened by the unexpected: a Golden Anniversary Salute to Warner Bros. Animation by the New York Museum of Modern Art in September, 1985, honoring Friz Freleng, Mel Blanc, and the subject of this unvarnished biography. . . .

"Perhaps the most accurate remark about Mr. Jones was uttered by Ray Bradbury at his 55th birthday party. In answer to the question, 'What do you want to be when you grow up?' he replied: 'I want to be 14 years old like Chuck Jones.'"

Another Hollywood pinup.

From the animated TV special "Daffy Duck's Easter Show," presented on CBS, April 16, 1984.

During an interview with Rachel Koenig, Jones' detailed his upbringing, his craft and his philosophy.

"My first ten years were spent in Ocean Park on Washington Street, off the old Speedway. A vacant lot separated our house from the ocean. We became students of the ocean and were wild young things.

"My father taught us an important lesson. 'The ocean doesn't care,' he used to say. 'It's not out to kill you or to save you. It just doesn't care.' We always swam together, and wore a string with a small lead weight around our necks. If you got caught in a big wave and tossed around and the little weight hung against your chest, you were pointing up and if it hung in front of your nose, you were facing down. 'Chance favors the prepared mind,' according to my father. Swimming, he said, was a form of transportation, not a sport. To swim for sport was ridiculous in his mind. Why, there are so many creatures who swim faster than man, why would he bother?

"He also taught us to read. I read at four years of age, but lagged behind my sister who read at three. My father liked children but didn't want to amuse them. He figured the best way to get us out of his hair was to teach us to read. He never allowed us to talk at the breakfast table. 'It's no time to talk,' he'd say. 'It's too early in the day. If you can't think of anything better, read the cereal box.' He didn't care what we read, he just wanted us to read. He was right. You can't get an education by following a prescribed route for reading. I once protested. I memorized all the cereal boxes. When his inevitable, 'Read the cereal box,' comment was made one morning, I quipped, 'I've already read them.' 'Do you have a rubber heel?' he asked. 'Well, take off your shoe and read *that*.' My habits continue. I still can't speak at breakfast, and a book with lunch is wonderful.

"I read Dickens and Twain and Trollope and Dumas before I even went to school. You see, in those days it was common to rent houses with the owner's belongings still in them—sheets, dishes,

Wile E. Coyote and The Road Runner.

and of course, books. Books were in when we were kids. There was no radio, no television. Motion pictures were a once-a-week deal if we were lucky, so we read books and magazines. Father always looked for a house full of books to rent, and we'd get straight to reading the minute we moved in. By the time the last of us had finished the last of the books, we'd move on to a new house. I recall the owner of one house was the world's leading expert on the island of Guam. There must have been fifty books on Guam, and I still know quite a bit about it!

"I was always at war with my schools because they tried to teach me things I already knew, or to make me read things I already read, or worse, to read something I didn't want to read. A librarian once told me of a little girl who came in to tell her that she had just finished reading *Alice in Africa.* 'Oh, would you like another book about Africa?' asked the librarian. 'No,' said the little girl, I'm not reading about Africas, I'm reading about Alices. I would like another book on Alice.' I had a similar experience as a child. I read *Uncle Vanya*, figuring it would be a sequel to *Uncle Wiggly.* I found it very boring and was very upset that Alexander was spelled, 'Alexandr.' It was an outrage that the writer couldn't even spell.

"My father never allowed us to go to church on Sunday, because the scriptures declared Sunday a day of rest. Raised a Baptist, he knew the Bible by heart. Then he became an atheist. He'd approach the most intelligent of clergymen and try to convert them to atheism. He actually succeeded with one Catholic priest. He likened the Pope to a dishonest insurance agent who was publically betting his clients would not die, when his company knew damn well they would.

"We always had a lot of paper around the house. Everybody in the family drew. My father encouraged us. 'Draw on one side,' he used to say, 'and maybe you'll do something right. What if da Vinci had painted "The Last Supper" on one side of the paper and the "Mona Lisa" on the other?' He was appalled that other children used both sides of paper.

"Mother had the facility for drawing and was a gentle critic. She was a fine dollmaker, as well. The night before she died, there on her worktable was an unfinished doll, and two books: *Peter Rabbit* and Thomas Mann's *The Magic Mountain.* You see, she could enjoy the whole realm of books; her taste was universal. Never did she over criticize or over praise to the extent that we might lose respect for her opinion. She always made comments that we could understand. In one way or another, all four of us children went into graphics. My sister is a weaver and a teacher, my other sister a sculptress and a painter, and my brother, a painter and photographer, is now in audio-visual education.

"[Our progression] followed the usual path of copying things and making wonderful changes. But we kept drawing, which most people don't. I remember a teacher in art school telling us, 'You have a hundred thousand bad drawings in you, and the sooner you get rid of them, the better.' It didn't bother me, because by that time, I was already on my three hundred thousandth drawing. Parents, and people in general, don't understand the number of errors you have to make in any line of work.

"Growing up in Los Angeles we were very much aware of films. It was, after all, the city's industry. We used to go up to the Hollywood Hotel and watch the stars sitting out on the porch. The 160th Infantry in California with Mary Pickford as mascot used to parade on horses down Sunset Boulevard to cheering crowds. We'd squat on our front porch and watch. Cowboy actors would fist fight from one saloon to the next. I don't think they ever hurt each other much, but they knew how to tumble. Eucalyptus trees and big red flowers ran up the hills where the Hollywood freeway is now on a pass of winding road that followed the contour of the hills.

"I was a victim of the I.Q. Aptitude Test from Stanford University. My score moved me from fourth to seventh grade. At twelve I entered high school a small, skinny kid, socially out of the picture. I was transparent, which is worse than being disliked. When you're disliked, at least you exist. I was invisible. Aside from social hardships, it was very difficult for me to keep up, especially with subjects like algebra, which I really wasn't ready for. My father, who had turned down a full scholarship to Carnegie Tech had high expectations and demanded straight A's. I didn't get them. I learned instead to forge his name on report cards. After three years, he finally realized that I wasn't going to school. He decided I was a failure, but

came up with the idea of art school as a last resort. Art school was the best thing that ever happened to me.

"What was most important at Chouinard was not the individual teachers but the character of the school itself. In the classical tradition, the school offered painting and drawing and anatomy. Chouinard did not teach cartooning, it taught the human figure. The feeling was that if you can draw the human figure, you can draw any vertebrate because all the vertebrates have the same bones and the same muscles. The big difference is head structure.

"A large number of people who went to work with Disney came from Chouinard, because they knew the human figure. A comic strip artist can find a style and go on with it forever. But the animator may have to draw a white seal one day and Bugs Bunny the next. Of course, animators have signature type touches, but the truth is that you cannot recognize a *bad* animator's work; you can only recognize the work of a good one. A bad animator tends to imitate other people's work, and not very well at that. A good animator can take the same scene, and bring his personality to the animation, not in a heavy way, but more like an actor who must put aside his personality to play a part, but whom we nevertheless recognize.

"I never decided on animation; circumstances decided. I came out of art school into the Depression. I considered myself lucky doing anything. Unemployment stood at about fifteen percent. I didn't know anything about animation, and neither did the people who did it. I started as a cel washer and worked my miserable way up.

"I always did the storyboards first, which consisted of about 150 drawings. I would lay each picture out and then write dialogue. I made about 300 drawings total for each six-minute cartoon. Then I would have someone type the dialogue directly from the drawings.

"With Bugs and Daffy, I always knew exactly what I wanted them to say. I worked with the actors to get a precise intonation and timing. Mel Blanc did both Bugs and Daffy, and I would read through the script with him. It must all be planned before it goes to the animator. The dialogue is in your head so clearly, and occasionally, when a line is spoken by an actor, you get a glimpse of something you did not foresee. Then you might change it. The pictures were laid out in musical terms. We'd go to the director and work out the tempo. The accent would always go on the down beat. The director had to time the entire picture. There's no room for method acting. We never overshot a film; we couldn't afford to. Our producer, Leon Schlesinger, was bright enough to figure out that if salaries went up because of demand, it would be cheaper to produce a shorter picture. He'd have made them two minutes long, if he'd had his druthers. Thankfully, the exhibitors insisted on six minutes, so our pictures averaged about 540 feet. Each unit made ten pictures a year. The directors had to learn to time the pictures before it went into animation, well within a few feet of sixty minutes. I got so much experience that I am now able to time a half hour of film within two or three seconds. You learn a rhythm of working and begin to recognize when to speed something up.

"I had no knowledge of music before I began to work in animation, but toward the end of my career with Warner Bros., I was able to read a piano score. I would suggest pieces of music, and basic notes were written out for me. I would make the characters move to the notes. We always played the music straight, even in something like 'What's Opera Doc?' where we squashed the entire fourteen-hour 'Ring of Nibelung' into six minutes. The music was honest.

"[Comparing animated humor] with Chaplin films, the same holds true. It all comes down to the most profound statement I've ever heard about humor. It was Ed Wynn who said, 'A comedian is not someone who opens a funny door, he's someone who opens a door funny.' That is an important distinction. Our characters are not funny to look at, they are not like comic-strips, they are personalities who evoke humor by the way they move. Even when people see a static image of one of our characters, they find it funny because they remember how the character moved, and they remember the funny things that character did. Would I be interested in a photograph of Chaplin if I'd never seen his work? It's a trick of memory.

"A professor of neurology at the University of California, San Diego, recently wrote to me, 'I've watched with fascination Daffy's growth from his

Tom and Jerry a la Chuck Jones.

earliest haphazard plural personality, through adolescence, to the splendid maturity in the fifties. Daffy has become a spokesman for the egoist in everyone, but he remains undaunted by the fear of consequences and is as cowardly as the rest of us.' That's what Daffy is about. There is a Daffy in all of us, just as there is a Grinch in all of us. Believability invokes sympathy, and if you don't have sympathy, you can't have humor.

"Most of my characters are failures, as are Chaplin's. They are wimps and nerds, and regardless of how kind and decent they are, they are fighters. They fight to get something to eat, they fight to win the girl. They are trying to live within the establishments of 'City Lights' and 'Modern Times,' to maintain dignity in dehumanizing environments. From ancient comedy to Robin Williams and Richard Prior, comic characters have fought to maintain their dignity.

"Elmer Fudd is funny for several reasons. First, he is very much afraid someone is going to interrupt him in his pursuit of his sport, hunting. Second, his voice is funny, because he always sounds as if he is about to cry. He wants to be understood, and his way of getting attention is by crying. Well, what do kids do when they want mommy's attention, when they want the candy that mommy is dead set against? They cry. But Elmer is a grown man and he cries. Everything he says is related to that little sob.

"Porky Pig started out as a juvenile character. His debut was in a little picture called, 'I Haven't Got a Hat,' in which he recites the 'Midnight Ride of Paul Revere,' while fending off his need to go to the bathroom. In his race to get through the recitation, he begins to stutter, and that was the birth of Porky's speech characteristic. Porky continued to stutter, until I directed a few episodes. Stuttering just didn't work for me; I don't find it funny. So I transformed his stutter from a speech impediment to an exaggerated form of what we all go through when we are searching for a word we can't find.

"Bugs Bunny, Tweetie Bird, and Pepe le Pew are comic heroes. Comic heroes are actually quite rare; we tend rather to turn ineptitude, inefficiencies, and defects into humor. Bugs, on the other hand, manages to make *success* funny—and that's not easy. In order to accomplish that, he's got to take a few lumps himself. And, while a character like [Walter Lantz's] Woody Woodpecker goes out and intentionally bedevils people, Bugs simply fights back. He is a counterrevolutionary, but does not aggress people without provocation. That

would make him a wise-ass, and that would get tiring.

"My reason for using animals is very simple. Human beings are very complex. You have to work at getting a person to strike a general attitude. With an animal, you start from scratch. You can say, 'I want Daffy to be like "x."' But we are too familiar with human behavior to ever have such freedom to create. Take Disney's 'The Seven Dwarfs.' The picture began with complex characters. The queen is evil, but has the human attribute of fear that someone might be more beautiful than her. If she did not have this frailty, she wouldn't be believable.

"Like La Fontaine, you can assign human characteristics to animals. And you can play with people's assumptions about animals. For instance, people assume that gorillas are evil because they find them ugly. We assume that snakes are bad, but the chances of being bit by a rattlesnake are the same as being hit by lightning. We admire bees, though they hurt us. We hate flies and they are harmless. These cliches open up animation to new areas of comedy—one must simply contradict the general assumption to get a laugh.

"Pepe le Pew would never work as a real skunk. He works because he is a black cat with a white stripe on his back. The humor that arises from the situation of his desire for a female is legitimate.

"Most characters start out one way and then evolve into more sophisticated behavior. Yosemite Sam is a victim of his own inability to control his bad temper. Daffy Duck believes the world owes him a living.

"I recall how on my sixth birthday I got a big cake. As I result I figured I was being initiated into manhood. After blowing out the candles, my mother gave me a knife and told me to cut as big a piece as I wanted. I gave her the knife back and said I had no interest in sharing the cake. I was a man, and it was my cake. There is the origin of Daffy Duck's obstinate behavior. I said I did not want to share, I was fed up with sharing, I had shared enough in my life to that point. Then my father came in. He seemed to be nine feet tall and looked like a moose without antlers. He took me to my room and revealed to me a word I had never heard before: Selfish. I then discovered, as Daffy did once, that in order to survive, you must learn certain rules. That in a cake—even your own birthday cake—there is a piece that is completely surrounded by corporal punishment. If you deviate, even one thousandth of an inch, *you're in*

Porky, Sylvester, and Daffy starred in the 1950 Warner Brothers spoof "The Scarlet Pumpernickel."

trouble. And this also relates to timing films; I have a great respect for that thousandth of an inch.

"Porky is an observer. In pictures like 'Buck Rogers' he watches with a kind of amused intelligence and comments on what is happening around him. Daffy as Buck Rogers started out as a third string, sub-Boy Scout type, but evolved into an interesting character. Sylvester and Coyote represent the fanatic type who becomes so obsessed that he doubles his effort and forgets his aim.

"The Road Runner has no meaning at all. He is simply a *force*; he is something to eat. The Road Runner ignores the Coyote. He just goes along on his way. We made structural rules about how the Coyote and Road Runner could behave. The Road Runner could never personally harm the Coyote; the Coyote being a victim of his own ineptitude and inability in getting the right product from the 'ACME' company. The Road Runner must stay on the road unless he is lured off by something relevant like a 'detour' sign or a white line. The Coyote is only after the Road Runner. The land-scape was always the southwestern American desert. As Don Graham of Cal Arts pointed out, the Road Runner is the only character in film who establishes himself as a form moving in deep space. You always know how deep the space is by the way the Road Runner moves, and *not* by what the background tells you.

"Jam sessions were unique at Warner Bros. I don't know who started them, but the way it worked was that after you came up with a story or an idea for an animated picture, the director and writer would call in other directors, usually six or seven, as well as the production crew, and the producer (a spector at the feast). We'd come together for a two-hour session to decide if the idea might work. It was not like brain storming where anyone can say anything. In our jam sessions you could only say something of a contributory nature. You had to think in terms of the word, *yes.* No one was allowed to say anything negative whatsoever. It really worked.

"It wasn't long before everyone realized that if you began to horde ideas in the jam session, everyone else would horde, too. This realization fostered a more open atmosphere. Ideas began to pour in, and sometimes, you could almost write the entire story after one session. We worked on what we called character 'business' rather than on story structure.

"Some ideas did not catch fire. The director who brought in the original idea was the monitor. As director, you could detect an embarrassing silence or a futile effort on everyone's part to get the idea up and working. If it didn't begin to fatten up after half an hour, it was back to the drawing board. There was never any embarrassment involved in leaving the session with a failed idea.

"There are only two really bad words in the English language. One is 'no,' and the other is 'why.' How the baby ever survives the first 'no' is beyond my comprehension. Everything has been going very smoothly, milk and mommy and all that great stuff, and then suddenly he tips over a wastebasket and somebody screams 'No!' at him. He stops what he's doing. He feels bad; he is free no longer. He suddenly knows what life's about, and damn it, he has to start obeying the rules. It's awful.

"'Why' is such a perfect word to ask yourself. 'Why did I do that? Why can't I write better? Why don't you like me?' Kids often ask, 'Why did you spill the ink?' There's no answer to that. I could invent a myth, say that something happened to my ancestors eons ago that cause me to spill the ink. But it would be false. But if someone asks 'What happened?' Well, you can answer in honest detail. 'I was playing around, and spilt the ink, period.' We connect everything to motivation, even when it's completely nonexistent or irrelevant.''

Approaches to animating the same characters are uniquely different. "Humphrey Bogart once said that the Academy Awards were nonsense because if you *really* wanted to judge acting, you should get five actors and have them all play one role, like Hamlet and then decide. In terms of animation, I could see subtle differences between the Bugs Bunny cartoons that Ken Harris directed and those that I did. The action would vary a bit; Friz Freleng broadened what Bugs could do, and the character grew that way, which is only right. We had to be consistent, but characters nevertheless developed through accidents of style and creativity by mutation. Most mutations are bad—in animation, in

drawing, in anything, but you still must constantly be on the alert for the good ones, and use them.

''The half-closed eyes of my characters are very important to me. Daffy laughed with his mouth and the front of his eyes. The contradiction worked very well. The half-glance of the Coyote also worked well—he did not want the audience to see his disgrace. John Singer Sargent was once asked the difference between a portrait and a painting, 'A portrait is a picture in which something is wrong with the eyes.' We expect to see eyes moving. When painting, it is very difficult to portray where the eyes have been and where they will go. It's a problem of starting point. Lautrec and other painters came up against the same problem when portraying action. When does the horse jump? When does the discus thrower let go? Either it's ready to happen, or it has already happened—there is no in between. We used to start with that old hand on the hip. Things could go anywhere from there. You'd look at Bugs and think, 'What'll he do next?' The hip is a natural place for the hand to rest.

''Nobody performs an action immediately. If you pull a bow and arrow, you may not be aware of it, but you bring it back, hesitate ever so slightly and let it go. That is a 'field of action.' None of us are so damn confident that we execute an action without some hesitation. It's not intellectual, it's just natural, and probably a function of our eye movement. So to portray character, it is essential not to mechanize such nuances of action. None of us know precisely what we are going to do at any time, whether we are making love or eating cake or driving home. Watching my wife eat a plate of scrambled eggs is fascinating to me; she does all sorts of rearranging before she ever gets to the first bite. I am more direct than she. I eat what comes next. But still I hesitate. A bad director flattens out such characteristic behavior.

"Gesture is very important. For instance, Bugs eats his carrot with his pinky extended. It's a contradiction, and its funny. It's not like eating caviar, it's like eating a hot dog with your pinky extended.

"At Warner Bros. the director was the composer and the performer. We had a great deal of artistic freedom and control, not because we were given it, but because we *demanded* it. The absolute control of the director was a vital factor.

"We never wrote for a 'target' audience. We never made pictures for children or for adults; we made them for ourselves. We couldn't know what an audience would react to because we were not

december morn

"December Morn." (Portrait by Chuck Jones.)

allowed to preview. We made the pictures for ourselves, and if we kept our jobs we took it as an indication that we were doing something right. The only response we ever got was not from the front office or the distributors but from the exhibitors. It took about two years from the time we began an animated cartoon until the time it hit the screen. That's one reason why our pictures have no temporal connotations or references. We knew that that would date the pictures and so avoided it."

The directors who worked at Warner Bros. with Jones shared a diverse background. "Friz was raised in a middle-class Kansas City neighborhood; McKimson was from a ranch family in Denver; Carl Stallings was an organist from Kansas City; Ken

Harris was a race track driver; Ben Washman was a short order cook; Tex Avery was raised in the middle of Texas and had all the prejudices that went with it. But we all drew. And so we were able to live together and to work.

"We learned from each other. It was like playing tennis. You can't play without an opponent. We never tried to beat each other. Competition never played any part. There was a spirit of intense cooperation in all the animation units.

"We had very little to do with each other socially. We were one wonderful head at work, but after work, we went our separate ways. Because our lives were so different, we maintained distinct points of view, and that of course enriched our work.

"In terms of editing, we worked more like Alfred Hitchcock, who said that his films were finished when he starting shooting them. [For us, too] everything was timed and ready by the time it went to the animator."

Jones enjoys sketching animals at the zoo. "Show me the skeleton of an animal and I'll show you how it must move. You could take two men, put them in a perfect horse suit, and they may actually look like a horse as long as they stand still. But the minute they move they will look like two men in a horse suit, because you can't move any differently. Years after I'd left Warner Bros. I met a girl who was the world's leading expert on road runners. She told me that our animation was actually accurate, with a slight difference in the shape of the head."

Jones feels that perspective affects the accuracy of a painting. "We don't see the way we think we do. We don't see in perspective; we *can't*. Motion pictures give you a sense of vertigo because the whole image is in focus; our eyes don't work that way. Look at a Native American, African, or Middle Eastern painting and the perspective will be much more accurate than the so-called Italian masters. In Japanese erotic art, the sexual organs are magnified—nobody has sexual organs like that, except perhaps the horse! But the artists convey what they feel is important. Think of the reverse; Chinese culture is much older, and they diminish the centrality of the sexual organ in their art, and opt to portray an overall feeling. In African painting, if a lion is in the landscape, no matter how far away, it will be emphasized. But no matter how close you are to an elk or an elan, it will appear very small because these gentle creatures are not dangerous.

"Likewise, if something was dangerous in our cartoon, we'd emphasize it by using a close up. Proportion of sound was also important. When we first started making cartoons, the sound effects were all hugely exaggerated. Then one day we were dubbing a 'Road Runner' cartoon and the Coyote fell off a cliff. I felt that one or two frames could make the difference in the gag. He'd go off the cliff and fall for thirty-two frames and then disappear for eighteen. I felt in twenty-four frames, it wouldn't be as funny. While we were working on the timing, the sound editor accidentally left the sound down. When the Coyote hit the ground, instead of a big 'PLOP' we heard a little 'plip.' Well, we never laughed so hard. Then the mixer shook his head, wiped his tears away and said, 'Well, we'd better fix that.' 'Bob,' I said, 'if you fix that I will stuff your shirt in your mouth. I will give

you writer's cramp....What the hell were you just doing?' 'Laughing,' he said. 'Why?' I asked. 'Because it was funny. Why should we change it, then?' He said, 'Well, it's not the way we do things.' 'It's the way we do things from now on,' I said.

"Animation is a uniquely American art form. You see, people like Chaplin, Buster Keaton, and Laurel and Hardy made short subjects until 1930. When sound came in, they began to make features. The Keystone Cops faded out because they couldn't sustain feature length. Around 1930, there was suddenly an opening for short subjects. That is why animation took off. It's always that way—animation came into its own because there was a place for it to fit into. Exhibitors needed something of entertainment quality that was six minutes long and so animation became big.

"When Disney made 'The Three Little Pigs' it was a turning point for all of us. Up until then, good characters were cute and sweet, and evil characters were ugly and bad. The only way you could tell who the characters were was by their appearance. Character animation was born with 'The Three Little Pigs,' in which three characters with completely different personalities looked exactly alike. It was their movement and their personalities that distinguished one from the other, not their appearance.

"Voice has surprisingly little to do with character. If voice makes the character, why isn't Barney Rubble as famous as Bugs Bunny? Both are portrayed by the same voice actor. It is the quirky action that contributes to character, the funny visual effects like the dancing mushroom in *Fantasia* or the weird way that Goofy walks.

"The Warner Bros. cartoons became popular after World War II. Up until then, we were learning our trade. We weren't imitating Disney, but we were struggling with character. Then we realized that personalities were important. Our cartoons are more insouciant than those of the other studios. We seldom made pictures that were cute or pretty. Because after the war, everybody was saying, 'The hell with it, let's go do things.' We were an impertinent generation. We didn't believe in patriotism or ideology. Bugs, Daffy, and all the rest of our characters reflected that spirit of the post-war period. You cannot ignore the place or the time you live in.

"I am the only one of my generation of animation directors who refused to compromise. After Warner Bros. [disbanded], the characters were farmed out and they were cheapened. They were poorly animated and unprofessional. The tool of my trade is character animation. I left Warner Bros. in 1963 after thirty years. I didn't know what I would do. I decided to pursue Dr. Seuss to see if he'd allow me to make *How the Grinch Stole Christmas* into an animated picture. It took some persuasion.

"That led to doing 'Horton Hears a Who,' 'The Cricket in Times Square, 'Yankee Doodle Cricket,' 'A Very Merry Cricket,' and three stories from Rudyard Kipling's *The Jungle Book*

"Every Disney film I've seen has had something of interest to me. An animator can always watch another's work with confidence that he will learn something. But the Disney Studio's respect for authors was very thin. Their 'Jungle Book' had zero to do with Kipling. I remember being so surprised by their pronunciation of 'Mowgli.' My father had always said, 'Mowgli' as in 'how,' yet the Disney characters said, 'Mogli' as in 'toe.' When it came time to do my own work on *The Jungle Book*, I called up Kipling's daughter, who was eighty-five

years old. I introduced myself and told her what we were working on. Finally I confessed that I was calling to find out how to pronounce, 'Mowgli.' After a pause, this lovely old English lady said, 'Mowgli.' Then she added, 'And I hate Walter Disney.' I had never heard anybody call him Walter before.

"We used the dialogue exactly as written in the original text. I wrote a few bridges to connect the material, because the actual 'Jungle' stories are very short. Orson Welles did the narration. I sent the script to him with an invitation to do a recording session, and what came back was a cassette tape of his reading. There were several things I didn't like, so I made a tape, sent it back to him, and I later got a new reading with all the corrections I had requested. Unfortunately, the tape was made in San Francisco, and I could hear lots of trolley bells in the background. I sent the tape back, and received his answer from Spain. He had recorded this second try on a machine that was not standard. I managed to transfer it, and sent it

Porky Pig signs off.

back for final corrections to an address in Paris. June Foray did the female voices. June is my all-purpose female voice, she is as versatile as Mel Blanc.

"I believe in my characters. As far as I'm concerned, they're alive. Tom Sawyer is not an illusion to me, he is not simply an image. He is vivid and alive. I feel the same about Daffy as I do about Tom Sawyer.

"It's very difficult for young artists to understand that every artist must have an audience, and that he may not get it in his own lifetime. Van Gogh, Gaugin did not live to see their work find an audience. Very few artists have been as lucky as I. The public is there, it is just a question of when the artist will make contact. The best analogy is the bullfighter, who can spend hours in the pasture, but he does not become a matador until he performs for an audience. Now that doesn't mean he has to fight the bull in a way that pleases the audience. But he does require an audience. What the bullfighter—or the artist for that matter—supplies to the audience is courage. Audiences are cowards. People would love to have the courage of a matador, or even the courage of Daffy or Bugs."

Jones' advice to young would-be animators is to, "learn the anatomy of vertebrates. As one great animator once said, '[You] should have at least two thousand tools.' By tools he meant, for instance, the gait of a horse, the amble of a dog. Once you learn these tools and the laws of movement, you will gain a lot of independence. Learn as many simple truths as you can. How *not* to use perspective, for instance. And don't tell the story with the background, tell the story with the action. Action is one's relation to the environment."[1]

Footnote Sources:

[1] Based on an interview with Rachel Koenig for *Authors and Artists for Young Adults.*

■ For More Informations See

Daily News, March 3, 1970, May 31, 1984, September 8, 1985.

Alan Bunce, "ABC-TV Planning 'Sesame Street' Rival," *Christian Science Monitor*, November 2, 1970.

Tom Mackin, "Don't Call This 'Kid Vid,'" *Newark Evening News*, January 12, 1971.

"An Interview with Chuck Jones," *Funnyworld*, spring, 1971.

Dictionary of Film Makers, University of California Press, 1972.

World Encyclopedia of Film, A. & W. Visual Library, 1972.

J. Cocks, "World Jones Made," *Time*, December 17, 1973.

Film Comment, January/February, 1975, December, 1985.

Chuck Jones, "Diary of a Mad Cel Washer," Program Book to the Third International Animation Festival in New York, 1975.

New York Times, February 8, 1976, October 7, 1979.

Richard Koszarski, *Hollywood Directors, 1941-1976*, Oxford University Press, 1977.

Wayne Warga, "Chuck Jones—Director behind the Animated Stars," *Los Angeles Times*, August 27, 1978.

C. Jones, "Confessions of a Cel Washer," *Take One*, September, 1978.

William Scobie, "Animal Crackers," *Observer*, April 8, 1979.

Jeff Millar, "The Biggest Laugh," *Houston Chronicle*, April 15, 1979.

Film Encyclopedia, Crowell, 1979.

World Encyclopedia of Cartoons, Volume 1, Gale, in association with Chelsea House, 1980.

Joe Adamson, "Chuck Jones Interviewed," in *The American Animated Cartoon*, edited by Danny Peary and Gerald Peary, Dutton, 1980.

John Lewell, "The Art of Chuck Jones," *Films and Filming*, September, 1982.

Atlantic, December, 1984.

International Motion Picture Almanac, 1984, Quigley, 1984.

"Animator Chuck Jones in Conversation with David Colker and Chris Gulker," *Los Angeles Herald Examiner*, January 21, 1985.

Time, September 9, 1985.

Leonard Maltin, "What's Up, Doc?" *American Film*, July-August, 1985.

Ron Givens, "Honoring a Daffy Auteur," *Newsweek*, October 21, 1985.

Timothy Onosko, "The Rise and Fall of the Classic Cartoon," *Video*, March, 1986.

June Jordan

Born July 9, 1936, in New York, N.Y.; daughter of Granville I. (a postal clerk) and Mildred Maude (maiden name, Fisher) Jordan; married Michael Meyer, 1955 (divorced, 1965); children: Christopher David. *Education:* Attended Barnard College, 1953-57, and University of Chicago, 1955-65. *Politics:* "Politics of survival and change." *Religion:* "Humanitarian." *Residence:* New York, N.Y. *Agent:* Roberta Pryor, International Creative Management, 40 West 57th St., New York N. Y. 10019.

■ Career

Poet, essayist, editor and author of children's books. Assistant to Frederick Wiseman, producer of motion picture "The Cool World," New York, N. Y., 1964; Mobilization for Youth, Inc., New York, N.Y., associate research writer in technical housing department, 1965-66; City College of the City University of New York, New York, N.Y., teacher of English and literature, 1966-68, writer-in-residence, assistant professor of English, 1975-76; Connecticut College, New London, Conn., teacher of English and director of Search for Education, Elevation and Knowledge (SEEK Program), 1967-69; Sarah Lawrence College, Bronx-

ville, N.Y., teacher of literature, 1969-74; State University of New York at Stony Brook, Stony Brook, N. Y., associate professor of English, 1981—. Visiting lecturer in English and Afro-American Studies, Yale University, New Haven, Conn., 1974-75; Reed Lecturer, Barnard College, New York, N. Y., 1976. Has also been a visiting poet at State University of New York at Stony-brook. Has given poetry readings in schools and colleges around the country and at the Guggenheim Museum. Co-founder and co-director, Voice of the Children, Inc. (creative writing workshop for children); co-founder, Afro-Americans against the Famine, 1973—; member of board of directors, Teachers and Writers Collaborative, Inc., and Center for Constitutional Rights. *Member:* National Coalition for Land Reform, American Civil Liberties Union, Poets and Writers (member of board of directors), PEN American Center (member of executive board, 1981—), American Writers Congress.

■ Awards, Honors

Rockefeller Foundation Fellowship for Creative Writing, 1969-70; American Library Association Best Young Adult Book, 1970, for *Soulscript,* and 1971, for *His Own Where;* Prix de Rome in Environmental Design from the American Academy in Rome, 1970-71; Nancy Bloch Memorial Award, 1971, for *The Voice of the Children;* National Book Award finalist, and selected one of *New York Times* Outstanding Young Adult Novels, both 1971, both for *His Own Where; New Life: New Room* was selected a Notable Children's Trade

Book in the Field of Social Studies by the National Council for Social Studies and the Children's Book Council, and one of Child Study Association of America's Children's Books of the Year, both 1975; Award from the New York Council of the Humanities, 1977; *His Own Where* was selected one of New York Public Library's Books for the Teen Age, 1980; National Endowment for the Arts Fellowship, 1982; Fellowship in Poetry from the New York Foundation for the Arts, 1985; Award from the Massachusetts Council for the Arts, 1985, for essay "On the Difficult Miracle of Black Poetry, or Something Like a Sonnet for Phillis Wheatley."

■ Writings

Who Look at Me (juvenile poetry; ALA Notable Book), Crowell, 1969.
(Editor)*Soulscript: Afro-American Poetry* (ALA Notable Book), Doubleday, 1970.
(Editor with Terri Bush) *The Voice of the Children* (a reader; ALA Notable Book), Holt, 1970.
Some Changes (poems), Dutton, 1971.
His Own Where (young adult novel), Crowell, 1971.
Dry Victories (young adult), Holt, 1972.
Fannie Lou Hamer (juvenile biography; illustrated by Albert Williams), Crowell, 1972.
Poem: On Moral Leadership as a Political Dilemma (Watergate, 1973), Broadside, 1973.
New Days: Poems of Exile and Return, Emerson Hall, 1973.
New Life: New Room (juvenile; ALA Notable Book; illustrated by Ray Cruz), Crowell, 1975.
Okay Now, Simon & Schuster, 1977.
Things That I Do in the Dark: Selected Poetry, Random House, 1977.
Passion: New Poems, 1977-1980, Beacon Press, 1980.
Civil Wars (autobiographical essays), Beacon Press, 1981.
Kimako's Story (juvenile; illustrated by Kay Burford), Houghton, 1981.
Living Room, Thunder's Mouth, 1985.
On Call: Political Essays, South End Press, 1985.
High Tide—Marea Alta, Curbstone, 1987.

Plays:

"In the Spirit of Truth," first produced at Public Theatre, New York, May, 1979.

"For the Arrow That Flies by Day" (staged reading), first produced at Shakespeare Festival, New York, April, 1981.

Also author of "The Issue."

Recordings:

"For Somebody to Start Singing," Black Box/Watershed Foundation, 1980.

Contributor of stories and poems (prior to 1969 under name June Meyer) to national periodicals, including *Esquire, Nation, Evergreen, Partisan Review, Negro Digest, Harper's Bazaar, Library Journal, Encore, Freedomways, New Republic, Ms., American Dialog, New Black Poetry, Black World, Black Creation, Essence*, and to newspapers including *Village Voice, New York Times*, and *New York Times Magazine*. Author of column "The Black Poet Speaks of Poetry," *American Poetry Review*, 1974-77; contributing editor, *Chrysalis, First World*, and *Hoo Doo*.

■ Adaptations

"Things That I Do in the Dark" (cassette), Spoken Arts, 1978.

■ Sidelights

Jordan was born on July 9, 1936 in Harlem, the only child of immigrants from the British West Indies. When she was five, the family moved to the Bedford-Stuyvesant area of Brooklyn, where she grew up in a brownstone on Hancock Street. "When I try to understand why or how I arrived where I am, one image keeps recurring. At nights, in Brooklyn, in our home, I would sit, studying, or eating in the kitchen, as my mother, her progress a slow and heavy tread on the wooden stairs, came up from the basement, carrying heavy pails of ashes from the furnace. This ritual nightmare never ended; even after a stroke, my mother carried the ashes up from the basement furnace, her breathing short and ragged, her thin frame crooked and lopsided from the weight of those filthy pails. Carrying the ashes up, and outside, you see, was her responsibility, as my father defined things. What would you have him do? Stay home from work to empty the ashes? Or switch to a day shift, which would mean less money, a few dollars less even, than he earned by working nights? These were rhetorical questions only. The ashes remained the responsibility of my mother, who, I must add, also worked, whenever her health allowed, as a private duty nurse, also at night. Later, she worked the so-called midnight shift. Why?

Because nighttime was, otherwise, incredibly barren for her, with my father away, and because nighttime duty meant a little more money for the family. Throughout my growing up, my parents worked as hard as they could devise, and yet we never had a car, my parents never had a vacation, our family never knew what it was to feel satisfied, or proud, or basically secure. In fact, more than anything else, my father felt himself a man despised, a man whose maximal efforts to achieve would be regarded by the powerful as pitiful, as ridiculous. He suffered for this, and he made my mother suffer for this."[1]

"When I was a child I never wanted to grow up because it was obvious that grownups were these very unhappy people. All the time they did things they didn't want to do. They went to work. They woke up early. They pretended to like neighbors. They stayed married. They had babies. They paid their income tax. They made sacrifices. They controlled themselves. And then there was my father, for example, who used to say, just before beating me, 'This hurts me more than it will hurt you.' And I thought, 'Why does he have to do this to himself, I mean, why does he have to do this to me?'

"Certainly I did not want to remain a child, to remain powerless, that is. I wanted to grow so that I could take my revenge or so that I could decide things for myself, so that I could be different from my mother and my father. What I never realized was that, the longer I lived, the more similar I would become, the more I would lose my own ideas about being happy, about how to be happy. I would even lose the idea that it was good to be happy. And the only way I could change into somebody powerful was this: I had to imitate the powerful people around me. It was a circular dilemma that left me, thinking about it, grim to the point of blank staring at the ground or, as adults saw me, daydreaming, again."[2]

"For a long while during childhood I was relatively small, short, and, in some other ways, a target for bully abuse. In fact, my father was the first regular bully in my life and there were many days when my uncle pounded down the two flights of stairs in our house to grab the chair, or the knife, or whatever, from my father's hands.

"But outside intervention has its limits and, consequently, my uncle decided to teach me how to fight for myself. He showed me numerous ways to disarm/disable an assailant. But what he told me is what I best remember: 'It's a bully. Probably you can't win. That's why he's picking the fight. But if you go in there, saying to yourself, "I may not win this one but it's going to cost you; if you hit me you'd better hope to take me out. Because I'll be going for your life."—If you go in there like that they'll leave you alone. And remember: it's a bully. It's not about fair. From the start: it's not about fair.'

"I quickly, and repeatedly, learned that jumping into a showdown breeds, and requires, a decent degree of optimism, or affirmation, if you prefer: The outcome matters less than the jumping into it; once you're on, there's an adrenalin pumping of self-respect that compensates for terror. I learned, in short, that fighting is a whole lot less disagreeable than turning tail or knuckling under. It feels better. Besides, he was right; I lost a lot of fights as a kid in Bedford-Stuyvesant. But nobody fought me twice. They said I was 'crazy.'

"While my uncle was teaching me literal pugilistics, my parents were teaching me the Bible and sending me out for piano lessons, voice lessons, and the like. Early on, the scriptural concept that 'in the beginning was the Word and the Word was with God and the Word was God'—the idea that the word could represent and then deliver into reality what the word symbolized—this possibility of language, of writing, seemed to me magical and basic and irresistible. I really do mean 'early on:' my mother carried me to the Universal Truth Center on 125th Street, every Sunday, before we moved from Manhattan. I must have been two years old, or three, when the distinctive belief of that congregation began to make sense to me: that 'by declaring the truth, you create the truth.' In other words, if you lost your wallet you declared, 'There is no loss in Divine Mind'—and kept looking. Those words, per se, possessed the power to change the facts; the wallet would turn up again.

"I loved words and I hated to fight. But if, as a Black girl-child in America, I could not evade the necessity to fight, then, maybe, I could choose my weaponry at least."[1]

Jordan chose the pen as her weapon and poetry as her medium. "I was good at writing quick rhymes and things and the kids around me accepted it. It was not anything my peers considered weird. I would write things for them that they wanted to give to somebody, whether it was a love note or a putdown."[3]

At home, where she had been introduced to poetry at a young age, her decision met with resistance. "My father wanted me to grow up to be a doctor;

my mother wanted me to marry one. *Being a poet did not compute for them.*"[3]

She received encouragement from "Uncle Teddy [who] lived upstairs in our house. He was, is, a master of Black English. Anytime he wanted to say anything at all of interest, or that really mattered to him, he said it in Black English. Times at home, like Thanksgiving, when there were a lot of men and women around and the men were all vying, my uncle would tell a story and no one else had a chance—partly because of this language he was speaking. The first time I heard him talk like that I was stunned. I said, 'What do you call that?' He said, 'Preachin'.' Nobody else in the house could do it. They could imitate anybody who was West Indian, but they couldn't imitate Uncle Teddy. I didn't even try to, but I listened, and I watched.

"Every summer I went to Camp Robinhood, a Y camp upstate New York where the schedule was rigid and camp life totally structured. It was my father's idea. He thought that a disciplined life was good for the character. The combination of going away to prep school and going to camp for the

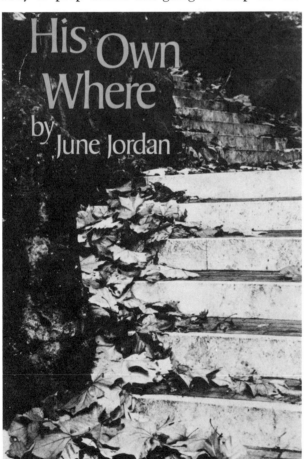

Photo by June Jordan for the jacket of her novel.

whole summer meant that, in effect, I had been sent away from home."[3]

By the time she entered high school, Jordan was traveling one hour and twenty minutes by trolley from her home to Midwood High School, where she was the only Black student among 3,000 pupils. She attended one year until her father enrolled her at Northfield School for Girls in Massachusetts. "...In other words, I began my life in a completely Black universe, and then for the three years of prep school, found myself completely immersed in a white universe."[1] There her interest in poetry was encouraged, although she was exposed to only white male poets.

From prep school, Jordan entered Barnard College in New York City. "When I came to Barnard, what I hoped to find...was a connection; I hoped that Barnard College—which I attended while living at home, in Brooklyn—I hoped that Barnard College would either give me the connection between the apparently unrelated worlds of white and Black, or that this college would enable me to make that connection for myself.

"Let me say, at once, that whereas Barnard, or in other words, a relatively conventional, elitist education, gave me friends (and one of them introduced me to architecture as environmental control); whereas Barnard gave me the father of my son (that is also to say that Columbia College was, even in 1954, right across the street); whereas Barnard trained me to think independently, honed my capacity for ingestion of materials, forced me to master any analytical skills, and taught me the difference between an Ionian and a Corinthian column; whereas Barnard College changed me in these various respects, not listed according to importance, please note, it did not, none of the courses of study, nothing about the teaching, made the connection for me, or facilitated my discovery of a connection.

"After school, every day, I went home via the subway. That was the only connection I encountered: a dirty, alive, underground trip between the Parthenon and what was subsequently termed the ghetto.

"It was quite a ride. But, at Barnard, there was one great teacher whom I was privileged to know, Barry Ulanov. And in freshman English I remember to this day two assignments for which I will always feel gratitude. One was the assignment of a paper to pull together, I think he said 'somehow,' Alfred North Whitehead's *Aims of Education* and Edith Hamilton's *Mythology*. Many of my classmates

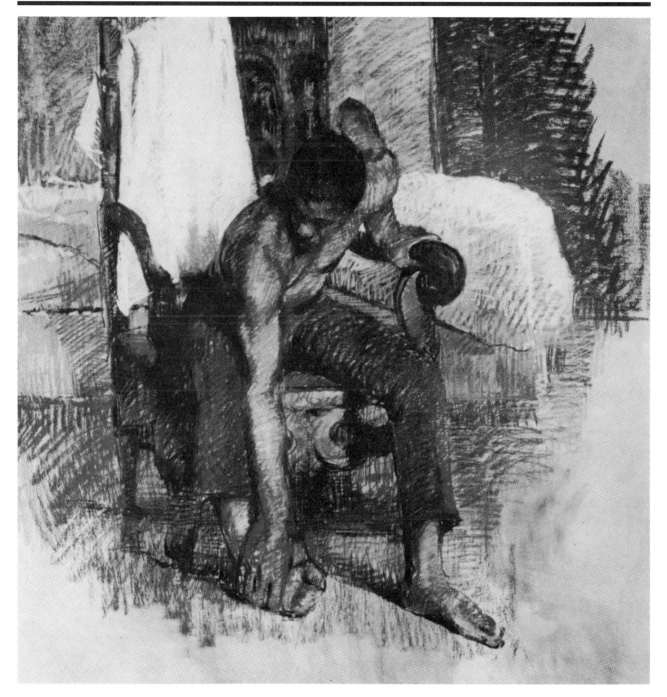

"Tony Seated." Painting by Albert Handell from Jordan's first book.

became more or less suicidal as they reflected on this task. But I thought, damn, if you can synthesize Whitehead with Greek mythology, then maybe you can bring the Parthenon to Bedford-Stuyvesant, and make it *all* real.

"The other assignment Barry Ulanov gave to us came in the form of a surprise, in-class exam: write about anything you want, without using any forms of the verbs *to be* and *to have*. That's extremely difficult, in case you don't know. And I learned more about the functions of our concepts of Being and Having, from that fifty minutes of class, than I had ever known, or considered, until that moment, altogether.

"On the debit side of things, the farce side of Barnard, I must mention a required zoology lab. You had to take three hours of lab. That was in addition to three hours of standing room only lectures in zoology, held in the Minor Latham Playhouse. But the lab was amazing; every experiment was rigged. It turned out there were predetermined right answers and wrong answers. I mean, they gave you these ears of corn, see, and you were supposed to count the blue kernels, the white kernels, the red kernels, and the yellow. Can you imagine a more weird way to spend time? If you came up with too many blues, or reds, you were wrong. I couldn't believe it. What kind of a rigged, pro forma, nonexperiment was this? Counting corn kernels that had already, long ago, been counted, and summed up into some kind of an unassailable genetic principle? Pure farce.

"But to return to the credit side. The one year of sociology that I took was helpful even though the woman teaching the course on the family, or marriage, used to show up in dark glasses that failed to conceal her black eyes (and she seemed to have a black eye, at least one black eye, throughout the semester). Even so, I remember Professor Samuel Barber telling us that, if you really assimilated the perspectives and assumptions of that discipline, you could never be bored. He was telling the truth. Sociology even helped me to get through a lot of classes that, pre-sociology, I would have cut, without thinking twice about it. Plus, it gave me a new way of thinking about everything.

"But nothing at Barnard, and no one at Barnard, ever, once, formulated, and expressed, the necessity, the political necessity, if you will, for the knowledge they required you to absorb. Precedent and tradition, after all, are not of themselves sufficient justification for anything whatever. And nobody, and not a single course of study at Barnard, ever spoke to issues judged critical, or to possible commitments evaluated as urgent. More specifically, no one ever presented me with a single Black author, poet, historian, personage, or idea, for that matter. Nor was I ever assigned a single woman to study as a thinker, or writer, or poet, or life force. Nothing that I learned, here, lessened my feeling of pain and confusion and bitterness as related to my origins: my street, my family, my friends. Nothing showed me how I might try to alter the political and economic realities underlying our Black condition in white America.

"And because Barnard College did not teach me necessity, nor prime my awareness as to urgencies of need around the world, nor galvanize my heart around the critical nature of conflicts between the powerful and the powerless, and, because, beyond everything else, it was not going to be school, evidently, but life-after-school, that would teach me the necessities for radical change, and revolu-

tion, I left. I dropped out of Barnard. It was, apparently, an optional experience."[1]

In her junior year at Barnard, Jordan married Michael Meyer, a white student at Columbia University. "My parents utterly opposed the marriage. His parents opposed the marriage. Our friends (an unruly mix of Black and white students) thought we must be kidding: why get married? Nobody thought either of us was old enough to do anything so serious as that. (And I would have to agree with them, at this remove.) But our friends came. The Episcopal minister came. At the last minute, my parents came. His parents did not. And we got married to the accompaniment of wedding presents that included the four-volume *Social History of Art* and a snakebite kit for camping.

"Now I look back on those two kids who fell in love and went ahead and married each other, he wearing an awkwardly fitted but spotless tuxedo and she wearing the highest spike heels and the best $35 wedding gown from Brooklyn, and both of them, in every sense, obvious virgins in a cruel land. From that moment in 1955, where, I wonder, should the cameras cut? To the white mothers screaming invectives at fifteen year old Elizabeth Eckford as she approached the school yard in Little Rock, Arkansas? To the mutilated bodies of the Black and white SNCC volunteers found below the Mississippi highway? To the Birmingham police and the police dogs and that white violence that killed the four Black children in the Birmingham church?

"Thinking only about what to wear, exactly, or what reading to pack on the honeymoon trip they couldn't afford and about brand new sleeping bags, those two kids quietly did something against the law, against every tradition, against the power arrangements of this country: they loved each other.

"Apparently, this is where the rest of us get into the story. When two people do something the rest of us don't like or some of us feel real nosy about, then the rest of us interpose ourselves in any way we can. We call out the law. We produce experts. We maintain an attitude. We ostracize. We whisper. We develop jargon such as Interracial Marriage or Sleeping White or Niggah Lover or Identity Conflict or Acting Out or Patterns of Rebellion. And if possible, we kill them, the ones who love each other despite sacrosanct rules of enmity and hatred.

"Well, my marriage to that young man...lasted ten and a half years, which is, of course, longer than many. And I think ours was more interesting in some ways. And I know that in America, one out of two marriages fails nowadays: the institution itself is not well, evidently. And I know that I do not regret my marriage. Nor do I regret my divorce.

"Hardly anyone talks about love anymore, but I know that I did love that particular young man and that he loved me."[2]

Prior to their divorce in 1965, Jordan had already assumed full responsibility for supporting her son, Christopher David, who had been born in 1958. Her emergence as a working mother began in 1964; the year that also marked the "...Harlem Riot of 1964, a week of lurching around downtown streets like a war-zone refugee (whenever I heard a police or fire engine siren I would literally hit the pavement to flatten myself before the putative level of the flying bullets) that I realized I now was filled with hatred for everything and everyone white. Almost simultaneously it came to me that this condition, if it lasted, would mean I had lost the point: not to resemble my enemies, not to dwarf my world, not to lose my willingness and ability to love.

"This was self-interested, to be sure. As Mrs. Fannie Lou Hamer said, years later, as she stood on her porch in Mississippi, 'Ain' no such a thing as I can hate anybody and hope to see God's face.'

"So, back in 1964, I resolved not to run on hatred but, instead, to use what I loved, words, for the sake of the people I loved. However, beyond my people, I did not know the content of my love: what was I *for*? Nevertheless, the agony of that moment propelled me into a reaching far away to R. Buckminister Fuller, to whom I proposed a collaborative architectural redesign of Harlem, as my initial, deliberated movement away from the hateful, the divisive.

"At about the zenith of my preoccupation with [Buckminister] Fuller's ideas on the one hand, my involvement with Harlem on the other, and the ongoing, central concerns of raising my son, keeping the house, fathoming my huband, from whom I would be, shortly, divorced, working at my poetry, fighting with my parents, developing skills as a political journalist, and the overwhelming assault of the daily news, my friend Huck arrived with another brainstorm.

"She had landed a job as a gofer on the motion picture 'The Cool World' and, convinced that I should write scenarios and, thereby, combine poetry and architecture in a medium accessible to most people, she tried to persuade me to hang out, on location, and watch the making of this movie. It was being filmed in Harlem, my old homeground. Directed by a white woman, Shirley Clarke, and produced by a white man, Frederick Wiseman, the film 'starred' Black kids from the streets; it was the only feature film about what it means to be Black in a racist white country from 1954 to 1964 that I can recall."[1]

Life as a working mother proved to be a formidable challenge. "...As a mother without a husband, as a poet without a publisher, a free-lance journalist without assignment, a city planner without a contract, it seemed to me that several incontestable and conflicting necessities had suddenly eliminated the whole realm of choice from my life.

"My husband and I agreed that he would have the divorce that he wanted, and I would have the child. This ordinary settlement is, as millions of women will testify, as absurd as saying, 'I'll give you a call, you handle everything else.' At any rate, as my lawyer explained, the law then was the same as the law today; the courts would surely award me a reasonable amount of the father's income as child support, but the courts would also insist that they could not enforce their own decree. In other words, according to the law, what a father owes to his child is not serious compared to what a man owes to the bank for a car, or a vacation. Hence, as they say, it is extremely regrettable but nonetheless true that the courts cannot garnish a father's salary, nor freeze his account, nor seize his property on behalf of his children, in our society. Apparently this is because a child is not a car or a couch or a boat. (I would suppose this is the very best available definition of the difference between an American child and a car.)

"Anyway, I wanted to get out of the projects as quickly as possible...My mother, against my father's furious rejections of me and what he viewed as my failure, offered what she could; she had no money herself but there was space in the old brownstone of my childhood. I would live with them during the summer while I pursued my crash schedule for cash, and she would spend as much time with Christopher, her only and beloved grandchild, as her worsening but partially undiagnosed illness allowed.

"After she suffered a stroke, her serenely imposing figure had shrunk into an unevenly balanced, starved shell of chronic disorder. In the last two years, her physical condition had forced her retirement from nursing, and she spent most of her days

Dust jacket from Jordan's 1972 novel.

on a makeshift cot pushed against the wall of the dining room next to the kitchen. She could do very few things for herself, besides snack on crackers, or pour ready-made juice into a cup and then drink it.

"In June, 1966, I moved from the projects into my parents' house....This is how we organized the brownstone; I fixed a room for my son at the top floor of the house. I slept on the parlor floor in the front room. My father slept on the same floor, in the back. My mother stayed downstairs."[2]

That summer Jordan faced yet another separation: her mother committed suicide. "I wanted to be strong. I never wanted to be weak again as long as I lived. I thought about my mother and her suicide and I...wanted to live my life so that people would know unmistakably that I am alive....

"And I thought about the idea of my mother as a good woman and I rejected that, because I don't see why it's a good thing when you give up, or when you cooperate with those who hate you or when you polish and iron and mend and endlessly mollify for the sake of the people who love the way that you kill yourself day by day silently.

"And I think all of this is really about women and work. Certainly this is all about me as a woman and my life work. I mean I am not sure my mother's suicide was something extraordinary. Perhaps most women must deal with a similar inheritance, the legacy of a woman whose death you cannot possibly pinpoint because she died so many, many times and because, even before she became your mother, the life of that woman was taken; I say it was taken away.

"...I am working for the courage to admit the truth that Bertolt Brecht has written; he says, 'It takes courage to say that the good were defeated not because they were good, but because they were weak.'

"I cherish the mercy and the grace of women's work. But I know there is new work that we must undertake as well: that new work will make defeat detestable to us. That new women's work will mean we will not die trying to stand up: we will live that way: standing up.

"I came too late to help my mother to her feet.

"By the way of everlasting thanks to all of the women who have helped me to stay alive I am working never to be late again."[2]

Working to pay her rent, Jordan still managed to keep writing, and her reputation as a young freelance writer grew. Before the 1969 publication of her first book, Jordan supported herself as a college teacher. "In the fall of 1966, Herb Kohl called me at home, very late one night. He was supposed to begin teaching at City College the next morning and he had decided that was impossible: He needed to write, full-time. Would I, he asked me, take the job instead?

"I was sure Herb was kidding. I had never taught anywhere, had no college degree, and what in the hell would I be teaching anyway?

"'Freshman comp,' he answered me, calmly. 'What's that?' I wondered. But Herb is pretty persuasive and, at the last, after he promised to check with the Chairman of the English Department, and then let me know the outcome of their conference, I agreed to take the class.

"The Chairman said he would be very pleased if I'd join the faculty so I spent the night crash-rummaging among my books in order to choose a course curriculum reading list. The next day we began, the freshmen and I, with Whitehead's *Aims of Education.*

"In this way I began my teaching career on a university level. At the time, the English faculty of City College included these poets and writers and thinkers: Toni Cade Bambara, Addison Gayle, Jr., Ray Patterson, Barbara Christian, David Henderson, Adrienne Rich, Audre Lorde, and Mina Shaughnessy. Tony Cade Bambara walked with me to my first class. 'Are you nervous?' she asked. I laughed, nervously, 'Anything you have to give, just give it to them,' she said. 'They'll be grateful for it.'

"All of these people were soon to become much more than colleagues. City College was split between faculty and Third World students who wanted to inaugurate an Open Admissions policy, on one side, and faculty and students who viewed the Open Admissions concept as an intrinsic atrocity which, if implemented, would catapult the University into a trough of mediocrity, at best. Those opposed to Open Admissions argued, in effect, that the people, as in a democratic state, preclude excellence: excellence of standards and of achievement.

"In every sense, from faculty petitions to student manifestoes, to the atmosphere in the cafeteria and the bathrooms, City College signified a revolution in progress. Nobody was eating, sleeping, thinking, or moving around anything except the issues at stake.

"When the Third World Students raised the red and green and black nationalist flag on the campus flagpole and closed the campus until our demands were met, we opened what we called A Free University at Harlem's P.S. 201. It was exhilarating: we were furious and fighting. And we won."[1]

With the publication of her first book, *Who Look at Me,* Jordan became known as an advocate of fine literature for young people—and she also became the director of the Voice of the Children, Inc., a Brooklyn-based creative writing workshop for Black and Puerto Rican children. "That book was important to me. I had problems with what was being published as Black poetry at that time. It seemed to me very narrow and confined. There was an orthodox idea of Black poetry, and if you did not meet that idea, then you were not a Black poet, even though you *were* Black. And certainly you were not going to be published as a Black poet. I was being published by *Negro Digest* and *Black World,* which was surprising to me because I was not in that school of writing. One thing I wanted to do very consciously with *Who Look at Me* was to make my own statement as a Black poet about

Black life in a way that I thought would be dignified, for kids as well as their parents.

"Working with those kids in Brooklyn was the revolutionary moment for me, as far as my commitment to Black English."[3]

"We had some trouble finding a place of our own: someplace warm with a window, tables, and an outlet for the phonograph. But finally, The Church of the Open Door gave us a room of our own. Then...The Doctor White Community Center [gave]...us space....

"We had no trouble finding children who would come to rap, dance, snack, browse among the books lying around, and write their stories, poems, editorials, and jokes.

"After a few months, after our group grew in steady and serious attendance, the children decided to produce a weekly magazine; they called it *The Voice of the Children.* With this magazine, they began their publishing career. Throughout, their writings have never been subjected to adult 'cor-

Cover photo by Sara Miles for Jordan's 1980 book.

rection.' If requested by the children, the purpose of a paragraph might be described, or the use of quotation marks might be explained. Spelling errors were corrected, as an informal rule initiated by the writers. Spelling is one problem they want to solve; they want to avoid adult errors of understanding; they want people to receive the message, and no mistake about it."[4]

Eventually the children gave poetry readings on local radio stations, at Hunter College and Queens College. Their poetry was published in magazines, the *New York Times*, and collected by Jordan and co-director Terri Bush, into a book. "By 1970, in addition to *The Voice of the Children,* I had completed *Who Look at Me, Soulscript, Some Changes,* and *His Own Where.* I had also completed the research and then written the scenario for a half-hour documentary on American slavery that I called 'The Crimes of Dollar Blood.' The script was revised, without my permission, and later released by the producers, Milton Meltzer and Doubleday & Company, under the title *Slavery and the Man.*

"These works emerged while I was managing full-time responsibilities as Christopher's mother—the proverbial female head of household—and regularly teaching at City College, then Connecticut College, and then Sarah Lawrence College. I was, in fact, by 1970, ready for a serious change of situation.

"Toward the end of 1969, Bucky Fuller had urged me to accept the Prix de Rome in Environmental Design, for which he was planning to nominate me. I could not imagine what I would do, or why, or how, outside this country, but his urgings to the effect that a year away, based at the American Academy in Rome, would yield a usefully revised perspective on everything dear to me here finally prevailed.

"My novel, *His Own Where,* was the immediate reason for my receiving the Prix de Rome. I wrote it as a means of familiarizing kids with activist principles of urban redesign or, in other words, activist habits of response to environment. I thought to present these ideas within the guise of a Black love story, written entirely in Black English—in these ways I might hope to interest teenagers in reading it.

"My projects for the year in Rome were these: To transmute this novel into a scenario for a commercial feature film, and to study alternative urban designs for the promotion of flexible, and pacific, communal street life.

"From Rome, I traveled to the Greek island of Mykonos, in January, by myself. It was while I stayed on that cold white island (an island virtually devoid of vegetation) that the idea of land reform in Mississippi came to me.

"Mykonos is nothing but a rock. Rowboats carry oranges and meat, and other perishables, into the tiny harbor whenever the sea allows. But if the water becomes too rough, the boats cannot make it to the island and the peoples of Mykonos have to endure a diet consisting mainly of bread, olive oil butter, honey, and coffee, or hot chocolate.

"As I walked across and around Mykonos, easily crisscrossing my own steps, I marveled at the clear obduracy of these islanders: Why would anybody settle there, in a place of such inhospitality, a place of no arable land? The vista of sky and sea in Mykonos is stunning, but feeds no one. If the sea permits, the men haul their handwoven, many-times-mended nets out on the waters, and fish. But fish and bread do not constitute a happy routine of nourishment, even supposing you can find either one of these to eat.

"A year earlier, in 1969, I had crisscrossed Mississippi, much as I was doing on Mykonos, to write a piece for the *New York Times Magazine* called 'Black Home in Mississippi,' meeting with leaders and families, everywhere, and driving alone through the long hot roads of the delta. The people of Mississippi, the Black people of Mississippi, especially Dr. Aaron Henry and Mrs. Fannie Lou Hamer, had given me so much, I had wanted to give them something in return, something that might transform the facts of material despair into realistic prospects for an ample, self-sufficient life.

"After the publication of the article in the *Times,* Bob Gottlieb at Knopf commissioned me to write a book on Black Mississippi: The idea was to expand upon those interviews and anecdotes, bearing the good news of militant Black determination to remain in Mississippi on newly won terms of freedom and public safety. But that good news was only one facet of the Mississippi situation. Another, equally important dimension of Mississippi life was the fact that the largest number of hunger counties in America were concentrated right there, in Mississippi, one of the most fertile land areas in the United States.

"As I stood on the rock of Mykonos, the horrible absurdity of hunger in Mississippi hit me hard: here, in Mykonos, the people were surviving with dignity where there were no natural support systems for such survival. There, in Mississippi,

Black people were perishing from forced dependency and kwashiorkor while big time landowners let arable land lie idle, so they could collect government subsidies! Black poverty and hunger in Mississippi were the obscene, absurd consequence of political arrangements whereby private property rights preempted the rights of human beings to life itself.

"I cut short my year in Rome and returned to New York City hellbent upon the compilation of a manual for land reform in Mississippi. I finished this in the late spring of 1971 and called the manuscript 'More than Enough.' The publisher refused to accept it. 'Who are you,' he asked me, 'to write on land reform?'

"The hateful shock of this reception threw me into an abyss of rage and depression not much alleviated by the development, that August, of interest from another publisher in underwriting a 'fictional' version of the manual. This was to become my second novel, "Okay Now," which is still unpublished.

"But *His Own Where*, meanwhile, was gaining praise and notoriety, both. Black parents in Baltimore joined together to ban the book—a finalist for the N.B.A.—from the public school libraries. Its use of Black English, they reasoned, would encourage their children to shirk the diligent mastery of standard English that college entrance exams and the job market both require. Elsewhere, related objections to the book arose, and this mild furor overtook my own activities. I began meeting with parents and teachers in various circumstances but soon, wearing out on the road and the microphone, I decided to write down my thinking on Black English and let these statements, in general, answer for me.

"I published articles on Black English in places as diverse as *Blackstage* and *Leaflet*, the journal for the National Conference of the Teachers of English.

"In 1979, the Michigan courts ruled that Black English is, indeed, an identifiably different language system from that of Standard English and that public schools presuming to teach Black children must present these children with teachers and language studies positively oriented to the distinctive language skills these children bring into the classroom. At last!"[1]

Written entirely in Black English and combining personal interests in architecture and urban design, *His Own Where* told the story of Buddy and

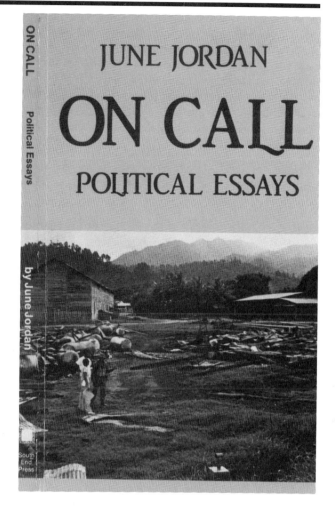

Jordan views the aftermath of contra bombing in Teotecacinte, Nicaragua.

Angela, two teenagers resembling two students from Jordan's workshop. The love story also drew from Jordan's own Bedford-Stuyvesant experiences. Sixteen-year-old Buddy is left virtually on his own, abandoned by circumstances. Angela, just fourteen, is abandoned by her parents. Together they move into an abandoned building near a cemetery with no money, but with a belief in each other. *Kirkus Review* called it a "kind of cross between Black English and streams of consciousness. . . .In a scant 90 pages, a rich and moving experience from a rare talent."

Jordan described it as a "survival manual for the young people who confront the hopelessness of the ghetto.

"Buddy acts, he moves. He is the man I believe in, the man who will come to lead his people into a new community. . . .All of the concepts suggested in *His Own Where* were governed by the principle that they should really be possible.

"They should cost no more money than anyone who is truly poor could afford. They would really depend on will, rather than on material resources, and not only would these ideas affect the immediate block where you live, but they would also change the big city concept. All these proposals are feasible—nothing that Buddy undertakes in the book is impossible.

"This is a shout—a testament to survival and some suggestions on how to assure that survival for all of us."[3]

Three more books in Black English for young adults (*Dry Victories, Fannie Lou Hamer, New Life: New Room*) and another collection of poems, *New Days, Poems of Exile and Return* followed.

Dry Victories studied the use of violence by whites to suppress black freedom. Two black boys, Kenny and Jerome, analyze the Reconstruction and Civil Rights eras. *School Library Journal* commented: "They provide dates and statistics; discuss civil rights legislation enacted on everything from voting to housing and such figures as Charles Caldwell and Martin Luther King...and point up important events....[The] natural dialogue of the two boys provides an excellent, unique teaching tool for casually informing kids about history."

The biography *Fannie Lou Hamer* gives a more positive heroic view of the Civil Rights era. *New Life: New Room* refers literally to a new baby, the Robinsons' fourth child. But, literally, there is no "New Room"; they can't move to a bigger place even though the present apartment is too crowded. By rearranging the limited space, they are able to feel a genuine sense of control.

New Days: Poems of Exile and Return contains political poems. Honor More in *Ms.* magazine called it "...a substantial book of five sections: 'Conditions for Leaving,' 'Poems of Exile,' and three sections written after her return from Rome. 'Poems of Exile' culminates with the long 'Roman Poem Number Five,' about visiting the ruins of Pompeii. In it Jordan describes her contradictory feelings on seeing mummified citizens in the lava-frozen horror of unexpected death: *living visitors admire the poise/of agony is/absolute.* And there are love poems, breathtaking in their simplicity...."

Despite an increased literary output, Jordan continued teaching. "When I received an unexpected invitation to teach at Yale, I was surprised because I knew no one on the English or the Afro-American Studies faculty. But, by 1974, teaching no longer

seemed to me an accident, a stunt, or primarily a distraction from my real work as a poet. Teaching had begun to alter even the way I approached things as a writer. The vast innocence of my students, Black and white, signified vulnerability that I became increasingly determined not to violate with endless bad news.

"And it is not possible really to teach both Black and white students but to sustain a loving commitment only to some of them. This fact began to change my conception of the community I wanted my lifework to encompass. I found myself becoming self-consciously concerned to dent the extremely low self-esteem, and the commonplace sense of impotence, that seriously disfigured the formulating world view of my students, regardless of race.

"To be sure, I attempted to identify elements of responsibility in different ways, depending upon whether we were examining questions of white or Black experience in American history. I mean, if there is slavery then there are two factors, two realms of responsibility, at least. And if you teach the descendants of slavery, the descendants of the slaves as well as the descendants of the slaveowners, then you have a double obligation to try and illuminate what happened by considering the implications of what did *not* occur, or what continues *not* to occur.

"But teaching at Yale was special, as it turned out. There I encountered every traditional orthodoxy imaginable so that, as a kind of flamboyant affirmation, rain or shine, I made myself wear very high heels. Let the hallowed halls echo to the fact of woman, a Black woman, passing through!"[1]

Jordan's major collection of poetry and her tenth book, *Things That I Do in the Dark*, appeared in 1977. In a *New York Times Book Review*, Hayden Carruth commented: "Even in free poems Jordan is best when she retains this hint of tradition, working creatively, newly, with the span of poetry....Just as black musicians have changed, augmented and reformed Western music, making it functionally their own without quite abandoning it, so Jordan and other black poets are taking to themselves, rightly, the formal impulse that was Shakespeare's, Wordsworth's, Browning's. But *taking* it, *commanding* it; not imitating it."

"*Things That I Do in the Dark*, my selected poems [spanned] twenty years....Only *Freedomways* and the *New York Times* reviewed it; no other Black periodical, and not a single feminist periodical, acknowledged the book. It was an unexpected silence that pushed me to further re-examine my assumptions of community, since at the time I was a contributing editor for *First World* and *HooDoo* (both of them Black journals) and *Chrysalis* (a feminist magazine)."[1]

Whether ignored or not, Jordan is a poet, compelled by her art. She claims that "everything I do, I am a poet doing it."[3]

"Nailed to my wooden bedroom door is a poem by Adrienne Rich, a response to my new book from the Black critic Stephen Henderson, a glossy of Monique Wittig and myself talking together, excitedly, a torn-out article on Alaska as an example of environmental crisis, a love poem from a friend, and a recent, angry limmerick that I wrote 'after cleaning the house on a Sunday afternoon by myself, as usual.' This particular door separates my room from the kitchen; it is seldom shut. On the floor around my bed you can find the poems of John Ashbery, a novel by Mishima, two books by Alta, the first issue of *Conditions*, a recent issue of *Black Scholar*, and Jarrell's *Poetry and the Age.*

"'What,' I sometimes wonder, 'am I trying to do, exactly?' I think that I am trying to keep myself free, that I am trying to become responsive and responsible to every aspect of my human being. I think that I am trying to learn whatever I can that will make freedom of choice an intelligent, increasing possibility. Often, these desires, these needs, translate into the sweltering sensation of a half-assed effort to explore and accomplish everything at once. But, thankfully, not always.

"At first, say roughly from the age of seven through my mid-twenties, poetry was the inside dictator to whom I more or less simply submitted myself, writing down whatever the poem turned out to be, wording myself as precisely, and with whatever ambiguity, as was necessary in the interest of truthfulness. For example, the poem entitled 'Pygmalion' came to me, entirely given, after reading Huxley's *Doors to Perception,* in my freshman year at Barnard....

"Exceptions to this quasi-automatic process were the regular exercises that I invented for myself so that I should feel competent, as regards craft, to write in the manner of Herrick, Shelley, Eliot, or whoever, and whenever. These disciplined emulations/transmutations absorbed a great part of my working time, as a poet, although I did not consider them achievements of any kind; they served as means, strictly, and not ends. I guess my theory was that if apprenticeship was essential to painting then apprenticeship was essential to being a

poet, an identity I assumed from childhood with rather unquestioning, and even religious, feelings of sobriety. It is certain that I did not regard these studies as optional...."[1]

"Words interest me. I hear and see and think with words. Like musicians who hear music in everything, I hear words. So I have to be a poet because being a poet means you are working in the most intense way with language. I never thought of it as a way of getting rich but as a way of life, as a consecration to the idea of words, as something that can create and change your reality. I'm not sure that I've ever called writing a career to myself. It's my life. I see it as my life's work....

"All art is mysterious to some degree because it participates in magic and when you are using what everyone uses every day—words—to create this or that feeling, that is magical. You are beginning with something that is so humdrum, and you can take it someplace unforgettable.

"Most people, when pressed about something, will say, 'I can't explain it' or 'I don't know if you know what I mean.' Well, a poet or writer is saying exactly what she means and, with luck, is saying exactly what a lot of other people mean. So you have spoken not just for yourself but for a lot of people.

"My work is closely related in purpose to the traditional work. It just takes a different form. I would be very proud if people found in my poetry things that were as useful to them as a decent breakfast before they go to work."[5]

In 1981 the first collection of political essays by a Black woman to be published by an American publishing company, *Civil Wars*, was published. It is an autobiographical chronicle of "one black person's reactions to the experiences she's gone through intellectually and emotionally.

"Obviously some of the things I said 10 years ago I no longer feel, see or think about. But it's still me. There's continuity after all.

"Anyone who's alienated by anything I've said in my essays or poetry *ought* to be alienated. If he or she wants to fight—then let's fight! Review me...attack me...but don't fight me with your silence."[6]

Four years later, Jordan published her second volume of essays, despite the fact that many of the essays had been previously censored by national magazines. "I am learning, first hand, about American censorship. In a sense, this book must compensate for the absence of a cheaper and more immediate, print outlet for my two cents. If political writing by a Black woman did not strike so many editors as presumptuous or simply bizarre then, perhaps, this book would not be needed. Instead, I might regularly appear, on a weekly or monthly schedule, as a national columnist. But if you will count the number of Black women with regular and national forums for their political ideas, and the ideas of their constituency, you will comprehend the politics of our exclusion: I cannot come up with the name of *one* Black woman in that position."[2]

Although a leading political writer, Jordan is also a leading poet of international acclaim. She is a member of the board of directors for Poets and Writers, Inc. and the Center for Constitutional Rights. Her poems speak honestly about experiences. "As a child I was taught that to tell the truth was often painful. As an adult I have learned that not to tell the truth is more painful, and that the fear of telling the truth—whatever the truth may be—that fear is the most painful sensation of a moral life."[2]

Footnote Sources:

[1] June Jordan, *Civil Wars*, Beacon Press, 1981.
[2] J. Jordan, *On Call: Political Essays*, South End Press, 1985.
[3] Alexis De Veaux, "Creating Soul Food: June Jordan," *Essence*, April, 1981.
[4] J. Jordan, "Afterword," *The Voice of the Children*, collected by J. Jordan and Terri Bush, Holt, 1970.
[5] Pamela Bragg, "June Jordan," *Publishers Weekly*, February 21, 1972.
[6] Stella Dong, "June Jordan," *Publishers Weekly*, May 1, 1981.

■ For More Information See

June Jordan, "Writing and Teaching," *Partisan Review*, Volume XXXVI, number 3, 1969.
New York Times, April 25, 1969.
Kirkus Reviews, August 15, 1969, September 15, 1971, July 15, 1972, December 1, 1981.
School Library Journal, February, 1970, December, 1971, November, 1972, April, 1973, May, 1975, September, 1981.
Horn Book, February, 1970, December, 1971, April, 1973.
Negro Digest, February, 1970.
J. Jordan, "Mississippi 'Black Home': A Sweet and Bitter Bluesong," *New York Times Magazine*, October 11, 1970.
Saturday Review, April 17, 1971.
Christian Science Monitor, November 11, 1971.
Redbook, August, 1972.
Booklist, January 1, 1973, June 15, 1975.
Poetry, February, 1973.

Jennifer Farley Smith, "New Biographies for Children: 'What's the Author's Angle?'" *Christian Science Monitor*, February 7, 1973.
Janet Harris, "Dry Victories," *New York Times Book Review*, February 11, 1973.
Alice Walker, "Can't Hate Anybody and See God's Face: *Fannie Lou Hamer*," *New York Times Book Review*, April 29, 1973.
J. Jordan, "Young People: Victims of Realism in Books and in Life," *Wilson Library Bulletin*, October, 1973.
Ms., April, 1975.
Theressa G. Rush, and others, *Black American Writers: Past and Present*, Scarecrow, 1975.
Contemporary Literary Criticism, Gale, Volume 5, 1976, Volume 11, 1979, Volume 23, 1982.
Reading Teacher, April, 1977.
Hayden Carruth, "Politics and Love," *New York Times Book Review*, October 9, 1977.
Washington Post, October 13, 1977.
San Francisco Examiner, December 7, 1977.
J. Jordan, "June Jordan," *Wilson Library Bulletin*, October, 1978.
Virginia Quarterly Review, winter, 1978.
D. L. Kirkpatrick, editor, *Twentieth-Century Children's Writers*, St. Martin's, 1978, 2nd edition, 1983.
Doris de Montreville and Elizabeth D. Crawford, editors, *Fourth Book of Junior Authors and Illustrators*, H. W. Wilson, 1978.
Ellen Tremper, "Black English in Children's Literature," *Lion and the Unicorn*, winter, 1979-80.
Publishers Weekly, October 17, 1980.
Library Journal, December 1, 1980.
Mildred Thompson, "Book Reviews: *Passion: New Poems, 1977-1980*," *Black Scholar*, January-February, 1981.
Joan Larkin, "Women's Poetry: Once More with Form," *Ms.*, March, 1981.
Toni Cade Bambara, "Chosen Weapons," *Ms.*, April, 1981.
Susan McHenry, "...The Jumping into It," *Nation*, April 11, 1981.
Patricia Jones, "June Jordan's Faith Healing," *Village Voice*, May 27, 1981.
Darryl Pickney, "Opinions and Poems," *New York Times Book Review*, August 9, 1981.
J. Jordan, "South Africa: Bringing It All Back Home," *New York Times*, September 26, 1981.
Childhood Education, March-April, 1982.
Elaine Dallman and others, editors, *Woman Poet: The East*, Women-in-Literature, 1982.
"Brooklyn, Borough of Writers," *New York Times Book Review*, May 8, 1983.
J. Jordan, "Black Folks and Foreign Policy," *Essence*, June, 1983.
J. Jordan, "Living: Report from the Bahamas—Conflicts of a Black American Tourist," *Ms.*, November, 1983.
J. Jordan, "Nicaragua: 'Why I Had to Go There,'" *Essence*, January, 1984.
J. Jordan, "In Our Hands," *Essence*, May, 1985.
Children's Literature Review, Gale, 1986.
Gerard J. Senick, editor, *Children's Literature Review*, Volume 10, Gale, 1986.

Garrison Keillor

S urname is pronounced *Kee*-ler; born Gary Keillor on August 7, 1942, in Anoka, Minn.; son of John Philip (a railway mail clerk and carpenter) and Grace Ruth (a homemaker; maiden name, Denham) Keillor; married Mary C. Guntzel, September 11, 1965 (divorced, May, 1976); married Ulla Skaerved (a social worker), December 29, 1985; children: (first marriage) Jason, (stepchildren) Morten, Malene, Mattias. *Education:* University of Minnesota, B.A., 1966, graduate study, 1966-68. *Politics:* Democrat. *Religion:* Plymouth Brethren. *Home:* New York City and Copenhagen, Denmark. *Office:* Minnesota Public Radio, 45 East 7th St., St. Paul, Minn. 55101. *Agent:* Ellen Levine, Ellen Levine Literary Agency, 432 Park Ave. S., New York, N.Y. 10016.

■ Career

Writer. KUOM-Radio, Minneapolis, Minn., staff announcer, 1963-68; Minnesota Public Radio, St. Paul, Minn., producer and announcer, 1969-70, 1971-73, host and principal writer for weekly program "A Prairie Home Companion," 1974-87.

■ Awards, Honors

George Foster Peabody Broadcasting Award, 1980, for "A Prairie Home Companion"; Edward R. Murrow Award from the Corporation for Public Broadcasting, 1985, for service to public radio; Grammy, 1988, for best spoken-word recording; Minnesota Book Award, 1988, for fiction.

■ Writings

Happy to Be Here: Stories and Comic Pieces, Atheneum, 1982, expanded edition, Penguin, 1983.
Ten Years: The Official Souvenir Anniversary Program for a Prairie Home Companion, Minneapolis Public Radio, 1984.
Lake Wobegon Days, Viking, 1985.
Leaving Home: A Collection of Lake Wobegon Stories, Viking, 1987.
Don: The True Story of a Young Person, Redpath Press, 1987.

Contributor of articles and stories to *New Yorker* and *Atlantic Monthly.*

■ Adaptations

"News from Lake Wobegon" (cassette), Minnesota Public Radio, 1983.
"Gospel Birds and Other News of Lake Wobegon" (cassette), Minnesota Public Radio, 1985.
"Lake Wobegon Days" (cassette), Minnesota Public Radio, 1986.

"Happy to Be Here" (cassette), Minnesota
Public Radio, 1987.

"Prairie Home Companion: The Final
Performance" (cassette), Minnesota Public
Radio, 1987.

"Ain't That Good News" (record; cassette),
Minnesota Public Radio, 1987.

"A Prairie Home Companion: The Last Show,"
(videocassette; also broadcast on the Disney
Channel), Disney Home Video, 1987.

"Second Annual Farewell Performance of *A
Prairie Home Companion*," Radio City Music
Hall, New York, N.Y., June, 1988.

■ Work In Progress

A collection of stories, *We Are Still Married*; a
novel about the death of live radio; a novel
entitled, *Lake Wobegon Loose*.

■ Sidelights

Born August 7, 1942 in Anoka, Minnesota, and
christened Gary by his parents, John and Grace
Denham Keillor. "I've lived all of my life in
Minnesota. As a child, the Laura Ingalls Wilder
books were special to me because they were set so
close by. These stories led me to other books
written by Minnesota authors, and later I read
Sinclair Lewis and F. Scott Fitzgerald. I've loved
all kinds of books—including books that are far
better than anything Lewis or Fitzgerald ever
wrote—but it amazed me as a boy that people
could make books out of the terrain and population
where I lived. It just amazed me, to think that you
could write books about Minnesota."[1]

"When I was four years old, I fell through a hole in
the haymow into the bull pen, missing the stan-
chion and landing in his feed trough full of hay, and
was carried into the house and laid on my grandma's sofa, which smelled like this quilt, and so did a
warm shirt handed down to me from my uncle.
When I was little I didn't think of grownups as
having bare skin; grownups were made of wool
clothing, only kids were bare-naked; now I'm older
than they were when I was little and I lie naked
under a quilt made of their clothes when they were
children. I don't know what makes me think I'm
smarter than them."[2]

"I grew up in the Plymouth Brethren Church. The
Brethren were a tiny minority for whom life was
strictly an upstream paddle. A great many things
that the people of other creeds got to do were
forbidden to us. I've felt that restriction as far back
as I can remember. Still, being part of a minority—

of whatever sort—is not the worst thing that can
happen to somebody.

"I still believe what I was brought up to believe. I
don't go to a Brethren assembly anymore, but I
think that's more my fault than theirs. I doubt I'll
ever go back, but you never know. People make
some unusual turns in their forties, and so could I.

"I'm uncomfortable with churches more liberal
than what I was brought up in. I have a hard time
sitting still when a preacher's talking about the
value of being a good person. Church is for sinners
like me. Good people ought to stay home and read
the *Times*.

"Religion *is* rigorous, whether a lot of people see it
that way or not. That's not to excuse the cruelties
committed in the name of rigor and doctrinal
purity. If those people had *really* been rigorous
themselves, they wouldn't have been intolerant.

"Most people think of fundamentalists as narrow-
minded, unhappy, sexually frustrated, embittered
people who are intolerant of everything that's
different, hypocrites, to boot. That's a novelist's
point of view, though. It's not based on the church
I grew up in."[3]

"...The storyteller in our family was my Uncle
Lew Powell, who was my great uncle, my grandma's brother, who died only a couple of years ago,
at the age of 93. In a family that tended to be a
little withdrawn, taciturn, my uncle Lew was the
friendliest. He had been a salesman, and he liked to
drive around and drop in on people. He would
converse, ask how we were doing in school, but
there would be a point when he would get
launched, and we would try to launch him. There
were two different house-burning stories. I worked
in a little bit of one in the book, the one where
Great Grandpa came back from the Colorado gold
fields, is the legend, and the gold dust was all lost
in the blaze.

"My parents would be in the living room, and my
Aunt Ada and my brothers and sisters. We would
be eating popcorn. I remember lying on the floor
when it got late so my mother wouldn't see me and
send me to bed. Uncle Lew would stop for a while,
and then someone else would spell him, my dad or
my Aunt Ruth. And then Uncle Lew would come
back. The period he talked about so well was about
ten years on either side of the turn of the century.
A beautiful time, I still think so. I just wanted him
to tell more and more and more. I wanted to know
everything. What it looked and smelled like, what
they ate and what they wore.

The star of "Prairie Home Companion." (Photo courtesy of Minnesota Public Radio.)

"I remember Uncle Lew's stories not as coming to a moral, really, but to a point of rest, a point of contemplation. As I got older, of course, life was becoming strange. I looked to those stories of his, and to the history of the family, as giving a person some sense of place, that we were not just chips floating on the waves, that in some way we were meant to be here, and had a history. That we had standing."[4]

"As I got older, more and more often I hear my father's voice coming out of me, and I find myself saying things he would say. I write things that seem to me to be something my father would have said, or my Uncle Lew would have said—sort of an apotheosis of what they would have said if they had been writers. I find a satisfaction in doing that, that I don't get from writing funny stories."[1]

"New York was the first place I traveled as a boy. My dad took me...and I got to see the Brooklyn Dodgers play at Ebbets Field, to see Coney Island. I never forgot it. Especially because he didn't really want to take me, but he did. And it's the trip of my life, that trip I took...to the big city. It's the trip against which all other trips are compared. I could tell you everything about that trip, where we stayed, and almost everything that we did. So if you have 11-or-12-year-old kids, keep that in

mind. Whatever you do for them may likely turn out to be permanent and memorable."[5]

"When I was fourteen, I was happy to read all day every day and into the night. I hid in closets and in the basement, locked myself in the bathroom, reading right up to the final moment when Mother pried the book from my fingers and shoved me outdoors into the land of living persons.

"She was right to do that. If she hadn't, I would be four feet tall, have beady little eyes and a caved-in chest and a butt like a bushel basket.

"...Our family subscribed to *Reader's Digest*, *Popular Mechanics*, *National Geographic*, *Boys Life*, and *American Home*. My people weren't much for literature, and they were dead set against conspicuous wealth, so a magazine in which classy paragraphs marched down the aisle between columns of diamond necklaces and French cognacs was not a magazine they welcomed into their home. I was more easily dazzled than they and to me the *New Yorker* was a fabulous sight, an immense glittering ocean liner off the coast of Minnesota, and I loved to read it. I bought copies and smuggled them home, though with a clear conscience, for what I most admired was not the decor or the tone of the thing but rather the work of some writers, particularly the New Yorker's great infield of Thurber, Liebling, Perelman, and White.

"They were my heroes: four older gentlemen, one blind, one fat, one delicate, and one a chicken rancher, and in my mind they took the field against the big mazumbos of American literature, and I cheered for them. I cheer for them now, all dead except Mr. White, and still think (as I thought then) that it is more worthy in the eyes of God and better for us as a people if a writer makes three pages sharp and funny about the lives of geese than to make three hundred flat and flabby about God or the American people."[6]

Submitted poetry to his junior high school newspaper under the byline Garrison Keillor. "It was in a school and at a time when boys didn't write poetry. So I used the name Garrison. It sounded a little stiffer, a little bigger. Flags flying. I think I was trying to hide behind a name that meant strength and 'don't give me a hard time about this.'"[1]

1960. Studied at the University of Minnesota, at Minneapolis, working as a parking lot attendant to help pay for tuition. He dropped out for one year, because he was low on funds, but returned when he became employed at the campus radio station, KUOM. "I put myself through school working for the University of Minnesota radio station. I got the job, I think, because I was able to imitate the voice that they were looking for. I could broaden a few vowels and get a kind of cultivated, funereal tone with a very slight British sound to it.

"Radio announcing is easy indoor work. You sit in the studio and you say, 'We have just heard "Appalachian Spring," by Aaron Copland, and we now turn to the music of Beethoven.' Announcing is much easier than parking cars or washing dishes, and yet it has a kind of status attached to it that I've never understood."[3]

"When I burst upon the radio business in 1963 as the friendly announcer of 'Highlights in Homemaking,' I badly wanted my voice to sound like that of Orson Welles, as rich and smooth as my mother's gravy on Sunday pot roast, and I succeeded so far as to sound at least brown and thick and lumpy, and then the pretense was too hard to keep up, and by the time 'Prairie Home' rolled along, my voice had drifted back toward center and sounded more like my dad's."[2]

That same year he became fiction editor for Ivory Tower, the campus literary magazine and interned briefly with the St. Paul Pioneer Press. "I loved newspaper writing, I did my share of weather, lots of obits, called hospitals to see if people in traffic accidents had died, and I interviewed authors. That's no way to live. Interviewing celebrities is just a step above calling the morgue."[7]

1965. Married fellow student Mary Guntzel, a music major and sometime contributor to Ivory Tower.

1966. Received a B.A. in English from University of Minnesota. "It was a mistake to have gone to the university, to expend the time I did....It had a corrupting influence on me on what I wrote. It removed me from what I had to write about and what I still have to write about—which is people that I came from and the class of people that I have some feeling about."[7]

Keillor traveled East by bus seeking employment with a nationally known magazine, and interviewed with the Atlantic Monthly in Boston. "...I rode the bus up from New York City and struck Boston early in the morning. I changed my clothes and washed my face in the Greyhound bus terminal. And I think that during the interviews they could tell that I was somebody who had just changed in a public rest room. I had a kind of hangdog look about me. I looked a little bit stiff, too, because I had to keep my hand on my leg where I had spilled some Orange Julius two days before. Well, they said they didn't have any jobs just then and they would let me know...."[8]

1968. Hosted a three-hour morning classical music show for Minnesota Public Radio. "Part of this had to do with money—it's not easy to earn a living freelancing humorous fiction—but also with an attraction to radio. There's a wonderful simplicity about radio which cuts through my own pretenses.

"I had an early-morning radio show. You sit at a microphone with your favorite music, talk to people and wish them a happy birthday and try to create something pleasant and happy for them. Seemed to me to be a simple, decent service to mankind. Whereas sitting at a typewriter and writing often seems to me to be particularly ambitious, in sort of a scheming, crafty way. So much in humor and comedy is manipulative. But I love to write, I do it every day and I have since I was a little kid. So I've had to resolve these things somehow."[1]

"Radio makes me feel competent. A writer feels like an amateur every morning. He has to relearn his craft every time he sits down. When someone tells a writer, 'Hey, that was a terrific story,' he thinks of all the silly stuff he's written and all the

Dust jacket for Keillor's collection of thirty-six stories, a farewell tribute to life in Lake Wobegon. (Jacket illustration by Peter Thorpe.)

blank paper he's stared at, and he thinks, 'How can that be so?' With radio it's different. When I do a show, I feel competent in something."[9]

1969. Son, Jason, was born. "Being a parent is not something that people ever feel confident or secure about."[10] Keillor told students at Gettysburg College. "When you were tiny children, we started to read about tremendous advances in prenatal education. And when you got a little bit older, we started reading great books about early childhood and fantastic things that parents can do. We've always been a step behind in bringing you up....We wanted to bring you up with information about sex that we never had. Our parents only told us that if we listened to rock 'n' roll, we would have babies—and they were right."[10]

A parody of small town newspaper stories, called "Local Family Keeps Son Happy," about a family that hired a local prostitute to keep their seventeen-year-old son company so he wouldn't leave home was published in the New Yorker. It was the first of many Keillor stories published by the magazine. "When you write...fiction for the New Yorker and you feel as I did then about the New Yorker, you tend to be an extremely careful writer. I went through a great many drafts, and I studied every sentence, and it was work that I enjoyed doing, but it was also very difficult."[11]

"I still love the New Yorker and love writing for them, and want to write anything I can for them. But there's another style of writing that I cannot do for them, which is to me more Midwestern, more colloquial. My Lake Wobegon monologues, which all start out as writing, are humor that is also sentimental. They have an emotional base you don't have in short, satirical fiction. Satire to me has a moral base but not an emotional base. And the monologues, always do."[1]

March, 1971. Left broadcasting to try writing full time. "I would sell a story and then wait two weeks and call and ask for the money. It bothered me that I was spending so much time doing what seemed like humiliating, adolescent things...to look through the New Yorker to get ideas on how to write another story they would want. It did me no good and I knew that, but just to be busy and neurotic and try to have a plan about it and go at things straight."[7]

Months later he returned to Minnesota Public Radio, this time to KSJN, the flagship station in St. Paul. He attributed this upgrading to his having been published in the New Yorker. "I would never have been able to get away with playing the music

I did unless I happened to be associated with a magazine which, although it has changed, still, in the Midwest, stands for being Uptown."[7]

1974. Keillor was assigned by the New Yorker to do a feature story on the Grand Ole Opry, and returned with a format in mind for "The Prairie Home Companion." "It occurred to me then that I needed a hobby...and I thought I'd like to talk for a hobby. I'd like to say funny things that couldn't be edited, that no researchers would examine— and that led me to live radio."[8]

The first live broadcast of "The Prairie Home Companion" took place on July 6th of that year, and included favorite local musicians as well as scripted radio sketches, with Keillor as the host. One Saturday in the summer of 1975, he delivered a monologue, seemingly unscripted, which began "It has been a quiet week in Lake Wobegon..." and told of the residents of that mythical town. "I stood at the microphone, looked up into the lights, and let fly. If the crowd got restless, I sat down on a stool, which caught their interest, and if they rustled again, I stood up. After twenty minutes or as soon as the story came to an extremely long pause, I stopped and said, 'That's the news from Lake Wobegon, where all the women are strong, the men are good-looking, and all the children are above average,' and walked off."[2]

"[Lake Wobegon's] residents include almost all of the people I've known in my life. The town also incorporates most of what has ever happened to me. My childhood, my education, my belief, and my disbelief all go back to that place, and from Lake Wobegon I get my voice."[8]

"The place is an invention between myself and the audience and we are all aware of this. I don't really do too much, just draw out a few lines, and the audience fills in everything else. Lake Wobegon is a screen we have set up. We are really looking for something beyond that screen, though. It would be pretentious if we tried to say exactly what that is, but it's always there."[12]

The challenge of performing for a live audience holds a particular significance, since Keillor considers himself a shy person. "Shy is beautiful, for the most part....A lot of people who are not shy think that those of us who are would simply like to be uninhibited. That's not true. What a lot of shy people really dread is talking nonsense."[13]

"An audience is intimidating, really intimidating....But I never want to see the day when it isn't. Sometimes the thing that you dread and are

"I never lived outside of Minnesota before, and I learned that no matter how smart or tolerant we think we are, down deep we find it strange and unpleasant that other people are not like us." (Photo by Kevin Horan/*People Weekly*, copyright © 1987 by Time, Inc.)

afraid of is the very thing you should do, just in order to not have to think about it."[14]

"As terrifying as getting up in front of an audience was—and still is today—nobody can resist laughter. The chance to make people laugh has a powerful attraction."[11]

1976. Divorced wife.

1978. "A Prairie Home Companion" found a permanent home in the World Theatre in St. Paul. "The World Theater, our home for half of those thirteen years, was the right place for that sort of seance, a classic Shubert two-balcony house from 1905, inhabited by two bats and the ghost of a stagehand, all seats within eighty feet of the stage, closer than first base to home. Standing at stage center with your toes to the footlights, you're as close to a thousand people as you can conceivably be. Out there on the prairie where even close friends tend to stand an arm's length apart, such intimacy on such a grand scale is shocking and thrilling and a storyteller reaches something like critical mass, passing directly from solid to radio

waves without going through the liquid or gaseous phase. You stand in the dark, you hear people leaning forward, you smell the spotlights, and you feel invisible.

"No script, no clock, only pictures in your mind that the audience easily sees, they sit so close. You come to be so calm out there, it is more like going to bed than going out to work. It is like crawling under [the] quilt that my grandma Dora Keillor made for me from scraps of clothes worn by my aunts and uncles, which is soft and thin from years of sleep, which comes easily to me when I lie under a smell that goes back to my earliest times lying in bed between my mother and father."[2]

"A Prairie Home Companion" was first heard nationwide in 1980. "I always thought that one of the most wonderful things about the show was that I didn't know many people who listened to it, and they would tell me about their kids and talk about walleye fishing and complain about work and compare automobiles and discuss gas mileage. From this and my memories, I derived a town and populated it. I didn't invent anything. I simply took what I saw around me and put it in another form and came up with fiction.

"I would take a small thing and make it stand for something. To me, that's what a writer does. I think that I was put here on Earth to do that, to write in extravagant praise of common things."[15]

1982. *Happy to Be Here* published. "I can't think of stories in formal terms until they're written. Then I can look at a story that I have written or that someone else has written, and I can describe its form, as I did when I was in school and was asked to write term papers. Every story finds its own form. Finding that form is the great struggle of writing, for which there is no prescription. I would say that the essential element in storytelling is the passion of finding out how to tell it. If you don't have that passion to tell a story, you will settle for telling it not very well, which is almost worse than not telling it at all. But if you have the passion to tell a story, it becomes a wonderful problem in your life like being in love. It becomes an irritation, a splendid misery, that might get some work out of a person to do his little part in adding to the world's knowledge."[16]

"Writing is still a pleasure after all these years. I've stuck an awful lot of paper into typewriters, and still get a little thrill with each fresh sheet. One never knows what might result. It's usually dreary but in writing, unlike teaching, we get to destroy the failures. In teaching, all the failures graduate anyway, as I well know, having been one of them."[17]

"At some point in the writing, I will sit down with a manuscript and go over it, word for word, more than once—sometimes many times. Writing consists of very small parts pieced together into a whole, and if the parts are defective, the whole won't work. But that's a mechanical view. What really comes first is feeling and passion and curiosity.

"If the writer is true to personal experience, the reader is offered something recognizable. It's only as you are faithful to the peculiarities and the exact description of personal experience that you create something that other people will be able to take as their own."[16]

1985. *Lake Wobegon Days* published. "I'm more comfortable put into the third person. There's no

Keillor and bride, Ulla, pose with their children after their wedding. (Photo courtesy of Wide World Photos, Inc.)

The continuing saga of "Buster the Show Dog" is a regular feature of "A Prairie Home Companion." Performers: Garrison Keillor, Kate MacKenzie, Dan Rowles, Stevie Beck and Tom Keith (as "Buster"). (Photo by Rob Levine.)

one character that's more me than another; there are a lot of characters to whom I ascribe what happened to me; there's not one character I'm especially fond of over another. There's not one hero in the piece. In fact, there aren't many heroes around Lake Wobegon at all."[17]

"The book has what I believe to be the longest footnote in American fiction [a 12-page parody of Martin Luther's 95 theses]. I was pleased with the footnotes in the book and that one in particular. I think footnotes have a place in fiction. There is supporting material which can be read in sequence or earlier or just glanced at or eliminated entirely, and that can go into footnotes. It really allows a person freedom of digression that you want in a book. And I like the idea of a book being packed and rich and having layers."[1]

Attended his twenty-fifth high school reunion where he became reacquainted with Ulla Skaerved, a Danish social worker who had been an exchange student in Anoka when he was a senior. They were married months later. "I met my wife Ulla...in 1959 when we were seventeen. She was an AFS exchange student come from Denmark to Anoka, Minnesota, and I was a classmate who admired her and suffered mute ecstasy and un-

speakable torment over her, oftentimes simultaneously. I was a writer. Long before I dared say hi to her in the hallway, I had written poems about her red hair and brown eyes, her stunning smile and grace, her sweetly accented voice, and about my love for her which was spiritual and fine, being secret, was also unrequited. I was 6'3" tall and weighed 150 pounds, all of it pure feeling struggling to get onto paper. It wasn't easy. I felt that I was one of the first people in the world to ever fall in love like that, and it was hard to put such an extraordinary phenomenon into mere English words such as are used by other people.

"Twenty-five years passed, and one warm day in August, 1985, I drove north from Minneapolis along the Mississippi River to a friend's house to meet [her] again who had returned from Denmark for the silver anniversary reunion of our high school class. I got out of the car, walked toward the house, and she opened the door and came down the steps into the sunshine. We embraced each other. We walked along the shore and around our old neighborhood, and on my way home I stopped and got about ten pounds of books about Denmark out of the library. I learned the phrase *jeg elsker dig* for 'I love you' and, in case that made me spill my coffee, *undskyld* for 'Excuse me.' I had gone along all this time knowing nothing about Denmark except Hans Christian Andersen, strong beer, Hamlet, and flat furniture with skinny legs, but what I felt for her was tumultuous and overpowering and the rest of my life became clear to me.

"I wrote her two or three poems that week, nothing so original because—at the age of forty-three you start to understand that love isn't unique or individual but is common as dirt, which is what is most beautiful: to know that our love for each other is the same stuff that other people's lives are made of, an ordinary, mysterious everday transcendent quality, the stuff of music. So I sang. I sang '*Jeg Fik En Sorg Sa Stor*' to her and the next day after saying goodbye, I drove around Minneapolis singing 'Lovesick Blues' at the top of my voice— 'That last long day she said goodbye, Lord, I thought I would die'—and sang it the next Saturday on 'A Prairie Home Companion,' and 'Let Them Talk' and 'Slow Days of Summer.' I sang 'Tell Me Why' alone in hotel rooms touring with the show, sang 'The Water Is Wide' to her on the telephone, sang 'Whoopi Ti Yi' on a visit to Copenhagen in September, and again in October, and 'Ain't That Good News' in November when she visited me. I sang a love song every Saturday on the show because I was happy. We married in December at a little church north of Copenhagen, with great festivity, attended by our four elegant children, in a shower of rice and a chorus of *Skols*, amid speeches and songs. The organ played 'What a Wonderful World' as we receded, and here we are, one more husband and wife in the sweet history of marriage, not so different from all the others."[18]

"My true love doesn't know anything about 'A Prairie Home Companion,' and she doesn't read English well enough to know that I am a humorous person. She thinks of me as passionate and sweet and a terrific singer, which is what I have wanted to be all my life."[19]

"I've had sort of a running disagreement with the two newspapers in town over what constitutes private life, and there really isn't any way to resolve it. . . ."[20]

"The hometown newspaper decided that, being a published author, I was a credit to the community and should be paid close attention, so it announced my romance with my wife and published a photograph of our house, our address, and interviews with the neighbors. I felt watched. Felt mistaken for somebody else. It dawned on me that life might

be better elsewhere. That winter it was warm, there was no snow, the landscape was dry and brown and bleak. We left Saint Paul in June, as soon as school was out."[2]

"It wasn't the fact of being known that was so hard. I think a person who does a radio show can expect to be known beyond friends and family. . . .It was the feeling that I had of being punished, in a way, for having done better than I was supposed to.

"I had thought for many years that I would live all my life in Minnesota. I had no particular wish to go elsewhere. But I couldn't live in my hometown under those circumstances. When your home is no longer a place you feel secure, a place you're understood and people respect you, it's like not having a front door."[20]

Keillor also sensed that his contribution to the show was not what it had been or could be. "I've simply come to the point where my material isn't as good as I want it to be. It's time to pull away, listen to the way people talk. I need the discipline of reporting to get back my ear for dialogue."[21]

"Then, you see, you lose your ability to gather material. Suddenly people don't talk to you about all these interesting things. They talk about, 'Isn't this interesting what's happening to you?' I don't know that it is so interesting, actually."[15]

"You do something for 12 years and maybe you learn how to do it too well. Then you need something else to come along to create new problems."[22]

In 1987, he decided to move his family to Denmark, thus ending the run of "The Prairie Home Companion." The adjustment to life in a new country was one he felt ready to make. "Some days it seems that I am living the immigrant dream in reverse, starting with success in America, then the voyage, then the life of servitude in the Old World. It's hard work setting up housekeeping in a foreign language. But then I take my shopping bag down to the open market on Frederiksborggade and one look down the avenue of booths heaped with crates of produce and I'm home in Lake Wobegon, back in the land of tomatoes and cucumbers. Cucumbers are *agurker* in Danish, but tomatoes are *tomater* and I see *meloner* and *nektariner*, *bananer*, *radiser*, *broccoli*, *selleri*, and plenty of *aebler* (both 'Golden Delicious' and 'Granny Smith'). For *vandmelon*, you pay ten kroner, almost $1.50, and they're as big and thump as well as what I remember from our *vandmelon* patch at home. *Mais* is ten kroner

Keillor prepares to enter New York's giant showplace to do "The Second Annual Farewell Performance." "It was so much fun leaving, we're coming back to say good-bye again."

for three ears, a little expensive, but when it comes to *mais* who counts the cost?

"Sweet corn was our family's weakness. We were prepared to resist atheistic Communism, immoral Hollywood, hard liquor, gambling and dancing, smoking, fornication, but if Satan had come around with sweet corn, we at least would have listened to what he had to sell. We might not have bought it but we would've had him in and given him a cup of coffee."[2]

"...In Denmark, a country that I have been trying to figure out, and a country that I felt so much more certain of my opinions about it the first week I was there than I did a month later. I felt after a week in Denmark that I could write a book about it, then after a month or so I thought I could write a magazine article about it; and now I'd be satisfied to say three true things about that country."[5]

1987. *Leaving Home*, a collection of stories from "A Prairie Home Companion," published. "It

seems to me that in a great many of these stories, even before I was aware of it, I was showing signs of being ready to pick up. Some of the characters in the stories are thinking the same thing. And others are coming to realize that this is where they'll be the rest of their lives.

"I wrote these as stories and then performed them on the show—not from a script, but from an imperfect memory. I felt that they were better as stories than they were in performance. I want them to appear in the best way they can, which is in print. My aim was not to transcribe a performance and put it in print; some of the best stories that I did on the show really were performances and I've not included them here.

"My fear was that the longer I did the show and talked about Lake Wobegon, the more I would cut corners and not do justice to the characters in the town. But I feel that I did give them my best effort as a writer. If I were to sit down and write another book about Lake Wobegon, I might do many things differently, and it might have a different feeling to it, especially now that I'm so far away, but I was pleased with the way the characters came across in print."[20]

In the fall, Keillor and his wife moved to New York City. He subsequently addressed the National Press Club in Washington, D.C. "It's lovely to come here and break my retirement with you. It's a frightening thing to get up in front of a microphone and be on radio and talk to a roomful of people after months of not doing it; months of being in another country...where if an American can say 'Good Morning' and 'Thank You' and 'where is the railway station,' they think you are just brilliant. Especially your mother-in-law does.

"I've had three months off—more than that, five months—to sit and contemplate all of those people whom I've told stories about; and a storyteller has to keep working. If you ever stop and think about what you've done, you just feel such guilt about not having done better by these people.

"I miss ['The Prairie Home Companion']. I miss it terribly. I could not find any work in Denmark that I was the least bit useful at, except for washing dishes. As we see these headlines in the paper [i.e. the stock market crash of October 1987], we start to think about other career skills we might have, and washing dishes is one of mine. I put myself through a part of college washing dishes, which is why I do it so seldom now that I'm married, because I'm a professional. I can handle large amounts of them, but to do just a few really doesn't interest me that much. Same reason that journalists don't write letters. But I did dishes in Denmark."[5]

Keillor discussed some future plans with *Publishers Weekly*, including a screenplay based on Lake Wobegon. "I've never written a script before and it feels awkward, the times I've given it a try. It came from my interest in doing something I'd never done before, and also being able to see this town. People who listened to the stories on the radio claimed they could see the town, but I only had a hazy view. I wanted to put the characters up on screen so I could take a look at 'em.

"But I'm finding it's hard to move them in and out [of scenes]. Mainly it's hard to move them out. They tend to walk in and just hang around, same as I do in real life. I never know how to leave a party.

"I'm working on a novel that is set in a radio station which I started almost 10 years ago. I'm going to throw out the characters and keep the radio station—fire the staff and start over again. They just didn't interest me long enough.

"...I want to get back to writing fact pieces for the *New Yorker*. I've been fiddling with a piece about coming to Denmark and the experience of feeling stupid.

"...I'll have to get back to doing something in front of an audience in the near future, or else accept that I couldn't do it anymore. I don't think you can lay off for too long—it's too scary, too terrible. I'd hate to think of not performing again right now, but it could happen. It's something that you need other people in order to do; it's not like writing. I miss the link with people."[20]

Footnote Sources:

[1] Diane Roback, "PW Interviews: Garrison Keillor," *Publishers Weekly*, September 13, 1985. Amended by G. Keillor.
[2] Garrison Keillor, "A Letter from Copenhagen" (introduction) in *Leaving Home*, Viking, 1987.
[3] Peter Hemingston, "The Plowboy Interview," *Mother Earth News*, May-June, 1985. Amended by G. Keillor.
[4] John Skow, "Lonesome Whistle Blowing," *Time*, November 4, 1985. Amended by G. Keillor.
[5] National Press Club Speech, Washington, D.C., 1987.
[6] Garrison Keillor, "Introduction" in *Happy to Be Here*, Atheneum, 1982.
[7] Ira Letofsky, "For Garrison Keillor Fantasy Is a Lot More Fun Than Reality," *Tribune* (Minneapolis), July 29, 1976.
[8] James Traub, "The Short and Tall Tales of Garrison Keillor," *Esquire*, May, 1982.
[9] Paul Judge, "Portrait: Garrison Keillor," *Life*, May, 1982.
[10] "Education: Lake Wobegon Chronicler Garrison Keillor at Gettysburg College, Gettysburg, Pa.," *Time*, June 22, 1987.
[11] *Current Biography*, H. W. Wilson, August, 1985.
[12] Les Lindeman, "In a Lake Wobegon Daze," *Chicago Sun Times*, September 13, 1985. Amended by G. Keillor.
[13] Edward Fishe, "Small-Town America," *New York Times*, October 31, 1982.
[14] Jon Pareles, "Prairie Humor Comes to the Big City," *New York Times*, May 13, 1983.
[15] Peg Meier, "Wobegon and the Burden of Celebrity," *Newsday*, April 20, 1987.
[16] Michael Schumacher, "Sharing the Laughter with Garrison Keillor," *Writer's Digest*, January, 1986. Amended by G. Keillor.
[17] John Bordsen, "All the News from Lake Wobegon," *Saturday Review*, May-June, 1983. Amended by G. Keillor.
[18] "Line Notes" from "Ain't That Good News" (record album), Minnesota Public Radio, 1987.
[19] "Lake Wobegon's Garrison Keillor Finds a Love That Time Forgot and the Decades Can't Improve," *People*, November 25, 1985.

[20] Alan Bunce, "Denmark-Bound Keillor Chats about His Plans," *Christian Science Monitor*, March 3, 1987.

[21] Diane Roback, "Leaving the Shores of Lake Wobegon," *Publishers Weekly*, August 21, 1987.

[22] Dirk Johnson, "With Singing, Satire and Sentiment, Lake Wobegon Fades," *New York Times*, June 14, 1987.

[23] Steve Schneider, "'Prairie Home Companion' Exits," *New York Times*, March 1, 1987.

■ For More Information See

Time, November 9, 1981, February 1, 1982, September 2, 1985, October 26, 1987, March 28, 1988 (p. 88).

Country Journal, January, 1982.

Washington Post Book World, January 18, 1982.

Chicago Tribune Book World, January 24, 1982.

Chicago Tribune, May 20, 1982.

Christian Century, July 21-28, 1982, November 13, 1985.

Linda Feldmann, "Radio's 'Prairie Home': City Slickers Like It, Too," *Christian Science Monitor*, May 23, 1983.

Louise Lague, "Garrison Keillor: Favorite Son of the Town Time Forgot," *People*, February 6, 1984.

New York Times, July 8, 1984, August 20, 1985, October 31, 1985, November 1, 1987.

Detroit News, September 1, 1985.

Detroit Free Press, September 8, 1985.

Dan Cryer, "America's Hottest New Storyteller," *Newsday*, October 13, 1985.

Michael Walker, "Interview: The Met Grill," *Metropolitan Home*, November, 1985.

"Door Interviews Garrison Keillor," *Wittenberg Door*, December-January, 1985-86.

Wayne Lee Gay, "Voice of the Prairie," *Continental*, February, 1986.

Bill Barol, "A Shy Person Says So Long," *Newsweek*, June 15, 1987.

"Leaving Lake Wobegon," *Time*, June 29, 1987.

Video, September, 1987.

Eric Levin, "Goodbye to Lake Wobegon," *People*, October 12, 1987.

Daily News, October 25, 1987.

Garrison Keillor, "How to Write a Personal Letter," *Reader's Digest*, November, 1987.

"Garrison Keillor: Beyond Lake Wobegon," National Public Radio, 1987.

Michael Fedo, *The Man from Lake Wobegon*, St. Martin's, 1987.

Variety, March 16, 1988.

Parade, May 29, 1988.

M. E. Kerr

Born Marijane Meaker May 27, 1927, in Auburn, N.Y.; daughter of Ellis R. (a mayonnaise manufacturer) and Ida T. Meaker. *Education:* University of Missouri B.A., 1949. *Home:* 12 Deep Six Dr., East Hampton, N.Y. 11937. *Agent:* Julia Fallowfield, McIntosh & Otis, Inc., 475 Fifth Ave., New York, N.Y. 10017.

■ Career

Worked at several jobs, including assistant file clerk for E. P. Dutton (publisher), 1949-50; free-lance writer, 1949—. *Member:* Ashawagh Hall Writers' Workshop (founder), P.E.N., Authors League of America, Society of Children's Book Writers.

■ Awards, Honors

Dinky Hocker Shoots Smack was selected one of *School Library Journal's* Best Books of the Year, 1972, *The Son of Someone Famous,* 1974, *I'll Love You When You're More Like Me,* 1977, *Little, Little,* 1981, and *What I Really Think of You,* 1982; *If I Love You, Am I Trapped Forever?* was selected one of *New York Times* Outstanding Books of the Year, 1973, *Is That You, Miss Blue?,* 1975, and *Gentle-*

hands, 1978; *Book World's* Children's Spring Book Festival Honor Book, and one of Child Study Association of America's Children's Books of the Year, both 1973, both for *If I Love You, Am I Trapped Forever?; Media and Methods* Maxi Award, 1974, for *Dinky Hocker Shoots Smack; Is That You, Miss Blue?* was selected one of American Library Association's Best Books for Young Adults, 1975, and *Me Me Me Me Me—Not a Novel,* 1983; Christopher Award, 1979, and one of New York Public Library's Books for the Teen Age, 1980, and 1981, both for *Gentlehands;* Golden Kite Award for Fiction from the Society of Children's Book Writers, 1981, and one of New York Public Library's Books for the Teen Age, 1982, both for *Little, Little.*

■ Writings

Young Adult Fiction; Under Pseudonym M. E. Kerr:

Dinky Hocker Shoots Smack! (ALA Notable Book), Harper, 1972.
If I Love You, Am I Trapped Forever?, Harper, 1973.
The Son of Someone Famous, Harper, 1974.
Is That You, Miss Blue? (ALA Notable Book), Harper, 1975.
Love Is a Missing Person, Harper, 1975.
I'll Love You When You're More Like Me, Harper, 1977.
Gentlehands, Harper, 1978.
Little, Little, Harper, 1981.
What I Really Think of You, Harper, 1982.

Him She Loves?, Harper, 1984.
(Contributor) *Sixteen,* edited by Donald R. Gallo, Delacorte, 1984.
I Stay Near You, Harper, 1985.
Night Kites, Harper, 1986.
Fell, Harper, 1987.
Fell Back, Harper, 1989.

Young Adult Nonfiction; Under Pseudonym M. E. Kerr:

Me, Me, Me, Me, Me—Not a Novel (autobiography), Harper, 1983.

Adult Fiction:

(Under name, M. J. Meaker) *Hometown,* Doubleday, 1967.
Game of Survival, New American Library, 1968.
Shockproof Sydney Skate, Little, Brown, 1972.

Adult Nonfiction; Under Name M. J. Meaker:

Sudden Endings, Doubleday, 1964, paperback edition under pseudonym Vin Packer, Fawcett, 1964.

Nonfiction; Under Pseudonym Ann Aldrich:

We Walk Alone, Gold Medal Books, 1955.
We Too Must Love, Gold Medal Books, 1958.
Carol in a Thousand Cities, Gold Medal Books, 1960.
We Two Won't Last, Gold Medal Books, 1963.
Take a Lesbian to Lunch, MacFadden-Bartell, 1972.

Adult Fiction; Under Pseudonym Vin Packer:

Dark Intruder, Gold Medal Books, 1952.
Spring Fire, Gold Medal Books, 1952.
Look Back to Love, Gold Medal Books, 1953.
Come Destroy Me, Gold Medal Books, 1954.
Whisper His Sin, Gold Medal Books, 1954.
The Thrill Kids, Gold Medal Books, 1955.
Dark Don't Catch Me, Gold Medal Books, 1956.
The Young and Violent, Gold Medal Books, 1956.
Three-Day Terror, Gold Medal Books, 1957.
The Evil Friendship, Gold Medal Books, 1958.
5:45 to Suburbia, Gold Medal Books, 1958.
The Twisted Ones, Gold Medal Books, 1959.
The Damnation of Adam Blessing, Gold Medal Books, 1961.
The Girl on the Best Seller List, Gold Medal Books, 1961.
Something in the Shadows, Gold Medal Books, 1961.
Intimate Victims, Gold Medal Books, 1962.
Alone at Night, Gold Medal Books, 1963.

The Hare in March, New American Library, 1967.
Don't Rely on Gemini, Delacorte Press, 1969.

Teacher's guides are available for *Dinky Hocker Shoots Smack!, If I Love You, Am I Trapped Forever?, Is That You, Miss Blue?* and *Love Is a Missing Person.*

■ Adaptations

"Dinky Hocker" (television film; based on *Dinky Hocker Shoots Smack!*), starring Wendie Jo Sperba, Learning Corporation of America, 1978.
"If I Love You, Am I Trapped Forever?" (listening cassette), Random House, 1979.

■ Work In Progress

An adult book set in Oak Ridge, Tenn. in 1942.

■ Sidelights

Marijane Meaker was born on May 27, 1927 in Auburn, New York. The only daughter of Ellis and Ida Meaker. Her father owned Ivanhoe Foods, whose chief product was mayonnaise, and she often joked of the family monopoly, as her grandfather owned many of the local grocery stores. "I grew up always wanting to be a writer. My father was a mayonnaise manufacturer, with a strange habit, for a mayonnaise manufacturer, of reading everything from the Harvard Classics, to all of Dickens, Emerson, Poe, Thoreau, Kipling, and John O'Hara, Sinclair Lewis, John Steinbeck, all the Book-of-the-Month Club selections, plus magazines like *Time, Life, Look,* and *Fortune,* and all the New York City newspapers, along with the local Auburn, New York *Citizen Advertiser.*"[1]

Meaker's father was not the only one who encouraged her interest in reading and writing. "So did English teachers. . .and librarians who had to pull me out of the stacks at closing time. And there were my favorite writers like Thomas Wolfe, Sherwood Anderson, the Brontes, and our hometown hero, Samuel Hopkins Adams. (I'd pedal past his big house on Owasco Lake, just to see where a real writer lived!) But in my heart, I know who was responsible for this ambition of mine to become a writer: it was my lifelong abettor. . .my. . .mother.

"One of the most vivid memories of my childhood is of my mother making a phone call. First, she'd tell me to go out and play. I'd pretend to do that, letting the back door slam, hiding right around the corner of the living room, in the hall. She'd have her pack of Kools and the ashtray on the desk, as she gave the number of one of her girlfriends to the operator. . . .My Mother would begin nearly every conversation the same way: 'Wait till you hear this!'

"Even today, when I'm finished with a book and sifting through ideas for a new one, I ask myself: Is the idea a 'wait till you hear this?'"[1]

On Saturday nights in summer mother and daughter would drive downtown together and park in different spots, observing their neighbors and collecting gossip. "Then home. . .and a lesson from my mother on the importance of fiction. Fiction, I learned early on, spins off grandly from fact. Our trip downtown would be related over the phone, beginning, 'Wait till you hear this! Carl Otter sent poor little Polly off to see 'Brother Rat' so he could have a night on the town, that dear little woman with her face down to her shoes, standing in line by herself while he treats Ellie Budd to old-fashioneds down at Boysen's.'

"Long before the character in one of Salinger's short stories ever peeked into someone else's bathroom cabinet to inspect its contents, I'd learned from my mother that that was the first thing you did once the bathroom door was closed in other people's homes.

"'What are you looking for?' I'd ask.

"She'd say, "Shhhh! Run the water!'

"I learned that the first thing you look for is prescription medicine, then all the ointments and liquids that tell you what ailments are being treated in the house you're visiting.

"My mother taught me all a writer'd need to know about socio/economic/ethnic differences, too.

"She taught me to cut out all the labels from my coats and jackets, anything I might remove in Second Presbyterian Church on a Sunday morning, so that no one knew that we often bought out-of-town.

"My mother'd come from a poor immigrant German family twenty-six miles from Auburn, where she'd been raised in a convent. She'd taken a step up in her marriage, a fact she was always defensive about in Auburn, always proud of in her hometown, Syracuse; and the labels she'd cut out were sewn back in for visits there.

"She took an unusual interest in the boys who came to call on me when I was in my early teens. She warned me that if I married a Catholic, there'd be one baby right after the other; that if I married

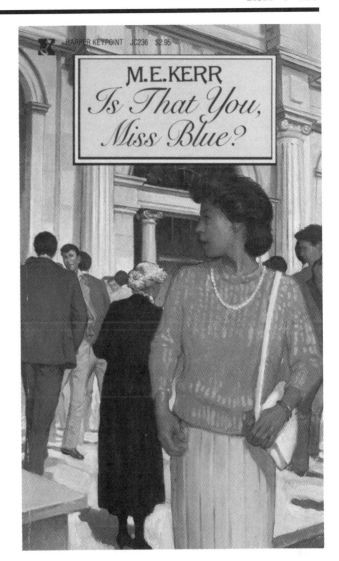

Cover art by Richard Williams from the Harper Keypoint edition.

an Italian I wouldn't be allowed to wash the salad bowl, they just wiped it dry; and that any boy whose father was bald, would be bald himself one day."[1]

At age ten, Meaker and her friends were in love with the movie star, Ronald Reagan. She wrote him a letter pretending to be a little crippled girl in the hope of getting his autograph. He wrote back:

"Dear Marijane,
    Thank you for your letter.
    Remember that a handicap can be a
    challenge.
    Always stay as cheerful as you are now.
                    Yours truly,
                    Ronald Reagan"[2]

Her parents found the letter and she was forced to admit she had lied to the actor. "After my father read the letter, and got the truth out of me concerning my correspondence with Ronald Reagan, he told me what I was to do.

"What I was to do was to sit down immediately and write Ronald Reagan, telling him I had lied. I was to add that I thanked God for my good health. I was to return both the letter and the photograph.

"No Saturday in my entire life had ever been so dark.

"My father stood over me while I wrote the letter in tears, convinced that Ronald Reagan would hate me all his life for my deception. I watched through blurred eyes while my father took my letter, Ronald Reagan's letter, and the signed photograph, put them into a manila envelope, addressed it, sealed it, and put it in his briefcase to take to the post office."[2]

1939-1940. Her younger brother, "Butchie," was born and Meaker's life changed. "Twelve was the age I was when my baby brother was born, and my older brother went off to military school.

"Thirteen was the year I became a hundred.

"Three things contributed to my rapid aging: the new baby in the house, the dramatic change in my older brother's personality, and my forced enrollment in Laura Bryan's ballroom dancing classes.

"No new budget was going to make up for the fact that both my parents were suddenly swooning daily over Butchie, my baby brother.

"No new budget was going to make me feel better about the sight of my older brother coming through the door on vacation from military school, a Riverside Military Academy cadet, caped and epauletted and sabered.

"I was suddenly the nothing, sandwiched between two stars.

"Locked in my room, I wrote stories about murder and suicide, tried on clothes, daydreamed about boys, and listened to records like 'Blues in the Night' and 'Let's Get Away from It All.'

"I was in a slump, and my mother's answer to this was to enroll me in Laura Bryan's school, this time for ballroom dancing. I had already suffered through toe and tap dancing, with Laura Bryan wincing while I performed grotesque tour jetes and did the buck-and-wing to any rhythm but the one the pianist was playing. Dancing was not one of my gifts."[2]

1943. Another answer to Meaker's "slump" was to send her to boarding school at Stuart Hall in Staunton, Virginia. She resented the move and soon got into trouble at the Episcopal, all-girls' school.

1944. Meaker's family bought a summer cottage on Owasco Lake, at Burtis Point, a point of land farthest away from town. Meaker was isolated from her friends. "The summer of 1944 I became Eric Ranthram McKay.

"I think one reason for this was all the sailors pouring into our small town. There were some soldiers and marines around, too, but we knew them. They were hometown boys, coming and going from war. The sailors were another matter. On leave from nearby Sampson Naval Base, they came to us fresh from boot camp, lonely and looking for fun.

"'The kind of fun a sailor is looking for might fill a few empty hours for him, but you could pay for it the rest of your life,' my father said."[2]

Meaker, naturally, wanted to be where the sailors were, instead of babysitting for her kid brother. "There, at the beginning of the summer, I was marooned. My father drove into work every morning at seven, and returned at six every evening. Gas rationing made it hard for anyone to get to and from Burtis Point. There were no buses. Hitchhikers didn't fare well on the empty roads at night, which discouraged local boyfriends from visiting. 'Life' was going on back in town, at the movies, at the Teen Canteen and the USO, at the kids' hangouts like Murray's.

"By day I swam and sailed and looked after my kid brother, listening to my girl friends' accounts of what was happening, for hours on the telephone. By night I wrote, using my first pseudonym: Eric Ranthram McKay.

"The pseudonym was chosen because my father's initials were E. R. M. After I wrote a story, I mailed it off to a magazine with a letter written on my father's stationery, engraved with his initials and our home address.

"I don't know why I chose Eric, Ranthram, or McKay—I guess I just felt the name had a good ring to it.

"All of Eric Ranthram McKay's stories were sad, romantic ones about the war. I subscribed to a magazine called *Writer's Digest*, which listed the needs of publications like *Good Housekeeping*, *Ladies' Home Journal*, and *Redbook*. I mailed off my stories in manila envelopes with a stamped, addressed envelope enclosed, and they came back

From the television film "Dinky Hocker," based on *Dinky Hocker Shoots Smack*, starring Wendie Jo Sperber. Courtesy of Learning Corporation of America.

like boomerangs, with printed rejection slips attached.

"Sometimes these rejection slips had a 'sorry' penciled across them, or a 'try again.'

"These I cherished, and saved, and used to buoy my spirits as I began new stories, and kept the old ones circulating.

"At the same time Eric Ranthram McKay was writing stories, Marijane Meaker was writing servicemen—a soldier named Bob McKeon from my hometown, and a sailor named Eddie Herbold. Herbold was considered an okay sailor, since my family knew him. These 'romances,' by mail, were in full swing that summer."[2]

1945. On her return to Stuart Hall, she continued to be rebellious to school authorities, and in February of her senior year she was suspended for throwing darts at photographs of faculty members. From February to March she worked at American Locomotive, a local defense plant, as a file clerk. Her mother's manipulations allowed her to be reinstated in time for graduation. "I think my years at Stuart Hall were a provocative experience for both Stuart Hall and me. I was the class reprobate, assigned a single room the size of a large closet on Middle Music Hall to keep me out of trouble. Nevertheless, I was very familiar with Mrs. Hodges' office, where I would go after finding in my mailbox, many a morning, a note exclaiming, 'See me at once! APH.'...In my senior year I was

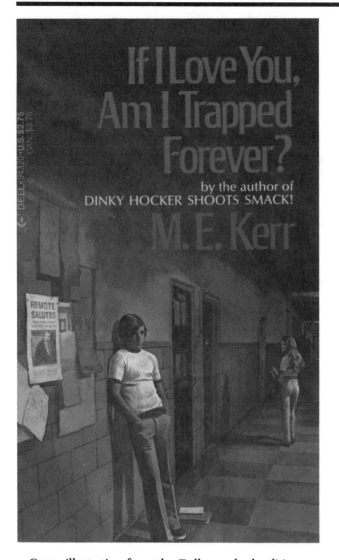

Cover illustration from the Dell paperback edition.

expelled, and only my mother's intervention with a bishop had that changed to a suspension, so I could return to graduate with my class....I had, while I was there, and well after, a great infatuation with Stuart Hall, a lover's quarrel with its rules and certain stern faculty members, and now I read it's changed and not so strict, and wonder would I love it so well these days? I don't know, but there was something stimulating and amusing, and very like life, as I came to know it, in its regulated, intense, dutiful and peculiar ambiance. I went there during World War II, and I remember so well getting there on overcrowded trains jammed with boys just a few years older than I, on their way to war. Many of us had brothers away at war. It was a difficult time...and I remember Mrs. Hodges calling an assembly to announce Roosevelt's death, and dear Miss Dean, the science teacher, correcting her former opinion that atoms could not be split.

"In the school yearbook, *Inlook,* 1945, I am distinctively out of place, since it was put together during my expulsion. At the very end of the seniors' photographs comes Kathryn Walters, my roommate; then Wellford, Worthy and Yates ...then Marijane Meaker, on record forever, the out-of-line black sheep."[2]

After graduation, Meaker went to Vermont Junior College where she edited the school newspaper, which published her first story. "I was too overwhelmed by the idea there were boys on campus (local ones, about a dozen, who were day students) and too amazed that I could wear jeans to class, and to the dining room, and that I could carry a pack of cigarettes in my shirt pocket, though I could smoke them only in the 'smoker.'

"I felt like someone who'd been let out of prison. I was finally going to school again with Yankees who talked like me, knew what deep snow was, and owned skis, skates, and toboggans. (Winters you could take skiing for gym, go off on skis before breakfast with the class, and come in to a feast of pancakes with real Vermont maple syrup poured over them.)

"I was too busy clearing out an old storage room the dean allowed me to convert into a press room.

"Before the autumn leaves had stopped falling, my first article appeared in the first issue of the school paper.

"It was called 'The Air and I,' and it was about my flying lessons, which I'd talked my father into giving me that past summer. (My father'd bought a small plane for my older brother and him to enjoy, and I suppose I was in another phase of 'brother envy.')

"I hated flying, managed to solo, then never went up again."[2]

1946. Transferred to the University of Missouri. She had to join a sorority because housing was so scarce due to the war. Her father refused to send her trunks until he was sure she had joined up, and therefore had a place to live. "At the University of Missouri, where I went despite my father's warning that if I did go there, I'd end up marrying someone from Missouri, I switched my major from Journalism to English...partly because I failed Economics, which one had to pass to get into J-School, and partly because I realized I didn't want anything to do with writing fact. I wanted to make up my own facts. I wanted to do creative writing.

"It was the end of World War II, and Columbia, Missouri, was a real college town, filled with kids right off the farm, or coming from little towns like Bolivar and Poplar Bluff, plus an abundance of young men straight out of the service. Girls who'd never been any farther than St. Louis or Kansas City were matched on blind dates with fellows who'd fought in Okinawa, or already seen London and Paris, as sorority/fraternity life commenced. My very first week there I went with some classmates to a popular hangout called The Shack, and learned the game of Chug-a-Lug, which was a beer drinking contest, in which you drained your full glass in one breather, while everyone sang 'Here's to Marijane, she's true blue, she's a drinker through and through!'"[1]

But Meaker hated the sorority teas and their process of elimination. "The sorority system, to my mind, is still one of the cruelest introductions to college life that I can imagine, and I'm not particularly proud of my participation in sorority life, even though I made my closest friends in the Alpha Delta Pi sorority.

"...I tried to think what it was sororities were saying to their members, and it seemed to me they were all saying not to be individuals, but to be as much like the group as possible."[2]

Being as much like the group as possible was not Meaker's strong suit. "Although it was very much a party campus in those postwar years, it was still the end of the 1940s, and there were rules: a time to be in at night, no men above the first floor in a sorority house, no alcoholic beverages...and in our sorority, Alpha Delta Pi, dating men who were not in fraternities was frowned on. They were called 'independents'; they were unwelcome (though tolerated) at major sorority functions.

"I found someone to date (and fall in love with) who gave my father far more to worry about than the boy from St. Louis or Kansas City whom he'd envisioned. George was from Hungary originally, a Jew who'd barely managed to escape the Nazis in his teens by being smuggled into Venezuela.

"By the time he arrived on the Missouri campus, he was an ardent Communist....

"Under his spell, I joined the Communist party, and voted for Henry Wallace for President of the United States, the only one in Cayuga County, New York, to do so.

"I stayed on for summer sessions, too, because of George, and although he'd politicized me, he hadn't cured me of my wish to be a writer."

Cover art by Michael Deas from the Harper Keypoint edition.

"I wrote story after story, sending them off to New York-based magazines, accumulating so many rejection slips that I attended a sorority masquerade party as a rejection slip, wearing a black slip with rejections from all the magazines pinned to it."[1]

Meaker also volunteered at the local mental hospital, where she dated the hospital psychiatrist. She and George discussed marriage, but eventually he left the country without her, spurred on by an F.B.I. investigation of his Communist sympathies. Meaker implies that her mother may have instigated the investigation.

1949. After receiving her B.A. from the University of Missouri, Meaker moved to New York City with several of her sorority sisters. "In those days, New York City was still a place where you could take a subway at night and not fear getting mugged. You could also find a two-bedroom apartment for $150 a month, if you wanted to live in Washington Heights, where the four of us found ours.

"My roommates all got good jobs in advertising/publishing, because they knew shorthand. In those days, a good job, for a female, was a job as a secretary, at about fifty dollars a week.

"I had never been able to master shorthand, though I had studied it at my father's insistence....My first job was at Dutton Publishing Company, as something like an assistant to the file clerk, at thirty-two dollars a week....

"My job had no real title. I worked in the art department, in the bull pen, carrying my lunch every day in a paper sack, after a long subway ride with two station changes; it took me an hour to get down to lower New York from Washington Heights in hose, heels, hat, and gloves.

"I wasn't worth the thirty-two dollars Dutton paid me to file letters and answer phones and carry things from one floor to another. My own work came first with me. I was always sitting there scratching out short stories and poems. I think the only time I looked up was when an author came into the area to discuss the artwork on his/her cover. I was in awe of all the authors. I remember one young, tough fellow who never liked his covers, who always gave the art director a hard time. He was Mickey Spillane, not too well known yet."[1]

Her work continued to be rejected, but she kept on with it. "I couldn't get an agent, so I began sending out manuscripts under my roommates' names. I wanted a variety of names, and I wanted to be sure the manuscripts were safely returned to our mailbox.

"I wrote anything and everything in an effort to get published. I wrote confession stories, articles, 'slick' stories for the women's magazines, poetry and fillers.

"One manuscript was returned from *Your Life* magazine with a hopeful letter, telling me that with a little revision, they might publish it. It was one of the ones sent out under a roommate's name.

"She hit the roof when she saw the title: 'Masturbation Is Normal.'

"After that, none of my roommates wanted their names on my work."[2]

Meaker lost her job at this point. "In a year's time, I went from Dutton to Compton Advertising Company, to a medical house publishing the *Review of Gastroenterology* and the *Proctology Review*, to

Fawcett Publications, fired almost as soon as I was hired.

"Meanwhile, I'd found a way to get an agent: I'd become my own agent, print up stationery with my name on it and 'Literary Agent,' and send out stories under pseudonyms.

"My pseudonyms were my clients.

"On lunch breaks from Fawcett Publications, I visited editors and talked about Laura Winston (who wrote slicks for women's magazines), Mamie Stone (who wrote confessions), Edgar Stone, her 'husband' (who wrote detective stories), and Winslow Albert (who wrote articles)....They were all me.

"Finally, Fawcett fired me, tired of my two- and three-hour lunch breaks."[2]

1951. Meaker made an arrangement with her roommates to cook for them in exchange for food money, and she worked full time on her writing. Finally, at the age of twenty-three, she sold her first story. "On April 20, 1951, a letter came in the mail from the *Ladies' Home Journal*, to Marijane Meaker, Literary Agent, saying they were going to buy Laura Winston's story.

"I raced to the phone to call my roommates.

"I was so excited that I believed they were paying seventy-five dollars for the story.

"No one, in any office in New York City, was at their desks. General Douglas MacArthur was being welcomed in New York City with an enormous ticker-tape parade!

"When my roommates finally came home and read the acceptance letter themselves, one said, 'It isn't seventy-five dollars they're paying you. It's seven hundred and fifty dollars!'

"That night I took everyone out to dinner to Ruby Foo's for egg rolls, duckling chop suey, beef with snow-pea pods, et cetera, et cetera.

"I'd earned enough to keep on writing for another six months....

"I was on my way!

"In September 1951, when my story was published, I opened to the table of contents and cried out, 'Look, there's my name with John P. Marquand's and Dorothy Thompson's!'

"'There's Laura Winston's name,' a roommate said, 'and there's your picture, with Laura Winston's name under it!'

On pages 46 and 47, there was a large illustration depicting three characters from my story.
The *Journal* Presents
LAURA WINSTON
And
Her First Published Story
DEVOTEDLY, PATRICK HENRY CASEBOLT"[2]

1952. After this success, she never worked at a full-time job again. Her first novel, *Spring Fire*, was published by Gold Medal Books, a series by Fawcett Publications. "*Spring Fire* was an instant paperback success, selling 1,463,917 copies in 1952, more than *The Damned* by John D. MacDonald or *My Cousin Rachel* by Daphne du Maurier, both published that same year in the U.S.

"Long out of print now, *Spring Fire* enabled me to become a full-time free-lance novelist, enjoy a trip to Europe, and get my first apartment, sans roommates, on East Ninety-fourth Street, off Fifth Avenue, where I would live for eight years.

"The apartment building at 23 East Ninety-fourth was very small, only two apartments per floor, five floors altogether."[1]

Meaker began to write mysteries and thrillers under the pen names Vin Packer and Ann Aldrich. "I was writing some paperback originals. In those days it seemed like a phenomenal amount of money that you could get for them; hardcover, of course, didn't pay as much unless you were a best-seller. Then I heard that if you wrote mysteries and suspense you would be reviewed in the *New York Times* in the mystery and suspense column, whereas, you were never reviewed if you wrote just a paperback original. So I immediately started writing mystery and suspense for that reason, and that was how I got into it. And I did get reviews; I did get noticed."[3]

1950-1964. During this period, Meaker wrote twenty novels under her two pen names. She explained how she choose the name Vin Packer. "Years and years later, I discovered I wasn't the only one who felt a female wouldn't be taken seriously. When I first began writing suspense stories for Fawcett Publications, my editor suggested that I take a male pseudonym.

"'You tell a fast, tough story,' he said, 'and you'll lose your credibility with a name like Marijane Meaker.'

"I chose the pen name Vin Packer, after talking about the problem over dinner with one friend whose first name was Vin and another whose last name was Packer."[2]

A good friend, Louise Fitzhugh, encouraged her to write for young adults. "Louise was an artist turned writer, who had done a very successful book called *Harriet the Spy.* It was published by Harper & Row as a 'young adult' book. I had never heard of such a category.

"'You'd be a good young adult writer,' Louise would tell me, 'since you're always writing about kids.'

"'But not from their viewpoint,' I'd answer, and I'd dismiss her suggestions that I should try to write for this field."[1]

Meanwhile, she was studying psychology, sociology, anthropology and child psychology at The New School for Social Research.

1964. Meaker wrote a hardcover nonfiction book on suicide called *Sudden Endings* under the name M. J. Meaker. In her "Author's Note" she wrote: "When I was a child, there was a grand eight-sided white stone house at the end of our block, with a glass-roofed cupola on top, and a tall iron fence built all the way around the sumptuous grounds. It was an abandoned house, boarded up, the lawn a field of weeds. 'The Octagon' was always a source of eerie fascination to the children; we called it 'The Octopus,' and we went there to play despite our parents' warnings to stay away. What drew us to this house was not its eight sides, nor its cupola, nor even the fact it was empty; when we sat huddled under the large front porch in our secret clubhouse, we spoke of the mysterious Mr. Slater, who had owned 'The Octopus.' The mystery revolved around the fact that Mr. Slater hanged himself in an upstairs bedroom of the house.

"We had heard that Mr. Slater was very rich, that he had married a much younger woman, and that she had run off with another man. We made up many stories to supplement what we knew about Mr. Slater. We acted out versions of his life and even fought over who would be the one to commit suicide in our strange little plays.

"Our town was near Rochester, New York. One day our parents were all whispering over the suicide of George Eastman, the founder of Eastman Kodak. Every family had a Kodak; we children used to muse over the idea that the man who had made our cameras had done what Mr. Slater had done....Our town was a prison city; one of the stories about the prison, which we all knew, was that the state executioner who had sent 141 men to death in the electric chair, had shot himself.

"We used the word 'suicide' frequently; it sounded even more ominous than murder. It was a far more taboo subject, we sensed that. There was never anything about it on the radio, nor in the magazines; we sensed there was something shameful about the subject.

"I wanted to be a writer, and as I grew up I began to read whatever I could about the lives of the writers whose books and poems and stories and plays I had read. . . .

"I began to read as much as I could on the subject of suicide. . . .

"In college I read Virginia Woolf and Hart Crane; both of them had committed suicide—both in the same way, by drowing. My junior year in college, my classmates were all excited about 'a new Thomas Wolfe,'" a writer named Ross Lockridge, who had written a book called *Raintree County.* A few months after the book reached the bestseller list, Lockeridge killed himself.

"Primarily, *Sudden Endings* is an examination of the lives of thirteen victims of suicide; it cannot answer why people kill themselves; it can only suggest why these individuals killed themselves. Just as more can be known about the whole by studying the isolated part offering the most potential, so, I think, more can be known about suicide by examining the backgrounds of people who killed themselves, and whose prominence lent access to details of their private lives. There are patterns and similarities in their lives; there is a feeling of drift which is the same. Out of it all comes no *one* answer, but many glimpses—now sharp, now hazy—of that impulse toward self-destruction to which none of us is immune."[4]

1967. Meaker wrote *Hometown* under pseudonym Vin Packer, which was not successful. "It was described by *Publishers Weekly* as 'a long, boring novel, all the more surprising because it comes from the facile pen of Vin Packer.' I was beginning to believe that my real name was a jinx, though ultimately I went on to publish a successful novel called *Shockproof Sydney Skate* as a Marijane Meaker. It became a Literary Guild alternate, and a selection of the Book Find Club, and the paperback money was exceptional, enough eventually to buy me the house I live in today, in East Hampton, New York.

"Again, my friend Louise Fitzhugh was nudging me about writing a novel for young adults. Again, she reminded me that my protagonist, Sydney Skate, was a teenager.

"Louise, by that time was interested in writing mystery and suspense. She thought that maybe if we traded typewriters, a young adult book would emerge for me, and my typewriter would produce for her a crime story.

"We laughed about it. I took a look at some of these young adult novels and decided I could never write one. . .*until* I picked up one called *The Pigman* by Paul Zindel."[1]

1968. Meaker began to voluneer as a teacher one day a week as part of an experiment with writers in the schools. "I'd been assigned to some classes at Central Commercial High School, in New York City, on Forty-second Street. These kids worked half a day and went to school half a day. They were wild, unruly, wonderful kids who didn't give a fig for reading, but who responded to writing assignments with great vigor and originality.

"The star of one of my classes was a very fat black girl nicknamed 'Tiny.'

"She wrote really grotesque stories, about things like a woman going swimming and accidentally swallowing strange eggs in the water, and giving birth to red snakes.

"I always 'published' Tiny's stories in the little mimeographed magazine we ran off for the kids. One day her mother appeared, complaining that Tiny's stories were hideous and that I was encouraging her to write 'weird.'

"While we discussed this, I learned that Tiny's mother was an ardent do-gooder who worked with her small church helping drug addicts. Tiny would come home from school to an empty apartment, fix herself something to eat, watch TV, and wait for her mom to come home from her churchwork. Then they'd eat dinner, her mom would go back to her good works, and Tiny would eat and watch TV.

"Tiny was getting to be enormous. She was also glued to the TV all the while she was alone.

"In other words, while Tiny's mom was putting out the fire in the house across the street, her own house was on fire.

"I was thinking a lot about this.

"A book was coming to me.

"I had just read Zindel's books.

"That was the birth of my first book for young adults. Tiny translated into 'Dinky,' and since I knew that this story could be told about any family, black or white, rich or poor, I decided to stick close to home. I'd just moved to Brooklyn Heights, which abounded with lawyers because the courts were right nearby. I set my story there, and made Dinky's mother a middle-class lawyer's wife who was involved in rehabilitating dope addicts.

"The result was *Dinky Hocker Shoots Smack.*

"Since I love pseudonyms, I decided to call myself M. E. Kerr, a play on my last name, Meaker."[1]

1972. *Dinkey Hocker Shoots Smack* was published and Meaker decided she would now write for young adults. "To my astonishment, this 'sideline' made money. The paperback sale was enormous. It was optioned for the movies (many times) and ultimately made into an afternoon special. It is still going strong today.

"I decided to take a second look at this new, to me, young adult category. I was in my forties, by then, and not very interested any longer in murder and crime. The passion I had brought to that interest was waning, as I became more mellow, more liable to see the light in the dark, or the light *and* the dark. As I looked back on my life, things seemed funnier to me than they used to. *I* seemed funnier to me than I used to, and so did a lot of what I'd 'suffered.'

"Miraculously, as I sat down to make notes for possible future stories, things that happened to me long ago came back clear as a bell, and ringing, and making me smile and shake my head as I realized I had stories in me about *me*—no longer disguised as a homicidal maniac, or a twisted criminal bent on a scam, but as the small-town kid I'd been, so typically American and middle class and yes, vulnerable, but not as tragic and complicated as I used to imagine.

"So I had a new identity for myself in middle age: M. E. Kerr.

"I also moved to a new place, East Hampton, on Long Island, New York, which would eventually become Seaview, New York, in many of my novels. My old hometown, Auburn, would appear from time to time as Cayuta, New York."[1]

1975. Published two books under the name M. E. Kerr. *Love Is a Missing Person* came from an idea she got while attending a high school football game. "At halftime I'd watched a pretty blond girl run up to the pom-pom cheerleaders, greeting them as though she hadn't seen them in a long time. She was carrying something in her arms, in a

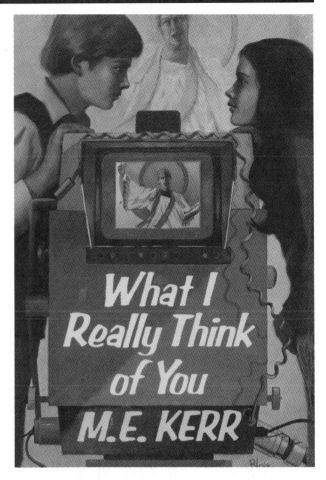

Robert Blake's dust jacket painting for the Harper & Row hardcover edition.

blanket. Behind her, a tall black guy was waiting for her, not joining in the reunion.

"When this blond girl unfolded the blanket, there was a tiny black baby gurgling up at everyone.

"I was standing beside my dentist's wife, and I said something about supposing that was inevitable in a community where there were blacks and whites going to school together: intermarriage.

"She said, 'Ah, but that's not the real story. The real story is the anger black girls here have because white girls date "their men."' She said many of the black boys were sports heroes, and the white girls went out with them, but white boys didn't in turn date black girls.

"This incident, on an ordinary autumn afternoon, was the background for a book called *Love Is a Missing Person*. It was the story of a girl whose sister fell in love with a black boy, and ran off with him at the end of the novel. Not a lot of local teachers and parents were thrilled about this Kerr, but it has elicited many letters from kids familiar with the problem of interracial dating."[1]

A second book was about life in a boarding school, *Is That You Miss Blue?* Meanwhile, *Dinky Hocker Shoots Smack* was banned in Randolph, New York, from the district high school library.

1978. Meaker published *Gentlehands*. She explains some of its inspiration. "I've never married nor had children, and I've lately thought this has been a great asset. If I'd had children, I'm sure I would have been tempted to keep them tied to something in an upstairs room, so no harm would come to them. I think the youngster in me remains vivid because I've never raised any children to compete with her, or compare with her, and I have not had to pace the floor nights worrying where they are or with whom, and what has happened to the family car.

"Again, these experiences come to me through osmosis. When I first moved to East Hampton, a sweet seventeen-year-old kid next door to me was going through his first love affair with a very rich girl who spent summers in our community. His family disapproved of this girl; his dad was a policeman, and Kippy was brought up strictly. He was working as a soda jerk the summer he met this rather sophisticated young lady. He had a new bicycle; she had a new Porsche.

"Kippy would come over to my house, agonizing about what to wear, what fork to pick up on the table when he was invited to her house for lunch. She had a butler. She lived by the ocean. She was a year older than Kippy. She'd gone to high school in European boarding schools.

"That same summer, I was reading a book by Howard Blum called *Wanted! The Search for Nazis in America.*

"That book, and what Kippy was going through, became all mixed together, until finally I sat down to write a novel called *Gentlehands.*

"*Gentlehands* was about a boy in Kippy's situation, who looked up a grandfather the family was estranged from, in order to impress this girl. The erudite, opera-loving grandfather proved to be a Nazi war criminal the Immigration Service was investigating.

"Of any book I've ever written, *Gentlehands* was the easiest. It poured from my typewriter as though a tape was inside with the whole story put down on it."[1]

1981. In this year she published *Little Little,* a book about teen-age dwarfs. Meaker says it was her most difficult to write but her favorite. "...I don't know why it was so difficult, except I couldn't seem to get much humor into it, and what was there often seemed too dark....Another thing was that I was afraid to tell *anyone* I was writing a book for young adults about dwarfs. I was afraid of the reaction, and of being discouraged by it. So I kept it to myself as I started the story over and over again, worked on it up to about fifty pages, then abandoned it. It seemed unworkable after several years of trying.

"One day I decided to write an essay about it for the Long Island section of the *New York Times.* It would be about the one story I wanted to write but couldn't.

"In the middle of this essay, I stopped, and started the book again, and this time finished it.

"Maybe it is my favorite book, not because I think it's better than the rest, but because it was such a struggle. Maybe a parent, who's finally raised a particularly difficult child, feels this same affection and pride when that kid turns out okay."[1]

Meaker's inspiration for the story comes from a hometown experience. "I grew up in a small town in upstate New York, and the golden boy of our town went to Harvard and came back with a wife. They were everybody's idea of the marvelous young couple. And then they had a child who was a midget. This always held me fascinated: watching them cope, watching them change from an almost Scott and Zelda Fitzgerald-type of carefree couple with everything in the world, watching them having to fight for this little girl and find her friends. They joined the Little People of America, and then we had what I described in *Little Little,* an invasion by the little people. They would come every summer, which caused all sorts of problems because the town was trying to sell itself as a town for industry. We already had a prison and a Japanese steel plant, so people who were looking the town over would ride with midgets, prisoners, and Japanese businessmen! They would not think our town was a very typical small American town; they would reject it as a place for industry. Anyway, that story held me; I never forgot it."[3]

1982. Meaker's next work was *What I Really Think of You,* a book about "P.K.'s" or preacher's kids. "Right now I just want to say that my interest in preachers' kids probably started when I roomed with Kay Walters, the first P.K. I ever really knew.

"Preacher's kids figure in *Is That You, Miss Blue?* and are the main characters in *What I Really Think of You.*

"In my book *Little Little,* a young evangelist preacher is featured who is also a dwarf, and the grandfather of the main character is a preacher.

"While I came from a religious background (with one aunt who was a Roman Catholic nun) and attended an Episcopal boarding school, I always seemed to have a quarrel with organized religion.

"I suppose the reason was simply that I always had a quarrel with authority of any kind.

"I remember visiting Kay Walters' family in Sayre, Pennsylvania, one vacation from Stuart Hall, and accouncing to her father that I was an atheist. I tried very hard to persuade Kay to declare herself an atheist while we were there. When I hinted at the idea, Reverend Walters said there was no reason, then, for either of us to go to his church for Sunday services. He took my pronouncements in good spirits, shrugging and smiling, and not giving me the fight I was probably looking for.

"At the clanging of the church bell, Kay decided she really wasn't in my camp, and went along to church, as she always had, with her family—leaving me back at their house, abandoned and lonely in my 'avowed atheism.'

"Religion still fascinates me, whether it's a book by Paul Tillich, a local church service, a seder I'm invited to by Jewish friends, a talk with a Moonie on the street, a Billy Graham appearance, or one of the Sunday-morning TV preachers. I don't yet 'believe'—and some of what I see I love or hate, but I'm rarely indifferent, which leaves me more involved than not."[2]

Kenneth L. Donelson and Alleen Pace Nilsen commented on the controversy raised by the book. "Kerr's *What I Really Think of You* was simultaneously criticized for 'copping out' with a 'spiritual' ending and for 'taking cheap shots at religion.' What some people interpreted as 'cheap shots' were incidents and comments that other readers responded to as 'healthy skepticism' about the connections between religion and money. In the spiritual ending, Opal Ringer, the P. K. (preacher's kid), finds herself speaking in tongues and enjoying a celebrity status when television cameras roll into her father's church to film her. Throughout the rest of the book she was terribly embarrassed at the 'strangeness' of her family. She hated being a 'have-not' living among 'haves,' and she was humiliated when some of the affluent kids from her high school came to her father's shabby little church acting as if they were on a field trip.

"The real power of the book is its portrayal of Opal's ambivalent feelings. One of our graduate students grew up in a family much like Opal's. She has a brother who is now a famous—and as she's quick to add very wealthy—evangelist. She swears by the authenticity of Kerr's presentation of the preacher's family and the girl's feelings, at least in the first nine-tenths of the book. She was less pleased with the ending, but she couldn't honestly tell whether her reaction was due to a literary disappointment in that Kerr failed to make the conclusion ring true or whether she felt uncomfortable simply because Opal's early life closely resembled her own and reading the book gave her such a strong feeling of 'What if?' that she couldn't be objective about it. She wanted Opal's choice to be the same as her own.

"The kind of confusion experienced by a well-read, sophisticated adult must be all the stronger for young people when they come across books that touch their deepest religious feelings. Adults working with young readers need to be extra sensitive to the potential problem because it's easy to blur the line between criticizing the literary skill with which an author presents an experience and criticizing the experience itself...."[5]

1983. Meaker published her teenage autobiography, *Me, Me, Me, Me, Me: Not a Novel.* "...It's sort of to tell kids that there was one bad kid out there! I was really a troublemaker. When I look back now, I pity the boarding school that I went to. I was always thinking of things to do to it and to my parents; I didn't have very good grades; I was just trouble. I originally called the book 'Yesterday Me,' but as I was working on it I kept seeing this T-shirt that I'd seen years ago with Me, Me, Me, Me, Me written on it. So we're calling it *Me-me-me-me-me.*

"...I think the badness was probably a reaction to a lot of things I saw and felt. But I've always been interested in kids who were having a hard time. I didn't seem to have a hard time getting along with other kids—they cheered me on because I did all the awful things, got into all the trouble. But I was aware of other kids that weren't in the *in* group, weren't accepted.

"I have to have faith that kids are the same today as they were when I was a kid, because I have no contact with kids now. I just write for myself when I was that age. And I trust that while the mores are different, kids are the same; they face the same problems in their teens that I faced all those many years ago. Also I try not to use jargon because it goes out too fast. And I try not to build a story around something like a marijuana problem because you never know if that's going to be with us: It has its 'in' years and its 'out' years. When I was a teenager we had beer."[3]

1985. *I Stay Near You* was her next work. "I had always hesitated writing a book for kids set in the forties, when I was growing up. I remembered how I hated reading 'historical' novels, when I was a kid. Still, the years during World War II haunt me, and I am filled with stories about what happened to teenage girls back then. There have been so many, many stories about what went on in the lives of young men...so few about 'us.'

"Finally, I decided to tackle the problem by attempting a novel that would begin in the forties and end in the eighties. I didn't want to write a long three-generational type thing, so I came up with a new approach, for me. I wrote three short stories about the same characters: one set in the forties, told from the first person; one set in the sixties, told from the third person; the last, a letter in the second person, written by a boy to his dad, set in the eighties.

"The three stories, read together, are a novel.

"I called this *I STAY NEAR YOU*—one story in three."[1]

1986. In *Night Kites*, Meaker explores a family's discovery that their eldest son is gay and has AIDS. Audrey B. Eaglen, in the *New York Times Book Review* said of the novel: "In less sure hands, this moving and understated examination of the angst of first love and first sex, of the effects of a catastrophic illness on one family, especially an illness like AIDS with its undercurrents of irresponsibility on the part of its victims, could have been just another problem novel. M. E. Kerr, the author of *Dinky Hocker Shoots Smack!* however, has managed to transcend that young adult genre, and has, with sensitivity and delicacy, described an issue that may face many more families if predictions about AIDS come true. This is a fine story, beautifully told, with characters that ring true. Mrs. Kerr has simply never been better in her long and lauded career; she too is a 'night kite,' unafraid to soar into the darkness of the human predicament."[6]

And *Horn Book* reviewed it equally favorably: "...Like Robert Cormier and Richard Peck, M. E. Kerr is one of the few young adult writers who can take a subject that affects teenagers' lives, can say something important to young readers about it, and can craft what is first and foremost a good story, without preaching and without histrionics. Consequently, *Night Kites* is an important part of the Kerr canon and an important contribution to the literature for young adults."[7]

1987. Meaker's most recent M. E. Kerr offering is *Fell*, described by *Publishers Weekly* as a: "...surprise-filled love story/mystery. After being stood up for the senior prom by Keats, his rich and snobby girlfriend, Fell, literally runs into her next-door neighbor, Woodrow Pingree, who offers to pay him $10,000 to attend exclusive Gardner prep school—as his own son, Woodrow Pingree Jr., known as 'Ping'—and will add another $10,000 if Fell gets into Gardner's elite fraternity, the Sevens. During the summer, Fell falls heavily for Delia Tremble, who works as an *au pair* for acquaintances of the Pingrees. In the guise of Ping, Fell goes off to Gardner, while Ping goes to school in Switzerland as Fell. Fell makes it into the Sevens and enjoys his new identity and life, until his cover is blown. The totally unexpected events that follow will have readers looking forward to further books in this new series. Ages 12-up."[8]

Meaker found that, since moving to Long Island, she missed other writers, so she established The Ashawagh Hall Writers Workshop. A nonprofit group, its member fees go to a scholarship fund for disadvantaged students. "We meet once a week for two hours, fall and spring sessions running for twelve weeks at a time. Our group age ranges from the early twenties to the seventies, twenty members in all, everyone from the minister at the Amaganset Presbyterian Church, to the bartender from a hotel in Sag Harbor, to a famous artist's wife, a beautiful young girl who only writes horror stories, and local teachers, a real estate salesperson, a retired editor, etcetera.

"Probably none of us would have ever met each other socially, but all of us are focused on each other's work, as well as what's current, and what's being published in the various genres from suspense to literary. We have our own literary agency, though no one has to pay a ten or fifteen percent fee...and each semester we try to take in one or two new members."[1]

Meaker has few interests that aren't related to writing. "I read like a fat person eats. I read everything from magazines like *Time, Rolling Stone, Interview, New York Magazine, Redbook, Fortune, Business Week, Vanity Fair, Woman's Day,* and *Ms.* to the best-sellers—Anne Tyler (a particular favorite), Raymond Carver, Elmore Leonard, Eudora Welty, Robert Cormier, Alice Munro, Bobbie Ann Mason, Alice Walker, Joyce Carol Oates, Barbara Pym—on and on and on. And I reread wonderful Carson McCullers. I love poetry, too—Yeats and Auden and Kastner and Rilke and Wakoski and Leo Connellan.

"I watch a good deal of television, talk shows and news programs like Ted Koppel's. I'm a movie fan. . .I guess I'm just a media freak.

"Long ago, despite my WASP training, I learned that motion isn't work, that sitting at the typewriter when you have no clear idea of what you want to write, is wasted time. When I'm 'stuck' between novels, I mostly read, walk by the ocean, and complain that I can't work to other writers who complain back that they are finding what they're working on too hard, impossible, or not worth it."[1]

"I love to cook. And when you live out in the country it's especially fun. . . .Even when I lived in New York I enjoyed cooking. I come from a food family. . . .and we talked food a good deal of the time and tasted food and loved food. It's a wonder we weren't all fat, but none of us were."[3]

She also likes to keep up with teenagers' interests: "One great advantage in writing for kids is keeping up with the times. I've developed a very enthusiastic interest in today's music. I listen faithfully to the top ten, and I follow all the groups from pop to rock to heavy metal. I'm an MTV watcher, mesmerized by all the groups from Police, Duran Duran, Wham!, Van Halen, and Aztec Camera, to Twisted Sister, Kiss, and Motley Crue. Some of the videos I love, and some I really hate, but all of them teach me about kids today. It's a whole new world for me, one I probably wouldn't have investigated if I wasn't a Y.A. writer."[1]

Although she likes to watch television herself, Meaker worries about her own works appearing on it. "I really hate everything that's on television, and I hate the way it's controlled. They did *Dinky Hocker Shoots Smack!* as a television production, and they've done a couple of pilots. But I have no interest in screen or television. It's too collaborative and I'm not a good collaborator."[3]

"I *hope* I can woo young adults away from the boob tube and Pac Man not just with entertaining stories, but also with subject matter which will provoke concern and a questioning about this complicated and often unfair world we live in. I would like my readers to laugh, but also to think; to

Jacket illustration by Fred Marcellino from Harper & Row's hardcover edition.

be introspective, but also to reach out. . .and I hope I can give them characters and situations which will inspire these reactions. Now that the young adult field seems to have grown up, I hope it will grow out and touch, and that I'll be contributing."[5]

Her first love is still writing: "I love writing, and I particularly love writing for young adults. I know other young adult writers who claim that their books are just slotted into that category, and claim there's no difference between an adult novel and a young adult one. . . .I beg to disagree. When I write for young adults I know they're still wrestling with very important problems like winning and losing, not feeling accepted or accepting, prejudice, love—all the things adults ultimately get hardened to, and forgetful of. I know my audience hasn't yet made up their minds about everything, that they're still vulnerable and open to suggestion and able to change their minds. . . .Give me that kind of an audience any day!"[1]

Footnote Sources:

[1] "M. E. Kerr," *Something about the Author, Autobiography Series*, Gale, 1986.
[2] M. E. Kerr, *Me, Me, Me, Me, Me: Not a Novel*, Harper, 1983.
[3] "Marijane Meaker," *Contemporary Authors*, Volume 107, Gale, 1983.

[4] M. J. Meaker, *Sudden Endings*, Doubleday, 1964.

[5] Kenneth L. Donelson and Alleen Pace Nilsen, *Literature for Today's Young Adults*, second edition, Scott, Foresman, 1985.

[6] Audrey B. Eaglen, *New York Times Book Review*, April 13, 1986.

[7] *Horn Book*, September-October, 1986.

[8] *Publishers Weekly*, June 26, 1987.

■ For More Information See

Horn Book, February, 1973 (p. 56), August, 1975 (p. 365), June, 1977 (p. 288).

Times Literary Supplement, November 23, 1973, September 19, 1975, December 1, 1978.

Washington Post Book World, May 19, 1974, July 11, 1982.

English Journal, December, 1975, February, 1986 (p. 26).

School Library Journal, January, 1977 (p. 40), September, 1986 (p. 46), November, 1986 (p. 30).

Jerry Tallmer, "An Old Question for Young Adults," *New York Post*, July 8, 1978.

Lion and the Unicorn, fall, 1978 (p. 37).

Doris de Montreville and Elizabeth D. Crawford, *Fourth Book of Junior Authors and Illustrators*, H. W. Wilson, 1978.

D. L. Kirkpatrick, editor, *Twentieth-Century Children's Writers*, St. Martin's, 1978.

Kenneth L. Donelson and Alleen Pace Nilsen, *Literature for Today's Young Adults*, Scott, Foresman, 1980.

Contemporary Literary Criticism, Volume 12, Gale, 1980.

Suzanne Freeman, "Growing Up in a Small World," *Washington Post Book World*, May 10, 1981 (p. 15).

David Rees, *Painted Desert, Green Shade: Essays on Contemporary Writers of Fiction for Children and Young Adults*, Horn Book, 1984 (p. 17).

Kathy Piehl, "The Business of Religion in M. E. Kerr's Novels, *Voice of Youth Advocates*, February, 1985 (p. 307).

Alleen Pace Nilsen, *Presenting M. E. Kerr*, Twayne, 1986.

Collections:

Kerlan Collection at the University of Minnesota.

Norma Klein

of the Year, 1978; O. Henry Award, 1983, for short story "The Wrong Man."

B orn May 13, 1938, in New York, N.Y.; daughter of Emanuel (a psychoanalyst) and Sadie (Frankel) Klein; married Erwin Fleissner (a biochemist), July 27, 1963; children: Jennifer Luise, Katherine Nicole. *Education:* Attended Cornell University, 1956-57; Barnard College, B.A. (cum laude), 1960; Columbia University, M.A., 1963. *Politics:* Democrat. *Home:* 27 West 96th St., New York, N.Y. 10025. *Agent:* Elaine Markson, 44 Greenwich Ave., New York, N.Y. 10011.

■ Career

Author of novels, short stories, and children's fiction. *Member:* Phi Beta Kappa.

■ Awards, Honors

Girls Can Be Anything was selected one of Child Study Association of America's Children's Books of the Year, 1973; *Media & Methods* Maxi Award for Paperback, 1975, and selected one of New York Public Library's Books for the Teen Age, 1980, both for *Sunshine; Love Is One of the Choices* was selected one of *School Library Journal*'s Best Books

■ Writings

Novels, Except As Indicated:

Mom, the Wolf Man and Me, Pantheon, 1972.
Love and Other Euphemisms (novella and five short stories), Putnam, 1972.
Give Me One Good Reason, Putnam, 1973.
It's Not What You Expect, Pantheon, 1973.
Confessions of an Only Child (illustrated by Richard Cuffari), Pantheon, 1974.
Taking Sides, Pantheon, 1974.
Coming to Life, Simon & Schuster, 1974.
What It's All About, Dial Press, 1975.
Hiding, Four Winds Press, 1976.
Girls Turn Wives, Simon & Schuster, 1976.
It's Okay If You Don't Love Me, Dial, 1977.
Love Is One of the Choices, Dial, 1978.
Tomboy (sequel to *Confessions of an Only Child*), Four Winds Press, 1978.
Breaking Up, Pantheon, 1980.
A Honey of a Chimp, Pantheon, 1980.
Robbie and the Leap Year Blues, Dial, 1981.
Domestic Arrangements, M. Evans, 1981.
Wives and Other Women, St. Martin's, 1982.
The Queen of the What Ifs, Fawcett, 1982.
Beginner's Love, Dial, 1982.
Baryshnikov's Nutcracker (adaptation of the *Nutcracker* Ballet; photographs by Ken Regan, Christopher Little, and Martha Swope), Putnam, 1983.
Bizou, Viking, 1983.

Sextet in A Minor (novella and short stories), St. Martin's, 1983.
The Swap, St. Martin's, 1983.
Lovers, Viking, 1984.
Snapshots, Dial, 1984.
Angel Face, Viking, 1984.
The Cheerleader, Knopf, 1985.
Family Secrets, Dial, 1985.
Give and Take, Viking, 1985.
Going Backwards, Scholastic, 1986.
Older Men, Dial, 1987.
My Life as a Body, Knopf, 1987.
American Dreams, Dutton, 1987.
Now That I Know, Bantam, 1988.
No More Saturday Nights, Knopf, 1988.
That's My Baby, Viking, 1988.
The World As It Is, Dutton, 1989.

Novelizations:

Sunshine: A Novel (based on a television special written by Carol Sobieski), Holt, 1974.
The Sunshine Years (based on television series), Dell, 1975.
Sunshine Christmas (based on a screenplay by C. Sobieski), Futura, 1977.
French Postcards (based on screenplay of the same title), Fawcett, 1979.

Juvenile:

Girls Can Be Anything (Junior Literary Guild selection; illustrated by Roy Doty), Dutton, 1973.
If I Had It My Way (illustrated by Ray Cruz), Pantheon, 1974.
Dinosaur's Housewarming Party (Junior Literary Guild selection; illustrated by James Marshall), Crown, 1974.
Naomi in the Middle (illustrated by Leigh Grant), Dial, 1974.
A Train for Jane (illustrated by Miriam Schottland), Feminist Press, 1974.
Red Sky, Blue Trees, (illustrated by Pat Grant Porter), Pantheon, 1975.
Visiting Pamela (illustrated by Kay Chorao), Dial, 1979.

Work has been anthologized in *Prize Stories: The O. Henry Awards*, 1963, and 1968, and *The Best American Short Stories of 1969*, 1969. Contributor of about sixty short stories to magazines, including *Sewanee Review, Mademoiselle, Cosmopolitan, Prairie Schooner*, and *Denver Quarterly*.

■ Adaptations

"Mom, the Wolf Man and Me" (record or cassette), Caedmon, 1977, (film) Time-Life Productions, 1979.
"Confessions of an Only Child" (cassette), Caedmon, 1977.

■ Work In Progress

Give Me a Yes (tentative title), a novel about a sixteen-year-old girl who is very close to her grandmother.

■ Sidelights

"I was born on May 13, 1938, in New York City and grew up on 88th Street between Park and Madison Avenue. By a strange coincidence, when my husband and I found our present apartment in 27 West 96th Street, my mother told me that it was the same building in which I had lived between the time I was born and when I was three when we moved to 88th. I suppose if I was more spiritually inclined, I would say I must have been drawn to that building for that reason. I loved the city as a child and therefore thought of it later as a wonderful place in which to raise children. But when I use the city as a background for my novels, I try to show the side of it I knew, not the extremes of wealth and poverty which have grown ever more acute in the heartless Reagan era, but simply middle class families, living in slightly shabby, bookish, rent-controlled apartments.

"I was very much influenced by the fact that both of the schools I attended, Dalton from age three to thirteen, Elizabeth Irwin for high school, were progressive schools, run in less extreme form somewhat along the lines of the famous English school, Summerhill. We called teachers by their first names, classes were small, the emphasis was on writing papers, not on cramming for exams. Even when you were very young, independent study was emphasized. At Dalton, for instance, you were given all the work assignments for a month ahead and could do them at your own pace. Unlike the English classes my daughters had, ours offered a chance to do a lot of creative writing as well as literary essays. I regret now that, when I applied to college, I decided I wanted a complete change and attended very rigid, conventional schools, (at least by contrast to Dalton and E.I.). I was at Cornell for my freshman year (1956-1957), and finished up at Barnard (1957-1960), but was miserable at both places and hated the style of education both offered which was filled with absurd do's and don'ts. You couldn't, for instance, take studio art at all, just art history. You could only study literature if you knew the language in which it was originally written. I wish now that I had gone to Antioch, as my younger daughter has, or to a college that emphasized the arts, like Bennington or Sarah Lawrence.

"Elizabeth Irwin was, in an educational sense, more conservative than Dalton and less imaginative. There were grades and exams, though the emphasis was still on a relaxed atmosphere in which you studied because you were inspired to, not because you were forced. The parents of most of the students at E.I. were like my own, extremely liberal left wing Jews. If you had parents who had voted for Adlai Stevenson, you were considered weirdly conservative; Eisenhower was beyond the pale. I thought then that the world was like the milieu in which I grew up, very understanding of differences between people, accepting of homosexuality or alternate life styles. When I began writing about this world, far from meaning to shock, I was simply describing what to me was 'real life.' I now realize that to many Americans this is shocking, though the kids who like my books often find it fascinating as well. Growing up in small, repressive communities, they look to my books, I think, as a glimpse of a wider, more rational, freer world which they hope to reach in adulthood.

"Few of the kids in my high school class dated. We were the class of 1956, conformity and repression were in vogue. Girls wore very full skirts with horsehair crinolines underneath. This was still an era of garter belts and padded bras. Since we had grown up in the city, virtually no one knew how to drive. Thus the whole car culture of America, so celebrated in movies like 'American Graffiti' was totally unknown to us; we took subways or buses.

"In addition, like most of my friends, I was completely unaware of popular music except for folk music like the ballads sung by Pete Seeger or social protest songs such as those sung by Paul Robeson, the famous black singer of that era. I assumed teenagers across America were singing 'I Ain't Gonna Study War No More,' or 'We Are the Peat Bog Soldiers.' In addition I listened to the same classical music I love today, went to chamber music concerts and the opera with my parents (my favorite opera then, as now, was 'The Marriage of Figaro,' not only for its exquisite music, but because it is one of the few operas whose plot resembles that of a good realistic novel).

"My daughters, partly through their total immersion in rock music, are much more in touch with the contemporary culture of their time than I was of mine.

"Being the daughter of a Freudian psychoanalyst had a profound influence on me. Just as I inherited my parents' liberal political beliefs and their love of books and music, so I was raised in a home where Freud had replaced the God in whom my father had decided early on he didn't believe. My brother, Victor (who is sixteen months younger than I am), and I went to psychoanalysts even as children for problems which I would now consider simply a normal part of growing up: he wet his bed, I was afraid of the dark. We both voluntarily underwent psychoanalysis as adults. After my father died, in 1977 when I was forty, I began to question and ultimately reject much of psychoanalytic theory and practice. I believe Freud was an inspired thinker who developed some fascinating and important theories about human life such as the importance of early childhood sexuality, but I don't feel, from the evidence I've seen, that psychoanalysis, or 'talking' therapy, really helps people very much with their emotional problems, especially the kind of analysis my husband and I endured in which the patient rambles interminably on for close to a decade (or longer) and the therapist occasionally clears his throat and says, 'We'll continue next time.'

"Though I have rejected many of my father's beliefs, I am grateful to him for the immense support he gave me in my intellectual endeavors. Now I see that encouragement as deriving simply from the fact that he loved me and thought whatever I did—I loved painting and writing from the time I was very young—was wonderful. The effect this had on me was to make me feel that ultimately I would find people in the outside world who would be like my father, who would love my work. Like most self-created hypotheses, this has proved true, or to put it another way, I have an extraordinary amount of persistence in the face of rejection, based in part on the underlying thought that somehwere, out there is that person, if only I can just hang in there long enough. My mother, a creative and talented person, did not come into her own until after my father's death. In the past decade she blossomed and received her B.A. from Baruch College at the age of seventy-seven. She is still extremely active, writes, has friends of all ages, and travels (she went to China a few years ago).

"I think my daughters and their contemporaries are not only growing up in a world more hospitable to women, they also often have mothers who have had active professional lives throughout their childhood. Thus, they grow up with a sense that they, too, can achieve, though they often choose different fields than the ones in which their mothers excelled. It's interesting to me that though both my daughters are wonderful writers, thus far, they write mainly poetry or literary criticism, the two areas of writing I haven't explored.

"Since most of the women writers I admired while I was growing up, such as Jane Austen and Virginia Woolf, were either unmarried, or married and childless, I wasn't sure when I got married at the age of twenty-five that I wanted to have children. I felt then that if I had to choose between writing and children, I would choose writing. But as my marriage continued, like so many people who are happy in their marital choice, I gradually felt I *did* want children. By the time my daughters were born (Jen arrived when I was almost twenty-nine, Katie three and a half years later), this desire had grown to the point that I greeted their arrival with

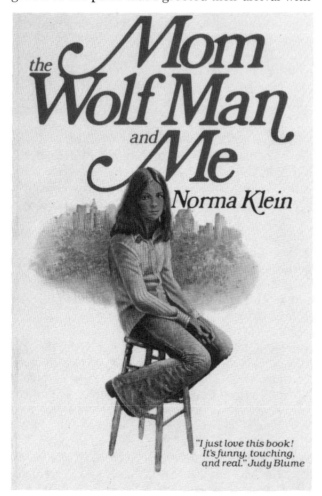

"I just love this book! It's funny, touching, and real." Judy Blume

Cover for the paperback edition of Klein's first novel.

extreme delight, a delight which has only deepened over the years. Although I still love writing as much as ever, I feel being a parent has been an enormous joy to me.

"Until I entered college, painting was as important to me as writing. I've read nursery school reports which state that when I was three or four, I would immediately, upon coming to school, march over to the table where the poster paints and paper were kept and spend the morning happily immersed in an imaginary world, scarcely paying any attention to what was going on around me. That sensation, of being able to lose oneself in an imaginary world of art or writing, has remained central to my identity.

"There were two main reasons I chose writing rather than art as a profession. One was that Barnard, although it offered creative writing courses, did not 'believe' in studio art. I took several writing classes with writers such as George P. Elliott and Robert Pack (who now runs Breadloaf). Both were very encouraging to me. George, in particular, suggested I send my work out to literary magazines which I began doing when I was still a teenager. As fate would have it, the first story I sent out (I was nineteen), 'Ceremony of Innocence,' was accepted by a literary magazine, *The Grecourt Review*. I assumed from that experience that being accepted would be a matter of course. It wasn't. Some of my short stories were rejected as many as forty-five times and even today, as a much published writer, my work is still often rejected. I expect this will always be the case but, if acceptances are mixed in, it's a tolerable combination.

"I also found the process of submitting my work as a writer easier than what I had heard artists had to undergo. A writer can just slip his stories or novel into a book bag, send it out and suffer rejections privately; no one need know of them. An artist has to stand around while bored gallery owners browse through slides of their work. The thought of that terrified me. To this day I hate being in a room when someone is reading something I've written.

"Because my parents were not happy together, I didn't really believe in the possibility that two adult human beings could live together contentedly. Perhaps this is why some friends have commented that the short stories I wrote in my twenties are more bleak in tone than my novels. I feel marriage (I've now, as of 1988, been married twenty-five years), has softened and mellowed my feeling about life. Although I am an ardent feminist and deplore the macho ethic which dominates our society, I take pleasure in the fact that individual

From the television movie "Mom, the Wolf Man and Me," starring Patty Duke Astin, David Birney and Danielle Brisebois. Copyright © 1979 by Time-Life Productions.

men, like my husband, can be exceptions to this rule. I believe my marriage was helped by the fact that my mother-in-law, though born at the turn of the century, got her Ph.D and taught at the college level throughout her long and active life. Thus, my husband grew up with an example before him of a woman who was able to maintain loving and warm relationships with a husband and children while fulfilling herself intellectually. He accepted this as a given and I have never had to experience a day without writing, unless I felt ready for a break between books.

"Although my books are frequently perceived as wildly daring by the children's book establishment, I feel I've led an almost tediously conventional life, which happens to have suited me. I've enjoyed having children, look forward eagerly to having grandchildren, and hope to be married to the same man for the rest of my life. Throughout their lives, I lived only five minutes away from my parents and I would love, though I know I can't count on, being that accessible to my daughters when they have families of their own. My brother, who married late and now has a four-year-old daughter, also lives

near by. Family ties have always been crucial for me, and this may explain why they play such an important role in my books.

"From the age of nineteen, when my first short story was accepted, until the birth of my daughter Jen in 1967, I devoted full time (except for the years from 1960-1963 when I was getting an M.A. in Slavic languages from Columbia), to writing short stories, several anthologized in *Prize Stories*, the *O. Henry Awards* and *The Best American Short Stories.* I had only limited success with the 'big' magazines: a few in *Mademoiselle* and *Cosmopolitan.* My list of rejections from the *New Yorker* (I've saved all of them), is equal to almost any living writer, I imagine.

"As I began reading picture books to my daughter, the idea entered my head that I might try writing and illustrating my own picture books. None of these manuscripts (*Girls Can Be Anything, Dinosaur's Housewarming Party*) were accepted until after the success of my first novel for 'middle-aged' (eight- to twelve-year-old) children, *Mom, the Wolf Man and Me.* Because the heroine, Brett, has an unmarried mother, *Mom* was forced into the young

FAMILY SECRETS

Norma Klein

Jacket painting by Ed Martinez for Klein's novel of teenage love and friendship.

adult category where I strongly feel it does not belong. I wrote *Mom, the Wolf Man and Me* simply because a children's book agent to whom I submitted my picture book manuscripts felt there was more of a demand for books for middle age readers. My only preparation was to read a few novels which had been published in the 60s, after the era in which I had been a child. Although some advances had been made, it was clear to me then (as, alas, it still is), that the level of writing in many of these books was inferior. 'Hey, I can do as well as that,' was my first, perhaps egotistical thought. I think, in fact, that I have.

"Like many writers who have an unexpected sudden success with a first book, I have now been able to analyze in retrospect what led to that success. I was lucky, I think, as were many of my contemporaries in the field like Judy Blume or Bob Cormier, in breaking in at a time when, due to the delayed influence of the 60s, openness and boldness were actually encouraged. Possibly a decade earlier, *Mom, the Wolf Man and Me* and certainly many of my later YA novels, would never

have been published, or would have been published for adults. Censorship, which has become rife in the era of Reagan, was virtually unknown. I sailed forth, naively and happily, into a world I thought would greet my books for kids only with delight, certainly not with condemnation or outrage.

"Now, at the age of fifty, having been published as a children's book writer for sixteen years, I am less naive, sadder, wiser, but still undaunted. I want to write excellent, literary novels for teenagers. That, really, is my only goal. I loathe books that try to 'teach' or end with a moral lesson. My feeling is if you want to preach, become a preacher. Books should entertain, move, delight, not hammer the reader over the head. I still feel there are not enough fine, realistic novels for kids of any ages, and I now see that the few there are will always, to some extent, be under attack for doing precisely what they set out to do, describing the world as it is.

"Comparisons have been made and probably will continue to be made between my books for kids and Judy Blume's. Judy is a friend so it's almost as hard for me to be objective about her work as it is for me to be objective about mine, but I would say that, though both of us see similarities—humor, frankness, a colloquial narrative style—the differences are just as great. Basically Judy's forte, the area she has honed in on, is junior high, age ten to fourteen, where anxieties focus on getting a first bra, masturbating, being kissed at a spin the bottle party. I feel my own YA novels are much more akin to Salinger's *Catcher in the Rye*. They are about the last two years of high school or, increasingly, college and the anxieties are about what profession one will enter, how to evaluate one's parents as one approaches adulthood, what direction one's burgeoning sexuality will take. I don't think either set of anxieties is more important, they're just different.

"I also feel the world in which Judy's characters live is unlike the world of my heroes and heroines. Judy's characters usually grow up in the suburbs where a great effort is made to conform and fit in, to do what everyone else is doing when they are doing it. My heroes and heroines tend to grow up as I did, in Manhattan, in a world which cherishes and encourages individuality. My characters are usually intellectual, thoughtful, responsible and, occasionally, sexually active.

"To have sexual activity take place in a young adult novel is still to arouse total horror in the eyes of most children's book librarians and book reviewers. I think what bothers them most about my books is that there is no crime and punishment. That is, I don't see making love as a crime which must be punished by the book's end, either by a disastrous abortion which ages the heroine by several decades, or by an unwanted and miserable teenage marriage. I'm also, which perplexes and disturbs some, not writing about promiscuous kids or kids who are too careless or uninformed to use birth control. Somehow it's worse in the eyes of certain people in the field, to portray teenagers who are making love because, not only are they in love, but perhaps they are actually in tune with their sexual feelings and accept them joyfully.

"The advent of AIDS has, I am disturbed to notice, been greeted with barely concealed glee by a sizeable portion of the children's book world. Their thinking appears to be: great, now teenagers won't engage in sexual activity or think a sexual thought until the day they get married! It's a massive back swing to those ghastly Rosamund du Jardin romance novels of the 50s. The new version is 'Sweet Valley High' where the heroines are all white, well to do, sexy-looking and adored by a handsome boy who has no intent other than an occasional good night kiss. The dishonesty and hypocrisy of these books struck me even thirty years ago. To see it return is very sad.

"Luckily for me not all kids want to 'escape' into a fantasy never never world. Some actually love, as I did, books about real life, books which don't pull punches, which don't end happily but ambiguously, where heroes and heroines are allowed to be physically imperfect, where parents are sometimes cruel and erratic. When I reread my past books, I feel critical only of the extent to which I tried, usually unsuccessfully, to conform to what I was told were the 'rules' of the children's book world. In my more recent books like *My Life as a Body* or *Going Backwards* I've tried to be more muted, to create a tone of greyness, not black or white.

"Because my books are funny, some of my editors have found the element of tragedy at odds with the rest of the book, as, for example, the suicide of Jason's mother at the end of *Angel Face*. I don't see this as a discrepancy. I find life funny, I laugh a lot, but I also am increasingly aware of its darker sides, the way people so often suffer, or bring suffering upon themselves. In my early years as a children's book writer, I gave way to editors' demands and thus to some extent emasculated my books. Now I resist and, although my editor for *Angel Face* pressured me for a removal of the mother's suicide,

I refused. My primary aim is to write the kinds of books I would have liked to read when I was in my teens, not the ones editors feel the 'average' (what an absurd term!) teenager wants to read.

"Unlike some of my writer friends, I never submit a partial manuscript or describe my ideas to my editors before I write the book. I prefer to have the months of writing a totally private time where I can focus my energies only on the book itself, not on the marketing problems with which editors have to concern themselves. One reason I've always had several different publishers for my YA novels is I don't want anyone to publish me half heartedly. If a particular editor doesn't like a particular book, there are no hard feelings. I simply publish it elsewhere, but feel free to return to the first editor on the next book. I've always been able to find editors who support me in what I'm trying to say. Jean Feiwel, Beverly Horowitz and Frances Foster

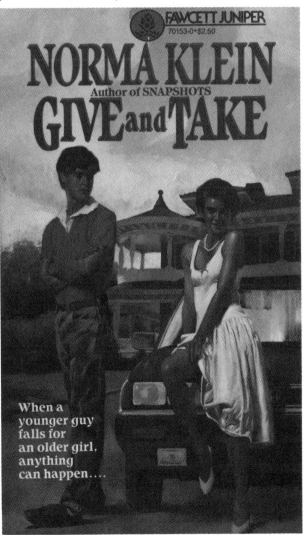

Cover for the 1985 paperback edition.

are among those I now value highly; Phyllis Fogelman, Amy Ehrlich and Fabio Coen gave me a start when I was beginning my career.

"There are a lot of absurd 'rules' that are handed to writers of YA novels: don't make the book longer than 200 pages, always have a single narrator, usually first person, don't allow the adult characters to play a prominent part, just focus on teenage concerns, but downplay or avoid description of sexual feelings or actions. Phooey! I now include as many main characters as I want, make the book as long as it needs to be, allow the adult characters to be central, and include sexual thoughts and feelings, as well as actions, if I feel they are central to the book's purpose. Many of these rules are carryovers from an earlier time. For instance, in the beginning of this century, middle class kids often were raised mainly by servants and had little contact with, or knowledge of their parents as people. Hence the many English novels like *Mary Poppins* or those of E. Nesbit in which the nurse is a prominent character and is often an emotional substitute for the parent. To know one's parents intimately, as many kids do now, is not always to admire and respect them wholeheartedly. Therefore, the parents in my books are not, nor are they intended to be 'role models'; they are fallible, complex human beings, engaged in as difficult a struggle to live a meaningful life as are the teenage characters.

"I think I write well about sex, but my sex scenes are, as often as not, humorous and awkward. I don't incline toward the lyrical or the pornographic, but I try to show what sex is like between two often inexperienced, nervous teenagers. I have no fear that if I portray sex as an occasionally enjoyable activity, my readers, be they fourteen, twelve or eight will instantly rush out and 'do it,' thereby neglecting their piano lessons or hockey practice. Many of my readers are the way I was at their age, intellectually far ahead of their social development. These are the teenagers who can recite chapter and verse from *Lady Chatterly's*, but are still waiting for someone to ask them out.

"The term 'problem novel' came into existence because too many YA novels raised important and complex issues only to 'answer' them very superficially. I don't think I ever did that, though I was always prodded toward the conventional happy ending editors believe kids prefer. If I were to write some of these novels now, I would end them differently. Caroline in *Love Is One of the Choices* (a ghastly title; I will never again use love in a title), falls in love with and marries her high school

science teacher and, at the end of the book, is expecting her first child. I meant to imply an unhappy future for Caroline in which she would become increasingly dissatisfied with her husband and ultimately divorce him. I wanted to end the book just as she is beginning to see that, in some sense, she has dug her own grave. But I left this so vague that many readers have written saying, 'What are you implying at the end?' This was not literary ambiguity, but failure of nerve.

"Similarly in *Breaking Up*, one of the few novels I've ever written from the point of view of a popular, pretty girl (since I know little of what it's like to be such a girl, I feel this is one of my less successful books), the heroine's father attempts to get sole custody of her after he learns his wife is engaged in an ongoing lesbian relationship. If I were to write the book now, I might well have the father succeed in his attempt and leave the reader a sense of horror at an action directly opposed to the heroine's own happiness.

"Recently I completed a novel in which there are flash forwards which tell what will happen, not only to the heroine, but to the boy she eventually marries and to all her best friends twenty-five years hence. 'My God,' said a friend, 'you've created a new unmarketable genre, a middleage YA.' The paperback editor to whom it was submitted asked via my agent, 'But will the average thirteen-year-old girl be interested in these melancholy projections into the future?' I realized, by my indifference to that question, that I have never written for any audience except, possibly, myself at a given age or my daughters. I am writing about kids who are intellectually knowledgeable and sophisticated, but that doesn't mean that the kids who read my books are. I think all of us read partly to find out about people unlike ourselves. That's how we stretch our horizons, which is one of the important functions of reading. I've never conceived of my audience as 'average' because I don't think there is such a thing as an 'average' teenager any more than there is an 'average' adult. If one aims one's books at an average, one ends up with a stereotype.

"I have definitely been influenced by the fact that my daughters, who are now both in college, find the style and subject matter of most YA's, including some of mine, too young, simplistic, or lacking in complexity. I am trying, as it were, to capture their attention or the attention of young people like themselves who are also reading adult fiction, but would delight, as kids of my generation did, in books like *Catcher in the Rye*, which focus on teenage characters. This is an audience (sixteen to twenty-two year olds) which, thus far, publishers refuse to acknowledge. Kids are supposed to leap from S. E. Hinton to Joan Didion in one fell swoop.

"I also feel that many young people read 'ahead,' that good readers of eight or nine are often reading adult fiction and finding it fascinating, as I did. We all grow up at different rates, one reason why denying books to kids on the grounds that they are 'too young' to know about certain subjects is ridiculous. Just as kids mature at different ages sexually, some having love affairs at fourteen, others waiting until they are in their twenties, so people read, not according to a rigid set of guidelines, but according to their own personal tastes and preferences. Teenage readers, like adult readers, can have many different tastes simultaneously. Think only of the vast number of English professors who love murder mysteries, or the readers of literary fiction who are occasionally engrossed by best sellers. We need gourmet cuisine as much as we also like to indulge in a yen for junk food. A book reviewer once called me 'the thinking child's Judy Blume.' I would like to think that my books are not restricted to future intellectuals. I believe that teenage girls who are simultaneously reading romances may sometimes want a breath of real life so their teeth won't rot with too much sugar. Let's encourage diversity and not try to shove square pegs into round holes.

"In 1983 I published a novel, *Beginner's Love*, that represented a new departure for me in that the main character, Joel, was a teenage boy. Writers of YA fiction are often encouraged to write about girls on the grounds that girls are more likely to read fiction than boys. I'm sure there is some truth to this, just as women read more fiction than men, but I wanted to explore teenage life from a male point of view not only to interest male readers whose literary tastes might be more sophisticated than 'Bang, bang, you're dead,' but to reveal to young women some insights into the other sex. I've always had male friends, usually writers or editors, read these books carefully to make sure the male point of view seemed authentic or to point out any place where it wasn't.

"I suppose you could say that the teenage boys who people my novels incline toward being what our society perjoratively calls wimps. I myself love wimps since to me it is a term meaning a man who is sensitive, thoughtful, and rebellious against the macho posturing that is put forward as a male ideal in our society from birth onward. This doesn't mean that my male protagonists never hurt their girl friends or feel confused by sexual feelings, but,

like my heroines, they are thinking human beings, trying to make sense of life as it unfolds before them. My most recent novel told from a male point of view is *No More Saturday Nights* in which eighteen-year-old Tim Weber takes his pregnant girl friend to court when he learns she is going to sell their baby for adoption and sues for sole custody which he gains, the result being that he sets off for Columbia on a scholarship with a six-week-old infant. A woman friend to whom I showed the book protested loudly: no teenage boy would ever, *ever* do such a foolish thing. The man to whom I showed it said, simply, 'I would have, at that age.' My mother, right after reading the book, saw a teenage boy walking down the street with a baby in a back pack, just like the cover of my book. Sometimes, life imitates art which imitates life, and so on.

"Most of my teenage characters are not only urban, but Jewish, and have a wry, Woody Allenish sensibility based on a mocking inner commentary on the world and oneself. Charles Goldberg in *Going Backwards* is a good example of this. Everyone I knew while I was growing up was Jewish and I thought this stance toward the world was universal. From twenty-five years of being married to a non-Jew who grew up in a small town in upstate New York, I have come to realize it isn't. We have gone back to my husband's home town (population 300) every summer and I feel now that I know it as well, if in a different way, than I know New York City. I feel able, through this knowledge, to write about boys like Tim in *No More Saturday Nights* or Spencer in *Give and Take* who are slightly more earnest, naive and straightforard than my urban Jewish heroes. The basics of growing up are the same, no matter what the size of the population or the ethnic group from which one derives, but I enjoy switching settings occasionally and attempting to see life through the eyes of young protagonists who are different than I was or am.

"Because I idealized my father when I was growing up, I tended to present in my early novels an idealized portrait of fathers or grandfathers such as the grandfather in *Mom, the Wolf Man and Me,* or the father in *Confessions of an Only Child*, and *Tomboy*. I took the good traits of my father and husband and deftly air brushed out the bad or more troublesome ones. Now, rereading these books, I feel a bit impatient at some of these portrayals. It wasn't sadly, until after my father's death that I was able to begin writing about fathers who were more negative, sometimes even downright unpleasant. I see the beginnings of this trend in *Breaking Up*

Paperbound cover for Klein's 1986 novel.

where the heroine's father, a lawyer, is manipulative and dishonest, attempting to destroy her bond with her mother which threatens his own domination of her. But the book which carries this darker side of fatherhood most vividly thus far is the father in *Older Men,* a doctor who 'adores' his daughter and has contempt for his wife whom he places against her will in a mental hospital. It might be hard for someone to see my father in both the grandfather in *Mom, the Wolf Man and Me* and the father in *Older Men,* but I think both represent different sides of his character. The father in *No More Saturday Nights* is based more on my father-in-law, a withdrawn, unsocial man who, in the course of the book, becomes more fully human through his experience as a grandfather.

"As the daughter of a psychoanalyst and as someone who spent the better part of her adult life, to little avail, on an analytic couch, I am interested in the emotional problems of teenagers which are clearly extreme, given the teenage suicide rate and rate of mental breakdown. To some people, disturbed by emotional disturbances in themselves or family, the very concept 'mental illness' is terrifying. They try to perceive such young people as beyond the pale, completely unlike their own hopefully perfect teenage sons or daughters. In *Learning How To Fall,* I have portrayed a troubled teenage boy, Dustin, whose father has placed him in a mental hospital after he has had a psychotic episode. The book deals mainly with Dustin's first year after he gets out of the hospital (he is only there a few weeks) and how he tries to put his world together again. In fact, I don't think Dustin is any more disturbed than the characters in my other YA novels, and I hope that readers, in identifying with him, will have a greater understanding of what leads young people to go over the thin edge separating sanity from madness.

"My work schedule has only varied slightly in the years since I began writing novels, around 1970. I type ten pages a day, five days a week, always allowing myself two days off each week, though these days may vary. I write from the beginning to the end, not skipping ahead to scenes in the middle or end of the book. I find that when I finally arrive at those scenes, they are quite different due to what has happened earlier. I usually write three novels a year, one in the fall, one in the winter and one in the spring. I enjoy the alternation of writing novels for adults, novels for kids in their early teens and those in between late-high-school, early-college novels I described earlier. I think the ten-page-a-day schedule derived from the fact that I was originally a short story writer. It helped me to say to myself, 'You will never have to write a novel. You just have to write thirty ten-page scenes about the same characters which go in chronological order.' I like the six- to twelve-week gap between novels in which I can do what one friend describes as 'noodling around.' Noodling around can mean anything from writing an essay or book review to relabeling the spice jars or going out to see a movie at noon when the theatre is almost deserted. I've never been someone who holds with the view that writers are always writing. I think I spend far more time noodling around than I do writing and find it just as enjoyable an activity.

"When my daughters were growing up, the time I had to write was much more limited. They would be taken to the park by a babysitter in the morning and would return for lunch, a meal I liked to have with them. I knew, therefore, that I had to work quickly and efficiently in the morning hours. Since I'm a morning person, this suited me, but even now when I could work at any time of day or night for as long as I want, I find I still prefer the hours before noon.

"People sometimes ask why I write, and the answer to that question is, of course, complex, but essentially I think *I* write because I love the feeling I get when I am writing. For me it's as though, simply by going into my study and sitting in front of the typewriter, I am transported into a world peopled by human beings whom I will know much more intimately than I can ever know anyone in real life because I am simultaneously inside their heads and far outside, knowing things about them they themselves don't know. There is something indescribably thrilling about this. One aspect of sexuality is obviously the need to merge with another human being. Writing affords a way of actually doing this, of *becoming* another person.

"I still think of writing a novel as being like going on a trip. You have a general idea where you're going, but you don't know what will happen along the way, except that some of these experiences will be fascinating and by the end you will have learned a great deal and be, to some extent, a different person than you were before. Like most writers, I frequently have the experience, always delightful, that a character just marches into a book from somewhere unknown and begins saying and doing things which I listen to with total surprise and fascination. Just as the novel begins to slow down, such a character appears, as though waiting in the wings, though what 'the wings' are I don't really know, nor I think, does anyone.

"Writers sometimes worry about running out of ideas. I've never had this worry because, to the best of my knowledge, I've never had an idea. What I have are situations such as 'Write a novel about a teenage boy who gains sole custody of his son.' Once that sentence is written down, or even once it's a formed thought, the novel, in effect, exists. It's only a matter of going into my study and watching it unfold, perhaps in the way a sculptor feels the statue he is carving is *in* the piece of marble; he just has to take away the part that isn't the statue. The great thing about writing (and it's a good thing I enjoy it because I am totally devoid of marketable skills, never having had a 'real' job of any kind), is that all you need is time, a pad of paper and a typewriter or word processor if that happens to be your chosen method of writing. You can be waiting to cross the street and suddenly, for reasons known only to them, your characters

Paperback edition of the novel Klein dedicated to her daughters.

appear and start 'writing' a crucial scene for you. Sometimes this is so interesting you forget to cross the street! I've been known to walk directly past close friends, stare right into their eyes and not see them, an experience, they tell me, which is distinctly unnerving.

"When people try to clobber me by saying, 'You write too fast,' or 'You'll never write anything good until you agonize more over your work,' I've learned to say, 'Poor Mozart. He wrote the Linz Symphony in just four days. Think what his music could have been like if he'd learned to slow down!' The fact is, I don't think either the method or speed with which a writer creates his world makes much difference. Great novels have been written with a quill pen and great novels assuredly will be written on word processors. Some writers allow their work to pour forth in a joyous stream while others spend two months putting in and taking out a comma. I've learned to live with my own method because, once I hand in the completed manuscript, I am eager and willing to make whatever changes my editor suggests. Quite often these suggestions lead to major rewritings of scenes, the removal of some, the addition of others. I have no sense that what I am writing is sacred. I only object to changes which do violence to my original intent.

"Having writer friends like Betty Miles, Bob Cormier and Steven Kroll has been, more than almost anything else, a help in getting through a life as a writer. It is wonderful to know that every single emotion you experience, in the course of writing and publishing a book, delight at its creation, incomprehension at its rejection, outrage at a hideous cover or poorly written jacket copy, is being experienced, or has been experienced by virtually every writer you know. As they say, it goes with the territory. I once asked Norma Mazer (who in addition to being a fine writer and a good friend is the only other Norma I know) what she would say if God appeared before her and said, 'If you sign here I will guarantee that your future writing career will be identical to what has gone before, you will write neither better nor worse, will receive reviews as good but no better.' After a moment she said, 'I'd sign in a minute.' Adding that I would reserve the right to keep on complaining into eternity, I realized I felt exactly the same way."

■ For More Information See

School Library Journal, December, 1972 (p. 60), April, 1976 (p. 90), May, 1977 (p. 83), November, 1979 (p. 96), October, 1980 (p. 156), April, 1983 (p. 125), October, 1983 (p. 180), November, 1983 (p. 94).

Library Journal, December 15, 1972, November 15, 1974, February 15, 1976, April 15, 1977, November 15, 1978 (p. 2351), October 15, 1979 (p. 2236), June 1, 1982 (p. 1112).

Booklist, January 1, 1973 (p. 449), July 15, 1974 (p. 1254), November 1, 1975 (p. 369), November 1, 1976, December 15, 1979 (p. 595), June 15, 1982 (p. 1364), February 15, 1983 (p. 763), August, 1983 (p. 1448), October 15, 1983 (p. 360).

Horn Book, February, 1973 (p. 57), December, 1976 (p. 629).

Best Sellers, May 15, 1973 (p. 98), November 15, 1975, September, 1982 (p. 218).

Ms., January, 1974 (p. 36).

Top of the News, April, 1975 (p. 307); spring, 1985 (p. 248).

Margery Fisher, *Who's Who in Children's Books: A Treasury of the Familiar Characters of Childhood,* Holt, 1975.

Children's Literature Review, Volume II, Gale, 1976.

English Journal, May, 1976 (p. 90).

America, July 10, 1976 (p. 18).

N. Klein, "Growing Up Human: The Case of Sexuality in Children's Books," *Children's Literature in Education,* summer, 1977.

Kliatt Young Adult Paperback Book Guide, winter, 1978 (p. 9).

D. L. Kirkpatrick, editor, *Twentieth-Century Children's Writers,* St. Martin's, 1978, 2nd edition, 1983.

Interracial Books for Children Bulletin, Volume XII, number 3, 1981 (p. 19).

Quill & Quire, October, 1981.

Voyager, October, 1981, October, 1983.

Voice of Youth Advocates, October, 1981 (p. 34), October, 1983 (p. 203).

Publishers Weekly, December 24, 1982 (p. 47), March 9, 1984 (p. 106); March 28, 1986 (p. 58), July 24, 1987 (p. 109).

Los Angeles Times, May 26, 1983.

Nation, June 11, 1983 (p. 738).

Sally Holmes Holtze, editor, *Fifth Book of Junior Authors and Illustrators,* H. W. Wilson, 1983.

Contemporary Literary Criticism, Volume XXX, Gale, 1984.

Lion and the Unicorn, Volume 10, 1986 (p. 18).

School Library Media Quarterly, spring, 1987 (p. 161).

Collections:

Kerlan Collection at the University of Minnesota.

Milan Kundera

orn April 1, 1929, in Brno, Czechoslovakia;
surname pronounced "Coon'-dare-a"; came
to France in 1975, naturalized French
citizen, 1981; son of Ludvik (a pianist and musicol-
ogist) and Milada (Janosikova) Kundera; married
Vera Hrabankova, September 30, 1967. *Education:*
Studied music under Paul Haas and Vaclav Kapral;
attended Charles University, Prague, and Film
Faculty, Academy of Music and Dramatic Arts,
Prague, 1956. *Address:* c/o Gallimard, 5 rue Sebas-
tien-Bottin, F-75007 Paris, France.

■ Career

Writer. Film Faculty, Academy of Music and
Dramatic Arts, Prague, Czechoslovakia, assistant
professor, 1958-69; Universite de Rennes II, Rennes, France, associate professor of comparative
literature, 1975-79; Ecole des Hautes Etudes en
Sciences Sociales, Paris, France, professor,
1980—. *Member:* Czechoslovak Writers Union
(member of central committee, 1963-69), American Academy of Arts and Letters.

■ Awards, Honors

Klement Lukes Prize, 1963, for *Majitele klicu;*
Czechoslovak Writers Union Prize, 1968, for *Zert;*
Czechoslovak Writers' Publishing House Prize,
1969, for *Smesne lasky;* Prix Medicis, 1973, for *La
Vie est ailleurs;* Premio Letterario Mondello, 1978,
for *The Farewell Party;* Commonwealth Award for
Distinguished Service in Literature, 1981, Prix
Europa for literature, 1982, and Preis Nelly Sachs
(Germany), and Oestereichische Staatpreis fuer
Literatur, both 1987, all for the body of his
novelistic work; honorary doctorate, University of
Michigan, 1983; *Los Angeles Times* Book Prize for
Fiction, 1984, for *The Unbearable Lightness of
Being;* Jerusalem Prize for Literature on the Free-
dom of Man in Society, 1985.

■ Writings

Zert (also see below), Ceskoslovensky Spisovatel
(Czechoslovak Writers Union, Prague), 1967,
translation by David Hamblyn and Oliver
Stallybrass published as *The Joke,* Coward,
1969, new complete translation by Michael
Henry Heim with author's preface, Harper,
1982.
Smesne lasky (selection of seven short stories
previously published in *Smesne lasky: Tri
melancholicke anekdoty, Druhy sesit smesnych
laske,* and *Treti sesit smesnych lasek*),
Ceskoslovensky Spisovatel, 1970, translation
by Suzanne Rappaport with introduction by
P. Roth published as *Laughable Loves,* Knopf,
1974, new edition, Viking Penguin, 1987.

Zivot je jinde, Sixty-Eight Publishers (Toronto), 1979, translation from the original Czech manuscript by Francois Kerel first published as *La Vie est ailleurs*, Gallimard (Paris), 1973, translation from the original Czech manuscript by Peter Kussi published as *Life Is Elsewhere*, Knopf, 1974.

Valcik na rozloucenou, Sixty-Eight Publishers, 1979, translation from the original Czech manuscript by Francois Kerel first published as *La valse aux adieux*, Gallimard, 1976, translation from the original Czech manuscript by P. Kussi published as *The Farewell Party*, Knopf, 1976.

Kniha smichu a zapomneni, Sixty-Eight Publishers, 1981, translation from the original Czech manuscript by F. Kerel first published as *Le Livre du rire et de l'oubli*, Gallimard, 1979, translation from the original Czech manuscript by M. H. Heim published as *The Book of Laughter and Forgetting*, Knopf, 1980, published with an interview with the author by Philip Roth, Penguin Books, 1981.

The Unbearable Lightness of Being, translation from the original Czech manuscript, *Nesnesitelna lehkost byti*, by M. H. Heim, Harper, 1984.

Other:

Clovek zahrada sira (poetry; title means "Man: A Broad Garden"), Ceskoslovensky Spisovatel, 1953.

Posledni maj (poetry; title means "The Last May"), Ceskoslovensky Spisovatel, 1955.

Monology (poetry; title means "Monologues"), Ceskoslovensky Spisovatel, 1957, revised edition, 1964.

Umeni romanu (study of writer Vladislav Vancura; title means "The Art of the Novel"), Ceskoslovensky Spisovatel, 1960.

Majitele klicu (play; title means "The Owners of the Keys"; first produced in Prague at National Theatre, April, 1962), Orbis, 1962.

Jacques et son maitre: Hommage a Denis Diderot (three-act play; first produced in Paris at Theatre des Maturins, 1981), published with an introduction by the author, Gallimard, 1981, translation by M. H. Heim published as *Jacques and His Master* (produced in Cambridge, Mass. at American Repertory Theatre, January, 1985), Harper, 1985, translation by Simon Callow produced as "Jacques and His Master" in Toronto at Free Theatre, May 14, 1986.

L'Art du roman, Editions Gallimard, 1986, translated from the French by Linda Asher, published as *The Art of the Novel*, Grove, 1988.

Kundera's narrative works have also been translated into German, Dutch, Danish, Norwegian, Swedish, Finnish, Portuguese, Spanish, Italian, Serbian, Slovene, Greek, Turkish, Hebrew, Polish, and Japanese. Contributor of essays to *New York Times Book Review*. Member of editorial board of *Literarni noviny*, 1963-68, *Literarni listy*, 1968-69, and *Messager europeen*, 1987—.

■ Adaptations

"The Joke" (also author of screenplay with Jaromil Jires), Smida-Fikar—Studio de Cinema de Barrandov, 1968.

"The Unbearable Lightness of Being" (film), starring Daniel Day-Lewis and Juliette Binoche, Orion, 1988.

■ Sidelights

Milan Kundera was born in Brno, Czechoslovakia in 1929. "I was born on the first of April. That has its metaphysical significance."[1]

"I come from a family of musicians. My father was a pianist, a very good pianist dedicated to modern music. He was one of the first to interpret piano compositions by Bartok, Stravinsky, Schonberg, and above all Janacek, whose young friend and student he was. Thus, I was imbued with music at home."[2]

"I was fascinated by [my father's] grasp of a composition, by the manner in which he played so that in his rendition each note was given a meaning....I have come to understand the essence of the interpreter's art, and I know that the concert public does not appreciate it properly....I am very fond of music but I have always disliked the musical environment, even in my early youth. Musicians are generally not particularly witty....Often rather limited, and I saw that my father suffered among them. The thought that I might spend my whole life only among musicians gave me goose pimples."[1]

"...I betrayed my father, so to speak—not personally, on the contrary, I still loved him very much, but I turned away from music. [He] never used his authority to impose the destiny of a musician on me, but he expected me to become one."[2]

From the movie "The Joke," directed by Jaromil Jires. Released in Prague, Czechoslovakia on the day of the Soviet invasion, August, 1968, and since banned.

"When I was fourteen or fifteen, I began to write poems....I think that my earliest poems were actually much better than many I published later; they had a strong surrealist cast...."[1]

"...I read [Kafka's] *The Castle,* I was bewitched. It was one of the first shocks literature has caused me."[3]

"...When I was 16, I read Marx. Communism enthralled me in much the way Stravinsky, Picasso and surrealism had. It promised a great, miraculous metamorphosis, a totally new and different world."[4]

1947. Joined the Communist Party. "All the Czech avant-garde were Communists....There was a certain beauty and poetry to the revolution."[5]

"...During my last year in the gymnasium, in the course of a political debate, I remarked that even though socialism might bring about a period of cultural darkness I would continue to support it since it represented a necessary phase in the liberation of the people. Coming from the mouth of a politician, such a pronouncement would sound like utter cynicism. Coming from a student totally devoted to culture, however, such words have a different inner meaning. They signify self-denial. And one cannot understand the psychology of intellectuals during revolutionary times without this key."[1]

"No Exit," a play by Jean-Paul Sartre sent "shivers running down my back. No theatrical piece since then has wrenched me to such an extent....Sartre's outlook was shaped primarily by the war and he was influenced by the immediate postwar atmosphere, and therefore Sartre was also fascinated by the story of man in history flux. For this reason, Sartre seems more contemporary to me than current writers such as Robbe-Grillet."[1]

February 19, 1948. Supported by Red Army contingents, the Communists demanded, on the threat of violence, that complete power be turned over to them. Only one list of candidates was presented, and elections were held as in a totalitarian country. "...We saw the terror, the hangings, the general degradation of life.

"...The pro-Soviet Putsch in 1948 in Prague was experienced by a very large part of the youth with

Cover illustration by Jerry Lo Faro from the Penguin paperback edition.

the same fascinating and pure enthusiasm as May 68: the same attitudes, the same radicalism, the same desire for absolute change, the same refusal of the fathers' old world, and also the same refusal of Western culture, which right off seemed guilty....

"You know, around 1948, I too had a short period of lyrical enthusiasm, I too exalted the revolution."[6]

"I lived through the Stalinist terror of the fifties...and I can't tell you to what extent the lyric spirit, the spirit of enthusiasm, the spirit of lyric identification with utopia was bound up with the terror. It is not at all interesting to say that the Gulag is bad....The real problem is to know how extremely intelligent and even very nice people, and even people full of good will can be enthusiastic not about the Gulag, but about what leads to the Gulag. It's not hell that interests me but the image of paradise that led to hell."[7]

"Oh, I condemn nothing! Lyrical enthusiasm is a necessary dimension of life, it is its beauty! But all things human are ambiguous, they have their hidden side. The novelist discovers the hidden side of things, that's his *raison d'etre*."[6]

Skepticism and humor were later to become crucial themes in Kundera's work. "The period...had no sense of humor, but unwittingly it produced some marvelous paradoxes. In art, the official doctrine was realism. But it was forbidden to speak of the real. The cult of youth was publicly celebrated, but our enjoyment of our own youth was frustrated. In those pitiless times, all we were shown on the screen was a series of tender and bashful lovers. Official slogans were full of joy, yet we didn't dare to play even the slightest prank. We went through the school of paradox. Today, when I hear anyone mention the innocence of childhood or one's sacred duty to increase and multiply or the justice of history I know what all this really means. I've been through the mill.

"Of course, my generation was far from uniform, and this is often forgotten nowadays. Some emigrated, others became silent; still others adapted themselves, while others—including myself—adopted a kind of legal, constructive opposition. None of these postures was very dignified, and none was really satisfactory."[1]

Fall, 1948. "I went to FAMU [the Prague film school, which virtually all members of the Czech 'New Wave' attended] and I remember the reflections which guided me at the time: I'll give up music and poetry, I thought, precisely because these are too close to my heart, and I will make films because cinema doesn't have any special attraction for me. In this way I will get rid of personal considerations and I will take part in the only art which is just, the 'art which serves the people.' Once again, a paradox, a self-denial. First I studied film directing and then scenario writing....Quite early I was given a few good kicks in the behind, and shortly after February [revolution] I was expelled from the party...."[1] And from the university as well.

"My early conflicts with the regime weren't ideological; they were those of an artist who didn't want to conform, who couldn't adjust to the idea of art engage, political art, that was required then. But in defending the rights to live the way you want and create the kind of art you want, against your will you enter into a conflict."[8]

"I think jazz has played in Czechoslovakia almost the same role as in other Western European countries....The doctrine of socialist realism completely drove jazz from the stage and from life. Jazz became either music one could listen to only privately or music one could play, but in a softened, compromised manner, a disguised jazz one could hear only in small towns, so that it wouldn't be too visible, because it was an art of 'rotten imperialism.'...I played piano in a small band that was doing disguised jazz. It was very bad jazz, but it was welcomed with great enthusiasm because it represented something fascinating and more or less repressed."[2]

"After my life calmed down a bit...I painted, I dabbled in films and in the theater, I wrote poetry, but nothing seemed to satisfy me."[4]

1957. Published *Monologues*, poems condemned for their eroticism and cynicism. Although the first printing sold out, seven years passed before a second edition could be published. "...The book also contained some romanticized verse, tending toward broad emotional gestures, and these later became repugnant to me. I removed them from later editions.

"In general, I have come to dislike my poems; also, I have lost the touch of writing poetry. To tell the truth, when people referred to me by that somewhat ridiculous title of Poet, I never felt quite right about it....And the moment I realized that I no longer had it in me to write poetry, the thought that this phase of my life was behind me came as a relief."[1]

Cover illustration by Jerry Lo Faro from the Penguin paperback edition.

1960. Published *The Art of the Novel*, an influential study of the Czech avant garde writer, Vladislav Vancura. "...To be perfectly frank, one reason for my devoting so much time to theory during that period was that I was having difficulty with the practice."[1]

April, 1962. First production of "The Owners of the Keys" performed at the National Theatre in Prague by a well-known director Otomar Krejca. "I was happy to notice that the public, especially in Prague, understood very well...the current meaning of these characters we so often brush by [in] modern life: these are the owners of truths, the owners of morality, the owners of the right to judge others, to draft certificates...the owners who have no idea what is really at stake, so much is their horizon obstructed by their elephantine virtues...."[9]

In 1963 an international conference aimed at rehabilitating the work of Franz Kafka in socialist countries was held in Czechoslovakia. Kundera participated in the cultural liberalization of the sixties. "...The fight for Kafka revealed the most intellectual wing of the large movement of a whole nation that fiercely defended its way of living. . . .

"Thanks to the enormous force of this popular cultural resistance, my country knew in the sixties one of the greatest periods of artistic creativity. The cinema and theatre were then among the best in the world and aroused in the public an interest no French artist would dare even dream of. And yet, the structure of the regime had remained the same, although slightly weakened. Those who confuse reality with the simple political system (and who doesn't today?) will never be able to understand what happened then. . . ."[10]

Spring, 1967. *The Joke* was published. ". . .And without a trace of censorship! How was that possible in Communist Czechoslovakia one year before the Prague Spring?

"I presented the manuscript of *The Joke* to the editors of a Prague publishing house in December 1965, and though they promised to do their best to bring it out, they never really believed they would succeed. The spirit of the work was diametrically opposed to the official ideology. . . ."[11]

". . .The novel was received with almost unanimous fervor. . . .A hardly known author until then, I saw, within a short time, three editions quickly go out of print and a total printing reach 121,000 copies. . . .In the already very liberal atmosphere of the fore-spring of Prague, my book didn't cause the slightest political sensation. . . ."[12]

"The plot. . .is itself a joke. And not only its plot. Its 'philosophy' as well: man, caught in the trap of a joke, suffers a personal catastrophe which, seen from without, is ludicrous. His tragedy lies in the fact that the joke has deprived him of the right to tragedy. He is condemned to triviality. . . .

"But if a character is condemned to triviality in his private life, can he escape to the stage of history? No. I have always been convinced that the paradoxes of history and private life have the same basic properties: Helena ends up in the hoax of the trap Ludvik has set for her; Ludvik and all the others end up in the trap of the joke history has played on them; lured on by the voice of utopia, they have squeezed their way through the gates of paradise only to find, when the doors slam shut behind them, that they are in hell. Those are the times that give me the feeling history enjoys a good laugh."[11]

September 30, 1967. Married Vera Hrabankova.

In the Spring of 1968 ". . .In their attempt to build socialism—for the first time in their history—without an omnipotent secret police, in their respect for the freedom of speech and writing, in their consideration of public opinion, in their conduct of a politic supported by people who are no longer afraid, the Czechs and Slovaks, for the first time since the Middle Ages, are rising again in the midst of world history in order to challenge it."[13]

August 21, 1968. About 500,000 Russian and other Warsaw Pact soldiers occupied Czechoslovakia. ". . .The visceral horror didn't come from the fact that Dubcek's reforms were done for, but from this infinite space felt behind the faces of the Russian soldiers, from this strangeness of a civilization that thinks differently, feels differently, lives in a different historic time, and that had come to swallow us up into its eternity. Political regimes are ephemeral, but the boundaries of civilizations are traced for centuries.

"My country is not capitalist, and I don't think it wants to become capitalist. And yet, it is an old Western country and means to remain one. The West is a common history, a culture.

"Not oppositional culture but culture as such was massacred. . . .Half a million Czechs lost their jobs. About two hundred writers, including the greatest, were not only forbidden to publish, but had their books removed from all public libraries and their names erased from history manuals. Instead of about forty literary and cultural reviews, there is only one now. The great Czech cinema no longer exists. The best playwrights were expelled from the country. The political and cultural history has been rewritten: one finds neither Franz Kafka nor Tomas Masaryk, who had created the Czech Republic in 1918, nothing that Russian totalitarianism couldn't digest."[14]

Following the Russian invasion, Kundera became increasingly outspoken not only on behalf of Czechoslovakia as a Central European nation wrenched out of its historical place, but also in behalf of the whole of Central Europe, which, with the exception of Austria, has been part of the Soviet bloc since the end of World War II. The invasion began to affect Kundera personally. ". . .*The Joke* had insults heaped on it during a long press campaign, was banned (as were my other books) and removed from public libraries."[12]

". . .After 68 [my father] was blacklisted because of me. The matrix of his Janacek record was destroyed because it carried my name."[2]

October, 1968. *The Joke*, which had won the Czechoslovak Writers Union prize, was published in France prefaced by Louis Aragon. "...Claude Gallimard [French publisher] invited me to Paris for the publication of my book. That is when I saw Aragon for the first time....[He said] 'Even if I wanted to go [to Russia], my legs would refuse!' I admired him. A few years later, his legs obediently took him to Moscow where he allowed Brezhnev to decorate him, and, a few years later still, they obeyed him again and carried him up to the podium of the Party Congress, which applauded another invasion, that of Afghanistan ....Nevertheless, without him *The Joke* would have never seen the light of day in France, and my fate would have taken an entirely different bath (and a less happy one, for sure)...."

"The reception in Paris...both flattered and saddened me: my novel was showered with praise but read in a one-sided, political way. The fault rested with the historical circumstance of the moment (the novel came out two months after the invasion), with Aragon's preface (which spoke only of politics), with the publisher's insert in review copies, with the translation (which could only eclipse the artistic aspect of the novel), and also with the gradual transformation of Western literary criticism in hasty journalistic commentary subjected to the dictatorship of the news...."[11]

A truncated British edition of *The Joke* prompted a letter to the *Times Literary Supplement*. "...The publisher (Macdonald) has merely considered my text as a free basis for bizarre inventions of manipulators....The mentality of a London bookseller and that of a Moscow official responsible for art seem to have a mysterious kinship. The depth of their contempt for art is equally unfathomable...."[15]

"At about the same time, the British translation was published in New York—but even more simplified, more mutilated! I was powerless. Contact with the outside world was becoming more and more difficult in occupied Prague, and what with house searches and arrests, I had other things to worry about."[12]

While Kundera was in Paris, he spent time in "left" circles. "...Full of contempt for my own lyrical youth...I found myself in the so-called left milieu: nice people and, so to speak, from the same family as I; and...with the same rhetoric, the same utopias, the same thinking in cliches I had had twenty years ago and of which I was ashamed.

"The meaning of this encounter was double: I listened to them skeptically, disagreeing, but I understood them perfectly, sympathetically. Their honesty paradoxically reconciled me with my own former stupidity. This lyrical stupidity wasn't any less stupid, but I suddenly saw it as an almost eternal dimension of man....

"Paradox is the sudden appearance of an unexpected meaning of a situation. It is in a paradox that the most deeply hidden truth is suddenly revealed."[6]

1970. Kundera was expelled from the Prague Film School and the Writers' Union, his passport was confiscated, his books forbidden. "Since I was blacklisted as one of the instigators of the counter-revolution, my books were banned and my name removed even from the telephone book. And all because of *The Joke*."[4] His wife, who had done clandestine broadcasts during the Russian invasion, lost her job as a television announcer.

He earned his living by writing under fictitious names. "I lived in a very modest way on savings, but yet I wasn't unhappy....For the first time in my life I wrote absolutely freely because I knew that these books would never be published in Czechoslovakia and would never be read by any censor...."[16]

"...I...was forced from then on to write for translators only. And, paradoxical as it may seem, I feel it has done my mother tongue a lot of good.

"Conciseness and clarity are, for me, what makes a language beautiful. Czech is a vivid, suggestive, sensuous language, sometimes at the expense of a firm order, logical sequence and exactitude....I made myself—at first unknowingly—write sentences that were more sober, more comprehensible. A cleansing of the language...."[17]

"...In Prague, in the final years before the '68 invasion I had quite a few well-defined, visualizable readers. I lost them rapidly and completely; I was suddenly without any public at all."[18]

"...Then, suddenly, I understood...a writer's *true* public must be kept completely abstract. The writer must always write for *everyone, always*; he wants to be understood anywhere at any time. Sartre's *litterature engagee*—the idea of influencing a concrete, specific public—is *absolutely* foreign to me. It ultimately reduces literature to journalism."[19]

"Persecution has freed me from the intellectual's common complex vis-a-vis politics, which seems to represent for him real life, culture being only an ivory tower. Culture is a people's memory, the collective consciousness of historical continuity, a way of thinking and living."[10]

"If you cannot view the art that comes to you from Prague or Budapest in any other way then by means of this idiotic political code, you murder it no less brutally than the worst of the Stalinist dogmatists....The importance of this art does not lie in the fact that it accuses this or that political regime, but in the fact that, on the strength of social and human experience of a kind people over here [in the West] cannot even imagine, it offers new testimony about the human conditions."[17]

"A theatre director suggested that I write, under another name, an adaptation of [Dostoyevsky's] The Idiot. I tried...but this world was definitely unbearable for me, and even in order to eat I couldn't do this work."[20]

"The great Russian irrationality was weighing on my occupied country, and then, this cult of suffering, of hysteria and depth, I couldn't bear it. And I threw myself into a passionate rereading of [Diderot's] Jacques le Fataliste, where all the depth...is

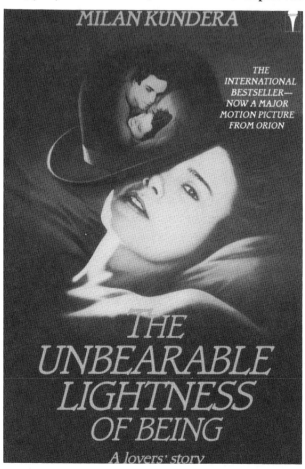

Cover from the Perennial Library paperback edition.

concealed by the surface....The enchantment of the French eighteenth century...came as a nostalgic reminder of my past life, of this spirit of play and freedom...which no longer exists anywhere.

"Not even in France, which resembles as little my 'idea of France' as a loved woman her lover's illusions. This country was for me only the sum of its artistic works, but does the artistic work still represent anything here?...One prefers, alas! ideas to works. Ideas eat works, received ideas eat ideas.

"What interested me in this novel was the spirit of entertainment. It's neither a lesson in philosophy nor a lesson in morality. It's a great game. But a game full of wisdom. A wisdom so wise that it refuses to teach lessons."[21]

Kundera's play "Jacques and His Master" was a homage to Diderot and the spirit of the novel. "I wrote 'Jacques and His Master' for my private pleasure and perhaps with the vague idea that it could one day be put on in a Czech theater under an assumed name. By way of a signature I dotted the text (another game, another variation!) with several mementos of my previous works....

"Renouncing strict unity of action, I sought to create a coherent whole by more subtle means: by the technique of polyphony (the three stories are intermingled rather than told consecutively) and the technique of variation (each of the three stories is in fact a variation on the others). And so this play, which is a 'variation on Diderot,' is simultaneously an 'homage to the technique of variation....'"[22]

Kundera later applied polyphony, variation, and other musical concepts in his novels. "It's not an adaptation. I played with Diderot's text. One could qualify this man as a non-pessimistic skeptic. He believed in the future. Very different is the attitude of the twentieth century skeptic, who no longer believes in a rosy future. All naive trust has disappeared. This play is a confrontation between two centuries, two moods. It's Diderot without his optimism."[23]

"The playfulness inherent in theatrical expression appealed to me. The theatre is a game, and playing games is an important source of pleasure. Real life is linked to a series of deceptions. It disappoints us with its futility. But when we consciously play games, as on stage, we already know that the game isn't serious. Thus, the tragic futility of life becomes the joyous futility of play...."[24]

When asked which of his novels he personally prefers, Kundera replied: "...Laughable Loves.

From the movie "The Unbearable Lightness of Being," starring Daniel Day-Lewis and Juliette Binoche. Released by Orion Pictures, 1988.

The happiest book. . .a book of euphoria, written in the unspeakable climate Czechoslovakia knew during. . .its precarious liberalization. Freedom expressed first of all in erotic life. This had nothing to do with this sexual liberalization which, here [in the West], seems to me artificial, deliberate, ideological, verbal, dogmatic, severe, serious."[3]

"Sexual liberation has certainly been a real liberation, but it has also been subjected to the cruel law of paradox. To liberate sexuality, one destroyed taboos and by getting rid of taboos one is destroying eroticism. One will soon discover (but too late) that taboos are there not to protect morality but eroticism. Eroticism, this fragile miracle! Why is one excited by a woman's body? Excitement, not pleasure, is the true mystery of eroticism. By getting rid of taboos (the taboos of nudity, the taboos of language, etc.) one also gets rid of obscenity, curiosity, sexual wonder, in short, excitement, the only source of eroticism."[6]

"...With me everything ends in great erotic scenes. I have the feeling that a scene of physical love generates an extremely sharp light which suddenly reveals the essence of characters and sums up their life situation."[25]

1971. Met Philip Roth in Prague, with whom he has remained friends. As editor of the Penguin series, *Writers from the Other Europe*, Roth brought Kundera to the attention of the English-speaking world.

1973. Published *Life Is Elsewhere* in France, for which he received the Prix Medicis. It was completed in 1969 and denied publication in Czechoslovakia. "...The most skeptical of all among my novels....Its subject is youth and poetry. The adventure of poetry during the Stalinist terror. Poetry's smile. The bloody smile of innocence."[19]

"...I turn to the destiny of old poets to tie the itinerary of my hero with that of lyric illusion of all times. The novel, for me, is the meeting place where present and past attempt to agree on what man is."[26]

1975. Was offered an associate professorship at the University of Rennes, France. "...We arrived in France with nothing; two suitcases, a few books and records, and that was it."[8]

"I'm a Francophile, an avid Francophile. But the reason I'm here is really because the French wanted me. I came to France because I was invited, because people here took the initiative and arranged everything. It wasn't the Germans or the English, it was the French. And I was lucky because I do feel good here—much better than I feel in, say, Germany."[27]

"You cannot imagine my euphoria after only my first fortnight....I could start my second life from the beginning, and everything was an adventure for me: people, language, landscape, even a chat with the neighbors."[16]

"We left by car with Vera, we crossed French cities all very beautiful, there were magnificent cathedrals, and then we entered the first ugly city of the trip, but really ugly, it was Rennes...."[3] "But love has nothing to do with esthetics. I am a real Rennes patriot."[28]

While at the University of Rennes, Kundera taught Kafka, in whose works he found "the alchemy that combines the free imagination of dreams with a precise analysis of the modern world."[4]

"In universities all over the world, every year several thousand pages about Kafka are scribbled. This discipline deserves its own name: kafkology. It's a pretentious, sophisticated, incredibly monotonous chatter, that thrives on itself and is completely blind to Kafka's art. Kafkology is the forgetting of Kafka."[3]

The Book of Laughter and Forgetting, written between 1976 and 1978, was published in France. "'The struggle of man against power is the struggle of memory against forgetting.' This sentence from [the book]...is often quoted as the message of the novel....Before becoming a political problem, the will to forget is an anthropological problem: ever since man has had the desire to rewrite his own biography, to change the past, to erase traces, his and those of others. The will to forget is far from being a simple temptation to cheat."[29]

"Forgetting, omnipresent, lies in wait for us every day to impoverish us by robbing us of our intimate but also collective past. Forgetting is an energy capable of devouring everything, and political power today knows how to use this immense energy."

"Laughter is one of the big subjects of the book. In the third part...a rather funny story is told, according to which there are two laughters: the laughter of the devil and the laughter of angels. The first is the product of distance, judgement; it comes from the sudden discovery of the absurd, the absence of meaning. The second...is the laughter of acquiescence: one agrees with the world, with its meaning, and one enjoys this agreement....Here are sketched two images of the 'end of the world.' The end in the enthusiastic laughter of angels, that is, fanatics who are so convinced of meaning that they are ready to hang those who aren't convinced enough. And the other image of decline appears in this diabolical laughter that no longer sees any meaning anywhere....The two laughters trace two abysses between which human life takes place."[30]

"[The seventh part of The Book of Laughter and Forgetting]...is a 'theme with variations.' The theme is the border beyond which things lose their meaning. Our life unfolds in the immediate vicinity of that border, and we risk crossing it at any moment. The fourteen chapters are fourteen variations of the same situation—eroticism at the border between meaning and meaninglessness.

"There is no unity of action, which is why it does not look like a novel....It's the unity of the themes and their variations that give coherence to the whole. Is it a novel? Yes. A novel is a meditation on existence, seen through imaginary characters. It's form is unlimited.

"...It is a novel because there is the desire, even if unsatisfied, to encompass a whole set of problems, compounded by the confrontation of different points of view that illuminate each other through irony."[31]

"Irony irritates. Not because it makes fun or attacks but because it deprives us of certainties by revealing the world as ambiguous."[29]

"...Irony is justified only on this condition: That nothing and no one be spared its illumination, neither men, nor women, nor the elderly, nor the young, nor the author himself. In its omnipresence consists the honesty of irony, which then is not meanness. If you think about it, it is in their intractable seriousness that things are frightening. On the other hand, in their non-sense, in their non-seriousness, they become touching and more human. Maybe the only true equality, the fraternity of all, the place of forgiveness are in the comic?"[30]

1980. Kundera was stripped of his Czech citizenship following the publication of The Book of Laughter and Forgetting. Left the University of Rennes to teach at the Ecole des Hautes Etudes et Sciences Sociales in Paris.

The Unbearable Lightness of Being, finished in 1982, was published in 1984 in France. It was on the best-seller list for months. "...I started this chase, this novel, 25 years ago. The idea was there, but I messed it up completely, ridiculously. All I was left with were two characters—the girl Tereza and the man Tomas—and one scene of Tomas looking out of a window and saying to himself *einmal ist keinmal...(one time is no time)....*Meaning that man, living his one life, is condemned to that one fatal experience. He can never know if he was a good man or a bad man, if he loved anyone or if he had only the illusion of love....."[30]

"...While writing the *The Unbearable Lightness of Being...*I thought of Descartes' famous phrase: man, 'master and possessor of nature.' After having accomplished miracles in science and technology, this 'master and possessor' suddenly realizes he possesses nothing and is master of neither nature (it gradually withdraws from the planet) nor history (it has escaped him) nor himself (he is guided by the irrational forces of his soul). But if God has gone away and man is no longer master, who then is master? The planet advances in the void without any master. Here it is, the unbearable lightness of being."[29]

"My ambition was the same one novelists have always had: to say about man and his existence what poetry, science or philosophy cannot say. Convinced that the novel has an extraordinary capacity for synthesis, I wanted to bring together various elements (story, dream, philosophy, poetry) and to juxtapose geographically distant places."[31]

"Every one of my novels could be entitled *The Unbearable Lightness of Being* or *The Joke* or *Laughable Loves,* the titles are interchangeable, they reflect the small number of themes that obsess me, define me, and, unfortunately, restrict me. Beyond these themes I have nothing else to say or to write...."[32]

With the exception of *The Farewell Party,* Kundera's novels are divided into seven parts. "...I am not indulging in some superstitious affection about magic numbers, nor making a rational calculation. Rather, I am driven by a deep, incomprehensible need, a formal archetype from which I cannot escape. All of my novels are variants of an architecture based on the number seven."[32]

1986. *L'Art du roman* ("The Art of the Novel") published in France. This collection of previously published essays and interviews, some revised, includes Kundera's personal dictionary. "The au-

thor who strives to keep an eye on the translations of his novels is running after countless words like a shepherd behind a herd of wild sheep; a sad figure to himself, laughable to others. I suspect my friend Pierre Nora, director of the review *Le Debat,* was aware of the sadly comic aspect of my existence as shepherd. One day, he said to me with ill-concealed compassion: 'Forget your torments and write something for me. The translations forced you to reflect on each of your words. So write your personal dictionary. The dictionary of your novels. Your key words, problem-words, love-words.'"[29]

About the fame that has overtaken him in exile, Kundera admitted: "When I was a little boy in short pants I dreamed about a miraculous ointment that would make me invisible. Then I became an adult, began to write, and wanted to be successful. Now I'm successful and would like to have the ointment that would make me invisible."[16]

"I am discreet to an almost pathological degree, and there is nothing I can do against that...."[19]

Footnote Sources:

[1] Antonin J. Liehm, *The Politics of Culture,* translated by Peter Kussi, Grove Press, 1967.
[2] Translation of Michel Contat, "Milan Kundera, La Musique e'est finiaujourd'hui," *Le Monde de la musique,* October, 1980.

Jacket design by the author from the Grove Press hardcover edition.

[3] Translation of Daniel Rondeau, "Entretien: Kundera: un Europeen a Paris," *Liberation*, April 18, 1983.
[4] Milan Kundera, "The Making of a Writer," *New York Times Book Review*, translated by Michael Henry Heim, October 24, 1982.
[5] *Current Biography*, 1983.
[6] Translation of Christian Salmon, "Milan Kundera et le piege du paradoxe terminal," *Liberation*, December 5-6, 1981.
[7] Translation of Nicole Casanova, "Milan Kundera le fataliste: 'Je suis vaccine contre toute croyance,'" *Le Quotidien de Paris*, September 28, 1981.
[8] James Atlas, "The Wounded Exile," *Vanity Fair*, January, 1985.
[9] Translation of Milan Kundera, "Kruta heros positif!," *Supplement a tep-actualite*, April, 1974.
[10] Translation of Amber Bousoglou, "Entretien avec Milan Kundera," *Le Monde des Livres*, January 19, 1979.
[11] M. Kundera, preface to *The Joke*, translated by M. H. Heim, Harper, 1982.
[12] Translation of Milan Kundera, "La Plaisanterie etait amere," *Le Nouvel Observateur*, August 23, 1985.
[13] Translation of Milan Kundera, "La destinee tscheque," *Lettres francaises*, March 19, 1969.
[14] Translation of Alain Finkielkraut, "Kundera: l'exode de la culture," *L'Express*, June 21, 1980.
[15] M. Kundera, "Letter to the Editor," *Times Literary Supplement*, October 10, 1969.
[16] Philip Roth, "In Defense of Intimacy, Milan Kundera's Private Lives," *Village Voice*, June 26, 1984.
[17] M. Kundera, "Comedy Is Everywhere," *Index on Censorship*, November-December, 1977.
[18] Francine du Plessix Gray, "Journey into the Maze: An Interview with Milan Kundera," translated by Susan Stout, *Vogue*, February, 1982.
[19] Olga Carlisle, "A Talk with Milan Kundera," *New York Times Biographical Service*, May, 1985.
[20] M. Kundera, "Le maitre de la derision," translated by Francoise Xenakis, *Le Matin de Paris*, February 20, 1981.
[21] Translation of Genevieve Coste, "Kundera oppose son humour a toutes les oppresions," *Tele-7 Jours*, October 31, 1981.
[22] M. Kundera, "Introduction to a Variation," *Jacques and His Master*, translated by M. H. Heim, Harper, 1985.
[23] Translation of Marion Thebaud, "Kundera: Diderot sans optimisme," *Le Figaro*, September 23, 1981.
[24] M. Kundera, "Interviewed by Arthur Holmberg," *Performing Arts Journal*, 1985.
[25] Philip Roth, "Interview with Milan Kundera," *New York Times Book Review*, translated by Peter Kussi, November 30, 1980.
[26] Translation of Ugne Karvelis, "Le romancier envie toujours le boxeur ou le revolutionnaire," *Le Monde*, January 23, 1976.
[27] Jane Kramer, "When There Is No Word for 'Home,'" *New York Times Book Review*, April 29, 1984.
[28] Translation of Pierre Sipriot, "Dialogue avec Milan Kundera, Pour un Roman Polyphonique," *Le Figaro*, February 7, 1976.
[29] Translation of Milan Kundera, *L'Art du roman*, Gallimard, 1986.
[30] Translation of Yannick Pelletier, "Un passe a visage humain, entretien avec Milan Kundera," *Les Nouvelles Litteraires*, April 26, 1979.
[31] M. Kundera, "The Book That I'm Writing," *New York Times Book Review*, December 6, 1983.
[32] M. Kundera, "The Art of Fiction LXXXI," *Paris Review*, summer, 1984.

■ For More Information See

Books:

Z. A. B. Zeman, *Prague Spring*, Hill & Wang, 1969.
Antonin J. Liehm, *The Politics of Culture*, translation from the Czech by Peter Kussi, Grove, 1972.
Lubomir Dolezel, *Narrative Modes in Czech Literature*, University of Toronto Press, 1973.
Milan Kundera, *Laughable Loves*, translation by Suzanne Rappaport with introduction by Philip Roth, Knopf, 1974.
P. Roth, *Reading Myself and Others*, Farrar, Straus, 1975.
Comtemporary Literary Criticism, Gale, Volume IV, 1975, Volume IX, 1978, Volume XIX, 1981, Volume XXXII, 1985.
Paul I. Trensky, *Czech Drama since World War II*, M. E. Sharpe, 1978.
Marketa Goetz-Stankiewicz, *The Silenced Theatre: Czech Playwrights without a Stage*, University of Toronto Press, 1979.
M. Kundera, *The Book of Laughter and Forgetting*, translation by Michael Henry Heim published with an interview with the author by P. Roth, Penguin Books, 1981.
Robert Porter, *Milan Kundera: A Voice from Central Europe*, Arkona (Denmark), 1981.
A. French, *Czech Writers and Politics, 1945-1969*, East European Monographs, 1982.
M. Kundera, *The Joke*, translation by M. H. Heim with author's preface, Harper, 1982.

Periodicals:

Nation, August 28, 1967, November 6, 1967, August 26, 1968, September 18, 1976, October 2, 1976, May 23, 1984.
New Republic, May 18, 1968, September 6, 1975, February 14, 1983.
Times Literary Supplement, October 30, 1969, March 3, 1978, July 21, 1978, February 5, 1982, May 25, 1984.
Saturday Review, December 20, 1969.
Newsweek, July 29, 1974, November 24, 1980, November 8, 1982, April 30, 1984, February 4, 1985.
Time, August 5, 1974.
Spectator, June 10, 1978, February 13, 1982, June 23, 1984.
New York Times, November 6, 1980, January 18, 1982, April 2, 1984.
Washington Post, November 22, 1980.
Commentary, December, 1980, October, 1984.
Village Voice, December 24, 1980, November 23, 1982.
Los Angeles Times, January 5, 1981, May 2, 1984.
National Review, March 20, 1981, January 21, 1983.

Washington Post Book World, December 19, 1982, April 22, 1984.
Dissent, winter, 1983.
Times (London), February 17, 1983, May 24, 1984.
World Literature Today, spring, 1983.
Voice Literary Supplement, November, 1983.
Critical Quarterly, spring/summer, 1984.

Globe and Mail (Toronto), April 28, 1984.
Macleans, May 14, 1984.
Commonweal, May 18, 1984.
Paris Review, summer, 1984.
New York Times Magazine, May 19, 1985.
Partisan Review, Volume LI, 1985, Volume LII, 1985.

Gary Paulsen

Born May 17, 1939, in Minneapolis, Minn.; son of Oscar (an army officer) and Eunice Paulsen; married second wife, Ruth Ellen Wright (an artist), May 5, 1971; children: James Wright. *Education:* Attended Bemidji College, 1957-58, and University of Colorado, 1976. *Politics:* "As Solzhenitsyn has said, 'If we limit ourselves to political structures we are not artists.'" *Religion:* "I believe in spiritual progress." *Residence:* Leonard, Minn. *Agent:* Ray Peekner Literary Agency, 2625 North 36th St., Milwaukee, Wis. 53210.

■ Career

Writer. Has also worked as a teacher, field engineer, editor, soldier, actor, director, farmer, rancher, truck driver, trapper, professional archer, migrant farm worker, singer, and sailor. *Military service:* U.S. Army, 1959-62; became sergeant.

■ Awards, Honors

Central Missouri Award for Children's Literature, 1976; *The Green Recruit* was chosen one of New York Public Library's Books for the Teen Age, 1980, 1981 and 1982, and *Sailing*, 1982; *Dancing*

Carl was selected one of American Library Association's Best Young Adult Books, 1983, and *Tracker*, 1984; Society of Midland Authors Award, l985, for *Tracker*; Parents' Choice Award for Literature from the Parents' Choice Foundation, 1985, for *Dog Song;* Newbery Honor Book, l986, for *Dogsong,* and l988, for *Hatchet; Dogsong* was chosen one of Child Study Association of America's Children's Books of the Year, 1986.

■ Writings

Novels:

The Implosion Effect, Major Books, 1976.
The Death Specialists, Major Books, 1976.
Winterkill, T. Nelson, 1977.
The Foxman, T. Nelson, 1977.
Tiltawhirl John, T. Nelson, 1977.
C. B. Jockey, Major Books, 1977.
The Night the White Deer Died, T. Nelson, 1978.
Hope and a Hatchet, T. Nelson, 1978.
(With Ray Peekner) *The Green Recruit,* Independence Press, 1978.
The Spitball Gang, Elsevier/Nelson, 1980.
Campkill, Pinnacle Books, 1981.
The Sweeper, Harlequin, 1981.
Clutterkill, Harlequin, 1982.
Popcorn Days and Buttermilk Nights, Lodestar Books, 1983.
Dancing Carl, Bradbury, 1983.
Tracker, Bradbury, 1984.
Dogsong, Bradbury, 1985.
Sentries, Bradbury, 1986.

Murphy, Walker, 1987.
The Crossing, F. Watts, l987.
Hatchet, Bradbury, l987.
The Island, F. Watts, 1988.
Murphy's Gold, Walker, 1988.

Short Stories:

The Madonna Stories, Van Bliet, 1988.

Nonfiction:

The Special War, Sirkay, 1966.
Some Birds Don't Fly, Rand McNally, 1969.
The Building a New, Buying an Old, Remodeling a Used Comprehensive Home and Shelter Book, Prentice-Hall, 1976.
Farm: A History and Celebration of the American Farmer, Prentice-Hall, 1977.
(With John Morris) *Hiking and Backpacking* (illustrated by Ruth Wright), Simon & Schuster, 1978.
(With J. Morris) *Canoeing, Kayaking, and Rafting* (illustrated by John Peterson and Jack Storholm), Simon & Schuster, 1979.
Beat the System: A Survival Guide, Pinnacle Books, 1983.

Neil Waldman's jacket painting for Paulsen's award-winning novel.

Juvenile:

Mr. Tucket, Funk & Wagnalls, 1968.
(With Dan Theis) *Martin Luther King: The Man Who Climbed the Mountain*, Raintree, 1976.
The Small Ones (illustrated by K. Goff and with photographs by Wilford Miller), Raintree, 1976.
The Grass-Eaters: Real Animals (illustrated by K. Goff and with photographs by W. Miller), Raintree, 1976.
Dribbling, Shooting, and Scoring Sometimes, Raintree, 1976.
Hitting, Pitching, and Running Maybe, Raintree, 1976.
Tackling, Running, and Kicking—Now and Again, Raintree, 1977.
Riding, Roping, and Bulldogging—Almost, Raintree, 1977.
Careers in an Airport (illustrated with photographs by Roger Nye), Raintree, 1977.
The CB Radio Caper (illustrated by John Asquith), Raintree, 1977.
The Curse of the Cobra (illustrated by J. Asquith), Raintree, 1977.
The Golden Stick, Raintree, 1977.
Running, Jumping, and Throwing—If You Can (illustrated by Heinz Kluetmeier), Raintree, 1978.
Forehanding and Backhanding—If You're Lucky (illustrated with photographs by H. Kluetmeier), Raintree, 1978.
Downhill, Hotdogging and Cross-Country—If the Snow Isn't Sticky (illustrated with photographs by Willis Wood and H. Kluetmeier), Raintree, 1979.
Facing Off, Checking and Goaltending—Perhaps (illustrated with photographs by Melchior DiGiacomo and H. Kluetmeier), Raintree, 1979.
Going Very Fast in a Circle—If You Don't Run Out of Gas (illustrated with photographs by H. Kluetmeier and Bob D'Olivo), Raintree, 1979.
Launching, Floating High and Landing—If Your Pilot Light Doesn't Go Out (illustrated with photographs by H. Kluetmeier), Raintree, 1979.
Pummeling, Falling and Getting Up—Sometimes (illustrated with photographs by H. Kluetmeier and Joe DiMaggio), Raintree, 1979.
Track, Enduro and Motocross—Unless You Fall Over (illustrated with photographs by H. Kluetmeier and others), Raintree, 1979.

(With Art Browne, Jr.) *TV and Movie Animals,* Messner, 1980.

Sailing: From Jibs to Jibing (illustrated by wife, Ruth W. Paulsen), Messner, 1981.

Plays:

"Communications" (one-act), first produced in New Mexico, 1974.

"Together-Apart" (one-act), first produced in Denver at Changing Scene Theatre, 1976.

Also author of *Meteor,* and more than 200 short stories and articles.

■ Adaptations

"Dogsong" (listening cassette; filmstrip with cassette), Random House/Miller-Brody, 1986.

■ Work In Progress

Collaborating on a book with a Soviet writer.

■ Sidelights

Gary Paulsen was born on May 17, 1939 in Minneapolis, Minnesota. "I'm only a second-generation American. My father's family came to this country from Denmark; my mother's people emigrated from Norway and Sweden. My father was a career military man who served as an officer on General Patton's staff during World War II. He spent most of my childhood years fighting the Germans, and my mother spent the war years working in a munitions plant in Chicago—'Rosie the Riveter' type stuff. I was reared by my grandmother and several aunts. I first saw my father when I was seven in the Philippines where my parents and I lived from 1946 until 1949.

"After we returned to the States, we moved around constantly. I lived in every state. The longest time I spent in one school was about five months. I was an 'army brat,' and it was a miserable life. School was a nightmare because I was unbelievably shy, and terrible at sports. I had no friends, and teachers ridiculed me. I wound up skipping most of the ninth grade and had to make it up during the tenth grade so I could graduate on time. As it was, I squeezed through with Cs and Ds. Again, I was sent to live with relatives. In order to buy clothes and have some spending money, I worked at a young age. For a while I sold the *Grand Forks Herald* in hospitals and bars; during junior high school I set up pins every night in a bowling alley."[1]

Paulsen harnessing a Husky.

"When I was fifteen, I started taking off. I'd go for a summer and hoe sugar beets, and during the school year I'd find things to do at night...."[2]

His teenage years were not totally bleak, however. He had "safety nets—all of them women. My grandmother and aunts were terribly important to me. And there was someone else. One day as I was walking past the public library in twenty below temperatures, I could see the reading room bathed in a beautiful golden light. I went in to get warm and to my absolute astonishment the librarian walked up to me and asked if I wanted a library card. She didn't care if I looked right, wore the right clothes, dated the right girls, was popular at sports—none of those prejudices existed in the public library. When she handed me the card, she handed me the world. I can't even describe how liberating it was. She recommended westerns and science fiction but every now and then would slip in a classic. I roared through everything she gave me and in the summer read a book a day. It was as though I had been dying of thirst and the librarian had handed me a five-gallon bucket of water. I drank and drank."[1]

The love of reading and the outdoors eventually took Paulsen to Bemidji College. "As I'd grown up hunting and trapping, I was able to pay my way through the first year by laying trap lines for the state of Minnesota."[1]

From college, Paulsen went into the army for three years. "I worked with missiles. When I got out of the service, I took extension courses and accrued enough credits to become a field engineer."[1]

Working in that capacity, Paulsen was employed in the aerospace departments of Bendix and Lockheed after the army. "I worked on the Gemini shots, the Mariner probes and on designing the guidance section for the Shrike, an anti-radar missile. I was good at my work, but didn't like it."[1]

"I was sitting in a satellite tracking station in California in front of a massive console and related computers. . . .I'd finished reading a magazine article on flight-testing a new airplane during an inactive period, and thought, *Gad*, what a way to make a living—writing about something you like and getting paid for it! I remembered writing some of my past reports, some fictionalized versions I'd included. And I thought: What the hell, I *am* an engineering writer.

Jacket illustration by Richard Cuffari from *The Foxman* by Gary Paulsen.

"But, conversely, I also realized I didn't know a thing about writing—*professionally*. After several hours of hard thinking, a way to earn came to me. All I had to do was go to work editing a magazine.

"I swung a typewriter around in the middle of all those consoles and computers, and typed up a *fictitious* resume showing I had been an editor for years! I mailed it to the publisher of a men's magazine in Hollywood. Within a short time, he *hired* me!

"However within a few days, the publisher quickly saw through me. I didn't even know what a layout sheet was!. . ."[3]

"My secretary—who was all of nineteen years old—edited my first three issues. They could see I was serious about wanting to learn, and they were willing to teach me. We published some excellent writers—Steinbeck, Bradbury, Ellison—which was great training and exposure for me."[1]

"I was there for about a year, and it was the best of all possible ways to learn about writing. It probably did more to improve my craft and ability than any other single event in my life.

"I consider formalized academic training for writing practically a waste anyway. Most academics I have run into seem to instruct incorrectly, and actually stifle the creative drive and discipline needed for becoming a professional writer."[3]

While living in California, Paulsen did a considerable amount of work as a film extra. "Once I played a drunken Indian in a movie called 'Flap' starring Anthony Quinn. I was on screen for about thirty-five seconds."[1] Paulsen also took up sculpting. "I don't sculpt anymore. I won a show several years ago in Santa Barbara for a piece of sculpture I did, and I became obsessed by it. I just kept sculpting and it was distracting from my writing. I don't think you can do more than one art at a time. . . ."[2]

His first book, *The Special War*, was based on interviews he did with servicemen returning from Viet Nam.

After twelve years as a writer, Paulsen had become one of the most prolific authors in the country, having published nearly forty books, over 200 magazine articles and short stories, and two plays. He wrote nonfiction on hunting, trapping, farming, animals, medicine and outdoor life, as well as juvenile and adult fiction. On a bet with a friend, he once wrote eleven articles and short stories inside four days and sold all of them. To burn off tension, he was given to long walks around his

Paulsen, numbered-up for the Iditarod.

Minnesota farm during which he would "blow the hell out of a hillside"[3] with a rifle.

Paulsen's life was changed radically and abruptly after the 1977 publication of his novel *Winterkill;* he was sued for libel. "My attorney, a full-blooded Chippewa, is now a reservation Magistrate. Our case went all the way up to the Minnesota Supreme Court, where we finally won. It was a good fight, and I'd do it all over again, but it brought me to the edge of bankruptcy. And I didn't get the support I'd expected from my publisher. In fact, the whole situation was so nasty and ugly that I stopped writing. I wanted nothing more to do with publishing and burned my bridges, so to speak.

"So there I was, living deep in the country in northern Minnesota with no way to earn a living. Having no choice in the matter, I went back to trapping for the state. It was predator control work, aimed at coyotes and beavers. The traps we used were snares, which kill the animals right away. It's not pleasant, but it's humane, if death can be humane. I was working a sixty-mile line mostly on foot, sometimes on skis, going out in the early morning and heading home at night. Very slow work.

"One day a guy named Bob McWilliams came to my house saying he had four dogs—a sprint team used to doing twelve-mile races—he couldn't keep. As we were so broke we didn't even have a car, the prospect of *any* sort of transportation was very inviting. And besides, the dogs were free. This team was real slow, but they did make my work much easier. One day about midnight we were crossing Clear Water Lake, which is about three miles long. There was a full moon shining so brightly on the snow you could read by it. There was no one around, and all I could hear was the rhythm of the dogs' breathing as they pulled the sled. We came to the top of a hill, the steam from the dogs' breath all but hid their bodies—the entire world seemed to glisten. It almost stopped my heart; I'd never seen anything so beautiful. I stayed out with the dogs for seven days. I didn't go home—my wife was frantic,—I didn't check line, I just ran the dogs, sixty to seventy miles an hour. We covered a lot of northern Minnesota. For food, we had a few beaver carcasses. You know, you don't train these northern breeds to pull sleds. It's part of their genetic make-up. When a puppy gets to be seven months old, you put a harness on him and he'll pull a sled. I was initiated into this incredibly ancient and very beautiful bond, and it was as if everything that had happened to me before ceased to exist. When I came off that seven-day run, I pulled all my traps, having resolved never again to kill.

"Shortly afterward, McWilliams told me about the Iditarod, a 1200-mile dogsled race that goes from Iditarod, an old mining town in the middle of Alaska, to Nome. On the spur of the moment, I announced, 'Sure, I'll run.' I had no idea what I was in for. And I certainly never figured I could raise the money it takes to get a team together. It was getting down to the wire when Richard Jackson, the publisher of Bradbury Press, called wanting to know what I was writing. Now I had never met or worked with Jackson. 'I'm not writing! I'm running dogs!' I told him. I was hard up for the upcoming Iditarod. 'I'll send you the money,' he said, 'and when you get around to writing something, let me be the first to see it.'

"So I ran the Iditarod—a mind-boggling experience. You don't sleep for seventeen days. You begin to hallucinate. You are not allowed any outside assistance. If you make a mistake, you are left to die. Even the CBS helicopters covering the event can't intervene. You have no physical contact with your dogs—it's all voice commands given from where you stand on the back of the sled. If your lead dog doesn't like and respect you, the odds are good that you will die. If the dogs sense that you are losing your nerve, they may simply stop, make craters in the snow, roll up in a ball and sleep for days. That's called 'cratering' and once they start, there's absolutely nothing you can do to stop it. The dogs may also go berserk and trash the sled. And there you are, all alone in the middle of Alaska. The dogs are deeply intuitive and incredibly smart, far more intelligent than most people.

"When you first start the race, you feel great, exhilarated by the unbelievable beauty of your surroundings. After about eight miles of navigating the Arctic Circle, you start to feel scared. After twelve miles, you realize that you are nothing and the dogs are everything. To survive, you must be in deep harmony with your team. The Iditarod may sound like a macho thrill, but it's the opposite. You go where death goes, and death doesn't give a damn about macho. Besides, the last two races were won by women.

"Here's something that was brought home to me: macho is a lie. It's testicular garbage. Core toughness and compassion are the opposite of macho. The absence of fear comes with knowledge, not strength or bravura. More people should be

telling this to young people, instead of 'climb the highest mountain and kill something.'"[1]

Paulsen's experiences with the dogs and the resulting transformations motivated him to continue with his writing. *Dancing Carl* was published in 1983 by Bradbury Press and had its first incarnation as a dance. "I began it when I was trapping beaver. It was a narrative ballet for two dancers with original music by John Collins and choreography by Nancy Keller. A seven-minute version of this piece was aired on Minnesota Public Television."[1]

Tracker, brought out a year later, deals with the metaphysics of tracking an animal. John, the thirteen-year-old protagonist, faces his first season of hunting alone, while his grandfather lay dying of cancer. Said Paulsen: "They're a farm family in northern Minnesota; they have always hunted their meat. 'We take meat with a gun,' John's grandfather tells him. 'It doesn't make you a man. It doesn't make you anything to kill.' What I'm exploring is the almost mystical relationship that develops between the hunter and the hunted. It's a relationship with its own integrity, not to be violated. There is, in the book, the concept of 'giving death' to the deer. I've seen this. At a certain point, the animal senses death coming and accepts it. This acceptance of death is something I was trying to write about in *Tracker*."[1]

Dogsong also deals with an adolescent boy struggling to become deeply humane. Russell, a fourteen-year-old Eskimo, has sought guidance from Oogruk, a tribal wise man, who counsels him to take his dog team across Alaska and back. Enroute, Russell finds a pregnant girl about his age dying of exposure. Helping her to give birth, he does his best to save her life. "I wrote *Dogsong* in camp while I was training my team for the Iditarod. It'd be twenty below, and there I'd sit by the fire writing longhand in my notebook. You know, I miss *Dogsong*. I wish I could keep writing it. It's like a friend who's gone away."[1] The book was named a Newbery Honor Book in 1986, and in 1988, *Hatchet* was also. "It's like things have come full circle. I felt like nothing the first time I walked into a library, and now library associations are giving me awards. It means a lot to me."[1]

One of Paulsen's latest books is *The Madonna Stories*, a collection of stories intended as a tribute to women who, by virtue of what he calls "core toughness" have deeply impressed him. "It started with Gloria, a friend of mine, who has two sons (out of a total of five kids) that were born with spina bifida, and a husband with a drinking problem. Not

Jacket drawing by Jon Weiman from *Tracker* by Gary Paulsen.

Jacket painting by Jon Weiman.

only has she kept her family together for twenty-five years, but she's recently gone to college for a nursing degree and has consistently been at the top of her class. That got me started looking at the ladies in my family. They amaze me. Women are inevitably emotionally tougher than men. I want to understand their kind of toughness, and so feel that I must write about it."[1]

"I don't think there's any attempt on the part of men (writers) to understand what women are or the influence they have on our lives. Incidentally, my grandmother taught me how to crochet. The male thing is to have an objective and go out and get it done. You can't stop. It's like the Iditarod, or combat, or all those stupid things that people do that are pointless. And when you try one of these things and you fail, and you do fail, you have this feminine influence to fall back on. You can lean back and say, all right, maybe the male side is crushed because I didn't make it, but I can also have compassion. I can try to understand my failure and I can try to learn from it."[2]

"I write because it's all I can do," admits Paulsen. "Every time I've tried to do something else I cannot, and have to come back to writing, though often I hate it—hate it and love it. It's much like being a slave, I suppose, and in slavery there is a kind of freedom that I find in writing: a perverse thing. I'm not 'motivated.' Nor am I particularly driven. I write because it's all there is."[1]

Paulsen writes for a youth market because, for his part, he feels that it's "artistically fruitless to write for adults. Adults created the mess which we are struggling to outlive. Adults have their minds set. Art reaches out for newness, and adults aren't new. And adults aren't truthful. The concept behind *Sentries* is that young people know the score. *Sentries* is mostly a lot of questions, and I'm betting that young people have the answers."[1]

His work habits have changed considerably over the years. He now does most of his writing on computer. "I even have a portable Radio Shack model I can take camping with me. When I was training dogs, we would run six hours on, four off. During my 'down time' in camp, I'd write. But

Sentries is mostly a lot of questions, and I'm betting that young people have the answers."[1]

His work habits have changed considerably over the years. He now does most of his writing on computer. "I even have a portable Radio Shack model I can take camping with me. When I was training dogs, we would run six hours on, four off. During my 'down time' in camp, I'd write. But these days, I'm camping less and less, and hardly running dogs at all. I'm building an office on my property with more advanced computers, modem links and the like. I find I do a lot more revision now that I work on computer. Diskettes are perfect for raw research. It's a new form and perfect for experimentation."[1]

A strict disciplinarian when he is writing, Paulsen, goes "'full bore' especially if there is a deadline looming. When I'm in such a work cycle, nothing in the world matters. You could burn the house down around me, and I wouldn't know it until the paper in the typewriter caught fire!

"When I work—I *work*. I actually sit down and write. That's what they pay me to do, and that's what I do!"[3]

Paulsen has several tips on writing for aspiring authors: "1. When writing fiction, let the *fingers* do the fast, mechanical work—your mind is really not strained when you work quickly.

"2. Stick to subjects you know best. . .so you can turn out clean work on the first draft. Rely on your experiences so you won't devote too much time to research.

"3. *Rewrite* and polish in *your mind*.

"4. Try to get your typing production up to 1,000 words an hour. Stick to deadlines and keep working.

"5. Stay away from antiquated typewriters. Get the best electric machine you can afford.

"6. Get a good agent. I've been told by some writers that they'd rather not use an agent, and keep the ten per cent. *Bull*-loney! In my experience, no writer should ever sell his own work. Writers are too close to it—too *personally* involved! And they are wide open to getting *ripped off*.

"My agent is, frankly, *dynamite*—the best. He spends a great deal of time researching markets, smelling them out, studying their needs. He then tells me what area to concentrate the novel in. I research it and send him two chapters and a synopsis. He sells it. Oh, we've had a few *bounces*,

but not very many. The method saves me a lot of time and he *earns* his ten per cent.

"There have been times—many times—when I was starving when I would have accepted subcontracts. Hell, I would have taken *anything!* But my agent held back, wouldn't accept anything he considered *nonprofessional*. I *would* have. As a result of his direction, I have come out considerably *ahead* of the ten per cent he charged.

"When you 'lock into' a good agent, you ride with him all the way. You do what he tells you, even if it means bouncing a contract if you are starving. If you respect the guy enough to have him sell your work—in a way *control* your life—then do what he says. Otherwise, dump him and get another one."[3]

When not writing, Paulsen gives public readings, performances, and does storytelling in small towns near his Minnesota farm. "It's real nice. Generally, it takes place in a town hall. People bring coffee, bake cakes and pies. There's a coal stove. Everyone sits around listening and swapping tales.

"I'm also building a garden. The first thing I do every day is go into my garden and meditate. I try to become serene and write from whatever reservoir of serenity I find within myself."[1]

Paulsen devotes a good deal of his time to nuclear disarmament causes. "I believe that governments are standing in the way of solving this thing. It's up to private citizens. We cannot let our children grow up terrified of being blown apart by a thermonuclear device. . . .My fifteen-year-old son and I sat down and wrote a letter to the Soviet Writers Union. A simple letter to let them know we have no desire to blow them up, that we do not consider them the 'Evil Empire.' Everyone should write letters—it makes a difference."[1] In response to the letter Paulsen was invited to discuss his work with a delegation of Russian writers who met in Minneapolis. Furthermore, one of the Soviet writers and Paulsen plan to collaborate on a book in an effort to spread good will between our two nations.

Besides world progress, Paulsen believes in spiritual progress. ". . .I have a spiritual belief which is really not explainable. I kind of live for a spiritual progress or perfection that has nothing to do with an organized religion. It is a personal thing. If you grow one inch, it's better than going back a half an inch.

"I've studied several [Eastern religions]. And I've studied the Bible, and I've studied American Indian beliefs. I went to several elders in the various tribes who were spiritual leaders and asked for advice. They were extremely helpful in guiding me. I don't think individuals have any strength on their own. I think they have to find strength from an outside spiritual source."[2]

Why does Paulsen continue to write? For two reasons, he claims: "I want my...years on this ball of earth to mean something. Writing furnishes me a way for that to happen. Secondly, I have not done anything else in my life that gives me the personal satisfaction that writing does. It pleases me to write—in the very literal sense of the word. When I have done well with it, and 'cooked' for a day so that it felt good when I put it down—it flowed and worked right. When all that is right, I go to sleep with an immense feeling of personal satisfaction.

"If you write, there is no substitute for work—damn hard work. No substitute for time with the machine—all else must be secondary. And the more you work, the better your craft—and the better your craft, the better your art. It's *that* simple."[3]

Footnote Sources:

[1] Based on an interview by Marguerite Feitlowitz for *Authors and Artists for Young Adults.*
[2] Maryann N. Weidt, "Gary Paulsen: A Sentry for Peace," *Voice of Youth Advocates,* August/October, 1986.
[3] Franz Serdahely, "Prolific Paulsen," *Writer's Digest,* January, 1980.

■ For More Information See

Horn Book, October, 1980, August, 1983, June, 1984, November/December, 1987.
Patty Campbell, "The Young Adult Perplex," *Wilson Library Bulletin,* January, 1988.

Marilyn Sachs

B orn December 18, 1927, in Bronx, N.Y.; daughter of Samuel (an insurance salesman) and Anna (Smith) Stickle; married Morris Sachs (a sculptor), January 26, 1947; children: Anne, Paul. *Education:* Hunter College (now Hunter College of the City University of New York), B.A., 1949; Columbia University, M.S. in L.S., 1953. *Politics:* "Changing constantly." *Religion:* Jewish. *Address:* 733 31st Ave., San Francisco, Calif. 94121.

■ Career

Author. Brooklyn (N.Y.) Public Library, children's librarian, 1949-60; San Francisco (Calif.) Public Library, part-time children's librarian, 1961-67. *Member:* American Jane Austen Society, English Jane Austen Society.

■ Awards, Honors

Outstanding Books of the Year Award, *New York Times,* 1971, for *The Bears' House,* and 1973, for *A Pocket Full of Seeds;* Best Books of the Year Award, *School Library Journal,* 1971, for *The Bears' House,* and 1973, for *The Truth about Mary Rose;* National Book Award, finalist, 1972, for *The Bears' House;* Jane Addams Children's Book Honor Award, 1974, for *A Pocket Full of Seeds;* Silver Pencil Award, Collective Propaganda van het Bederlandse Boek, Netherlands, 1974, for *The Truth about Mary Rose,* and 1977, for *Dorrie's Book;* Austrian Children's Book Prize, 1977, for *The Bears' House;* Garden State Children's Book Award, 1978, for *Dorrie's Book; A Summer's Lease* was chosen one of *School Library Journal's* "Best Book for Spring," 1979; *Fleet-Footed Florence* was selected as a "Children's Choice" by the International Reading Association, 1982; Association of Jewish Libraries Award, 1983, for *Call Me Ruth; The Fat Girl* was chosen one of American Library Association's Best Books for Young Adults, 1984; Christopher Award, 1986, for *Underdog.*

■ Writings

Amy Moves In (illustrated by Judith Gwyn Brown), Doubleday, 1964.
Laura's Luck (illustrated by Ib Ohlsson), Doubleday, 1965.
Amy and Laura (illustrated by Tracy Sugarman), Doubleday, 1966.
Veronica Ganz (ALA Notable Book; illustrated by Louis Glanzman), Doubleday, 1968.
Peter and Veronica (Junior Literary Guild selection; illustrated by L. Glanzman), Doubleday, 1969.
Marv (Junior Literary Guild selection; illustrated by L. Glanzman), Doubleday, 1970.
The Bears' House (illustrated by L. Glanzman), Doubleday, 1971.

The Truth about Mary Rose (illustrated by L. Glanzman), Doubleday, 1973.

A Pocket Full of Seeds (ALA Notable Book; illustrated by Ben Stahl), Doubleday, 1973.

Matt's Mitt (illustrated by Hilary Knight), Doubleday, 1975.

Dorrie's Book (illustrated by daughter, Anne Sachs), Doubleday, 1975.

A December Tale, Doubleday, 1976.

A Secret Friend (Junior Literary Guild selection), Doubleday, 1978.

A Summer's Lease, Dutton, 1979.

Bus Ride (illustrated by Amy Rowen), Dutton, 1980.

Class Pictures, Dutton, 1980.

Fleet-Footed Florence (illustrated by Charles Robinson), Doubleday, 1981.

Hello...Wrong Number (illustrated by Pamela Johnson), Dutton, 1981.

Beach Towels (illustrated by Jim Spence), Dutton, 1982.

Call Me Ruth (Junior Literary Guild selection), Doubleday, 1982.

Fourteen (Junior Literary Guild selection), Dutton, 1983.

The Fat Girl, Dutton, 1983.

Thunderbird (illustrated by J. Spence), Dutton, 1985.

Underdog (Junior Literary Guild selection), Doubleday, 1985.

Baby Sister, Dutton, 1986.

Almost Fifteen, Dutton, 1987.

Fran Ellen's House, Dutton, 1987.

Plays:

Reading Between the Lines, Children's Book Council, 1971.

Contributor to *New York Times* and *San Francisco Chronicle*.

■ Adaptations

"Veronica Ganz" (filmstrip with record or cassette and books), Insight Media Programs, 1975.

■ Work In Progress

"I am presently at work on a young adult novel about a girl who has a childish mother. I'm also trying very hard not to think about my next book. This is always a problem—how to keep a new work out of your head until the old one is finished."

■ Sidelights

Born December 18, 1927, in New York's east Bronx. Sachs grew up in the "railroad" apartment on Jennings Street. "Jennings Street had no trees, birds, or flowers. But it had kids. Every day after school and all day on the weekends, holidays, and during the summer vacation, the kids poured out of the apartment houses and filled the sidewalks, the playground, and the street itself. Hardly any cars ever came through so that the street served as a field for stickball or a rink for roller skaters."[1]

"I started kindergarten when I was four. My mother said I was five. Either she thought I was amazingly mature for my age or she wanted to get rid of me. I prefer the former reason.

"All was well in the beginning....But one terrible day, when I raised my hand and asked my teacher if I could go to the girls' room, she told me I would have to wait until somebody else needed to go as well. Evidently nobody else needed to go and my desperation grew. My teacher suggested we play Farmer in the Dell and as the game progressed, my self-control failed me....It was one of the most humiliating moments of my life. But humiliating moments are mother's milk to writers, and the episode ended up forty-five years later in the first chapter of my book *Class Pictures*."[2]

"I was a very skinny, cowardly kid. There were lots of bullies on our block and I never learned to stand up to them. They'd take advantage of me until my older sister came to my rescue, bash a few heads, and I would beat a hasty retreat. The only place I felt safe was our neighborhood branch library where I spent as much time as I could. I was not weak in the sense of not knowing what I wanted to do or not having the determination to do it, rather it was that I was not at all confrontational, particularly if the confrontations became physical. It's the weaklings who grow up to become writers, not the bullies. Of this I am sure.

"I knew from a very young age that I would be a writer. Reading and writing always seemed to me to go together. My teachers and librarians were impressed with my reading habits because I devoured the classics. It wasn't so much that my tastes were particularly 'refined,' or that I was exceptionally 'advanced,' but that I had no desire to read stories set in the present. As far as I was concerned, the whole point of reading was to transport out of the here-and-now. Historical fiction was my favorite genre. I read nothing that took place after 1700. I also loved fairy tales (particularly those in which the younger sister is the heroine). My favorite authors wrote swashbucklers. Dale Snedecker, Howard Pyle and Jeffrey Farnol wrote books with terrific heroines who could ride horses, swordfight and 'slay dragons' as well, if not better, than any man. When I was a little older, Sir Walter Scott and Alexander Dumas were also very important to me. *Rebecca of Sunnybrook Farm* is a book I came to love for entirely different reasons. My mother was quite often ill while I was growing up and she died when I was twelve. This was the one book she read aloud to me."[1]

"I could read very well by myself at that time, but it didn't matter. She would read me a chapter every day, usually in the afternoon. I would hurry home from school and carry a small chair into the living room. She sat on the sofa and I sat below, looking up at the book and her face above it. She loved that book. Sometimes she'd stop to laugh at parts she thought were funny, and I'd laugh too even though I didn't always understand what was so funny. It's still very sharp in my mind—sitting there with my mother, sharing that special book that I didn't quite understand, but knowing that my mother and I were doing something together that belonged to nobody else."[2]

"My mother's death was very hard on our family. It was she who had provided most of our stability. My father, who eventually remarried, was a colorful character, much like the father in *Amy Moves In*. He held a variety of jobs, or no job at all for periods of time. He was a storyteller and a dabbler in politics. He was a born organizer and loved to organize any kind of club from the Knights of Pythias to a variety of political organizations mostly for the Democratic Party.

"My father also did not believe that girls needed a higher education. My sister and I had to fight him very hard on this. Both of us held jobs throughout high school, and I left home at seventeen in order to go to college. I was an English major at Hunter College and knew that someday I would be a writer.

"Like many women of my generation, I married while still in college. My husband, Morris Sachs, is a sculptor. As newlyweds, we helped put each other through school. He had just gotten out of the Service, and paid his tuition with the GI Bill of Rights—an enormous help to us.

"I was at loose ends after graduation. I didn't feel I had anything to write about. The one thing I knew was that I needed a job. I found myself thinking back to all the pleasant, safe hours I had spent at the local library. When I saw an ad in the paper for a children's library trainee in the Brooklyn borough system, I applied. I had no idea what I was getting into. Looking back, the interview was quite comical.

"'Do you like children?' they asked me. 'I love children.' (What was I supposed to say? I needed a job.)

"But I took to it like a fish to water. I didn't know which I loved more, the books or the kids. I worked at the main building at Grand Army Plaza, in the Coney Island branch, the Brownville Children's branch and at various extensions. We were 'missionaries' as much as librarians. I worked on a bookmobile that went all over Brooklyn and I told stories in parks, playgrounds, housing projects, and hospitals. The Brooklyn system was extraordinary. Not only was the collection excellent, but the librarians were models of professionalism and dedication. I loved my job and stayed ten years.

"During this time I wrote my first book, *Amy Moves In*. I was twenty-five, very arrogant, and certain that my book would be better than anything else I was reading. I was absolutely astonished when no one immediately offered to publish it. I was also astounded at the amount of criticism and suggestions I got from editors who returned the manuscript. A number of them said they would consider buying the book if I made certain revisions. I had no idea publishing worked that way. By today's standards, *Amy Moves In* is a very mild book. But back then—this was the 1950s—apparently it wasn't mild enough. It was about a poor Jewish family, itself a problem since there were few Jewish families in children's books then. It was an unwritten rule that in 'realistic' novels, no one should be really poor, unless they overcame their poverty in the traditional happy ending. Amy's father—a perfectly nice father—doesn't work, and that too was a problem. Editors asked that I find him some suitable employment. They wanted all the 'loose ends' tied up, as though life were neat and tidy. I certainly wanted my book published, but I was unwilling to make the changes editors were asking for. After a year of submitting the book to various publishers, I put it in my desk drawer, where it stayed for ten years.

"I moved with my husband and two children to California where I worked in the San Francisco Public Library. Out of the blue, someone I had worked with in Brooklyn wrote to tell me that he was now an editor with Doubleday and would I please send the novel I had written so very long

Dust jacket for Dutton's hardcover edition.

ago. Two weeks later, on one of those 'impossible days' when everything that could go wrong did, there was a letter in my mailbox accepting my book for publication. I remember telling my children (who had been acting up all day) that I was 'going to be an author,' to which my daughter replied, 'You don't have the time.'

"Well, I did have time! Knowing that I had a book coming out was tremendously inspiring, and I have had a book published just about every year since 1964, when *Amy Moves In* came out.

"By then times had changed. The mid-sixties to the late-seventies were a kind of golden age for children's books. The civil rights struggles and victories, peace marches, the women's movement—all the things that made the sixties—were very good for publishing. Also, this was a time of prosperity and publishers could afford to take risks.

Reviewers were impressed with *Amy Moves In*. The *Virginia Kirkus' Service* noted that "[Sachs] follows Amy through her years of trial in a way that shows she's been there. The family scenes have the reality of relatives as they are rather than as the

articles on child psychology that Amy's mother reads would have them be....This is a very funny book that still offers readers valid insights into people and their behavior. Set near the end of the Depression, it is true to its time and true to the unchanging conditions of childhood."

"My working process is pretty much the same for every book. The first stage is always research. I prolong this phase as long as I possibly can, usually spending about a month. I read everything I can get my hands on. When I was doing a book involving Joan of Arc I even looked at the actual court records. After my library work is done, I do a first draft straight through. The aim here is to get the whole book roughed out. I draft each chapter by hand and then enter it into the computer.

"I start with a character, or a group of characters and in the first few chapters try to figure out why they belong in a book together. I have a vague plan in my head, and after drafting several chapters I can do a 'general outline' of the whole book. I map out what will happen in the first five chapters, then the second five, and finally the third five. But I am locked into nothing. Just the other day, a character I had assumed would be very minor began to take over the chapter I was working on. She's quite wonderful, actually, a poet. Perhaps this has something to do with the fact that my son-in-law is a poet and he and our daughter are currently staying with us. In any case, I have for a long time wanted to deal with a female character who writes. Whatever the reason, it's a marvellous surprise, and I'm going to follow her for a while.

"On a good day I can do a whole chapter. A more typical day, however, is half a chapter. When I sit down to write, I really write. I have friends who fuss over every word and by day's end have maybe half a page. I'm not like that. I generally send this initial draft to my daughter, Anne, whose criticism I value highly. I've done this for years, and for years she's wanted me to put more sex in my books. Perhaps I don't because I believe in too many books girl characters are measured by their romantic successes. I want my girl characters to be seen as important people with or without romance. First drafts usually take me about three months, sometimes less. I have done drafts of a couple of books in a matter of weeks. I send the corrected draft to my editor who generally returns it with suggestions for revisions. I usually spend a month or less on revisions.

"My style is much more stripped down than it used to be. This may be because at first I wrote in the third person, which allows for a considerable amount of description. My later books are first-person narratives, a form in which you have fewer stylistic choices. Everything must be subordinate to the character's voice. Nothing may compete with that. My first-person books tend to take place in the present, which means that the character is telling her story (or his story, as in *The Fat Girl*) with a certain amount of urgency. My protagonists are telling their stories because they are troubled and are trying to work out a problem. In that frame of mind, they aren't disposed to lyrical descriptions. As much as I have enjoyed writing in the first person, I think I would like to go back and do something in the third person again. I am curious as to how I would handle it after not having done so in a number of years.

"There is another way in which my writing has changed. I am much harder on myself than I used to be, and much more critical. My first books pretty much wrote themselves. I rarely stopped to rewrite a sentence. Now I am more aware and concerned with the craft of writing. Although I manage to keep up my momentum, I revise much more as I go along. I realize now that if I don't watch myself, I tend to use too many simple words and insipid, non-descriptive adjectives.

"You know, writers go through different periods. Sometimes the work goes well, sometimes it goes badly, and sometimes you feel like you'll never write again. About ten years ago, I hit a 'dry spell' that I was certain was the end. I couldn't get a handle on *A Secret Friend*. I had to struggle so hard that I really believed I had lost the ability to write. There's nothing you can do about these periods. You go to the library, go for long walks, try to make yourself write, try to make yourself have fun. Nothing works. Maybe I was tired and needed to recoup my energies. Mostly, though, I felt lost. All writers go through these times. You have to figure out a way to survive. A friend of mine takes a job during these periods so she won't brood. Other people I know travel. There really is no advice—you have to find your own way to survive until it passes. *A Secret Friend* has been rather popular but it's not one of my favorite books—it's too painful. The spell hit me like an ambush. There was no warning. And then one day it was over.

"Since then, I have had shorter periods when particular books were very difficult. I drafted *The Bears' House* three times before I came up with a version that worked. But the fourth time around, I wrote the book in two weeks flat. One of the hardest books I've ever done was *The Fat Girl*. It

took me a long time—and many pages—to get to the material I really wanted to write about. So often, writing is a process of 'excavation'—certainly it was in this case. The initial impulse for the book came from a newspaper article I read about an art teacher and his relationship with a fat young woman in his adult-education painting class. This woman showed extraordinary talent, which he was glad to acknowledge. Suddenly, however, she stopped coming to class, which mystified him. He went to her for an explanation. She told him she was dying of leukemia. The worst thing, she said, was that she had never been in love. Well, one thing led to another, and they were soon involved in an affair. She went back to her lover's painting class, did fine work, and shortly thereafter, died.

"That was the story I started to work from. About half-way through, it all seemed very trite—a rewrite of *Love Story*. I knew I couldn't go on in that vein, but there was something between the lines in that newspaper article that wouldn't let go of me. I decided to make a big change: the fat girl *says* she is dying, but really isn't. I made the class a

Dust jacket for Doubleday's hardcover edition.

ceramics class instead of a painting class and the import of the story was essentially the girl's deception. After more pages than I like to admit to, I again came to the conclusion that I hated what I was doing. There followed a host of other revisions—the fat girl became a fat boy; the fat girl was suicidal. The only thing that continued to ring true was the ceramics class. It's subtle, but the metaphor is there—in ceramics, you shape things, form things, attempt to exert control over inert matter. Not too terribly far removed from how we try to manage our lives. But all I had was this metaphor. Totally discouraged, I put the project aside for several months.

"Finally it came to me, and the ceramics-class metaphor was critical to my seeing the light. I didn't want to write a melodrama about young love and death, or anything remotely resembling that. I wanted to write about power. I wanted to deal with the classical myth in which the sculptor Pygmalion creates Galatea, the sculpture with whom he falls in love. He petitions the gods to bring her to life, and they do. Well, generally we look at this story from the viewpoint of Pygmalion. I wanted to see it through Galatea's eyes. After all, she was brought to life to please and adore Pygmalion. What kind of life is that?

"Of course, I made some big departures from the classical myth. The book is set in contemporary California. Ellen is fat, not beautiful. She isn't even very interesting, or talented. And Jeff ('Pygmalion') is a nice, but mixed-up and frustrated young man. His relationship with Ellen is based solely on his desire to possess and control her. She, at first, is more than happy to be his 'slave.' But this changes. Jeff's attentions gives Ellen the confidence she needs to lose weight, to become someone she herself can like and respect. Jeff is unable to accept this, and their relationship ends, rather brutally. Because Jeff and Ellen do not make love together, a lot of people have asked me if Jeff is gay. He is not. At first, I did have them involved in a sexual relationship, but I thought this clouded the issue. I wanted it to be clear that Jeff's interest in Ellen has to do with power, not sex. For him at this point, power is an even bigger high than sex.

"I didn't realize it for a long time, but there are links between *The Fat Girl* and a much earlier book, *Peter and Veronica*. Both protagonists, Jeff and Peter, reveal themselves to be at once kind and generous and dangerously tyrannical. As I grow older, I am increasingly suspicious of people who want to influence others, who strive to be leaders. And I am increasingly suspicious of, indeed frightened by, people who actually get power. Power corrupts. And this holds true of anyone in a position of power, be it Jeff Lyons, Peter Wedemeyer, or Adolf Hitler.''

Sachs is routinely praised for her handling of ambiguity and the strong social consciousness she brings to her books. "I think basically I like losers. Most of my protagonists, it is true, are characters who don't 'fit in,' who are either struggling hard to find out who they are, or are fighting for an ideal. One of my favorite characters is Marv. Two kids in the book are brilliant, but only Marv's sister, who gets the highest grades in her class and has a scholarship to a prestigious college, is generally recognized as such. Her achievements are not only conspicuous but predictable. She always has her nose in a book, hasn't time for ordinary mortals, and hasn't the merest hint of a sense of humor. Marv, on the other hand, always inventing things and building fantastical structures, is considered a little weird, particularly by his elder sister. But to my mind, Marv is the real genius. He sets out to execute ambitious projects of his own devising. Marv is a dreamer. And I believe that genius frequently feeds on dreams.

"That's not to say that my protagonists are perfect. Far from it. Take Veronica Ganz of *Veronica Ganz, Peter and Veronica* and *The Truth About Mary Rose,* for instance. Veronica started out as a composite of all the bullies who had tormented me as a kid. I created her with the express intention of eventually killing her. But no one is all bad or all good. Her unhappy family life came to figure largely in the books, as did her loneliness, the root of her aggressiveness. When my daughter (herself a child at the time) said she would never speak to me again if I killed Veronica, I rethought my plan. I did get a private 'revenge' on Veronica, though—in *The Truth About Mary Rose,* she grows up to become a dentist. Maybe that's an in-joke for cowards, but there you have it. Childhood Bully Becomes Dentist—it's perfect.

"And there's Peter in *Peter and Veronica* who is trying hard to counter what he perceives as his parents' bigotry against gentiles that he goes too far in the other direction. He goes out on a limb to ensure that Veronica is invited to his Bar Mitzvah, when to be the only gentile at the affair would make her feel very ill-at-ease. Veronica doesn't want to go, but Peter is too insensitive to realize this. Before one goes around helping people, one must make sure that it's help people want. Peter also reveals a possessive streak. When Veronica goes to visit her father in California and comes home with a new haircut, new clothes, and new-found confidence, Peter is not pleased for his friend. He is, in fact, disappointed, even bitter, that Veronica will no longer be the poor outcast he alone has befriended. Peter comes around, however, but it takes him awhile to overcome his fury at Veronica's progress towards independence.''

Dennis, the protagonist of *Thunderbird*, is another well-meaning character whose less admirable side Sachs exposes. ''Yes, he is anti-nuke; yes, he is for civil rights; yes, he is a vegetarian; yes, he wants to save the whales. He can say yes, yes, yes to all sorts of good causes. But he is also snobbish with regard to others who may not share his beliefs. He lacks a sense of humor. He is a missionary. For all his preoccupation with peace, he's harboring a lot of hostility. I wanted to break through the 'perfect veneer' of his activism to his anger and his problems, and then to break through his problems to show that he is really a very good human being.

''It's true that I have done a lot of political work in my time. I was active in the Civil Rights Movement, in the fight against the war in Vietnam, against the proliferation of nuclear arms, etc., etc. My kids say they grew up on peace marches. We 'socially conscious types' have to be careful that we don't take ourselves too seriously, that we don't turn into prigs and missionaries (I have been both). Yes, of course we want to make the world a better place, and we should bear in mind that a sense of humor goes a long way toward that goal. Towards that end, I do sometimes poke fun at activist characters who in some measure may be 'foils' for myself.

''In *Call Me Ruth*, a book which owes a lot to my immigrant heritage, I explored the question of what it meant for my grandparents' generation—largely a generation of immigrants—to be American. My grandmother came to this country from Russia at the turn of the century. As with the father in the novel, my grandfather had come over first to earn the money to bring over the rest of his family. My mother, like Ruth, was born on the other side. Fanny, Ruth's mother, is based in part on my grandmother, who, however, was not active in the labor movement, but she could have been. She was a dynamic woman, very forceful. It was she who told me stories of life on the Lower East Side. The family had left Russia not only because of economic hardship, but also because, as Jews, they were discriminated against and in constant danger of pogroms. The struggle between Fanny and Ruth is essentially their conflict over what it means to be an American. Ruth wants desperately to not be a

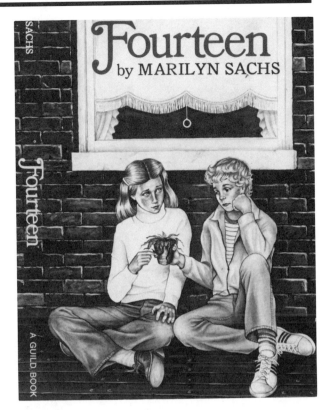

Jim Spence's illustration for Dutton's hardcover edition.

'greenhorn.' Her mother interprets this as a desire to shed her heritage like so much dirty clothing.

''America was supposed to have 'streets paved with gold.' I remember my grandparents talking about their expectations of America as a land of ideas, but what it came down to was cold cash, which wasn't so easy to come by. Sweatshops with dangerous working conditions were run by rapacious bosses. The Lower East Side was overcrowded. Bear in mind that many immigrants came from small villages in the countryside and had little, if any, exposure to city life. Such living conditions were a shock, to say nothing of a threat to health. In the old country, people knew what the dangers were; in America no one knew what to expect, and this drove many to desperation and early deaths.''

The book's final scene—in which Ruth once again, and more emphatically than ever, tells her mother not to call her by her Yiddish name—does not settle the question as to whether the conflict between Fanny and Ruth is irreconcilable. ''At that moment, Ruth is definitely separating herself from her mother. At first I had a far more devastating ending. I changed it. But I like to think, and really believe, that one day Ruth will understand what her mother was striving for, and that eventually she will arrive at a way of being American that doesn't

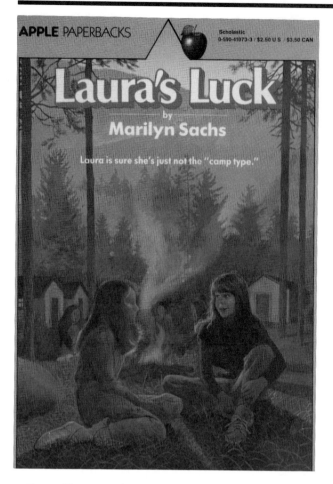

Cover illustration by Ruth Sanderson for the Scholastic paperback edition.

repress her own background. In that sense, although the final moment is one of conflict, I consider the ending open. If Fanny and Ruth were the same age, the ending would be closed, but Ruth is young and has time to change. As I've said before, I do not like endings in which all the 'loose strings' are 'neatly tied up.' Life is ambiguous and given to change. Why shouldn't stories be like that, too?

"For *Call Me Ruth*, I used not only my own family history but sources made available to me by the International Ladies Garment Workers. Because many characters in that novel worked in textile sweatshops I needed to know a great deal about the details of that life. I spent days reading about early textile strikes, many of which were led by women. I was even able to talk with a woman in her eighties living in a senior citizen housing project who had participated in some of those strikes and who had written a monograph on early efforts to organize textile workers. She told me all about how she had been arrested and how she and the other strikers sang songs in prison. The 1911 strike figures largely in *Call Me Ruth*. It was one of the more successful strikes, and, like many others, was led by women—twenty thousand young women—none experienced labor organizers, all of them immigrants. I read a number of diaries written by women involved in this strike. So many of their stories were tragic. They were in deep conflict over their desire for justice and the demands made on them by lovers, husbands and families. In those days, a woman's place was in the home. Even if she went out and worked every day, she was supposed to put her family first. It was very touching, often very sad.

"*A Pocketful of Seeds*, like many of my books, is based on an episode in the life of someone I know. In this case it is Fanny Krieger, a woman I met because of my son's frequent wildness in school. Since Fanny's son was at least as ill-behaved as mine, she and I tended to cross paths in the principal's office. And like me, she was active in the PTA. She stood out in a crowd, was outspoken, independent, unwilling to go along with generally accepted plans and projects she hadn't thoroughly questioned and thought through for herself. Her accent and her manner intrigued me, and we got to be friends. Fanny, a French Jew was trapped in France during World War II. Her family was rounded up by the Gestapo while Fanny was out visiting friends and eventually died in Auschwitz. Fanny lived in hiding and then was brought to America by a cousin. Originally, her cousin didn't want to get involved in her problems. After suffering a heart attack, however, he reconsidered the suggestion of a friend that God would look kindly on him if he were to do something that could save the girl's life. So he brought her to America unbeknown to his family. There was a lot of bitterness about this newcomer. Here she had narrowly escaped the Nazis, was in a foreign country where she didn't speak the language and where even members of her own family didn't want her. It was very hard on her, but Fanny is an admirable woman and repaid the evils with kindness.

"The book takes place entirely in France during the German occupation. I tried to deal with the fear people tend to have of those they perceive as 'different,' and the cruelty that is born of that fear. For *A Pocketful of Seeds*, I interviewed Fanny at length, on a number of occasions, about her experiences in France. (She has kept the tapes we made for her children and grandchildren.) I also did a lot of reading about France during that period. I needed all kinds of details—what people wore, what they ate for breakfast, what the subtle social dynamics in a village caught in a web of fear and peril were. Jews, of course, were terrified of being sent to concentration camps and dealt with that possibility in a number of ways—by going into hiding, by attempting to flee, by joining the Resistance, and some, by attempting to hide their Jewishness. There were non-Jews who sheltered Jews; others collaborated with the Germans; still others tried to walk a fine line by being cooperative with the occupying Germans, but not so cooperative that they would be vulnerable to accusations of collaboration after the war, if the Nazis were to lose (which, of course, they eventually did).

"After the book came out, Fanny and I went around to schools giving talks to students a little younger than she was during the Second World War. She explained how the Nazis came and took her parents away and went looking for her as well. Astoundingly, the kids asked, 'Why? What did you *do*?' 'We hadn't *done* anything,' she would reply. 'We were Jews.' 'Yes, but what did you *do*?' 'Our *crime*, if you want to call it that, was that we were Jews.'"

Sachs has had problems with censorship. "Several of my books have been banned by local school systems and occasionally I have received hate mail from parents and teachers. I once had a mother picket her local school protesting the presence of *Dorrie's Book* on its library shelves. She objected to the book's detailing the fictional mother's pregnancy. This particular incident actually turned out to be very good for me. The faculty, principal and school board all read the book and came to the decision that it deserved a spot on their school library shelves. There was lots of discussion and the book undoubtedly got more attention in that town than it otherwise would have. I have the photograph of the mother picketing hanging in my office to this day.

"I must say I think it's good when parents take an interest in what their kids read. Reading is terribly, terribly important. I always respond to people who would censor my books, either in person or by mail (unless their letters are abusive). I am one hundred percent against the censorship of books. While it remains a hotly-contested issue, all of us who feel strongly about protecting freedom of the press have a responsibility to speak out."

The term "woman writer" doesn't offend Sachs. "I know it offends some. I'm a pretty strong feminist and I've come to believe that there are some

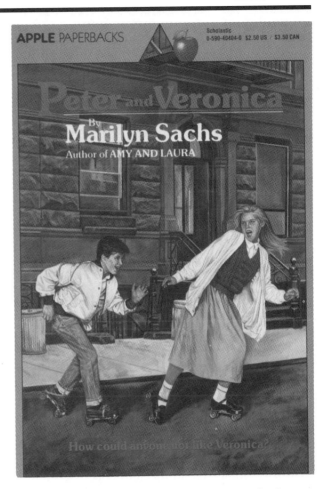

Cover illustration for Scholastic's paperback edition.

fundamental differences between the way women and men work. My daughter once asked me, 'Did having kids help or hinder you in your work?' 'It probably hindered me,' I told her, 'but that's all right.' I often speak at schools, and once I did an appearance with a male writer. We were asked about our work habits and he went on and on about how he has a room to himself and when he wishes to work there, locks the door. At that time he had a daughter about the students' age. 'What happens,' the kids wanted to know, 'when your daughter needs you?' And he said, 'She knows better than to bother me.' I thought then, 'This is an important difference between women and men.' My kids always knew that they could come in and 'bother' me if they needed to. I wanted it that way. And most of the women writers I know work in the same manner. Women's lives are not as compartmentalized as men's. You know, biology is on the side of woman. We have the babies. I very often think that on some submerged level women feel sorry for men because they cannot bear children.

"I think these differences are reflected in the work. And I'm feeling very positive about the things that seem to characterize a lot of women's writing. For one thing, it seems to me that women's books are filled with details that aren't found in men's books. (Of course, there are exceptions.) A male teacher once asked me, 'Why do women write so much about food?' Well, I thought about that. Food makes a big appearance in many women's books. Think about how important food is to us—it represents not only bodily nourishment, but nurturance, reward, consolation, celebration. Food is incredibly important, particularly during childhood. The thought of a particular food can summon memories from long, long ago. Think of Proust and his madeleine.

"Even though some of my books deal with the larger issues like prejudice and power, as in *The Fat Girl,* I like to feel that the everyday details of life come through strong and clear as well. I'm not always sure of the larger truths but I do believe in the preciousness of all the little everyday matters that enrich most of our lives. And humor—what a blessing laughter is! I'm proud of my funny books like *Veronica Ganz, Fourteen,* and *Almost Fifteen,* and I try, even in my more serious books always to balance pain with laughter. I learned this from Charlie Chaplin. Whenever things begin to get too heavy or mushy in his movies, a flower pot or a bag of garbage will fall out of a window and hit someone on the head.

"Books brought me great comfort as a child and still do. For many people, books are a place to go when things get tough. They can close doors as well as open them. I feel that I'm part of that continuing chain."

When not working, Sachs reads voraciously. "My favorite writer is Jane Austen. I am a member of both the American and English Jane Austen Societies. I never travel without a copy of at least one of her novels. Her books are treasures of detail. She has such a wonderfully subtle sense of humor and as a stylist, she is unparalleled.

"For about eleven years I have been part of a women's reading group—an extraordinary group. We have children book writers, a woman who just completed a children's biography of Georgia O'Keeffe, someone who writes Regency romances, a social worker, a teacher and Fanny Krieger. We read only books by women. I think, that like many women of my generation, I was educated, brainwashed!, if you wish, to believe that the great writers were men, that the work of women writers was inherently 'minor.' At first there was resistance to the suggestion that we read only women. People were skeptical that we would find enough good books, but after eleven years—and countless women's books under our belts—we despair of having the time to read a fraction of what still lies ahead of us. It is very inspiring!"

Sachs tells aspiring authors to, "Write a lot, but read as much as you write. Read and read and read and read. And don't be discouraged by peers who seem to have more talent than you. People develop at their own rates. Some 'early bloomers' do grow up to become writers, but many do not. And don't be intimidated by 'teacher's pets.' It takes time to find your own style, your own 'voice,' and this cannot be rushed.

"I recently received a letter from a sixth-grade teacher explaining that she had a class of 'gifted' students and requesting that I become this class' 'buddy.' I was to read and critique these children's writings. Well, I declined in a hurry. First of all, I have an aversion to the way the word 'gifted' is currently being used in our schools. Everyone is gifted in one way or another, and many people are gifted in areas the schools don't recognize as having value. Secondly, sixth graders should not be subjected to 'critiques' of their creative work. Children should be allowed to create in freedom, without fear of judgment.

"When P. L. Travers, who wrote *Mary Poppins,* was asked for her advice to young writers, she said something I agree with. To paraphrase—the best thing one can do for a writer is to leave him or her alone. She recounted how she had grown up in a traditional English family in which everyone was an extrovert and loved to ride horses. Only she liked to sit by herself and read. They were very kind to her, but troubled. However, this never bothered her. Her family went off for long gallops through the countryside and she stayed in the library doing as she'd liked, and was not plagued by adults meddling with her vision.

"As a writer, you keep learning more about your craft. It never stops. In fact, it becomes your way of life."[1]

Footnote Sources:

[1] Based on an interview by Marguerite Feitlowitz for *Authors and Artists for Young Adults.*
[2] *Something about the Author: Autobiography Series,* Volume 2, Gale, 1986.

■ For More Information See

Times Literary Supplement, October 16, 1969.
Library Journal, June 15, 1970, September, 1970.
Publishers Weekly, January 8, 1973, August 6, 1982, December 20, 1985, September 11, 1987.
Children's Literature Review, Volume 2, Gale, 1976.
Doris de Montreville and Elizabeth D. Crawford, editors, *Fourth Book of Junior Authors and Illustrators,* H. W. Wilson, 1978.

D. L. Kirkpatrick, *Twentieth-Century Children's Writers,* St. Martin's Press, 1978, 2nd edition, 1983.
Washington Post Book World, July 12, 1981.
Voice of Youth Advocates, February, 1982.
Horn Book, August, 1983, May-June, 1985, November-December, 1987.
Wilson Library Bulletin, May, 1984.
School Library Journal, August, 1986.

Collections:

Kerlan Collection at the University of Minnesota.

Carl Sagan

S urname is pronounced *Say*-gun; born November 9, 1934, in New York, N.Y.; son of Samuel (a cloth cutter and factory manager) and Rachel (Gruber) Sagan; married Lynn Margulis (a biologist), June 16, 1957 (divorced, 1963); married Linda Salzman (an artist), April 6, 1968 (divorced, May, 1981); married Ann Druyan (a writer), June 1, 1981; children: (first marriage) Dorion Solomon, Jeremy Ethan; (second marriage) Nicholas; (third marriage) Alexandra. *Education:* University of Chicago, A.B. (with general and special honors), 1954, S.B., 1955, S.M., 1956, Ph.D., 1960. *Politics:* Independent. *Religion:* Independent. *Office:* Laboratory for Planetary Studies, Space Science Building, Cornell University, Ithaca, N.Y. 14853. *Agent:* Scott Meredith Literary Agency, 845 Third Ave., New York, N.Y. 10022.

■ Career

University of Chicago, Chicago, Ill., lecturer, 1956-57; Armour Research Foundation, Chicago, physicist, 1958-59; University of California, Berkeley, Miller research fellow in astronomy, 1960-62; Harvard University, Cambridge, Mass., 1962-68, lecturer and assistant professor of astronomy; Smithsonian Institution, Astrophysical Observato-

ry, Cambridge, astrophysicist, 1962-68; Cornell University, Ithaca, N.Y., associate professor, 1968-70, professor of astronomy and space sciences, 1970—, David Duncan Professor of Astronomy and Space Sciences, 1976—, director of Laboratory for Planetary Studies, 1968—, associate director of Center for Radiophysics and Space Research, 1972-81; Carl Sagan Productions, Inc., president, 1981; writer.

Visiting professor of astronomy, Stanford University Medical School, 1962-68; National Science Foundation-American Astronomical Society visiting professor at various colleges, 1963-67; Condon Lecturer, University of Oregon and Oregon State University, 1967-68; National Aeronautics and Space Administration (NASA) lecturer in astronaut training program, 1969-72; Holiday Lecturer, American Association for the Advancement of Science, 1970; Vanuxem Lecturer, Princeton University, 1973; Smith Lecturer, Dartmouth University, 1974, 1977; Wagner Lecturer, University of Pennsylvania, 1975; Philips Lecturer, Haverford College, 1975; Jacob Brownowski Lecturer, University of Toronto, 1975; Anson Clark Memorial Lecturer, University of Texas at Dallas, 1976; Danz Lecturer, University of Washington, 1976; Stahl Lecturer, Bowdoin College, 1977; Christmas Lecturer, Royal Institution, London, 1977; Menninger Memorial Lecturer, American Psychiatric Association, 1978; Carver Memorial Lecturer, Tuskegee Institute, 1981; Feinstone Lecturer, United States Military Academy, 1981; Class Day Lecturer, Yale University, 1981; George Pal Lecturer, Motion Picture Academy of Arts and Sciences, 1982;

Phelps Dodge Lecturer, University of Arizona, 1982; H. L. Welsh Lecturer in Physics, University of Toronto, 1982; Distiguished Lecturer, U.S. Air Force Academy, Colorado Spring, 1983; Adolf Meyer Lecturer, American Psychiatric Association, 1984; Lowell Lecturer, Harvard University, 1984; Jack Distinguished American Lecturer, Indiana University (Penn.), 1984; Distinguished Lecturer, Southern Methodist University, 1984; Keystone Lecturer, National War College, National Defense University, Washington, D.C., 1984-86; Marshall Lecturer, Natural Resources Defense Council, Washington, D.C., 1985; Johnson Distinguished Lecturer, Johnson Graduate School of Management, Cornell University, 1985; Gifford Lecturer in Natural Theology, University of Glasgow, 1985; Lilenthal Lecturer, California Academy of Science, 1986; Dolan Lecturer, American Public Health Association, 1986; Distinguished Lecturer, The Japan Society, 1987; Cohen Lecturer, Moravian College, 1987; Barrack Lecturer, University of Nevada, 1987; Commonwealth Lecturer, University of Massachusetts, Amherst, 1988.

Member of committee to review Project Blue Book (U.S. Air Force), 1956-66. Investigator, Mariner mission to Mars, 1962, Mariner and Viking missions to Mars, 1969—, Voyager missions to the outer planets, 1979; designer of *Pioneer 10* and *11* and *Voyager 1* and *2* interstellar messages. President, the Planetary Society, 1979—; member, American Committee on East-West Accord, 1983—. Judge, National Book Awards, 1976. Member of Usage Panel, American Heritage Dictionary of the English Language, 1976-82; member of advisory panel, Civil Space Station Study, Office of Technology Assessment, U.S. Congress, 1982; chairman, Division for Planetary Sciences, American Astronomical Society, 1975-76; chairman, section D (astronomy), American Association for the Advancement of Science, 1975-76; member, advisory council, Smithsonian Institution, Washington, D.C., 1975-80; fellow, Committee for the Scientific Investigation of Claims of the Paranormal, 1976—; member, fellowship panel, John S. Guggenheim Memorial Foundation, 1976-81; member, board of directors, Council for a Livable World Education Fund, 1980—; commissioner, The President's Commission for a National Agenda for the '80's (McGill Commission), The White House, 1980; member, National Advisory Board, American Civil Liberties Union, 1981—; elector, National Women's Hall of Fame, 1981—; member, advisory board, American University, Washington, D.C., 1982—; member, advisory panel, Civilian

Space Stations and the U.S. Future in Space, Office of Technology Assessment, U.S. Congress, 1982-84; chairman, Conference on the Long-term Global Atmospheric and Climatic Consequences of Nuclear War, American Academy of Arts and Sciences, Cambridge, Mass., 1982-83; member, American Committee on U.S.-Soviet Relations, Washington, D.C., 1983—; sponsor, National Campaign to Save the ABM Treaty, Washington, D.C., 1984; member, advisory board, Educators for Social Responsibility, 1984; member, visiting committee, The College, University of Chicago, 1986—; member, national advisory board, Mothers Embracing Nuclear Disarmament (MEND), 1986—; member, national advisory board, Illinois Mathematics and Science Academy, 1986—; member, international advisory board, Institute for International Peace Studies, University of Notre Dame, 1986—; member, advisory board, Samantha Smith Foundation, 1987—; member, national advisory board, Americans for Religious Liberty, 1987—; member, advisory board, National Center for Science Education, 1987—; member board of directors, Spacewatch, Washington, D.C., 1987—.

Member:

International Astronomical Union (member of organizing committee, Commission of Physical Study of Planets), International Council of Scientific Unions (vice chairman; member of executive council, committee on space research; co-chairman, working group on moon and planets), International Academy of Astronautics, International Society for the Study of the Origin of Life (member of council, 1980—), P.E.N. International, American Astronomical Society (councillor; chairman, division of planetary sciences, 1975-76), American Physical Society, American Geophysical Union (president, planetology section, 1980-82), American Association for the Advancement of Science (fellow; chairman, astronomy section, 1975), American Institute of Aeronautics and Astronautics (fellow), American Astronautical Society (fellow; member of council, 1976), Federation of American Scientists (member of council, 1977-80; 1985—), Society for the Study of Evolution, British Interplanetary Society (fellow), Astronomical Society of the Pacific, Genetics Society of America, Authors Guild, Authors League of America, Phi Beta Kappa, Sigma Xi, Explorers Club, American Academy of Arts and Sciences (fellow), World Association of International Relations, World Academy of Arts and Sciences (fellow).

■ Awards, Honors

National Science Foundation pre-doctoral fellowship, 1955-60; Alfred P. Sloan Foundation research fellowship at Harvard University, 1963-67; A Calvert Smith Prize from Harvard University, 1964; Apollo Achievement Award, 1969, Medal for Exceptional Scientific Achievement, 1972, Medal for Distinguished Public Service, 1977, and 1981, all from the National Aeronautics and Space Administration; Prix Galabert (international astronautics prize), 1973; Klumpke-Roberts Prize from the Astronomical Society of the Pacific, 1974; John W. Campbell Memorial Award for "Best Science Book of the Year" from the World Science Fiction Convention, 1974, for *The Cosmic Connection*; Golden Plate Award from the American Academy of Achievement, 1975; Joseph Priestley Award from Dickinson College, 1975, for "distinguished contributions to the welfare of mankind"; D.Sc. (honorary) from Rensselaer Polytechnic University, 1975, Denison University, 1976, Clarkson College, 1977, Whittier College and Clark University, both 1978, American University, 1980, University of South Carolina, 1984, Hofstra University, 1985, Long Island University, 1987; D.H.L. from Skidmore College, 1976; Pulitzer Prize for Literature, 1978, for *The Dragons of Eden*; Washburn Medal from Boston Museum of Science, 1978; LL.D. (honorary), University of Wyoming, 1978, Drexel University, 1986.

Rittenhouse Medal, Franklin Institute/Rittenhouse Astronomical Society, 1980; The Explorer's Club 75th Anniversary Award for "achievement in furthering the spirit of exploration," 1980; *Cosmos* was named one of American Library Association's Best Books for Young Adults, 1980; *Broca's Brain* and *Murmurs of Earth* were both selected one of New York Public Library's Books for the Teen Age, 1980; "Cosmos" series received the Academy of Family Films and Family Television Award for Best Television Series of 1980, the American Council for Better Broadcasts Citation for Highest Quality Television Programming of 1980-81, Silver Plaque from Chicago Film Festival, 1981, President's Special Award from Western Educational Society for Telecommunication, 1981, three Emmy Awards from the Television Academy of Arts and Sciences, 1981, and Ohio State University Annual Award for Television Excellence, 1982; D.H.L. (honorary), Lewis and Clark College, 1980, Brooklyn College, 1982; George Foster Peabody Award for Excellence in Television Programming, University of Georgia, 1981; Glenn Seaborg Prize for Communicating Science from the Lecture Plat-

form, American Platform Association, 1981; Ralph Coats Roe Medal from the American Society of Mechanical Engineers "in recognition of contribution to planetary physics," 1981; American Book Award nomination for *Cosmos* (hardcover), and *Broca's Brain* (paperback), both 1981; Humanist of the Year Award from the American Humanist Association, 1981; Stony Brook Foundation Award (with Frank Press), for distinguished contributions to higher education, 1982; John F. Kennedy Astro-

Sagan at three.

nautics Award from the American Astronautical Society, 1983, for "outstanding contributions to public service through leadership in promoting...the exploration utilization of outer space," 1983.

Honda Prize, 1985, from the Honda Foundation for "contributions toward...a new era of human civilization"; Arthur C. Clarke Award for Space Education from Students for the Exploration and Development of Space, 1984; S.Sc. (honorary), University of South Carolina, 1984; Peter Lavan Award for Humanitarian Service, Bard College, 1984; The New Priorities Award from the Fund for New Priorities in America, 1984; Sidney Hillman Foundation Prize Award for "outstanding contributions [to] world peace," 1984; SANE National Peace Award, 1984; Regents Medal for Excellence, Board of Regents, University of the State of New York, 1984; Physicians for Social Responsibility Annual Award for Public Service, 1985; Leo Szilard Award for Physics in the Public Interest (with Richard P. Turco and others) for the discovery of nuclear winter, American Physical Society, 1985; Distinguished Service Award, World Peace Film Festival, Marlboro College, 1985; NASA Group Achievement Award, Voyager Uranus Interstellar Mission, 1986; Nahum Goldmann Medal "in recognition of distinguished service to the cause of peace and many accomplishments in science and public affairs," World Jewish Congress, 1986; Brit HaDorot Award, Shalom Center, 1986; Annual Award of Merit, American Consulting Engineers Council, 1986; Maurice Eisendrath Award for Social Justice, Central Conference of American Rabbis and Union of American Hebrew Congregations, 1987; In Praise of Reason Award from the Committee for the Scientific Investigation of Claims of the Paranormal, 1987.

■ Writings

(With W. W. Kellogg) *The Atmospheres of Mars and Venus*, National Academy of Sciences, 1961.

(With I. S. Shklovskii) *Intelligent Life in the Universe*, Holden-Day, 1963, reissued, 1978.

(With Jonathan Leonard) *Planets*, Time-Life, 1966.

Planetary Exploration: The Condon Lectures, University of Oregon Press, 1970.

(Editor with T. Owen and H. J. Smith) *Planetary Atmospheres*, D. Reidel (Amsterdam), 1971.

(Editor with K. Y. Kondratyev and M. Rycroft) *Space Research XI*, two volumes, Akademie Verlag (Berlin), 1971.

(With R. Littauer and others) *The Air War in Indochina*, Beacon Press, 1971.

(Editor with Thornton Page) *UFOs: A Scientific Debate*, Cornell University Press, 1972.

(Editor) *Communication with Extraterrestrial Intelligence*, MIT Press, 1973.

(With Ray Bradbury, Arthur Clarke, Bruce Murray and Walter Sullivan) *Mars and the Mind of Man*, Harper, 1973.

(With R. Berendzen, A. Montagu, P. Morrison, K. Stendhal and G. Wald) *Life beyond Earth and the Mind of Man*, U.S. Government Printing Office, 1973.

(Editor) *The Cosmic Connection: An Extraterrestrial Perspective*, Doubleday, 1973.

Other Worlds, Bantam, 1975.

The Dragons of Eden: Speculations on the Evolution of Human Intelligence (Book-of-the-Month club selection), Random House, 1977.

(With F. D. Drake, A. Druyan, J. Lomberg, and T. Ferris) *Murmurs of Earth: The Voyager Interstellar Record* (Book-of-the-Month Club selection), Random House, 1978.

Broca's Brain: Reflections on the Romance of Science (Book-of-the-Month Club selection), Random House, 1979.

Cosmos (also see below; Book-of-the-Month Club and Natural History Book Club selection), Random House, 1980.

(With R. Gawin and others) *The Fallacy of Star Wars*, Vintage Books, 1984.

(With P. R. Ehrlich and others) *The Cold and the Dark: The World after Nuclear War*, Norton, 1984.

Contact (novel), Simon & Schuster, 1985.

Comet, Random House, 1985.

Also contributor to several books on science. Author of radio and television scripts, including "Cosmos," Public Broadcasting System, 1980, and scripts for Voice of America, American Chemical Society radio series, and British Broadcasting Corp. Contributor to *Encyclopedia Americana*, *Encyclopaedia Britannica* and *Whole Earth Catalog*, 1971. Contributor of more than 350 papers to scientific journals, and of articles to periodicals, including *National Geographic*, *Saturday Review*, *Discovery*, *Washington Post*, *Natural History*, *Scientific American* and *New York Times*. *Icarus: International Journal of Solar System Studies*, associate editor, 1962-68, 1980—, editor-in-chief, 1968-79; mem-

"The cosmic explainer."

ber of editorial board, *Origins of Life*, 1974—, *Climatic Change*, 1976—, and *Science 80*, 1979-83.

Author of more than 600 published scientific papers and popular articles. Several of Sagan's books, including *The Cosmic Connection*, *The Dragons of Eden*, *Broca's Brain*, and *Cosmos* have been translated into numerous languages, including French, Spanish, Portuguese, German, Chinese, Hebrew, Greek, Japanese, Dutch, Russian, and Serbo-Croation.

■ Work In Progress

Nucleus for Random House; *Global Consequences of Nuclear War* (with R. P. Turco and others) for Random House; *The Search for Who We Are: The Gifford Lectures in Natural Theology*.

■ Sidelights

"We start out a million years ago in a small community on some grassy plain; we hunt animals, have children and develop a rich social, sexual and intellectual life, but we know almost nothing about our surroundings. Yet we hunger to understand, so we invent myths about how we imagine the world is constructed—and they're, of course, based upon what we know, which is ourselves and other animals. So we make up stories about how the world was hatched from a cosmic egg, or created after the mating of cosmic deities or by some fiat of a powerful being. But we're not fully satisfied with those stories, so we keep broadening the horizon of our myths; and then we discover that there's a totally different way in which the world is constructed and things originate.

"Today, we're still loaded down, and to some extent embarrassed, by ancient myths, but we respect them as part of the same impulse that has led to the modern, scientific kind of myth. But we now have the opportunity to discover, for the first time, the way the universe is in *fact* constructed, as opposed to how we would wish it to be constructed. It's a critical moment in the history of the world."[1]—Carl Sagan

November 9, 1934. Sagan was born in the Bensonhurst section of Brooklyn, N.Y. where his Russian-immigrant father was a cutter who rose to foreman in the garment industry. "It was during the Depression, and we were kind of poor. When I was very little, the basic thing for me was stars. When I was five years old, I could see them at whatever time bedtime was in winter, and they just didn't seem to belong in Brooklyn. The sun and the moon seemed perfectly right for Brooklyn, but the stars were different. I had the sense of something interesting, distant, strange about them. I asked people what the stars were, and I mostly got answers like 'They're lights in the sky, kid.' I could tell they were lights in the sky; that wasn't what I meant. After I got my first library card, I made a big expedition to the public-library branch on Eighty-sixth Street in Brooklyn. I had to take the streetcar; it was some big distance. I wanted a book on the stars. At first there was some confusion; the librarian mentioned all kinds of books about Hollywood stars. I was embarrassed, so I didn't explain right away, but finally I got across what I wanted. They got me this book, and I read it right there, because I wanted the answer.

"The library book had this stunning, astonishing thing in it—that the stars were suns, just like our sun, so far away that they were only a twinkle of light. I didn't know how far away that was, because I didn't know mathematics, but I could tell only by thinking of how bright the sun is in the daytime and how dim a star is at night that the sun would have to be very far away to be just a twinkle, and the scale of the universe opened up to me."[2]

"My parents always encouraged me to read. Every now and then I would think, gee, wouldn't it be terrific if I had a friend to talk to about the stars, but there wasn't one."[3]

"It must have been a year or two after this that I learned what the planets were. Then it seemed absolutely certain to me that if the stars were like the sun there must be planets around them. And they must have life on them. This was an old idea, of course. Christiaan Huygens, the Dutch astronomer, I found out later, had written about it in the sixteen-seventies. But I thought of it before I was eight. And once I reached that point, I got very interested in astronomy. I spent a lot of time working on distances, coordinates, and parallaxes."[2]

"By the time I was ten I had decided—in almost total ignorance of the difficulty of the problem—that the universe was full up. There were too many places for this to be the only inhabited planet. And, from the variety of life on earth (trees looked pretty different from most of my friends), I figured life elsewhere would seem very strange. I tried hard to imagine what that life would be like, but despite my best efforts I always produced a kind of terrestrial chimaera, a blend of existing plants or animals.

"About this time a friend introduced me to the Mars novels of Edgar Rice Burroughs. I had not thought much about Mars before, but here, presented before me in the adventures of John Carter, was another inhabited world, breathtakingly fleshed out: ancient seabottoms, great canal pumping stations and a variety of beings, some of them exotic. There were, for example, the eight-legged beasts of burden, the thoats.

"These novels were exhilarating to read. At first. But slowly, doubts began to gnaw. The plot surprise in the first John Carter novel which I read hinged on his forgetting that the year is longer on Mars than on earth. But it seemed to me that if you go to another planet, one of the first things you check out is the length of the day and the year. Then there were incidental remarks which at first seemed stunning but on sober reflection proved disappointing. For example, Burroughs casually comments that on Mars there are two more primary colors than on earth. Many long minutes did I spend with my eyes closed, fiercely contemplating a new primary color. But it would always be something familiar, like a murky brown or plum. How could there be another primary color on Mars, much less two? What was a primary color? Was it something to do with physics or something to do with physiology? I decided that Burroughs might not have known what he was talking about, but he certainly made his readers think. And in those many chapters where there was not much to think about, there were satisfyingly malignant enemies and rousing swordsmanship—more than enough to maintain the interest of a city-bound ten-year-old in a long Brooklyn summer.

"The following summer, by sheerest accident, I stumbled upon a magazine called *Astounding Science Fiction* in a neighborhood candy store. A glance at the cover and a quick riffle through the interior showed me it was what I had been looking for. With some effort I managed to scrape together the purchase price, opened the magazine at random, sat down on a bench not twenty feet from the store and read my first modern science-fiction short story, "Pete Can Fix It" by Raymond F. Jones, a gentle account of time travel into a postnuclear-war holocaust. I had known about the atom bomb—I remember an excited friend explaining to me that it was made of atoms—but this was the first I had seen about the social implications of nuclear weapons. It got you thinking.

"I found I was hooked. Each month I eagerly awaited the arrival of *Astounding.* I read Verne and Wells, read, cover-to-cover, the first two science-fiction anthologies that I was able to find, devised scorecards, similar to those I was fond of making for baseball, on the quality of the stories I read. Many ranked high in asking interesting questions but low in answering them."[4]

When he turned twelve, Sagan was asked by his aged grandfather what he planned to be when he grew up. "An astronomer," he replied. 'Fine,' said the old man, 'but how will you make a living?'"[5]

"I didn't make a decision to pursue astronomy; rather, it just grabbed me, and I had no thought of escaping. But I didn't know that you could get paid for it. I thought I'd have to have some job I was temperamentally unsuited to, like door-to-door salesman, and then on weekends or at nights I could do astronomy. That's the way it was done in the fiction I read, in which space science was practiced by wealthy amateurs. Then, in my sophomore year in high school, my biology teacher...told me he was pretty sure that Harvard paid [noted astronomer] Harlow Shapley a salary. That was a splendid day—when I began to suspect that if I tried hard I could do astronomy full time, not just part time.

"I had been receiving catalogues from various colleges, and I wanted one with good mathematics and physics. The University of Chicago sent me a booklet entitled 'If You Want an Education.' Inside was a picture of football players fighting on a field, and under it the caption 'If you want a school with good football, don't come to the University of Chicago.' Then there was a picture of some drunken kids, and the caption 'If you want a school with a good fraternity life, don't come to the University of Chicago.' It sounded like the place for me. The trouble was that it had no engineering school, and I wanted an education not only in astronomy and physics but also in rocket engineering. I went down to Princeton to ask Lyman Spitzer, the astronomer, his advice; he was involved in some early rocket studies. He told me that there was no reason an astronomer had to know every nut and bolt of a spacecraft in order to use it. Up until then, I had thought this was necessary—another holdover from the fiction I'd been reading, in which the rich amateur built his own spaceship. Now I realized that I could go to the Unversity of Chicago, even though it had no engineering school. I applied, and entered in the fall of 1951. In the early nineteen-fifties, the University of Chicago was a very exciting place to be. It was strong in the humanities—which I wanted—but it was also very strong in the sciences. Enrico Fermi and Harold Urey were both there, in physics and in chemistry. And it had a superb astronomy department, which operated the Yerkes Observatory."[2]

Through a friend, Sagan was introduced to Indiana University's Dr. H. J. Muller, who had won the 1946 Nobel Prize in Medicine and Physiology for discovering that X-rays caused mutations in genes. Since X-rays are produced by exploding stars, Muller's findings were linked to astronomy. Interested in those pursuits, Sagan spent the summer of his freshman year working for Muller at Indiana University. "Muller had me doing routine things, such as looking at fruit flies for new mutations. But he ran a real research group, and for the first time I got a feeling of what scientific research was like. Moreover, Muller was interested not only in the origins of life but in the possibility of life elsewhere; he didn't think the idea was the least bit silly. Muller encouraged me to learn genetics. Later, he sustained me through years of studying biology and chemistry, which I had thought were far removed from my main interest, astronomy. I always kept in touch with him. A few years before his death, he gave me a book about space flight by Arthur C. Clarke, and inscribed it, 'Perhaps we'll meet someday on the tundras of Mars.'"[2]

With Muller's letter of introduction to Dr. Urey, who had won the 1934 Nobel Prize in Chemistry for discovering hydrogen and who had gone on to study origins of life, Sagan returned to the University of Chicago to begin his sophomore year. "[Urey] was extremely kind to me when I was an undergraduate. I did an honors essay on how life began. I was very naive, and I remember Urey's comment: 'This is the work of a very young man.' I had the idea that in one fell swoop I could understand the origins of life, though I had not had much chemistry or biology. It was an attempt to learn by doing. Some other people at Chicago were more effective at this than I was. It was a time of great excitement, for this was when Stanley Miller was doing his work, under Urey, on the origins of life. He had filled a flask with methane, ammonia, water, and hydrogen—things you would expect to find in the primitive atmosphere of a young planet—and had passed an electrical discharge, like lightning, through it. The result was amino acids, the first step toward life. Miller had shown that the beginnings of life were not a matter of chance but could happen in any place where the conditions were right.

"Urey showed me through Miller's laboratory. Later, Miller was forced to defend his work before the University of Chicago's chemistry department.

They didn't take it very seriously; they kept suggesting that he had been sloppy, leaving amino acids all over his laboratory. I was outraged that something, as important as that could be received in such a hostile way. Urey was the only one who spoke up for him. He said, 'If God didn't create life this way, He certainly missed a good bet.'"[2]

Sagan received his master's degree in physics, and went on in 1956 to the University of Chicago's graduate school of astronomy at Williams Bay, Wisconsin, where he worked under the tutelage of Dutch astronomer Dr. Gerard Kuiper. "Kuiper was a respected man, and if he said it was possible for *any* sort of life to exist on Mars that was important. It was a tremendous boost to exobiology."[2]

In 1956 he spent the summer with Kuiper at the McDonald Observatory, in Fort Davis, Texas, where he had his first opportunity to see what Mars looked like through a big telescope. "As it turned out, there were dust storms in both places—Mars and Texas. I didn't find any canals. I was satisfied just to be able to see light and dark markings. The seeing was poor, even through the eighty-two-inch telescope at McDonald. There Mars was, though shimmering, squashed, distorted. Then, for an instant, the atmosphere steadied, and I caught a glimpse of the southern polar cap. I saw no fine details. It was no big deal. I realized that the telescopic technique, while interesting, was limited: Sitting under a blanket of air forty million miles from the target was not going to tell me much."[2]

At the age of twenty-one, published his first paper, "Radiation and the Origin of the Gene," in *Evolution*. It was during this time that Sagan met mentor Joshua Lederberg, then professor of genetics at the University of Wisconsin, an honored Nobel laureate and the inventor of the word 'exobiology' for the study of extraterrestrial life. It was Lederberg, as chairman of the Space Science Board committee studying ways of searching for life in space, who asked Sagan to become a member.

While Sagan was working for his doctorate under Kuiper, he married biologist Lynn Margulis. Two sons were born before the marriage ended in divorce in 1963. He received his doctorate in astronomy and astrophysics from the University of Chicago in 1960. His oldest son, Dorion recalled: "My father used to make up stories about black holes and tell them to my brother and me night after night. In fact, I was probably one of the first people that he experimented on in his attempts to popularize science."[6]

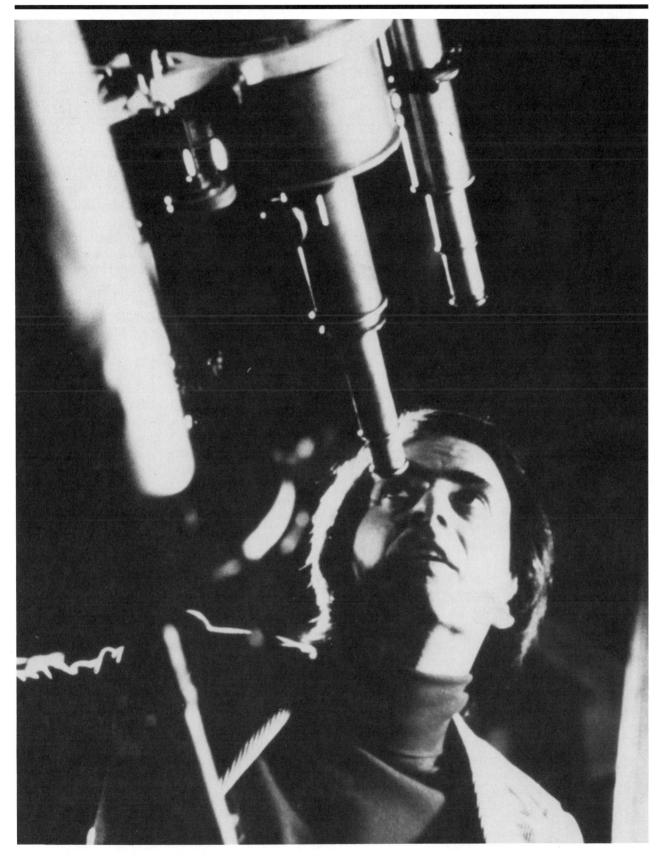

Sagan peering through a telescope at Arizona's Lowell Observatory. (William R. Ray/*Time* Magazine.)

During his years at Chicago, Sagan organized a highly successful campus lecture series on science, including himself as one of the speakers. Some faculty members dismissed it as "Sagan's circus."

He went on to become a research fellow at the University of California at Berkeley, and then, spent a year as visiting assistant professor of genetics at the Stanford Medical School. From 1962-68 he held a joint appointment as astrophysicist at the Smithsonian Astrophysical Observatory in Cambridge, Mass., and lecturer and later assistant professor of astronomy at Harvard. Sagan's flamboyant style did not go over well with old-line astronomy professors at Harvard, so when he was denied tenure in 1968, he moved on to Cornell. With one of his graduate students, James Pollack, Sagan concluded that the bright and dark patterns detected on Mars were not due to seasonal changes in vegetation, as some had theorized, but to winds swift enough to whirl up dust storms in the thin atmosphere and sculpt huge variations in surface elevations. Three years later, *Mariner* 9 confirmed his theory of the Martian winds. In his doctoral thesis, he argued that the observed radio emission from Venus was due to a very hot surface, the heat held in by a massive carbon dioxide/water vapor greenhouse effect. The Soviet *Venera* probes, and the American *Pioneer Venus* spacecraft confirmed his theory in the late '60s and '70s.

Sagan was asked about his quest to find life beyond Earth. "I think it's because human beings love to be alive, and we have an emotional resonance with something else alive, rather than with a molybdenum atom. Why are people interested in other animals? Why are we interested in the life history of the armadillo? Why do we go to Antarctica to find out what the emperor penguins have been doing lately? It's fun, because we are primarily drawn to things that are alive."[2]

"Life on Earth is the same, despite some external differences in form. In the essential biochemistry, every one of us—from bacterium to human being—is composed of the same proteins and the same nucleic acids, all put together in the same way. Therefore, the biologists have no idea what is possible in living systems—what ranges of biologies can exist. We have only one example.

"...We are all descended from a single instance of the origin of life. We're similar because we're related—we bacteria and we people.

"On another planet, the statistical factors work differently, the physical environment is different, evolution follows other pathways, and one would expect that the organisms, if any, would be astonishingly different—not just in their internal appearance, but more fundamentally in their internal make-up. The discovery of life on Mars—even very simple life—would work a fundamental revolution in biology which would have a wide range of practical implications for us here on Earth.

"If we find life on Mars, we will have looked at two planets and found life on both of them—the Earth and Mars. That would go a long way toward arguing for the grand conclusion of an inhabited cosmos. If so, it seems very likely that on many planets in other solar systems life would have evolved into advanced forms. The conclusion naturally presents itself that we might be able to communicate, using radio telescopes, with intelligent beings on planets of other stars. That's why it will be so exciting if we do find life on Mars. On the other hand, if we do not find life on Mars, that would hardly foreclose the possibilities of life on other planets."[7]

The Martian environment in Earth terms would go like this: "[A typical weather report]. In the Chryse Basin today, the wind was from the northwest at twelve miles an hour, changing at midnight to from the south at 19 miles an hour. The temperature just before dawn was -122 Fahrenheit, rising to -20 Fahrenheit at 2 p.m. The barometric pressure is constant at 7.7 millibars. Chances for rain: zero."[7]

"There is nothing about science that cannot be explained to the layman," says Sagan. However, the purists among his colleagues shudder at such popularization and simplification. His flamboyant style, the speculative nature of some of his work, and his celebrity profile (he's a regular on the Johnny Carson show) further fuel the controversy.

"There are at least two reasons why scientists have an obligation to explain what science is all about. One is naked self-interest. Much of the funding for science comes from the public, and the public has a right to know how their money is being spent. If we scientists increase the public excitement about science, then there is a good chance of having more public supporters.

"The other is that it's tremendously exciting to communicate your own excitement to others. It's satisfying. I find the letters I get from kids who have been excited by science extremely rewarding.

"We have a society which is built on science and technology and which uses science in every one of the interstices of national life and in which the public, the Executive, the Legislative and the

Judiciary have very little understanding of what science is about. That is a clear disaster signal. It has to be suicidal."[8]

American scientific illiteracy begins around the age of ten and twelve, according to Sagan. "Virtually every kid has an interest in science. It is an essential part of the nature of a human being—the sense of curiosity, discovery, understanding, manipulation of the environment. All kids are born with it, but then something happens in late grade school or junior high school that turns it off."[8]

"The most effective agents to communicate science to the public are television, motion pictures, and newspapers—where the science offerings are often dreary, inaccurate, ponderous, grossly caricatured or (as with much Saturday-morning commercial television programming for children) hostile to science."[1] Sagan's books, frequent appearances on television talk shows, and 'Cosmos,' his thirteen-part series for public TV are attempts at restoring balance.

"In the summer and fall of 1976, as a member of the *Viking Lander* Imaging Flight Team, I was engaged, with a hundred of my scientific colleagues, in the exploration of the planet Mars. For the first time in human history we had landed two space vehicles on the surface of another world. The results...were spectacular, the historical significance of the mission utterly apparent. And yet the general public was learning almost nothing of these great happenings. The press was largely inattentive; television ignored the mission almost altogether. When it became clear that a definitive answer on whether there is life on Mars would not be forthcoming, interest dwindled still further. There was little tolerance for ambiguity. When we found the sky of Mars to be kind of pinkish-yellow rather than the blue which had erroneously first been reported, the announcement was greeted by a chorus of good-natured boos from the assembled reporters—they wanted Mars to be, even in this respect, like the Earth. They believed that their audiences would be progressively disinterested as Mars was revealed to be less and less like the Earth.

Miniature set of the interior of the Alexandrian Library.

And yet the Martian landscapes are staggering, the vistas breathtaking. I was positive from my own experience that an enormous global interest exists in the exploration of the planets and in many kindred scientific topics—the origin of life, the Earth, and the Cosmos, the search for extraterrestrial intelligence, our connection with the universe. And I was certain that this interest could be excited through that most powerful communication medium, television."[9]

Hence, "Cosmos," the thirteen-part television series oriented toward astronomy with a broad human perspective, was born. The program, by 1987, had a world-wide viewing audience of one-third of a billion people. "[The program was] dedicated to the proposition that the public is far more intelligent than it has generally been given credit for; that the deepest scientific questions on the nature and origin of the world excite the interests and passions of enormous numbers of people. The present epoch is a major crossroads for our civilization and perhaps for our species. Whatever road we take, our fate is indissolubly bound up with science. In addition, science is a delight; evolution has arranged that we take pleasure in understanding—those who understand are more likely to survive. The...series...represents a hopeful experiment in communicating some of the ideas, methods and joys of science."[9]

1977. Pulitzer-Prize-winning *The Dragons of Eden*, Sagan's first popular book to delve outside the study of astronomy, examines the premise that "a better understanding of the nature of evolution of human intelligence just possibly might help us to deal intelligently with our unknown and perilous future."[10] To help achieve this understanding Sagan traces the evolutionary process of the intelligence of lower animals. He describes the brain evolution of three distinct brains of modern man. The reptilian brain (the oldest) plays a distinctive role in aggressive behavior, territoriality, ritual, and the establishment of social hierarchies. The mammalian brain which generates strong or vivid emotions and the neocortex, common to most higher primates at least in humans. The neocortex is most notably the recorder of culture which does not complement the functions of the earlier two brains but serves to obstruct, deny, repress, and frustrate them. Much of the book's attention is focused on the neocortex, especially the right and left hemispheres.

"...Unless we destroy ourselves utterly, the future belongs to those societies that, while not ignoring the reptilian and mammalian parts of our being,

enable the characteristically human components of our nature to flourish; to those societies that encourage diversity rather than conformity; to those societies willing to invest resources in a variety of social, political, economic and cultural experiments, and prepared to sacrifice short-term advantage for long-term benefit; to those societies that treat new ideas as delicate, fragile and immensely valuable pathways to the future."[11]

The inspiration for Sagan's next work, *Broca's Brain*, came during a tour of the Musee de l'Homme in Paris, where he came upon a collection of jars containing human brains. Examining one of the jars, he found he was holding the brain of Paul Broca, a distinguished nineteenth-century anatomist. *Broca's Brain* is a compilation of essays ranging in topic from ancient astronauts to mathematically-gifted horses.

1981. Married third wife, novelist Ann Druyan. Druyan was one of the writers on the "Cosmos" series and was creative director of the *Voyager* record. She had been Sagan's constant companion for two and a half years. "We were friends and collaborators for several years," said Druyan, "and suddenly we fell in love. At first we didn't allow ourselves to think about it. Once it was out, we moved heaven and earth to be together."[3] Added Sagan, "Until I met Annie I thought love was a hype to sell movie magazines to teenage girls. The idea that it really could be the kind of feeling that popular songs claim was a revelation."[3]

1983. Suffered a near-fatal condition as a consequence of an appendectomy that caused massive internal hemorrhaging. His blood was replaced twice and he had ten hours of surgery in the Upstate Medical Center in Syracuse.

1985. *Contact*, his first novel published. He tried writing fiction "for the same reason I've gone on the 'Tonight' show: to reach a different audience, millions of people."[6]

In recent years, Sagan has devoted much of his time to writing and lecturing about the long-term effects of nuclear warfare. He played a major role in the discovery of nuclear winter, the widespread cold and dark likely to be brought about by even a small nuclear war. The scientists' vision of the total devastation and widespread death made him a leading spokesman in the nuclear disarmament movement. In 1986 he was arrested for misdemeanor criminal trespass at the Nevada Test Site, seventy miles northwest of Las Vegas. He and 138 other protesters, most of them doctors, nurses and public-health professionals, were taken into custody after crossing security barriers to demonstrate against continued U.S. nuclear testing in the face of a Soviet moratorium. An underground bomb, the tenth that year, was set off while the protest was in progress. All of the charges were subsequently dropped. With his wife, Ann, he organized in 1987 the largest demonstration at the Nevada Test site ever held, with the largest number of arrests in non-violent civil disobedience in U.S. history.

"The nuclear issue really worries me because we discover, unexpectedly, that we've created a doomsday machine. Yes, there are assurances: 'Trust me—we won't use it.' But that's like giving a loaded revolver to a child.

"Precisely the same technology that we use to destroy our global civilization—nuclear and rocket technology—can also be used to take us to the planets and stars. We can choose either fork in the road. It's like a morality play from the Middle Ages."[12]

"Overall, the human species spends almost $1 trillion a year, most of it by the United States and the Soviet Union, in preparations for intimidation and war....We are at risk. We do not need alien invaders. We have all by ourselves generated sufficient dangers. But they are unseen dangers, seemingly far removed from everyday life, requiring careful thought to understand, involving transparent gases, invisible radiation, nuclear weapons that almost no one has actually witnessed in use—not a foreign army intent on plunder, slavery, rape and murder. Our common enemies are harder to personify, more difficult to hate than a Shahansha, a Khan or a Fuhrer. And joining forces against these new enemies requires us to make courageous efforts at self-knowledge, because we ourselves—all the nations of the Earth, but especially the United States and the Soviet Union—bear responsibility for the perils we now face...."[13]

Sagan's fantasy is to hole up with piles of photographs of the Saturn system. "I have this image of long winter nights with the snow falling outside and there I am lost in the haze layer of Titan [Saturn's largest moon]."[3]

He is currently the David Duncan Professor of Astronomy and Space Sciences and director of the Laboratory for Planetary Studies at Cornell. In addition to the commissions and conferences on extraterrestrial life, Sagan has participated in the work of an enormous number of boards and committees having to do with space exploration, including the groups that formulated the international procedures for sterilizing spacecrafts and

Sagan with wife, Ann Druyan.

several committees for NASA—most notably the imaging teams of *Mariner 9, Viking,* and *Voyager.* He has also become involved in the flights of *Pioneers 10* and *11.* Sagan and Cornell colleague Frank Drake designed plaques to be installed on the crafts depicting the time of launch in relation to the history of our galaxy and pictures of those who launched the crafts—delineations of a nude man and woman. He was also responsible for the Voyager interstellar records aboard the *Voyager 1* and *2* spacecrafts.

Footnote Sources:

[1] Jonathan Cott, "The Cosmos," *Rolling Stone,* December 25, 1980.
[2] Henry S. F. Cooper, Jr., "Profiles: A Resonance with Something Alive—I," *New Yorker,* June 21, 1976.
[3] "His 'Cosmos' a Huge Success, Carl Sagan Turns Back to Science and Saturn's Rings," *People,* December 15, 1980.
[4] Carl Sagan, "Growing Up with Science Fiction," *New York Times Magazine,* May 28, 1978.
[5] David Gelman, and others, "Seeking Other Worlds," *Newsweek,* August 15, 1977.

[6]Glenn Collins, "The Sagans: Fiction and Fact Back to Back," *New York Times Biographical Service,* September 30, 1985.

[7]"Beyond Viking: Where Missions to Mars Could Lead," *U.S. News & World Report,* August 30, 1976.

[8]Boyce Rensberger, "Carl Sagan: Obliged to Explain," *New York Times Book Review,* May 29, 1977.

[9]C. Sagan, "Introduction," to *Cosmos,* Random House, 1980.

[10]Richard Restak, "The Brain Knew More than the Genes," *New York Times Book Review,* May 29, 1977.

[11]Charles Weingartner, "A Dragon in Your Head: Carl Sagan's *The Dragons of Eden,*" *Media & Methods,* September, 1978.

[12]"Today's Technology May Find E. T. If He's Out There," *U.S. News & World Report,* October 21, 1985.

[13]C. Sagan, "The Common Enemy," *Parade,* February 7, 1988.

■ For More Information See

Christian Science Monitor, November 15, 1965, November 19, 1980.

Current Biography, 1970, H. W. Wilson, 1971.

Arthur Fisher, "Close-Up Photos Reveal a Turbulent Mars: A PS Interview with Carl Sagan," *Popular Science,* September, 1972.

Edward Edelson, "Star Struck," *Washington Post Book World,* November 25, 1973.

Time, January 24, 1974, September 29, 1980, December 14, 1981, October 13, 1986.

Richard Berendzen, "The Solar System and Beyond," *Bulletin of the Atomic Scientists,* April, 1975.

"The Authors," *Scientific American,* May, 1975.

"Lots of Space Mysteries Still Left to Explore," *U. S. News & World Report,* May 19, 1975.

"The Authors," *Scientific American,* September, 1975.

New York, September 1, 1975.

Henry S. F. Cooper, Jr., "Profiles: A Resonance with Something Alive—II," *New Yorker,* June 28, 1976.

Joseph F. Goodavage, "An Interview with Carl Sagan," *Analog Science Fiction/Science Fact,* August, 1976.

Meet the Press, September 19, 1976.

"The Vikings on Mars Provide Vicarious Adventure for a Would-Be Space Explorer," *People,* January 3, 1977.

Carl Sagan, "In Praise of Science and Technology," *New Republic,* January 22, 1977.

John F. Baker, "PW Interviews: Carl Sagan," *Publishers Weekly,* May 2, 1977.

New York Times, May 17, 1977.

Chicago Tribune, May 20, 1977.

Peter Stoler, "Brain Matter," *Time,* May 23, 1977.

Detroit News, May 27, 1977.

Washington Post Book World, May 27, 1977, November 17, 1980.

New York Review of Books, June 9, 1977.

Newsweek, June 27, 1977, August 22, 1977, October 6, 1980, November 23, 1981.

Atlantic, August, 1977.

R. J. Herrnstein, "Psycho-Physiology," *Commentary,* August, 1977, May, 1981.

John Updike, "Who Wants to Know?," *New Yorker,* August 22, 1977.

David Gelman and others, "Seeking Other Worlds," *Newsweek,* August 15, 1977.

C. Sagan, "'Miss Universe,'" *New York Times Magazine,* October 23, 1977.

New York Times Book Review, June 10, 1979, July 19, 1979, January 25, 1981.

R. Berendzen, "Astronomy and Other Subjects," *Science,* July 6, 1979.

Judy Klemesrud, "Behind the Best Sellers," *New York Times Book Review,* July 29, 1979.

National Review, August 3, 1979.

Astronomy, October, 1979.

Roger Bingham, "The New Scientist Interview," *New Scientist,* January 17, 1980.

Science Books and Films, March, 1980.

New Statesman, April 4, 1980.

Bruce Cook, "Carl Sagan's Guided Tour of the Universe," *American Film,* June, 1980.

J. Kelly Beatty, "Carl Sagan's 'Cosmos': Prime-Time Astronomy," *Sky and Telescope,* September, 1980.

David Roberts, "Carl Sagan's *Cosmos,*" *Horizon,* October, 1980.

Isaac Asimov, "Isaac Asimov on *Cosmos* Star," *Horizon,* October, 1980.

"The Cosmic Explainer," *Time,* October 20, 1980.

Alvin P. Sanoff, "A Conversation with Carl Sagan," *U. S. News & World Report,* December 1, 1980.

Frederic Golden, "Carl Sagan: Astronomical Superstar," *Reader's Digest,* February, 1981.

William J. O'Malley, "Carl Sagan's Gospel of Scientism," *America,* February 7, 1981.

Jeffrey Marsh, "The Universe and Dr. Sagan," *Commentary,* May, 1981.

William J. Harnack, "Carl Sagan: Cosmic Evolution Vs. the Creationist Myth," *Humanist,* July-August, 1981.

David Paul Rebovich, "Sagan's Metaphysical Parable," *Transaction: Social Science and Modern Society,* July-August, 1981.

William J. Broad, "A Star Fades for Entrepreneur Sagan," *Science,* January 8, 1982.

Science Digest, March, 1982.

C. Sagan, "Can We Know the Universe?" *Saturday Evening Post,* July-August, 1982.

Constance Holden, "Scientists Describe 'Nuclear Winter,'" *Science,* November 18, 1983.

Contemporary Issues Criticism, Volume II, Gale, 1984.

"Notes in an Interplanetary Bottle," *Harper's,* November, 1986.

C. Sagan, "Why We Must Continue to Be Explorers," *Parade,* November 22, 1987.

Daniel Cohen, *Carl Sagan: A Biography,* Dodd, 1987.

C. Sagan and Ann Druyan, "Give Us Hope," *Parade,* November 27, 1988.

J. D. Salinger

Born Jerome David Salinger January 1, 1919, in New York, N.Y.; son of Sol (an importer) and Miriam (Jillich) Salinger; allegedly married a French physician at the age of 26 and divorced in 1947; married Claire Douglas, February 17, 1955 (divorced, October, 1967); children: (second marriage) Margaret Ann, Matthew. *Education*: Graduated from Valley Forge Military Academy, 1936; attended New York University, Ursinus College, and Columbia University (where he studied with Whit Burnett). *Home and office*: Cornish, N.H. *Agent*: Harold Ober Associates, Inc., 40 East 49th St., New York, N.Y. 10017.

■ Career

Worked as an entertainer on the Swedish Liner *M. S. Kungsholm* in the Caribbean, 1941. Writer. *Military service*: U.S. Army, 1942-46; staff sergeant; awarded five battle stars.

■ Writings

The Catcher in the Rye (novel; Book-of-the-Month Club selection), Little, Brown, 1951.

Nine Stories, Little, Brown, 1953 (published in England as *For Esme—With Love and Squalor, and Other Stories*, Hamish Hamilton, 1953).

Franny and Zooey (two stories; "Franny" first published in *New Yorker*, January 29, 1955, "Zooey," *New Yorker*, May 4, 1957), Little, Brown, 1961.

Raise High the Roof Beam, Carpenters: and, Seymour: An Introduction (two stories; "Raise High the Roof Beam, Carpenters" first published in *New Yorker*, November 19, 1955, "Seymour," *New Yorker*, June 6, 1959), Little, Brown, 1963.

Four Books by J. D. Salinger (the four preceding books in one volume), Bantam, 1967.

Also contributor to *Harper's, Story, Collier's, Saturday Evening Post, Cosmopolitan*, and *Esquire*.

■ Sidelights

J. D. Salinger was born on January 1, 1919, the second child and only son of a Jewish father, a prosperous importer of hams and cheeses and a Scotch-Irish mother. Very little is known about Salinger. His silence is persistent. When pressed for biographical information, he has been known to spread false rumors: he was a goalie for the Montreal hockey team; the Marx brothers were a constant presence in his childhood home.

In 1932, he attended McBurney School, a private preparatory school in Manhattan. During the admissions interview, Salinger admitted to an interest in dramatics. He flunked out at the end of the first year. "He wanted to do unconventional things," recalled a friend. "For hours, no one in the family knew where he was or what he was doing; he just showed up for meals. He was a nice boy, but he was the kind of kid who, if you wanted to have a card game, wouldn't join in."[1]

Concerned about his education, Salinger's father enrolled him in the Valley Forge Military Academy in Pennsylvania. One of his classmates remembered crawling through the fence with him after lights out to poach local beer taps. Another mate recalled: "He was full of wit and humor and sizzling wisecracks. He was a precocious and gifted individual, and I think he realized at that age that he was more gifted with the pen than the rest of us.

"We were both skinny adolescents and must have looked terribly young and boyish. I was immediate-

Paperback cover from one of this century's classics.

ly attracted to him because of his sophistication and humor. His conversation was frequently laced with sarcasm about others and the silly routines we had to obey and follow at school. Both of us hated the military regime and often wondered why we didn't leave the school. I believe Jerry did everything he could not to earn a cadet promotion, which he considered childish and absurd. He enjoyed breaking the rules, and several times we both slipped off the academy grounds at 4 A.M. to enjoy a breakfast in the local diner. It was a great surprise to me that he returned to school for a second year.

"He loved conversation. He was given to mimicry. He liked people, but he couldn't stand stuffed shirts. Jerry was aware that he was miscast in the military role. He was all legs and angles, very slender, with a shock of black hair combed backward. His uniform was always rumpled in the wrong places. He never fit it. He always stuck out like a sore thumb in a long line of cadets."[2]

Salinger became literary editor of *Crossed Sabres*, the school's yearbook. It was here that he began writing short stories by flashlight under his blankets after "official lights" out. He presented the academy with a three stanza poetic tribute at graduation, which has since been set to music and is still sung by the cadets at last parade.

After graduation he enrolled for a summer session at New York University, followed by a visit to pre-*anschluss* Vienna, then Poland. "[I spent] most of the time in Vienna. . . .I was supposed to apprentice myself to the Polish ham business. . . .They finally dragged me off to Bydgoszcz [Poland] for a couple of months, where I slaughtered pigs, wagoned through the snow with the big slaughtermaster, who was determined to entertain me by firing his shotgun at sparrows, light bulbs, fellow employees.

"[I] came back to America and tried college for half a semester, but quit like a quitter. . . .I went to three colleges—never quite, technically, getting past the freshman year."[3] Frances Thierolf, a fellow student, recalled when this handsome, suave, and sophisticated New Yorker in the black Chesterfield coat (complete with velvet collar) hit the campus in 1938. "We had never seen anything quite like it. He gave the impression of having 'been around' more than the rest of us. We were enchanted by his biting and acerbic manner. . . .

"Most of the girls were mad about him at once—including me—and the boys held him slightly in awe with a trace of envy thrown in. Jerry Salinger

MIDSUMMER SELECTION

The Catcher in the Rye

BY J·D·SALINGER

PRICE: $3.00

Book-of-the-Month Club News called this selection, "An extraordinary first novel by a young American."

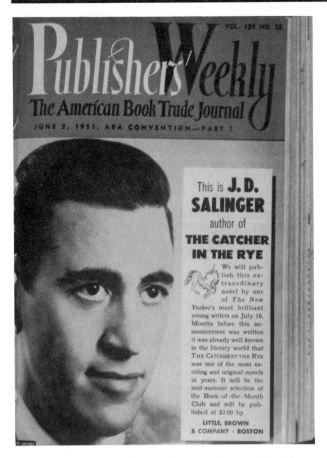

Advance promotion for Little Brown's original publication of *Catcher in the Rye.*

was a decidedly different phenomenon at Ursinus. His avowed purpose in life was to become a famous writer, and he declared openly that he would one day produce the Great American Novel. Jerry and I became special friends, mostly, I am sure, because I was the only one who believed he would do it. He felt that his English professors at Ursinus were more interested in how he dotted his *i*'s and crossed his *t*'s than they were in developing his literary style.

"When we knew Jerry, he was Holden Caulfield, although when *The Catcher in the Rye* burst upon the literary world, he expressed surprise when I recognized him as Holden. I guess he never knew his adolescence was showing."[2]

By 1939 Salinger was writing short stories in Whit Burnett's writing group at Columbia University, where he was remembered by Burnett as a quiet student who made no comments and was primarily interested in playwrighting; a student who spent one semester not taking notes, seemingly not listening, looking out the window, but who a week or so before semester's end, came to life.

For Salinger it was "a good and instructive and profitable year...on all counts....Mr. Burnett simply and very knowledgeably conducted a short-story course, never mugwumped over one. Whatever personal reasons he may have had for being there, at all, he plainly had no intentions of using fiction, short or long, as a leg up for himself in the academic or quarterly-magazine hierarchies. He usually showed up for class late, praises on him, and contrived to slip out early—I often have my doubts whether any good and conscientious short-story course conductor can humanly do more. Except that Mr. Burnett did. I have several notions how or why he did, but it seems essential only to say that he had a passion for good short fiction, strong short fiction, that very easily and properly dominated the room. It was clear to us that he loved getting his hands on *any* body's excellent story—Bunin's or Saroyan's, Maupassant's or Dean Fales' or Tess Slessinger's, Hemingway's or Dorothy Parker's or Clarence Day's, and so on, no particular pets, no fashionable prejudices. He was there, unmistakably, and however reechy it is almost sure to sound, in the service of the Short Story. But I would not ask Mr. Burnett to bear with any further hoarse praise from me. Not quite, anyway, of the same ilk.

"In class, one evening, Mr. Burnett felt himself in the mood to read Faulkner's "That Evening Sun Go Down" out loud, and he went right ahead and did it. A rapid reading, among other things, most singularly and undescribably low-key. In effect, he was much less reading the story aloud than running through it, verbatim, and very thoughtfully, with about twenty-five percent of his voice open. Almost anybody picked at random from a crowded subway car would have given a more dramatic or 'better' performance. But that was just the point. Mr. Burnett very deliberately forbore to perform. He abstained from reading beautifully. It was as if he had turned himself into a reading lamp, and his voice into paper and print. By and large, he left you on your own to know how the characters were saying what they were saying. You got your Faulkner story straight, without any middlemen between. Not before or since have I heard a reader make such instinctive and wholehearted concessions to a born printed-page writer's needs and, aye, rights. Regretfully, I never got to meet Faulkner, but I often had it in my head to shoot him a letter telling him about that unique reading of Mr. Burnett's. In this nutty, exploitive era, people who read short stories beautifully are all over the place—recording, taping, podiumizing, televising—and I wanted to tell Faulkner, who must have heard countless moving interpretations of his work, that not once, thoughout the reading, did Burnett come between the author and his beloved silent reader. Whether he has ever done it again, I don't know, but with somebody who has brought the thing off even once, the written short-story form must be very much at home, intact, unfinagled with, suitably content."[4]

At the end of the writing class Salinger submitted his first short story "The Young Folks," for which he was paid twenty-five dollars. "[Burnett] published my first piece in his magazine, *Story*. Been writing ever since, hitting some of the bigger magazines most of the little ones. Am still writing whenever I can find the time and an unoccupied foxhole."[3]

New Yorker purchased "Slight Rebellion Off Madison," the first Salinger story to mention Holden Caulfield. Its publication was delayed during the war years until 1946.

He was drafted into the United States Army in 1942. "I'm in the Officers, First Sergeants and Instructors Prep School of the Signal Corps, determined to get that ole message through....The men in my tent—though a damn nice bunch—are always eating oranges or listening to quiz programs, and I haven't written a line since my reclassification and induction."[5]

He was transferred to an aviation cadet air base in Georgia. "Finally passed all the examinations for transfer to the Army Aviation Cadets (Me in Aviation. Me what could never even put a Tinker-Toy together.")[6]

"Personal Notes of an Infantryman," reflective of Salinger's experience in the army, was published by Collier's. "It's almost impossible to write with the *Post* or Collier's or *Cosmopolitan* in mind. Those mags will let you scratch the surface, but they won't let you make an incision."[6] Salinger complained to Burnett that he was "tired—God, *so* tired—of leaving [characters] all broken on the page with just 'The End' written underneath."[6]

1943. Stationed in Nashville, Tennessee as Staff Sergeant. Kept up his writing during his stint. "I work on at least four stories at a time; whichever I finish first gets sent out first. Best system I ever had; avoids over-writing, going stale on a piece, draft-happy, etc."[6]

1944. After Counter-Intelligence training at Devonshire, England, Salinger landed with the 4th Division in Normandy on D-Day, six hours after the initial assault by the allies. He participated in five European campaigns, and was responsible for uncovering members of the Gestapo by interviewing civilians and captured Germans. "You never saw six-feet-two of muscle and typewriter ribbon get out of a jeep and into a ditch as fast as this baby can. And I don't get out till they start bulldozing an air field over me."[6]

"[I] am now in Germany with the Army. I used to go pretty steady with the big city, but I find that my memory is slipping since I've been in the Army. Have forgotten bars and streets and buses and faces; am more inclined, in retrospect, to get my New York out of the American Indian Room of the Museum of Natural History, where I used to drop my marbles all over the floor...."[3]

"This Sandwich Has No Mayonnaise," was published in *Saturday Evening Post*. "I have trouble writing simply and naturally. My mind is stocked with some black neckties, and though I'm throwing them out as fast as I find them, there will always be a few left over. I am a dash man and not a miler, and it is probable that I will never write a novel. So far the novels of this war have had too much of the strength, maturity and craftsmanship critics are looking for, and too little of the glorious imperfections which teeter and fall off the best minds. The

1961 photo of the reclusive author's mailbox...a lonely mile east of the the nearest paved road.

men who have been in this war deserve some sort of trembling melody rendered without embarrassment or regret. I'll watch for that book."[7]

Back in New York City, Salinger lived with his parents and spent his nights in Greenwich Village where he developed a reputation for taking many girls along. An older woman friend later recalled: "When there were other people around, he and I had complete rapport, but when we were alone our discussions always ended up lamely. I truly think that he was afraid. You see, I knew the routines and disguises he used with the college-age girls. He couldn't act for me. He had to be himself."[8]

"I never felt that he was a friend," recalled Hemingway biographer A.E. Hotchner who occasionally met Salinger for a game of poker or a drink. "He was too remote for friendship, but on a few occasions he invited me along on one of his night-clubbing sprees—he particularly liked the Blue Angels [on East 55th Street] and the Ruban Bleu [on East 56th Street], two of the clubs that featured young, unproved talent. On these occasions, we stayed up late drinking beer and enjoying the endless parade of beginning performers, some of whom were destined to have successful careers. In between the acts, Jerry talked, mostly about writing and writers, but sometimes he took on institutions, like the prep schools that had dismissed him, country clubs, writing classes that duped untalented boobs into thinking that one could learn to be a writer in the classroom, and so forth."[2]

"Down at the Dinghy" published by *Harper's*. The magazine requested that Salinger accompany the short story with a personal statement. "In the first place, if I owned a magazine I would never publish a column full of contributors' biographical notes. I seldom care to know a writer's birthplace, his children's names, his working schedule, the date of his arrest for smuggling guns (the gallant rogue!) during the Irish Rebellion. The writer who tells you these things is also very likely to have his picture taken wearing an open-collared shirt—and he's sure to be looking three-quarter-profile and tragic. He can also be counted on to refer to his wife as a swell gal or a grand person.

"I've written biographical notes for a few magazines, and I doubt if I ever said anything honest in them. This time, though, I think I'm a little too far out of my Emily Bronte period to work myself into a Heathcliff. (All writers—no matter how many rebellions they actively support—go to their graves half-Oliver Twist and half-Mary, Mary, Quite Contrary.) This time I'm going to make it short and go straight home.

"I've been writing seriously for over ten years. Being modest almost to a fault, I won't say I'm a born writer, but I'm certainly a born professional. I don't think I ever *selected* writing as a career. I just started to write when I was eighteen or so and never stopped. (Maybe that isn't quite true. Maybe I *did* select writing as a profession. I don't really remember—I got into it so quickly—and finally."[9]

1950. Goldwyn studios adapted his short story "Uncle Wiggily in Connecticut" into the movie "My Foolish Heart." Deeply disappointed with the film, Salinger never again granted permission to adapt his work.

July 16, 1951. *The Catcher in the Rye* was published, a story of a sixteen-year-old hero-narrator Holden Caulfied. Full of despair and loneliness because of the "phony" post war era in which he is living. Knowing that he is to be expelled from prep school for poor grades, Holden decides to run away just before Christmas. He spends the next few days wandering in New York City, describing in a mixture of schoolboy slang and poetry his feelings about himself, his family, the world that surrounds him, and his quest for the true, the good, the real, and the innocent. In the end, Holden comes to understand that despite the corruption that surrounds us, there is still the possibility of "goodness," and he finally decides to go home.

"I was much relieved when I finished [*The Catcher in the Rye*]. My boyhood was very much the same as that of the boy in the book, and it was a great relief telling people about it."[10]

Since that statement, Salinger's devotees have been trying to find parallels between his life as an adolescent, and that of Caulfield's. Memories about childhood play an important role in Salinger's work, and there are some unmistakable similarities between Salinger and his protagonist. Both grew up in a wealthy family living on the Upper West Side of Manhattan. Both had parents of different religions, both managed a fencing team in their teens, and both were kicked out of high school. At Valley Forge, one of Salinger's fellow cadets jumped from a window as does James Castle in *The Catcher of the Rye*. However, the book is not autobiographical. Holden Caulfield is a post World War II teenager; Salinger was not.

The negative reviews were outweighed by critics and fans who found in the novel the voice of their own generation. *The Catcher in the Rye* was

James McMullan's illustration for the 1981 *Esquire* magazine article which marked the thirtieth anniversary of "*Catcher's*" publication.

reprinted three times in the following month of its publication, and twice more a month later. In 1953, Signet issued the first paperback. Ten years later the book had sold 3,364,000 copies. It was translated into Finnish, Swedish, Russian, Hebrew, French, German, Polish, and Japanese, among others. There are more than ten million copies in print, and a mint copy of the first edition is a collector's item. A cult arose around Salinger who became the most sought-after author of his decade.

Despite its popularity, the book didn't escape censorious attacks from school officials and parents who found the language offensive. "I'm aware that a number of my friends will be saddened, or shocked, or shocked-saddened, over some of the chapters of *The Catcher in the Rye*. Some of my best friends are children. In fact, all of my best friends are children. It's almost unbearable to me to realize that my book will be kept on a shelf out of their reach."[11]

The book was temporarily banned on moral grounds in Australia and South Africa. In 1956 it was declared objectionable in Nevada by the National Organization for Decent Literature. In 1960, a Baptist minister of California denounced the book for its profanity and poor English and asked that it be removed from public schools. In 1961, it was banned from eleventh-grade English class in Oklahoma, and in 1965 from a Pennsylvania school. In 1970 a Carolina sheriff prohibited the book in his county for obscenity, and up to the mid-seventies, many small-town libraries kept their sole copy on a restricted shelf, long after the book had been adopted as required or supplementary reading by most colleges and high schools in the United States.

"Many of the letters from readers have been very nice. I feel tremendously relieved that the season for success for the *Catcher in the Rye* is nearly over. I enjoyed a small part of it, but most of it I found hectic and professionally and personally demoralizing."[12]

"My method of work is such that any interruption throws me off. I can't have my picture taken or have an interview until I've completed what I've set out to do."[13]

"A writer, when he's asked to discuss his craft, ought to get up and call out in a loud voice just the *names* of the writers he *loves*. I love Kafka, Flaubert, Tolstoy, Chekhov, Dostoevsky, Proust, O'Casey, Rilke, Lorca, Keats, Rimbaud, Burns, E. Bronte, Jane Austen, Henry James, Blake, Coleridge. I won't name any living writers. I don't think it's right. I think writing is a hard life. But it's brought me enough happiness that I don't think I'd ever deliberately dissuade anybody (if he had talent) from taking it up. The compensations are few, but when they come, if they come, they're very beautiful."[14]

In 1953, the influence of Zen Buddhism first appeared in his short story, "Teddy," first published in the *New Yorker*. Salinger's interest in Zen attitudes toward life and art began in the mid-'40s at the Rama Krishna-Vivekananda Center in New York.

Moved to Cornish, New Hampshire into a cottage overlooking the Connecticut River. Here he allowed himself to be interviewed by sixteen-year-old Shirley Blaney, for the New Hampshire *Daily Eagle*. When he first moved to New Hampshire, Salinger spent a lot of his time with local teenagers, and they would often come knocking on his door in the evening. Blaney remembered that "he seemed to be delighted. He cried, 'Come on in' and started bringing out the Cokes and potato chips. After a while he began playing some records on his hi-fi; he had hundreds of records, classics and show tunes. We were there a long time and I finally told my date, 'Come on, let's get out of here; Jerry doesn't want to be bothered with us.' But every time we started to leave Jerry would say, 'Stick around. I'll play another record.' I couldn't understand why he put up with us, but he didn't seem to want us to go.

"I never saw anyone fit in the way he did. He was just like one of the gang, except that he never did anything silly the way the rest of us did. He always knew who was going with whom, and if anybody was having trouble at school, and we all looked up to him, especially the renegades. He'd play whatever record we asked for on his hi-fi—my favorite was 'Swan Lake'—and when we started to leave he'd always want to play just one more.

"He seemed to love having us around, but I'd sit there and wonder, why is he doing this? Finally I decided that he was writing another book about teenagers and we were his guinea pigs. I don't mean that he was looking down his nose at us, or had us on a pin or anything like. He was very sincere. There's nothing phony about him. He's a very nice person. Once I told him that I thought I'd like to be a writer, that I was lying awake at night trying to think of ideas. He nodded very sympathetically and said, 'That's the best way. Be sure to get up and write them down, so you don't forget them.'"[8]

February 17, 1955. Married Claire Douglas, an English-born Radcliffe student. At the end of that year, his daughter, Margaret Ann, was born. The marriage lasted for twelve years.

Over the years, Salinger withdrew from the public world. The tremendous success of *The Catcher in the Rye,* and his intense desire for privacy pressed the curiosity of many fans, journalists, scholars, and researchers who showed up on his doorsteps unsolicited. He always refused to sign autographs, give lectures or interviews. He never consented to be in *Who's Who* and kept an unlisted phone number. To protect his privacy he eventually built a fence around his house, and a few years later, the house became inaccessible. "You can only get as far as the garage," acknowledges a neighbor. "The only way to get to the house is by going through a 50-foot cement tunnel from the garage. The tunnel is patrolled by dogs, and the way the house is situated, he could see you coming for miles."[15]

He also built a studio of concrete blocks. There he reportedly wrote from early in the morning, sometimes as much as fifteen hours a day, said his friend, artist Bertrand Yeaton. "Jerry works like a dog....He's a meticulous craftsman who constantly revises, polishes, and rewrites. On the wall of the studio, Jerry has a series of cuphooks to which he clips sheafs of notes. They must deal with various characters and situations because when an idea occurs to him he takes down the clips, makes the appropriate notation, and places it back on the proper hook. He also has a ledger in which he has pasted sheets of typewritten manuscript on one page and on the opposite one has arrows, memos, and other notes for revisions."[16]

February 13, 1960. Son, Matthew, was born. In autumn, *Franny and Zooey* was published and became the literary event of the year. "I love working on these Glass stories. I've been waiting for them most of my life, and I think I have fairly decent, monomaniacal plans to finish them with due care [and] all available skill.

"A couple of stories in the series besides *Franny* and *Zooey* have already been published in *The New Yorker*, and some new material is scheduled to appear there soon or Soon. I have a great deal of thoroughly unscheduled material on paper, too, but I expect to be fussing with it to use a popular trade term, for some time to come. ("Polishing" is another dandy word that comes to mind.) I work like greased lightning, myself, but my alterego and collaborator, Buddy Glass, is insufferably slow."[17]

The six "Glass family" stories, which were published between 1948 and 1965, are designed to work both as self-contained accounts, as well as part of a composite novel which the reader must assemble himself in order to derive an overall meaning. The family includes seven children, all prodigies and all having appeared at one time or another on a radio quiz show. Most of the stories focus on the two elder sons: Seymour, the genius poet-professor and God-seeker who is the spiritual guide for his siblings, and Buddy, a story writer and chronicler of Seymour's life.

Seymour's personality as a fiction hero was so popular that many readers believed him to be a real person. A British writer reported: "One night in Rome...an American friend noted for his sobriety and serious-mindedness phoned me in a state of great excitement to say that he had met Seymour Glass's brother-in-law in a bar and would I go and meet him. Feeling that the Salinger myth was getting out of hand, I said no...."[8]

June 19, 1965. Last known published story "Hapworth 16, 1924," appeared in the *New Yorker*. "There is a marvelous peace in not publishing. It's peaceful. Still Publishing is a terrible invasion of my privacy. I like to write. I love to write. But I write just for myself and my own pleasure."[18]

1974. An unauthorized edition of his previously uncollected stories published in California by John Greenberg. "Some stories, my property have been stolen. Someone's appropriated them. It's an illicit act. It's unfair. Suppose you had a coat you liked and somebody went into your closet and stole it.

"It's amazing some sort of law and order agency can't do something about this. Why, if a dirty old mattress is stolen from your attic, they'll find it. But they're not even looking for this man."[18] Salinger filed a civil suit against seventeen major bookstores who sold the unauthorized edition and asked for a federal search for John Greenberg.

Although Salinger had stopped publishing his works, rumors to the contrary were flying. In the February, 1977 issue of *Esquire,* an unsigned story "For Rupert—With No Promises," was widely believed to have been written by Salinger. However, when publicity reached its pitch, the fiction editor of *Esquire* revealed that he was the author. In 1981 the *New York Times* reported a rumor circulating that Salinger was publishing under the name of William Wharton. Wharton turned out to be a real author.

1981. *Newsweek* reported that Salinger's son, Matthew, a full-time undergraduate at Columbia, was also taking acting classes at Lee Strasberg Institute and one singing lesson a week. After brief stints on "Ryans Hope" and "One Life to Live," he opened in a small theatre in L.A. in a play called "One Night at the Studio." Said Matt, in an interview: "I won't let people try to get at my father—find out about his life—through me. I know how much he does not want public attention.

Cover for the paperback of Salinger's 1953 collection of stories.

He is a wonderful father and I respect him, so I won't talk about him."[19] Divorced when Matt was six, his mother still lived nearby and he divided his time between parents. "I was not the child of split parents. I was lucky, I thought. I liked the change of pace, and I got to know my parents as individuals."[19] His mother is now a Jungian psychologist in San Francisco.

1986. Filed a suit to stop publication of Ian Hamilton's *J. D. Salinger: A Writing Life.* Salinger objected to the use of personal letters he had written long ago as an invasion of his privacy. In response to Salinger's request, Hamilton deleted direct quotations from the letters, and instead used his own words to report the ideas and events they contained. Again, Salinger disapproved of the new version. By that time he had applied for copyright for all his correspondence housed in library archives.

1987. After deliberation, the judges blocked the publication of Salinger's biography on the ground that it depended mainly on his letters and on the paraphrasing which was so close to the original that it constituted infringement.

In 1988, Hamilton published *In Search of J. D. Salinger,* deleting all quotations from Salinger's personal letters. The book's main subject turned from Salinger to Hamilton: his views, his research, his legal battles with Salinger.

Salinger continues to protect his privacy. "It is my rather subversive opinion that a writer's feelings of anonymity-obscurity are the second-most valuable property on loan to him during his working years."[16]

Footnote Sources:

[1] Henri Anatole Grunwald, *Salinger: A Critical and Personal Portrait,* Harper, 1962.
[2] Ian Hamilton, *In Search of J. D. Salinger,* Random House, 1988.
[3] "Contributors," *Story,* November/December, 1944.
[4] Hallie and Whit Burnett, *Fiction Writer's Handbook,* Harper, 1975.
[5] "Contributors," Story, September/October, 1942.
[6] Salinger's Letters to Whit Burnett, Archives at Princeton University Library.
[7] "Contributors," *Esquire,* October, 1945.
[8] Ernest Haveman, "The Search for the Mysterious J. D. Salinger," Life, November, 1961.
[9] Arthur Mizener "The Love Song of J. D. Salinger," *Harper's,* February, 1959.

[10] "Shirley Blaney Interviews Salinger," *Daily Eagle,* November 13, 1953.
[11] *Twentieth Century Authors,* edited by Stanley J. Kunitz, H. W. Wilson, 1955.
[12] Warren French, *J. D. Salinger,* Twayne, 1963.
[13] Edward Kosner, "The Private World of J. D. Salinger," *New York Post Magazine,* April 30, 1961.
[14] William Maxwell, "J. D. Salinger," *Book-of-the-Month Club News,* July, 1951.
[15] "The Dodger in the Rye," *Newsweek,* July 30, 1979.
[16] "The Mysterious J. D. Salinger," *Newsweek,* May 30, 1960.
[17] J. D. Salinger, *Franny and Zooey,* Little Brown, 1961.
[18] Lacey Fosburgh, "J. D. Salinger Speaks about His Silence," *New York Times,* November 3, 1974.
[19] Paul Corkery, "Solitude May be Bliss for Author J.D. Salinger, But to Son Matt, All the World's a Stage," *People Weekly,* October 31, 1983.

■ For More Information See

Books:

F. L. Gwynn and J. L. Blotner, *The Fiction of J. D. Salinger,* University of Pittsburgh Press, 1958.
Maxwell Geismar, *American Moderns,* Hill & Wang, 1958.
Henry Anatole Grunwald, editor, *Salinger: A Critical and Personal Portrait,* Harper, 1962.
W. F. Belcher and J. W. Lee, editors, *J. D. Salinger and the Critics,* Wadsworth, 1962.
Frank Kermode, *Puzzles and Epiphanies,* Chilmark, 1962.
Alfred Kazin, *Contemporaries,* Atlantic Monthly Press, 1962.
Marvin Laser and Norman Fruman, *Studies in J. D. Salinger,* Odyssey, 1963.
Malcom M. Marsden, compiler, *If You Really Want to Know: A Catcher Casebook,* Scott, 1963.
Warren French, *J. D. Salinger,* Twayne, 1963.
Walter Allen, *The Modern Novel,* Dutton, 1965.
James Lundquist, *J.D. Salinger,* Frederick Ungar, 1979.

Periodicals:

Atlantic, August, 1961.
Mademoiselle, August, 1961.
Time, September 15, 1961.
Saturday Review, September 16, 1961, November 4, 1961.
Life, November 3, 1961.
Catholic World, February, 1962.
Horizon, May, 1962.
Harper's, October, 1962, December, 1962.
America, January 26, 1963.
Newsweek, January 28, 1963.
Critique, spring-summer, 1965.
Minnesota Review, May-July, 1965.
Book Week, September 26, 1965.

Todd Strasser

Born May 5, 1950, in New York, N.Y.; son of Chester S. (a manufacturer of women's dresses) and Sheila (a copy editor; maiden name, Reisner) Strasser; married Pamela Older (a businesswoman), July 2, 1981; children: Lia and Geoff. *Education:* Beloit College, B.A., 1974. *Home and office:* 310 West 79th St., New York, N.Y. 10024.

■ Career

Beloit College, Beloit, Wis., public relations, 1973-74; *Times Herald Record* (newspaper), Middletown, N.Y., reporter, 1974-76; free-lance writer, 1975—; Compton Advertising, New York, N.Y., copywriter, 1976-77; *Esquire*, New York, N.Y., researcher, 1977-78; Toggle, Inc., (fortune cookie company), New York City, owner 1978—. Speaker at teachers' and librarians' conferences and at high schools. Conducts writing workshops for adults and teenagers. *Member:* International Reading Association, Authors Guild, Freedom to Read Foundation, P.E.N.

■ Awards, Honors

Friends Till the End was selected one of American Library Association's Best Books for Young Adults, 1981, and *Rock 'n' Roll Nights*, 1982; *Friends Till the End* was chosen a Notable Children's Trade Book in the Field of Social Studies by the National Council for Social Studies and the Children's Book Council, 1982; *Rock 'n' Roll Nights* was chosen for the Acton Public Library's CRABbery Award List, 1983; Young Reader Medal nomination from the California Reading Association, 1983, for *Friends Till the End*; New York Public Library's Books for the Teen Age, 1981, for *Angel Dust Blues*, 1982, for *The Wave*, 1982, for *Friends Till the End*, 1983, for *Rock 'n' Roll Nights*, and 1984, for *Workin' for Peanuts*; Book Award from the Federation of Children's Books (Great Britain), 1983, for *The Wave*, and 1984, for *Turn It Up!*; Outstanding Book Award from the Iowa Books for Young Adult Program, 1985, for *Turn It Up!*; Colorado Blue Spruce Award nomination, 1987, for *Angel Dust Blues*.

■ Writings

Young Adult Fiction:

Angel Dust Blues, Coward, 1979.
Friends Till the End: A Novel, Delacorte, 1981.
(Under pseudonym Morton Rhue) *The Wave* (novelization based on the television drama of the same title by Johnny Dawkins), Delacorte, 1981.
Rock 'n' Roll Nights: A Novel, Delacorte, 1982.
Workin' for Peanuts, Delacorte, 1983.

Turn It Up! (sequel to *Rock 'n' Roll Nights*), Delacorte, 1984.

A Very Touchy Subject, Delacorte, 1985.

Ferris Bueller's Day Off (novelization based on feature film of the same title by John Hughes), New American Library, 1986.

Wildlife, Delacorte, 1987.

The Accident, Delacorte, 1988.

Cookie (novelization based on feature film of the same title by Nora Ephron), New American Library, 1989.

Moving Target, Fawcett, 1989.

Beyond the Reef, Delacorte, 1989.

Juvenile:

The Complete Computer Popularity Program, Delacorte, 1984.

The Mall from Outer Space, Scholastic, 1987.

Adult:

The Family Man (novel), St. Martin's, 1988.

Teacher's guides are available for *Angel Dust Blues* and *The Wave.* Also contributor to periodicals, including *New Yorker, Esquire, New York Times,* and *Village Voice.*

■ Adaptations

"Workin' for Peanuts," Home Box Office "Family Showcase," 1985.

"Can a Guy Say No?" (based on *A Very Touchy Subject*), "ABC Afterschool Special," February, 1986.

■ Work In Progress

Historical juvenile about a young Mexican diver in 1600s, for Scholastic.

■ Sidelights

Strasser was born on May 5, 1950 in New York City, and grew up in Long Island. His father, Chester S. Strasser was a dress manufacturer and his mother, Sheila Reisner Strasser, was an artist and copy editor.

"Looking back, I had a fine childhood in a very nice suburban setting. Like any kid I had my insecurities, but I also had a stable family life, attended good public schools and went to summer camp."

As a boy, Strasser was an avid collector of insects, amphibians and reptiles, much to his mother's chagrin, since they tended to escape in the house. A number were never found. His parents frequent-ly took him and his brother on skiing and fishing trips. Tennis also was, and is, an important family sport.

"Scholastically I was an underachiever and had a particularly tough time with reading and spelling. In general I did minimal amounts of homework, but if a subject excited me I would immerse myself in it. Those subjects included dinosaurs, sea shells and James Bond novels."

During his teen years he went through a period of "anti-establishment" feelings as did many of his peers. "I grew my hair long, listened to Led Zepplin and rode my motorcycle to the Woodstock festival. The Establishment said the war in Viet Nam was good and the counter culture (long hair, rock music, drugs) was bad, and in retrospect they were mostly wrong on the first count and sometimes right (concerning drugs) on the second. At the time they appeared to be dead wrong on both counts and I was about as countercultural as they came.

"I have small children of my own now, and I already wonder how I'll handle their teenaged years. Almost all my books, starting with *Angel Dust Blues* and *Friends Till the End,* and going through *A Very Touchy Subject* and *The Accident,* concern teens dealing with the kinds of choices I faced. Sometimes I think I write YA books because I'm still trying to resolve the conflicts of my own youth. When I say that I hope that each of my books shows an example of a young adult who learns good judgment, I sometimes want to add, 'because I wish I had when I was a teen.'

"Even in the midst of conflict and turmoil, we could usually share a laugh. I think this came from my grandfather, who profitted from every loss by turning it into a humorous anecdote. For instance, he used to tell the story of when I was three and he took me clamming near his summer home in Bayville. Leaving me in the boat, he hopped into the shoulder-deep water and began digging the clams with a rake and throwing them into a bushel basket in the boat. As fast as he threw clams in, I dropped them back over the side. He dug in the same spot for almost an hour, amazed at how plentiful the clams were. Of course, when he climbed back into the boat and found an empty basket, he realized what had happened.

"I guess it's no surprise that my characters sometimes turn to humor in a tough moment. When I think of Tony facing a new school in *The Complete Computer Popularity Program,* and Scott facing new hormones in *A Very Touchy Subject,* I know my grandfather would be proud.''

After high school, Strasser enrolled at New York University and began to write poetry and some short fiction, but it was done strictly as a hobby with no thought of being published. A few years later he dropped out. During the next two years he hitchhiked around most of Europe and the United States, taking odd jobs whenever money ran low. He was a street musician in France and Germany, worked on a ship in Denmark, lived on a commune in Virginia, worked in a health food store in New York and was kidnapped briefly by Jesus freaks in South Bend, Indiana.

During these wandering years he continued to write, as well as documenting his travels in journals and letters. ''Finally it occurred to me that perhaps I should give writing a try as a student and, possibly, some sort of profession. I enrolled at Beloit College and began taking literature and writing courses.''

He took a creative writing course and was encouraged by his professor to keep writing. During this time he wrote the first draft of *Angel Dust Blues.* He was to write eight more drafts before it was published in 1979. Meanwhile, he was trying to decide on a career. ''For many years after I started writing I never believed I would actually be a writer. I wrote the way some people sing in the shower. In a shower you don't think anyone is going to hear you. I wrote thinking no one was ever going to read me.

''I guess my becoming a writer was really process of elimination. I tried a variety of things in college. Medicine, law. Nothing worked.

''My family felt I had to be a business person, or if I was lucky, a doctor or a lawyer. I never really thought I would be a writer. In fact, even today I find it hard to believe that I manage to make most of my living by selling books.''[1]

After graduation, Strasser worked temporarily for the public relations department at Beloit, wrote for two years for the *Times Herald-Record,* Middletown, N.Y., and a year later became an advertising copywriter for Compton Advertising in New York City and a researcher for *Esquire.* ''I guess I decided I wanted to be a novelist while I was working at the newspaper. There were stories I wanted to tell that simply didn't fit into the newspaper format. Later I moved to advertising to give me more time to work on fiction. When I sold my first novel I quit my advertising job. And then I

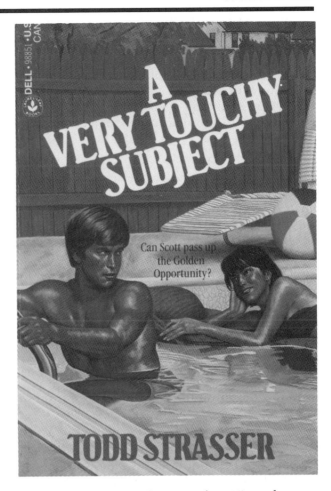

Paperback cover for Strasser's 1985 novel.

went the route of the poor struggling novelist. I used to do things like cut my own hair.''[1]

1978. *Angel Dust Blues* was accepted for publication. To supplement his income, he founded a fortune cookie business, Toggle, Inc. ''I started that business after I got a three thousand dollar advance for my first novel, *Angel Dust Blues,* and realized that it wasn't going to last me very long. Since I come from a business family, I had some idea of what to do. I just happened to start with fortune cookies.

''Before the fortune cookie business I was broke most of the time. You know in New York every penny you make goes toward rent. The first date I ever took [future wife] Pam on was to a bar in midtown Manhattan. They had free hors d'oeuvres if you bought a drink. I used to eat there two or three times a week. Buy a beer and get a free dinner.''[1]

The cookie business was more successful then he expected. ''It started as a way to come up with a little extra cash while I did my serious writing. In

October 1978 I started with 5,000 cookies hoping to sell them all by Christmas. I sold 100,000!

"To get it going I wore out a pair of shoes hiking from store to store in a seventy-block area of Manhattan. About thirty stores agreed to stock my cookies. They were immediately popular and before long I had sales reps around the city and all over the country."[2]

Strasser finds the business a perfect compliment to his writing. "It's good to get up from my typewriter and put my real work aside once in a while. And it's a way to supplement my serious writing. I must admit it's fun. When I look around at other friends who are waiting tables or driving cabs, it makes grinding out fortune cookie messages much more palatable. And I'll never be a starving writer. I can always eat my cookies.

"I recently dropped into one of the shops down the street that sells my fortune cookies and asked the proprietor how they were moving. He said, 'They're my bestseller!' So I thought—my first bestseller is a one-line manuscript wrapped in cookie dough!"[2]

1979. *Angel Dust Blues* was published. "When *Angel Dust Blues* was auctioned for paperback. I couldn't believe how much the publisher paid for it, but the hardcover house took half and my agent got her cut and then I didn't see all of my share for almost two years! It took forever.

"It was based on an incident that happened in high school to people I knew and I felt it was worth writing about....The funny thing is, the draft that Ferdinand Monjo bought, his assistant recommended that it be rejected. I only know that because when they gave me the manuscript back, the recommendation not to buy was under the first page!

"But Ferdinand decided to take a chance on me. What he bought and what he eventually got were very different books. I remember he took me out to lunch and told me, 'This is what you've done and this is what I think you really meant to do. Go ahead and do it.'

"He was amazing because he was able to see what I was trying to do even though I wasn't yet skilled enough to bring it off. He had that kind of vision.

"There aren't many editors like that. That book could not have been written without him. Unfortunately, he died without seeing the final version.

"For *Angel Dust Blues* the publisher did the paperback jacket without consulting me. It's a story of two boys and their relationship in terms of trust and friendship. One of the boys also has a strong romance. But the cover had two boys on it and no girl! I really wanted to have a girl because I felt the romantic aspect was very important. So I convinced the publisher to paint in a girl and she came out looking like a scarecrow.

"Ever since then I make sure early on that I let the publisher know what I hope the cover will look like. After that it's up to them. Sometimes they give me a cover before it's done. I point out what I think would be better. They generally make those improvements within the concept of the cover as it is. I can't say, 'I don't like this cover, give me a new cover.' I can say, 'Put in an amplifier, put in a guitar, change her hair,' and they'll do that."[1]

"*Angel Dust Blues* is about a group of fairly well-to-do, suburban teenagers who get into trouble with drugs." Explained Strasser. "(I grew up in a fairly well-to-do, suburban community and a group of kids I knew got into trouble with drugs.) My first story was based on that experience...and watching it occur."[3]

Reactions to this book about the drug culture were almost unanimously positive. Zena Sutherland wrote: "Phencyclidine, angel dust, is the drug that causes the violent climax of this trenchant and honest story....This is rough and tough, both in subject and language, but it is not didactic although Alex learns something from his bitter experience, and it's not overdone; Strasser's writing has a depth and candor that puts the book's focus on the intricate and at times compassionate development of the characters and their relationships."[4]

1981. On July 2, Strasser married Pamela Older, a production manager of *Esquire Magazine*. He also had another book published. "My second book, *Friends Till the End*, is about a healthy teenager who has a friend who becomes extremely ill with leukemia. When I moved to New York, I had a roommate...an old friend of mine. Within a few weeks, he became very ill. I spent a year visiting him in the hospital, not knowing whether he was going to live or die. I thought it was an experience that teenagers could relate to and one they *should* relate to."[3]

Mary K. Chelton, in *Voice of Youth Advocates*, praised the book: "It is nice to see one of the most promising authors of adolescent fiction...live up to his potential in this second novel....As David and his friends renegotiate their relationships, the pain of separating from peers as well as from parents is described beautifully. Told in the first person, this novel shows how well such narrative can be handled. Strasser's style is graceful and understated, and the adults, while not intrusive, are also not the usual cardboard stock characters of the genre....The book is well worth YASD Best Books consideration and should be useful in death and values clarification curricula as well as just a good read. I suspect that some creative adolescent medical specialists could also use the scenes at the hospital in medical education for dealing with friends and relatives of dying adolescents. A lovely and highly recommended book."[5]

In his next work, *The Wave*, Strasser adopted the pseudonym 'Morton Rhue.' "It was a novelization from a TV script. I only had three weeks to do the book. You have no objective view in that short period of time. The publisher wanted to put 'Todd Strasser' on the cover, but I didn't want my name on it because the book was not originally my idea. Ironically, the book has gone through dozens of printings and has been translated into something like nine languages.

"Why 'Morton Rhue?' In German, 'Todd' is very similar to the word 'dead' and 'Strasser' is the word for 'street.' Hence, Mort-du-Rue in French, or 'Morton Rhue.'"[1]

A review in *Publishers Weekly* explains the plot: "...The book is based on ABC-TV's dramatization wherein fiction teacher Ben Ross attempts to discipline careless students. Having stunned a class with films of Nazi atrocities and tried to explain how a minority achieved such power in Germany, Ross reads extensively on Third Reich indoctrination methods. They give him the idea for creating 'The Wave,' a select group who chivvy each other into excelling and bully others into joining them. The Wave's influence spreads incredibly and frighteningly until Ross takes steps to undo the mischief...."[6]

1982. His next work was *Rock 'n' Roll Nights.* "It's about a teenage rock and roll band—something with which I had absolutely no *direct* experience. However, I grew up in the 1960s when rock and roll was really our 'national anthem.' I relate much better to rock stars than to politicians. I always wanted to be in a rock band, as did just about everybody I knew.

Jacket illustration by Judy Clifford.

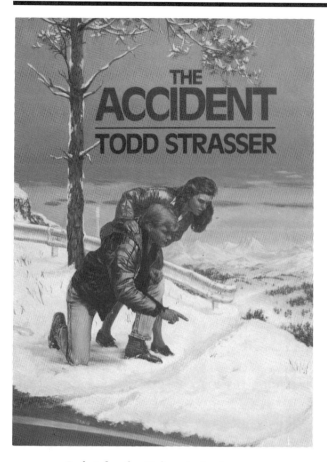

Jacket for the Delacorte hardcover.

"I think the kind of music teens listen to may change, or what they wear may change, but dealing with being popular, friends or the opposite sex, or questions of morality and decency...[I don't think] those things really ever change. I hate to say this, but I think authors tell the same stories—just in today's language and in today's settings."[3]

For Strasser, this work was a departure from the other two: "I wanted to do a different kind of book. *Rock 'n' Roll Nights* is a light book, probably more commercial than the first two and not as serious. I had a lot of fun writing it. I had just finished *Friends till the End*, which is about a kid who has leukemia and I wanted to write a fun, happy, up book. There are sequels, *Turn It Up!* and *Wildlife*.

"What I wanted to do is follow this rock-and-roll band from the days when they were playing in the street to the days when they are a super-group with ten thousand screaming kids in front of them, chronicling their lives, what it means to be a rock star, and how they are affected by their success.

In his review of the book, William G. McBride wrote: "Obstacles are realistic, and characters are quite well drawn. It is apparent that Gary has

talent; success is probable if he can get a break. Whether the break the band gets will suffice is left open, but that is a major strength of the novel.

"Younger students should find this an appealing story. It is a realistic career portrayal; being a first rate musician is extremely difficult, but it is not impossible. The story should appeal to both sexes."[7]

1983. *Workin' for Peanuts* was Strasser's next book. He describes problems he had with the jacket design. "In *Workin' for Peanuts* I originally described Jeff in the book as having black hair. On the cover he had brown hair. When I saw the cover I asked to have the hair changed to black. The publisher said, 'Hey, look. It's easier for you to go through the manuscript and change his hair to brown than to change his hair to black on the cover.' So I did. It only meant three or four changes. Of course, every other character in the book had brown hair so I changed a few others, too, so everyone wouldn't have brown hair."[1]

Diane C. Donovan praised the book in *Best Sellers:* "At first glance, *Workin' for Peanuts*, with its snappy title and first-person chatter, seems like a typical, trite 'confessional effect' novel: poor teen stadium vender Jeff Mead's attraction to rich-girl/boss' daughter Melissa poses problems for his job, family, and future career.

"Though the book holds the potential for trashy writings, its ability to portray economic realities and teen relationships in a realistic, moving manner places it a cut above the usual Young Adult problem-solving title. Protagonist Jeff's concerns about his unemployed father, breadwinning bus driver mother, and his own financial future are juxtaposed with Melissa's freer, unconcerned lifestyle, her uncertainties over a future unaffected by money concerns, and her genuine and growing affection for Jeff.

"Through such slow and deliberate comparisons of life styles, the reader is led to discern exactly how the presence or absence of money can affect interpersonal relationships and even love. . . .

"The result is a readable, engrossing tale which will capture and hold reader attention and provide unusual insight into the differences between poverty and wealth."[8]

"Over the years I had often complained to my wife that I wished that there were some easier way to do research on teenagers, especially in New York were, except for a few weeks each spring and fall, they seem particularly hard to find. Then. . .we had

From the movie "The Wave," starring Bruce Davison, on which Strasser based his novelization. Broadcast as an "ABC Afterschool Special," March 30, 1983.

our first child, a daughter. Shortly after we brought her home from the hospital, my wife turned to me and said, 'Just think, in thirteen years you won't have to leave the house at all to do your research.'

"Perhaps that's the best solution: grow your own."[9]

He also published a sequel to *Rock 'n' Roll Nights* titled *Turn It Up!* The reviews were mixed. Michael Healy wrote: "I do have some complaints. The 'music world' is a natural setting for drug use, vulgarity, and superficial relationships, but Strasser treats it as innocent and acceptable. His attempts to suggest that a few characters are struggling to define life's goals are his own fantasies. What he shows this reviewer contradicts what he thinks he tells the reader. He misses opportunities to give depth to characters and plot...."[10]

1985. *Workin' for Peanuts*, which had been sold to Scholastic Productions, was adapted by Home Box Office and was broadcast on "Family Showcase." Strasser also wrote a novelization of the film by John Hughes called *Ferris Bueller's Day Off.* Also during this year he published *A Very Touchy Subject.* In her *Horn Book* review, Ann A. Flowers wrote: "The author is an acute observer of the teenage scene and presents a humorous, no doubt accurate, rendering of the absorptions and conversations of teenage boys. Scott, though preoccupied with the very touchy subject, is a thoughful and decent young man, and the value of the book is the author's optimistic view of the basic kindness and good sense of young people."[11] In February, 1986, ABC-TV broadcast a dramatization of *A Very Touchy Subject* entitled "Can a Guy Say No?" as part of its "ABC Afterschool Special."

1987. Strasser published *Wildlife*, the third book in his trilogy about the rock band "Coming Attractions" featured in *Rock 'n' Roll Nights* and *Turn It Up!* He also wrote *The Mall from Outer Space*, a science fiction book.

Asked if he was interested in writing for the movies or television, Strasser replied: "*Workin' for Peanuts* was sold to Scholastic Productions for a one-hour made-for-cable movie. But the idea that Hollywood has unlimited amounts of money is an oversimplification. It does have a lot of money, but there are a lot of people competing for that money. The chances of you having a book made into a major two-hour theatrical release is pretty slim.

"It took S. E. Hinton fifteen years before anything of hers was made into a movie. Suppose she got one hundred thousand dollars for Tex. If you divide that by fifteen, it's about the same as earning minimum wage! It's not that I wouldn't mind writing for television or the movies. Television especially uses up an enormous amount of material and somebody has to keep coming up with it.

"I'm still living in a fool's paradise. I would not be motivated to write for TV except out of need. My desire is to write books. The only reason I would like to write for television is because someday I'll have to send my daughter to college....

"Another thing is, I spent a long time knocking on doors, trying to get people to read what I wrote, trying to get magazine articles published and trying to get books published. It was fun, an adventure. But it was also degrading. You're being put on hold all the time. You're trying to get your foot in the door.

"After I published a couple of books I didn't have to do that anymore. Now my publishers ask me if I'll have a book for next year. I don't have to go on my knees to them. That really makes a difference. And I'm not looking forward to starting over again. But I have a strong suspicion I'm going to have to!"[1]

"One of the great things about writing for young adults is that your books stay in print for so long. *Angel Dust Blues* was published in 1979 and still sells, and, of course, the paperback is still in print. All the money in the world can't replace the feeling of walking into a bookstore and seeing your books on the shelf."[1]

"I guess I originally wrote a lot of books for teens because that was where I had my first success and felt the most confident. But as I grow older, I find my interests widening not only towards writing books for older people, but for younger ones as well. I'd like to think that the day will come when I will write books for people of all ages, from three to eighty-three."[12]

His first adult novel, *The Family Man*, came out in late 1987 and was reviewed by *Publishers Weekly*: "Financial planner Stuart Miller, the hero of this enjoyable yuppie novel, has a charming wife with a career of her own, a beautiful baby daughter and a co-op apartment on Manhattan's Upper West Side. At the same time, he has problems: his wife admits to a mild flirtation with a business associate; his

parents quarrel; his best friends separate; and then there is the eternal need for a babysitter. Stuart is at first shocked when he glimpses a seductive beauty parading nude before a window in the sleazy hotel across the street. But the young woman's regular appearances make it clear she doesn't mind an audience, and Stuart becomes intrigued. As his problems at home mount, he develops a full-fledged obsession, complete with binoculars. Strasser...has done a fine job of portraying his young professionals without resorting to caricature. The book's tone is light, but there is a serious side that adds to the story's impact."[13]

But it is evident that writing for teenagers is a continuing interest for Strasser: "I am particularly interested in writing books for teenaged boys. By that I mean contemporary fiction and not sci fi or war stories. There are some very good writers writing for boys, but generally I'd say that most YA literature for the teenaged male is still in the Dark Ages. Many writers seem to have ignored the idea that a teenaged boy can be just as sensitive, just as mixed-up, just as curious as a teenaged girl. Well, I think he can (at least I know I was).

"I also think that books for teenagers today have to be very entertaining. We are dealing with kids who have been fed entertainment by the shovel-full, whether it comes from television, video games, or whatever the next fad will be. Books for teenagers have to compete or they simply will not get read. So when I write about an important subject like drug abuse or disease, I try to write a compelling story with humor and romance as well as serious matters."[14]

"A teenage boy from the age of about eleven to fourteen is discovering his masculinity and trying to understand the difference between himself as a male and others as females. In most families, the women are still *the readers*. The boy grows up saying to himself, 'Mom is reading and Dad is watching football on TV. I want to be like Dad.' A girl sees her mother reading and says, 'I can read just like Mom does.' Boys at that age aren't really *against* reading, but they want to do the things they envision as being masculine.

"What I try to do in my books is present boys the reader will admire, but I try to make them *real* boys, with emotions and sensitivities. If a boy sees a book that says on the cover, 'Tommy is a sensitive, caring young boy in a tumultuous relationship with his best friend and his girlfriend,' he's not going to pick it up. But if Tommy is the star of the soccer team and is a tough, good-looking guy, but is *still* in 'a tumultuous relationship with his best friend and his girlfriend,' *then* he's something boys will pick up on."[3]

Strasser says that his "characters grow out of the story. Each story requires a certain group of characters to make it progress from beginning to end, and I supply them based on need. I very rarely will pick a character and create a story around that character.

"I listen to teenagers whenever I have the opportunity. Also, I have a few nephews and nieces in the eleven- to thirteen-year-old range who supply me with information, whether they know it or not. I speak at schools a lot and sometimes I hang around for a few periods, go to some classes and listen to the kids."[3]

"People always want to know where I get my ideas....So I say I get my ideas from life or from the things I wish I'd done that I don't do. But I don't know where I get my ideas. Where does anybody get an idea from?"[1]

Strasser tries to maintain a regular working routine. "I start writing around nine in the morning and I usually keep busy with one thing or another until five P.M. Then my kids come home and later my wife gets home and by the time we've all eaten and my kids are in bed it's usually 9:30 or 10. If there's nothing else to do I can read for about an hour.

"Also, when it comes to teens, I am always looking for nonfiction articles and stories about them. I want to know what's going on in their lives; I'm looking for information I can use in my own stories about them. *Rolling Stone* and the *New York Times* are two of my best sources of information about teenagers."[1]

He finds he must leave home and forage in schools and teenage hangouts for information on his would-be readers. "For those of us who try to be factually accurate and who have never taught or had a teenager of our own, there is no avoiding it. I, for one, never even thought of research back in the old days when I was embarking on a career as a fiction writer. I just drew heavily on personal experience. My first couple of young adult books are based almost completely on factual experience and observation.

"But then I became intrigued by ideas and situations of which I had no firsthand knowledge. I also grew older, and my memories of my teen years grew dimmer and more difficult to understand. Soon I began to wonder if I really did know

Jacket illustration from *Friends Till the End* by Todd Strasser.

anything about teenagers. I worried that I was out of touch; I fretted too long over small details. What clothes should my characters wear? What music should they listen to? How should they speak?

"The day finally came when I woke up to the realization that the only way I could continue writing about teens was to leave my **IBM PC** behind and venture into the turbulent and misty world they inhabited. I put on the only pair of blue jeans left in my closet, grabbed a notebook and some pencils, kissed my wife good-by, and went out the door.

"In the last half-dozen years my desire to have realistic and contemporary settings for my books has forced me to infiltrate many bastions of youth. These places have included rock concerts, video arcades, the local Burger King at 3:30 P.M. on a school day, certain parts of public beaches—usually where the music is the loudest—dance clubs catering to the young, high school athletic events, and, of course, high schools. For one month several years ago I even took a job as a beer vendor at Giants Stadium to observe the teens who worked there."[9]

Strasser also finds that his frequent visits to schools help with his research. "When I'm invited to schools to speak on the craft and business of writing, I can stroll down crowded hallways and peek over the shoulders of students at their lockers. The boys hang mirrors and tape pictures of motorcycles and athletes inside their locker doors. The girls hang mirrors and paste up photos of bare-chested male movie stars. Schools are also good places to catch the latest developments in word usage. At one school recently I was referred to as 'that author dude.' At another I listened as a young lady explained why she had rejected an invitation to eat at a nearby diner—'It was too fluorescent.'

"With the start of each new book, I find it necessary to interview teens who might have special insights into the subjects or characters I have chosen. Thus, in recent years I have inter-viewed teenager soccer players, rock musicians, a boy who was in a two-week coma after a car accident, valet parkers, stadium vendors, and Westinghouse Science Prize winners."[11]

Strasser has a lot to offer the students, too: "When I speak at schools I bring a slide show that illuminates how I come up with ideas and write books, and also how the books are actually created in the publishing house, how the covers are created and the pages are set. A lot of times this helps get kids interested in reading and writing.

"What makes school visits rewarding to me is lively student response, both during the slideshow and afterwards when I ask questions. During the talk I try to make some jokes and show some funny slides. If the kids laugh and enjoy it, I know they're getting it. Sometimes, before I address a large assembly, the principal of the school will warn the kids to behave. I guess the principal thinks he or she is doing me a favor, but it usually intimidates the kids."[15]

"I also spend a lot of time speaking at conferences to groups of librarians and teachers. I really think publishers want writers to go out and sell them-selves these days. You almost have to because there are so many writers out there and the only way anyone is going to know who you are is if they've actually met you."[1]

Strasser is acutely aware that the reader's image of "the writer" is different from the real person who wrote the book. "The other day, someone who didn't know me well said that because I was a writer I must be a 'free spirit' and lead a wonderful life. At first I wanted to tell him he was wrong, but then I thought about it and decided he was only half wrong. In a way I am a free spirit, in that I am free to pick any idea or topic and write about it. That, indeed, is a wonderful freedom and I am grateful to have it. Along with that freedom, however, comes an awful lot of hard work. Unless you are fortunate enough to be one of the handful of perpetual best-selling writers in this world, you really can't make a living writing a book every two or three years. My work is about as close to 'nine-to-five' as my schedule allows. Being a writer is great, but I can't say it's easy."[12]

Strasser's image of himself is different: "I see myself as a typical person who just happens to sit in this room and pounds out books because he's basically unemployable. But other people seem to think if you're a writer you're something special.

"I write back to everyone. And sometimes they write back again to me. It's good, a way of researching. They tell me what books they like, what their lives are like.

"Just to show you how corny I am, I put the first fan letter I ever got in a scrapbook!

"I try and not think about the future too much because I don't know where I'm going to end up. If you're a doctor you set up your practice. The practice grows and you take on partners so you can play golf four times a week.

"If you're a writer, I don't know where you go. I don't know if I'm going to wind up in television or what. I know I'd like to stay in book writing, but sometimes I wonder if there will always be enough to write about or if there will be enough of an audience.

"But, for now, I'll just take it book by book."[1]

Footnote Sources:

[1] Jim Roginski, *Behind the Covers: Interviews with Authors and Illustrators of Books for Children and Young Adults,* Libraries Unlimited, 1985.
[2] Roy Sorrels, "The Writing Life: Cookie Funster," *Writer's Digest,* December, 1979.
[3] Nina Piwoz, "The Writers Are Writing: I Was a Teenage Boy: An Interview with Todd Strasser," *Media & Methods,* February, 1983.
[4] Zena Sutherland, "*Angel Dust Blues,*" *Bulletin of the Center for Children's Books,* February, 1980 (p. 120).
[5] Mary K. Chelton, "*Friends Till the End,*" *Voice of Youth Advocates,* June, 1981 (p. 32).
[6] "*The Wave,*" *Publishers Weekly,* November 27, 1981 (p. 88).

Matthew Broderick starred in the movie "Ferris Bueller's Day Off," from which Strasser adapted the novel.

[7] William G. McBride, "*Rock 'n' Roll Nights*," *Voice of Youth Advocates*, December, 1982 (p. 36).

[8] Diane C. Donovan, "*Workin' for Peanuts*," *Best Sellers*, May, 1983 (p. 75).

[9] Todd Strasser, "Young Adult Books: Stalking the Teen," *Horn Book*, March/April, 1986.

[10] Michael Healy, "*Turn It Up!*," *Best Sellers*, June, 1984 (p. 118).

[11] Ann A. Flowers, "*A Very Touchy Subject*," *Horn Book*, May-June, 1985 (p. 321).

[12] Contemporary Authors, Volume 123, Gale, 1988.

[13] *Publishers Weekly*, December 4, 1987.

[14] Kenneth L. Donelson and Alleen Pace Nilsen, *Literature for Today's Young Adults*, second edition, Scott, Foresman, 1985.

[15] Todd Strasser, "On the Road," *Voice of Youth Advocates*, December, 1986.

■ For More Information See

New York Times (travel section), January 4, 1976.

New Yorker, January 24, 1977 (p. 28).

School Library Journal, January, 1980 (p. 81), March, 1982 (p. 160), August, 1983 (p. 80), August, 1984 (p. 87), April, 1985 (p. 100), February, 1988 (p. 75), June/July, 1988 (p. 59).

Horn Book, April, 1980 (p. 178), April, 1983 (p. 175).

Wilson Library Bulletin, May, 1981 (p. 691), April, 1983 (p. 692), March, 1985 (p. 485).

Voice of Youth Advocates, October, 1983 (p. 209), June, 1984 (p. 98), June, 1985 (p. 136).

Publishers Weekly, April 24, 1987 (p. 73), December 4, 1987 (p. 63).

English Journal, September, 1982 (p. 87), January, 1985, December, 1985, December, 1986, November, 1987 (p. 93), March, 1988 (p. 85).

New York Times, October 2, 1983, June 19, 1985.

Children's Literature Review, Volume 11, Gale, 1986.

Library Journal, January, 1988 (p. 100).

Theodore Taylor

Born June 23, 1921, in Statesville, N.C., son of Edward Riley (a molder) and Elnora (Langhans) Taylor; married Gweneth Goodwin, October 25, 1946 (divorced, 1977); married Flora Gray Schoenleber (a library clerk), April 18, 1981; children: (first marriage) Mark, Wendy, Michael. *Education:* Attended U.S. Merchant Marine Academy, Kings Point, N.Y., 1942-43, and Columbia University, 1948; studied with American Theatre Wing, 1947-49. *Politics:* Republican. *Religion:* Protestant. *Home:* 1856 Catalina St., Laguna Beach, Calif. 92615. *Agent:* Gloria Loomis, Watkins Loomis Agency, Inc., 150 East 35th St., Suite 530, New York, N.Y. 10016.

■ Career

Portsmouth Star, Portsmouth, Va., cub reporter, 1934-39, sports editor, 1941-42; *Washington Daily News*, Washington, D.C., copyboy; National Broadcasting Co. Radio, New York City, sportswriter, 1942; *Sunset News*, Bluefield, W. Va., sports editor, 1946-47; New York University, New York City, assistant director of public relations, 1947-48; *Orlando Sentinel Star*, Orlando, Fla., reporter, 1949-50; Paramount Pictures, Hollywood, Calif., publicist, 1955-56; Perlberg-Seaton Productions,

Hollywood, story editor and associate producer, 1956-61; free-lance press agent for Hollywood studios, 1961-68; full-time writer, 1961—. Producer and director of documentary films. *Military service:* U.S. Merchant Marine, 1942-44; U.S. Naval Reserve, active duty, 1944-46, 1950-55, became lieutenant. *Member:* Academy of Motion Picture Arts and Sciences, Writers Guild, Authors League of America, Mystery Writers of America.

■ Awards, Honors

Commonwealth Club of California Silver Medal, 1969, Jane Addams Children's Book Award from Women's International League for Peace and Freedom, Lewis Carroll Shelf Award, Southern California Council on Literature for Children and Young People Notable Book Award, Woodward Park School Annual Book Award, and Best Book Award from University of California, Irvine, all 1970, all for *The Cay; Battle in the Arctic Seas* was selected one of *New York Times* Outstanding Books of the Year, 1976; Spur Award, Best Western for Young People category from Western Writers of America, and Commonwealth Club of California Silver Medal for the best juvenile book by a California author, both 1977, both for *A Shepherd Watches, A Shepherd Sings;* Award from the Southern California Council on Literature for Children and Young People, 1977, for his total body of work; George G. Stone Center for Children's Books Recognition of Merit Award, 1980, for "Hatteras Banks" trilogy (Teetoncey stories); Young Reader Medal from the California Reading Association, 1984, for *The Trouble with Tuck;* Jefferson Cup Honor Book from the Virginia Library Association, 1987, for *Walking Up a Rainbow*.

Writings

For Young People:

People Who Make Movies, Doubleday, 1967.
The Cay (ALA Notable Book; *Horn Book* honor list), Doubleday, 1969.
The Children's War, Doubleday, 1971.
Air Raid—Pearl Harbor! The Story of December 7, 1941 (illustrated by W. T. Mars), Crowell, 1971.
Rebellion Town: Williamsburg, 1776 (illustrated by Richard Cuffari), Crowell, 1973.
The Maldonado Miracle, Doubleday, 1973.
Teetoncey (illustrated by R. Cuffari), Doubleday, 1974.
Teetoncey and Ben O'Neal (illustrated by R. Cuffari), Doubleday, 1975.
Battle in the Arctic Seas: The Story of Convoy PQ 17 (Junior Literary Guild selection; illustrated by Robert A. Parker), Crowell, 1976.
The Odyssey of Ben O'Neal (illustrated by R. Cuffari), Doubleday, 1977.
(With Louis Irigaray) *A Shepherd Watches, A Shepherd Sings*, Doubleday, 1977.
The Trouble with Tuck, Doubleday, 1981.
The Battle of Midway Island (illustrated by Andrew Glass), Avon, 1981.
H.M.S. Hood Versus Bismarck: The Battleship Battle (illustrated by A. Glass), Avon, 1982.
Battle in the English Channel (illustrated by A. Glass), Avon, 1983.
Sweet Friday Island, Scholastic, 1984.
Rocket Island, Avon, 1984.
Waking Up a Rainbow, Delacorte, 1986.
The Hostage, Delacorte, 1988.

Other:

The Magnificent Mitscher (biography), Norton, 1954.
Fire on the Beaches, Norton, 1957.
The Body Trade, Fawcett, 1967.
(With Robert Houghton) *Special Unit Senator: An Investigation of the Assassination of Senator Robert F. Kennedy*, Random House, 1970.
(With Kreskin) *The Amazing World of Kreskin*, Random House, 1974.
Jule: The Story of Composer Jule Styne, Random House, 1979.
(With Tippi Hedren) *The Cats of Shambala*, Simon & Schuster, 1985.

The Stalker, D.I. Fine, 1987.

Author of television play "Tom Threepersons," TV Mystery Theatre, 1964, of screenplays "Night without End," 1959, "The Hold-Up," and "Showdown," Universal, 1973, of "Sunshine, the Whale," a television play for children, and of seventeen documentary films. Also author of books under the pseudonym T. T. Lang. Contributor of short stories and novelettes to magazines, including *Redbook*, *Argosy*, *Ladies' Home Journal*, *McCall's* and *Saturday Evening Post*.

Adaptations

"The Cay" (motion picture), starring James Earle Jones, NBC-TV, October 21, 1974, (filmstrip), Pied Piper Productions, 1975.
"The Trouble with Tuck" (filmstrip), Pied Piper Productions, 1986.

Work In Progress

Screenplay of *The Stalker*, for Charles Fries Productions; *For Fear of Lions and Tigers*, a young adult suspense novel; *Macki Jumbi Got Killed*, an adult novel set in the Caribbean.

Sidelights

"I believe that a writer should constantly feed his fires by being on the go, doing different things, seeking new experiences. In the way of practicing that philosophy, I have been, variously, a newspaperman, prize-fighter manager, merchant seaman, naval officer, magazine writer, movie publicist and production assistant and documentary filmmaker. I have worked in Japan, Taiwan and Hong Kong, as well as in most of the European countries. Some of the background in my novel, *The Cay*, came as a result of living in the Caribbean, principally in Puerto Rico and the Virgin Islands."[1]

"I was born in Statesville, North Carolina, last of six children of Edward Riley Taylor and Elnora Alma Langhans: four sisters and a brother, Edward, who had died of pneumonia two years previously, at the age of two. My mother was then in her early forties and I suppose I was spoiled by my sisters, especially Mary, the only one usually home when I was small. The others, Naoma, Eleanor, and Louise were off working; married.

"My father, though of absolute English descent, swore he was an Irishman and certainly had that temperament; never finished grade school. He went to work in a Pittsburgh foundry when he was barely twelve and became a molder, black-sheep of a moderately well-to-do family. He was an argumentative man; the highest wage he ever made in his life was in the fifty-dollar-a-week range.

"There were periods, especially during the Depression of the late 1920s and the early 1930s, when I would not see him for months. He was a blue-collar workingman's working man and became involved in the International Workers of the World, 'the Wobblies,' left-wing labor organization, in the 1920s. When I was only four or five I remember him coming home one night bloodied and bruised, results of tangling with police during a strike.

"My mother was so different that we children (when I was a little older) could never understand how these two people got together and got married. She, delicate and fragile; he, stocky and muscular. Mother, reciting poetry; father, talking about the 'working man' endlessly."[2]

Taylor recalls his childhood in rural North Carolina as, "one short happy adventure, knowing and caring little about what was going on in the outside world simply because there was so much going on in my inside world. I grew up with nature but wasn't really aware of it until much later. In terms of material wealth, we had very little, but there was a richness in the surroundings that money could never buy."

The American South forms the background for many of his books, especially the Carolinas, which are used as the locale for his "Hatteras" trilogy of historical fiction: *Teetoncey, Teetoncey and Ben O'Neal* and *The Odyssey of Ben O'Neal.* "Statesville, in the heart of the Piedmont area of North Carolina, red-earth flatlands before the western rises of the Blue Ridges, had about five thousand inhabitants when I was born. County seat of Iredell, it was centered in an agriculture economy, mainly: cotton, tobacco, corn, some orchards; truck farms. There was a brickyard and a foundry, where my father worked; knitting mills provided most of the jobs. It was a nice, God-fearing Waspish town of the upper South, related in some ways to 'Altamont,' Thomas Wolfe's town of Asheville, up in the Blue Ridges. Some of the people of *Look Homeward, Angel,* as I remember them, could probably have been found in Statesville.

"I have a foggy memory of a boxy little white clapboard house with a peanut field beside it and my father's first car. He only had two in his lifetime. This must have been 1924 or 1925. He went to work, saying it needed fixing. When he came home, I said, 'I ficked it.' I had, indeed,

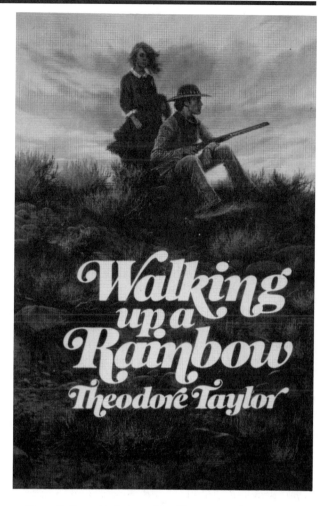

Darrell Sweet's dust jacket illustration for Taylor's adventure story set on the American frontier in the 1850's.

breaking all the glass. Headlights, windshield, instrument panel. He was so stunned I didn't get punished.

"Next we lived in a house on Walnut Street owned by a Dr. Anderson who lived next door in a truly grand house. His children were adults, gone from the hearth, and Dr. Anderson, an elderly man, became my companion on many occasions. He took me to Ringling Brothers, Barnum and Bailey, or whatever circuses came to town; took me to carnivals and to other events exciting to children. But most vividly I remember the day he pointed out 'The Hanging Tree' from which Tom Dula had been stretched in 1868 for the murder of Laura Foster. Others maintain Tom was stretched from a pine gallows. The Kingston Trio immortalized the Tom Dula ballad in 1958: 'Hang down your head, Tom Dooley....' I gathered research for a Tom Dula story in 1974 but have yet to write it. Statesville has a history of sorts.

"Other vivid memories when I was five or six years old, and we were living in the Anderson rental, were of the Ku Klux Klan riding by on horses one night, carrying pine knot torches; of a Model-T Ford, driven by a bootlegger, its rear end sagging with tins of booze, racing up Center Street toward the railroad station, laying a smokescreen, followed by cops in a black touring car. High times in old Iredell County! A fair amount of stills existed on the outskirts of Statesville.

"My affair with trees began during this period. There was a very tall one in our backyard and I climbed it to the top on many days, hanging up there to look over at Mitchell College, where two of my sisters were educated, working their way through. Eventually, I built a platform in the lower branches, my 'house' and fort.

"It was also during this period that I began playing with a boy named Phillip. We had fun together but I remembered, later on, his absolute hatred of black people. Man, woman, or child. Tragically, his mother had taught him that hatred. He became the 'Phillip' of *The Cay.*

"I never was a very good student and my memories of Mulberry Street School and Davie Avenue School are more of endurance than anything else. Fascinated with World War I (there were a few army trucks of that vintage in town), I spent a lot of time drawing Fokkers and Spads and Sopwith Pupus and Scouts in aerial battles; looping artillery fire into the Flanders trenches. When I should have been listening to the teacher I filled sheets of paper with war scenes: 'Dory,' of *The Children's War,* my least successful book.

"Earlier I had sort of a foster father in Dr. Anderson and now I had another one in a giant of a man. My next-to-youngest sister, Louise, had married another teacher, Hugh Beam, who was six-feet-four and weighed about 290. Ex-football tackle, he was a merry farmer's son who occasionally wrestled a black bear and did other feats of strength that held me in awe. Visiting them in Marion during summers, I spent some of the happiest days of my childhood in the company of the huge man from Lincolnton. Coaching winning football, even as superintendent of schools, he finally went into politics and served in the state assembly; then became a judge. Hugh Beam turned me into a rabid football fan and I remain one to this day.

"Moving to Johnson City, Tennessee—my father, a Spanish-American War veteran, had entered Soldier's Home, there to afford himself of free meals—Mother and I occupied two rooms in a private house. I saw something more of him during this period. We went fishing frequently, something we shared until he died. He hadn't been employed since the early part of 1928 and sister Mary had been, and was, footing most of our bills with a meager bookkeeper's salary. He visited us several times a week and made a wooden sled for me that Christmas in the Home's workshop. A red sled, I remember. I'd always wanted a steel-runged Flyer but I loved the wooden red sled.

"Again, I had that freedom to explore the countryside; hike up the mountains, which I sometimes did by myself. New kid in town, I didn't have many friends in Tennessee and spent a lot of time alone, making and flying kites; walking out three or four miles to several abandoned locomotives on rail spurs. I climbed all over those rusting engines, pretending I was the engineer.

"There was some kind of problem at the Soldier's Home and Father left after about a year. Mother and I returned to Statesville to live first on Davie Avenue and I entered the school of that name, which now corresponds to a middle school. I'm not sure where my father went for part-time work but he kept in touch by mail or occasional visits. He in no way ever deserted us; just wisely eliminated another mouth to feed, adding whatever money he could.

"About then into my life came Napoleon, a little black-and-white mongrel, auspices of Mary whose Chevrolet agency employer had a litter to give away. Nappy began my long love affair with dogs and many of the books I've written have canine characters in them, notably the *Teetoncey* trilogy, with 'Boo Dog'; 'Tuck' in *The Trouble with Tuck'* 'Rufus' in *Walking up a Rainbow.* Nappy had beagle, terrier, and some other breed mixed in."[2]

Early in 1934 Taylor moved to Cradock, Virginia when his father got a job as a molder's helper at the Norfolk Navy Yard in neighboring Portsmouth. He attended Cradock High School and began his writing career at the age of thirteen as a cub reporter for the Portsmouth *Evening Star.* "Until school began I explored. I highly recommend exploration to young and would-be writers. I followed the Norfolk and Western tracks down to the river, often hopping the slow coaljacks for a ride, to watch the small freighters that chugged down the Elizabeth toward North Carolina on the inland waterway; to see tankers unloading on the South Norfolk side. I followed the streetcar track on foot into Portsmouth and explored the water-

Dust jacket illustration by Milton Glaser for Taylor's multi-award-winning novel.

front, spending hours at the Isaac Fass fishing docks watching the boats unload. I watched the side-wheeler ferries, still coal-burners, plying the mile or so across to Norfolk. There was an all-encompassing excitement to this waterfront activity, so different from the flatlands of the Piedmont, and I was caught up in it.

"That late fall I saw the Atlantic Ocean for the first time in my life, an unforgettable thrill. The parents of a boy I'd met at school asked me if I wanted to go along to Cape Henry, forty miles or so east of Norfolk. I wasn't aware of it but the Jamestown settlers had first touched shore there in 1607. I couldn't wait to go. The day was sunny and chilly and there stretched the blue ocean. England on the other side of it. I remember that Sunday afternoon so clearly—a Coast Guard surfboat from the nearby Cape Henry Lighthouse station riding the breakers as the crew practiced, their long oars sweeping waves. Barefoot, I waded along the edge of the cold water, finding a horseshoe crab shell, taking it home. Later, I used that visual of the drilling surfboat crew in the *Teetoncey* trilogy.

"What changed my life, forever, occurred in the late spring of the next year, 1935, when I was offered a chance to write a sports column, usually for Sunday, a typewritten page and a half of copy, for the *Portsmouth Star.* The copy, to begin in the fall, was to be a report about the past week's activity in whatever sport was occurring at Cradock High. Football, basketball, baseball, track. For this, I was to receive fifty cents. Though I had the will to compete in sports, I was too skinny, less than a hundred pounds, to be a factor. Nor did I have the ability. Yet I was deeply interested in athletics and immediately said yes. That fifty cents a week loomed large. My allowance at the time was all of a dime.

"I remember studying the sports pages of the *Star* and the larger *Norfolk Virginian-Pilot,* just to see how the stories were written, then placing them down by the typewriter for constant referral. That is, in fact, a good way to learn how to write. Copy good writers.

"After laboring all morning and up to midafternoon on the page and a half, I nervously rode the streetcar to Portsmouth clutching my first story, mentally and probably physically crossing fingers that it would be accepted. One David P. Glazer, in his early twenties, though he seemed older, was sports editor of the *Star,* and 'Pete' took a long look at my work through thick-lensed glasses. His copy pencil then said more than words. Over the next

three years Pete Glazer was my patient teacher and fifty years later we remain in touch. In reviewing my first book, an adult biography, in 1954, Pete said, 'Ted Taylor was the rawest recruit we ever had. . . .'

"The staff was small: managing editor, city editor, Pete, as sports editor, and a part-time society editor. Everyone did double duty as general assignment reporters, even the managing editor, a little dynamo of a man. It was the perfect learning institution for me and I lingered around each time after delivering my copy, listening to newsroom conversations about sports and crime and politics; life in general, life on the seamy side and beneath it, the side that most often gets into newspaper print. The *Star* and another paper, a fast-paced metropolitan tabloid, were to be my college, my seamy-side university, my graduate schools. I've often regretted I didn't attend college. City rooms were the substitutes, newsmen were the teachers."[2]

Taylor left home at the age of seventeen to join the staff of the Washington *Daily News* as a copyboy. By the age of nineteen he was working as an NBC network sportswriter.

During World War II, he joined the United States Merchant Marine, "having no desire to slog around in army mud nor any great desire for navy discipline. But, at the same time, I became a member of the naval reserve. Over the next seventeen months, I served as a deck cadet and then an able-bodied seaman aboard a gasoline tanker in the Atlantic and Pacific areas, a freighter in the European theater, then obtained a third-mate's license, sailing for a trip each on two other ships. Returning to the United States in the fall of 1944, I found out I'd been called up by the Navy as a cargo office and soon reported as an ensign, USNR, to the USS *Draco,* a cargo attack vessel in the Pacific. Following the Japanese surrender, I heard about Operation Crossroads, the nuclear experiment at Bikini Atoll, and volunteered for duty out there. I wanted to see the bomb go off. Unfortunately, but typically, my ship, the USS *Sumner,* was ordered home before the big blast."[2]

In the Korean War, Taylor saw active duty as a naval officer.

During his entire military career, he served a total of five years at sea in both the Atlantic and Pacific Oceans. His experiences at sea form the basis for many of his fiction and nonfiction books. "*Battle in the Arctic Seas* [1976] is the result of wartime experience. I sailed in convoys, was both fascinated

Still from the television movie "The Cay," starring James Earle Jones. Presented on NBC, October 21, 1974.

and overwhelmed by them—this great family of ships at sea, moving as a single unit, performing like horses in a drill team. The drama was always incredible: the gathering together, the weighing of anchor, departure and forming-up; the escorts thrashing about; sometimes a U-boat attack, and then another type of drama. I'd always wanted to do a story about the most famous convoy of World War II, and PQ 17 qualified in every way. It is humanly impossible to tell this story and do it full justice. The elements involved defy words on paper. However, I tried to tell as much as possible by use of a single ship, the *Troubador*, and her unique crew."

In *Battle in the English Channel* (1983) Taylor tells the story of the 1942 episode in the English Channel when a group of German ships were able to successfully elude the Royal Navy and Royal Air Force while in route from France to Germany. In the conclusion, Taylor states its central theme: "Operation Fuller failed because of the command structure and not from lack of individual effort on the part of those who had to go out and fight."

While serving as a lieutenant in the navy during the Korean War, Taylor wrote his first book, *The*

Magnificent Mitscher, a biography of Admiral "Pete" Mitscher, a carrier group commander during World War II. A year after its publication, Taylor moved to Hollywood where he worked as a press agent, and later as a story editor and associate producer. He subsequently produced documentary films throughout the world and wrote books.

Using his war experiences, Taylor's second book, *Fire on the Beaches* told the story of the ships that fled from German submarines along the East Coast during the war, "ships like the Cities Service tanker, SS *Annibal*, the one I'd served on.

"I stopped off in New York to research *Fire on the Beaches* at the shipping companies and then in Washington at Coast Guard headquarters. One morning at the latter I was reading accounts of ships that were sunk along the Eastern seaboard and down in the Caribbean, over in the Gulf of Mexico, when I came across a paragraph that described the sinking of a small Dutch vessel. An eleven-year-old boy survived the sinking but was eventually lost at sea, alone on a life raft. That paragraph became *The Cay*, years later.

"In 1966, after devoting more than an exciting year to Robert Wise's 'The Sand Pebbles,' a Steve McQueen/Richard Attenborough film shot mostly in Taiwan and Hong Kong—marvelous experience in exotic locales—I decided to try a book for young readers. My own children were interested in how motion pictures were made and I thought others might be, too. *People Who Make Movies* was quickly sold to Doubleday and I was astonished some two years later, after the book began circulating in the schools, to receive mail from young readers. More than three thousand responded to that book, most seeking Hollywood careers....In writing for adults, I'd probably received a dozen letters.

"Two years later, after finishing a horrible Frank Sinatra film in Miami, and hearing Dr. Martin Luther King singing spirituals in the lobby of a hotel, I decided to go ahead with the long-brewing story of the boy on the life raft in the Caribbean. A few days after returning home from Florida, I rolled fresh paper into the typewriter. Three weeks later *The Cay* was completed and the printed version is little different from the first draft. By far it was the quickest and easiest book I've ever written, yet twelve years of occasional thought had gone into the work. I'm convinced that my subconscious or 'unconscious' does much of the writing for me. How else do I have half, or even well-formed, thoughts in the morning."[2]

The book is a two-character story about an eleven-year-old boy, Phillip, and a seventy-year-old black seaman who are stranded on a raft after their boat is torpedoed by German submarines in 1942. The two eventually land on a cay, or coral island. There, the boy, who has lost his sight, learns to trust the old man who trains Phillip to fend for himself, thus insuring his survival and rescue after the old man's death. Taylor dedicated the book to "Dr. [Martin Luther] King's dream, which can only come true if the very young know, and understand."

"I do not have the ability to write fantasy. My stories are taken from fragments of real-life though I do not expect anyone to accept them as more than fiction: nor do I place a greater value on them. The characters of the prejudiced white boy, Phillip and his prejudiced mother, were taken from real-life. Though I elected to change the circumstances, and add composites....The character of Timothy was developed from West Indian sailors, primarily one man, but also a composite.

"I lived in the Caribbean for a while: sailed it; roamed the area from Haiti to Grenada and Carricou; Curacao and Aruba to Coco Solo. The descriptions of the places, characters, and generally the events are not from guide books or lectures. From the Ruyterkade schooner market in Curacao (Venezuelan blacks and Indians mixed bloods, bi and multi-lingual) to carnival day and the *bambola* in Charlotte Amalie, St. Thomas, I was lucky enough to see it, hear it and taste it. I listened and I looked and I asked questions whenever I could.

"Between two separate experiences, one in the early forties, another in the early fifties, I met and talked at length with upwards of twenty bona fide West Indian sailors of several nationalities; sailed with one for a short period; fished with others; sat on the decks of several of those schooners and soaked up as much as I could, simply because of an interest in the ships and sailors, with no intention of doing a book a quarter century later. These expert seamen, a unique breed, were probably only amused with me but I was enchanted with the Caribbean sailor/merchants of that day and still am. The idea for *The Cay* evolved from research in 1955 and 1956 for Caribbean chapters in an adult book, published by W. W. Norton, 1958. The story of Phillip and Timothy was not written until 1968, so progression, from concept to completion, was not in undue haste."[3]

After its publication, *The Cay* received numerous awards and excellent reviews. The relationship between Timothy and Phillip was described by *Library Journal* as "a hauntingly deep love, the poignancy of which is rarely achieved;" and the *Washington Star* called the book "one of the best survival stories since *Robinson Crusoe.*"

The widely acclaimed novel was translated into nine languages and adapted into a successful film. However, it also attracted hostile criticism from some American critics, such as Albert Schwartz who called it "an adventure story for white colonists—however enlightened—to add to their racist mythology," in a 1971 article reprinted in *Racist and Sexist Images in Children's Books*, 1975. Attacks also came from the Interracial Council on Children's Books, who exerted enough pressure to ban the book in several libraries. Five years after Taylor received the Jane Addams Book Award, he was requested to return it. "Charges of 'racism' have been largely supported by the 'under-lining' of various passages in the book, usually descriptive of the black character, *Timothy;* then the broader contention that the white character, the boy *Phillip*, was not changed by his experience with the 70-

year-old West Indian. Needless to say, passages in any book can be underlined and utilized for whatever purpose the reader chooses. That purpose does not always coincide with what the writer had in mind; nor always with the total meaning; nor always with the majority of the readers.

"...On the occasion of the Bell Telephone television production of *The Cay*, a disappointing film for which I hold no brief, Mr. Samuel Ethridge, director of Civil and Human Rights for the National Education Assocation, took me to task for lacking the courage to get inside Timothy's head; to make known his private and innermost thoughts; to show that black people were capable of 'feeling, thinking and resolving.' Perhaps I cannot read my own work with a sense of fairness and reason: perhaps I am too conditioned to make proper judgment, but I truly believe that Timothy did all three from the first moment on the raft. One does not have true compassion without the ability to feel; one cannot make decisions (and he made many) without the ability to think and resolve.

"In my own mind, I did not set out to write a 'racist' novel, vintage 1942; harm any human being, black or white; damage the black struggle for human equality. Further, I am not at all convinced that I did write a 'racist' novel. The goal was to the contrary. Directed primarily toward the white child (thinking that the black child did not need to be told much about prejudice), I hoped to achieve a subtle plea for better race relations and more understanding. I have reason to believe that I partially achieved that goal, despite acknowledged omissions and commissions; flaws.

"I do think I clearly understand Mr. Ethridge's well-taken point on the depth of penetration of Timothy's character and his indirect questioning of my qualifications to write the story. Truthfully, I did not stop for a moment to even think about my qualifications, nor about whether I was white or black; whether or not I could step into Timothy's skin. Lengthy deliberations of this sort would lead to a frozen typewriter; fear of ever doing any story. None of us are really equipped to cross that barrier, even to crawling inside a person's skin when they are of the *same* color, but I think we should try.

"I had the story in mind for a long time and went about doing it to the best of my ability. I told the story from the viewpoint of the white boy because: (1) Timothy needed no lessons from the white boy about prejudice, survival or anything else. (2) I knew that Timothy would not be introduced until the third chapter and would die before the story ended. I needed a continuing narrator. (3) I felt that a needed intimacy could be gained by first person treatment. (4) I knew much more about the white boy than I did about Timothy.

"If a black writer were to handle this same story, or a variation of it, I'm inclined to think that he or she would tell it from the black point-of-view, simply because of that experience. Being white, I told it from the white boy's point-of-view. That being the case, right or wrong, Phillip could only be privy to Timothy's innermost thoughts as they were volunteered. Realistically, I doubt that a 70-year-old Indies schoonerman would share too many innermost thoughts with an 11-year-old white boy. For one thing, it was not the nature of the character, as I saw him, to say much beyond the comments of the moment.

"I can be faulted for not doing the story third-person but it never occurred to me to do it that way, enabling deeper penetration into Timothy's characters and his life. From the beginning, I was concentrating on what would come out, more or less naturally, once they met on the raft. By so doing, I was hoping to achieve a semblance of reality; dialogue and action as it might happen within the fictional scope.

"Space does not permit me to deal individually with each underlined passage that I have seen but those most used to support the disparaging 'racist' charge usually include my first description of Timothy, as seen by the racially programmed boy: *He was ugly. His nose was flat and his face was broad; his head a mass of wiry gray hair.* I don't think I am completely insensitive and realize why these words explode on paper for some people, both black and white.

"As a matter of story construction and nothing else, I purposely made Timothy facially ugly to enable what I thought would be an important change later on. To be blunt, had I made Timothy beautiful when Phillip awakened on that raft, I could see no valid reason for marked reaction or for the hateful fires of prejudice to be refueled. Timothy's appearance simply reinforced the poison planted by Phillip's mother.

"Quite purposely, I strengthened this a few paragraphs on with an even more unattractive description of Timothy. Given the same story circumstance, that of conflict and transformation, I would do it again. Also, quite on purpose, not carelessly, I had Phillip view Timothy as 'dumb and old and

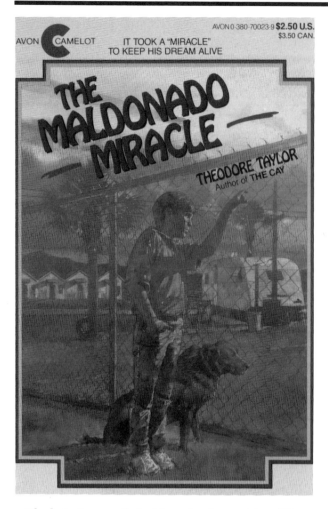

AVON C CAMELOT   IT TOOK A "MIRACLE"
TO KEEP HIS DREAM ALIVE

AVON 0-380-70023-9 $2.50 U.S.
$3.50 CAN.

THE MALDONADO MIRACLE

THEODORE TAYLOR
Author of THE CAY

The last nine months had been hard ones. (From *The Maldonado Miracle* by Theodore Taylor.)

black and different.' Given the lessons of his mother, how else could Phillip view Timothy?

"If conflict cannot be dealt with, on its many levels, pap will be the result. If a character cannot truthfully state a visual reaction to another character, one level of conflict is eliminated. If a white writer must view every black as 'beautiful, wise, young and the same as every white,' there can be no conflict; therefore no understanding which might possibly come out of conflict. If the black writer must say that every white is 'beautiful, wise, young and the same as blacks,' why bother with the story; why strive for truth?

"Terribly trite but true, facially, without getting into yellow, brown or red, we cannot all be Diahann Carroll or O. J. Simpson; Paul Newman or Faye Dunaway. Also worn, but true, human experience, time and time again, is that the facially unattractive person, of any hue, can become quite beautiful as the inner person emerges. I had hoped

that Timothy would emerge as a beautiful man. Obviously, for some, I failed.

"I have been faulted for the derogatory use of dialect by Timothy, even though most West Indian sailors of 1942 spoke dialect. To me, calypso is the single most pleasing, most musical dialect on earth; a black treasure, I would think. It may jar some white ears, and some black ears, but I would use it again without hesitation. I hope it is never laundered, sanitized and ironed flat on the boards of social change. Everyone will lose.

"Much has also been said about my purposely 'blinding' Phillip. Why could he not learn his lessons while sighted? In so far as prejudice is concerned, I honestly felt that Phillip was already blind, as was his mother, long before he suffered the injury. I believed that Phillip should dramatically know that much of prejudice is a matter of eyesight (as with ugliness)—my own opinion. Finally, I wanted him to reach the point where 'color' made no difference, leading to the line, 'Are you still black, Timothy?' I did not want to use a sledgehammer at this tender point of the story. I felt it best to let Phillip say it in his own way. I feel secure that the character of Timothy understood, as do most readers.

"It has been charged that I did not really show a change in Phillip; that he remained a total 'racist.' This can be argued for years, though I hope it won't be. Without preaching a sermon, because I've found that few people listen, including young readers, I attempted to show that change beginning with page 72. And for every so-called 'racist' passage, I believe I can underline one which shows the beginning of understanding; the growth of affection; the slow recognition of Timothy's humaneness, wisdom and courage as a distinct and valuable person. Despite novels and movies, people seldom change overnight. The process is slow and difficult but there is always a starting point. So it was, I believed and tried to write it, with Phillip and his superficial knowledge of Timothy.

"Of course, I could have written a summary, restating every change in Phillip, crossing the bridges, using a sledgehammer as we go off into the sunset. No thanks. For either young readers or adults, I prefer not to bang on anvils. The exercise is annoying, if not useless.

"Debating the obnoxious aspects of Phillip's character, his visual reactions, his verbal reactions, before Los Angeles county librarians some years back, an opposing spokesman said, 'He (Timothy) would have thrown that boy overboard.' I think

Jacket for the first of the Teetoncey novels.

Richard Cuffari's illustration for the dust jacket of Taylor's 1977 novel.

not. I doubt very much that the compassionate Timothy would have tossed Phillip to the sharks. I am compelled to think that he would, and did, handle it with wisdom and dignity. Had I committed that untruthful 'overboard' scene to paper the 'racist' charges would be entirely justified. I would have painted a picture of a black man who did not care about human existence; who could not cope with the mindless mouthings of a child.

"I do not know how much personal contact the members of the Interracial Council on Children's Books, Mr. Samuel Ethridge, or the Jane Addams committee, have with young readers. My own, gratefully, has been considerable. Since 1970, between visits to schools and libraries, book fairs, and in correspondence with complete strangers, I estimate that I have been enriched by contact with approximately 25,000 young readers, parents, teachers and librarians. In all that time, I have yet to see or learn of an indication much less of a *concrete example* of 'racism' promoted by *The Cay*;

of even that general type of damage done by *The Cay*. . . ."[3]

Taylor's stories are often tales of adventure and survival whose heroes are young boys challenged by the intrusion of the unfamiliar. He writes nonfiction as well as fiction, with one book very often leading to another book. "In the early seventies I'd come across a clipping from the *Fresno Bee* about a Basque shepherd who sang to his sheep. I sensed a story in this San Joaquin Valley man and after rereading the clipping in 1975, made contact with him. *A Shepherd Watches, A Shepherd Sings*, for Doubleday, resulted. In addition to extensive use of taped interviews for a book of this type I also independently do extensive research. That time, on sheep. Much to my surprise I learned that sheep were being driven across the United States from as far away as Vermont in the early 1850s to feed the gold miners of California. That bit of information became a novel, *Walking up a Rainbow*, published in 1986 by Delacorte.

"One night in 1974, I was having dinner at a friend's house in Laguna Beach and sat next to his lawyer stepson, from San Francisco. During the course of the meal, he said, 'Okay, you wrote a story about a blind boy in *The Cay*, now let me tell you a story about our blind dog.' Whenever someone says, 'Let me tell you a story,' I listen but ninety-nine times out of a hundred the listening is for naught. This time Tony Orser's story became a short story for *Ladies' Home Journal*, published in 1977, then a teleplay, after my agent sold it to NBC in 1979; finally, *The Trouble with Tuck* was published by Doubleday in 1981.

"Long ago I learned about discipline and have no trouble going to my office about eight-thirty each morning. With a half-hour off for lunch, I work until four or four-thirty; sometimes five. I do this seven days a week except during football season. September to Super Bowl Sunday. During this grunt-grind period on the gridiron, I work only five days weekly—*without guilt.* Otherwise, I feel enormous guilt if I don't work. Precious hours going to waste.

"Whereas I walked the beach alone, except for canine companions, for years, [my wife] Flora and I now take the early morning walks together. We especially enjoy the chill winter beach, sometimes treated to migrating gray whales blowing inshore. Our life is relatively quiet but we do try to take one fun and foreign trip each year. Traveling is our joint hobby. In 1982, we island-hopped around the world, ending up on quaint Sark in the English Channel after visiting such diverse cultures as Sri Lanka and the Seychelles and Bahrain.

"I often work on three [books] at once, switching from No. 1 to No. 2 if I write myself into a hole. An adult suspense novel, *The Stalker*, sprung from an episode of CBS' '60 Minutes,' and a book for young readers, *The Hostage*, was recently published by Delacorte. That idea was born of a story on the front page of the *Los Angeles Times* in 1980.

"There are always ideas, thank goodness."[2]

Footnote Sources:

[1] Anne Commire, editor, *Something About the Author,* Volume 5, Gale, 1973.
[2] Adele Sarkissian, editor, *Something About the Author, Autobiography Series*, Volume 4, Gale, 1987.
[3] Theodore Taylor, "To the Editor: Top of the News," *Top of the News*, April, 1975.

■ **For More Information See**

New York Times Book Review, June 26, 1969, July 11, 1971, November 15, 1981.
Saturday Review, June 28, 1969, August 21, 1971.
Top of the News, November, 1971, April, 1975.
Doris de Montreville and Elizabeth D. Crawford, editors, *Fourth Book of Junior Authors and Illustrators*, H. W. Wilson, 1978.
D. L. Kirkpatrick, editor, *Twentieth-Century Children's Writers*, St. Martin's, 1978, 2nd edition, 1983.
Washington Post, May 26, 1979.
Dorothy A. Marquardt and Martha E. Ward, *Authors of Books for Young People*, supplement to the 2nd edition, Scarecrow, 1979.

Collections: Kerlan Collection at the University of Minnesota.

Barbara Wersba

Born August 19, 1932, in Chicago, Ill.; daughter of Robert and Lucy Jo (Quarles) Wersba. *Education:* Bard College, B.A., 1954; studied at Neighborhood Playhouse with Martha Graham, and at the Paul Mann Actors Workshop. *Home:* P.O. Box 1892, Sag Harbor, New York 11963. *Agent:* McIntosh & Otis, 310 Madison Ave., New York, N.Y. 10017.

■ Career

Actress in radio and television, summer stock, off-Broadway, and touring companies, 1944-59; full-time writer, 1960—; Summer lecturer at New York University, 1976, writing instructor at Rockland Center for the Arts, 1978-83.

■ Awards, Honors

Run Softly, Go Fast was chosen one of American Library Association's Best Young Adult Books, 1970, *Tunes for a Small Harmonica*, 1976, and *The Carnival in My Mind*, 1982; German Juvenile Book Prize, 1973, for *Run Softly, Go Fast*; National Book Award Finalist, Children's Book Category, 1977, for *Tunes for a Small Harmonica*; D.H.L. from Bard College, 1977.

■ Writings

The Boy Who Loved the Sea (juvenile; illustrated by Margot Tomes), Coward, 1961.
The Brave Balloon of Benjamin Buckley (juvenile; illustrated by M. Tomes), Atheneum, 1963.
The Land of Forgotten Beasts (juvenile; illustrated by M. Tomes), Atheneum, 1964.
A Song for Clowns (juvenile; Junior Literary Guild selection; illustrated by Mario Rivoli), Atheneum, 1965.
Do Tigers Ever Bite Kings? (juvenile; verse; illustrated by M. Rivoli), Atheneum, 1966.
The Dream Watcher (young adult; ALA Notable Book), Atheneum, 1968.
Run Softly, Go Fast (young adult), Atheneum, 1970.
Let Me Fall Before I Fly, Atheneum, 1971.
Amanda Dreaming (illustrated by Mercer Mayer), Atheneum, 1973.
The Country of the Heart (young adult), Atheneum, 1975.
Tunes for a Small Harmonica (young adult; ALA Notable Book), Harper, 1976.
Twenty-Six Starlings Will Fly Through Your Mind (verse; illustrated by David Palladini), Harper, 1980.
The Crystal Child (illustrated by Donna Diamond), Harper, 1982.
The Carnival in My Mind (young adult), Harper, 1982.
Crazy Vanilla (young adult), Harper, 1986.
Fat: A Love Story (young adult), Harper, 1987.

Love Is the Crooked Thing (young adult),
   Harper, 1987.
Beautiful Losers (young adult), Harper, 1988.
Just Be Gorgeous (young adult), Harper, 1988.
Wonderful Me (young adult), Harper, 1988.
The Farewell Kid (young adult), Harper, 1989.
The Best Place to Live Is the Ceiling (young
   adult), Harper, 1990.

■ Adaptations

"The Dream Watcher" (play) starring Eva Le
Gallienne, first produced at White Barn
Theater, Westport Conn., August 29, 1975,
later produced by the Seattle Repertory
Theatre, 1977-78.

■ Work In Progress

"A trilogy centering on Heidi Rosenbloom who
lives on Manhattan's Upper East Side with her
divorced, chic, status- and clothes-conscious mother. Heidi and her mother see life very differently,
the cause of a lot of conflict between them. Heidi is
everything her mother wishes she were not. Heidi
buys her clothes in thrift shops, is passionate about
dogs, picking up every stray on the street. The
series deals with Heidi's growing up through
important relationships. The first book deals with a
twenty-year-old homeless man Heidi befriends. He
is homeless because of circumstance, not because
he is a bum. In fact, he is trying, in quite a naive
way, to break into show business."

■ Sidelights

"I was born in 1932, to a father whose parents
were Russian-Jewish, and to a mother who was a
Kentucky Baptist. The only child of this stormy
marriage, I grew up in almost total solitude. I
thought I was lonely when I was simply a loner—
and spent much of my childhood daydreaming,
writing poems, and creating dramas for my dolls.
We lived in California, in a suburb, on a hilltop,
and I would spend hours sitting in an almond tree
in the back yard—gazing at the glittering city of
San Francisco, miles away. I wanted to be a
musician, or a dancer, or a poet—anything that
would lift me out of what I considered to be a sad
life. At night, lying in bed, I would hear the sound
of trains passing in the valley, and imagine that I
was on one of them. Get away, get away, said the
wheels of the trains. Get away, get away, I echoed.

"Family photos show me, as a young child, happy
and obviously loved. But around the age of seven

or eight there was a change, and I became a
somber person whom people were always telling to
smile. Grammar school was a quiet, unspoken
torture. Children's parties were a torture, too. In
those days little girls were supposed to look like
Shirley Temple, with tight curls and starched
dresses. For reasons that I have never understood,
I looked more like a German refugee—my mother
choosing to dress me in knee socks, Oxfords and
dark wools. My long hair was skinned back into two
tight, unforgiving braids.

"I remember a blue bicycle with balloon tires,
which I rode like a fury up and down the California
hills. I remember the wonderful scrape of new
roller skates on smooth pavements. The fields of
wildflowers were being turned into developments,
and there was always the skeleton of a house to
climb....

"Then the evening came when a grownup, a friend
of my parents, turned to me at the dinner table and
asked the inevitable question. 'What do you want
to be when you grow up?' 'An actress,' I said
without blinking, and the minute the words were
out of my mouth, they had the ring of truth. I
would be an actress. Like Bette Davis and Joan
Crawford. Or even—like Greta Garbo.

"There was a community theatre in the town
where I lived, and it seemed the logical place to
begin. So one Saturday I walked through the door
and asked them for a job. Running errands, going
for coffee, handing out programs. I would work for
nothing, I said, as long as I could watch rehearsals.
Unable to turn down such a sweeping offer, the
directors gave me the job and my heart soared. I
was now a part of the American theatre and had a
place in the world. I was eleven years old.

"Within six months the theatre had given me a part
in a play, and from that day on I was stagestruck.
No matter that I did not like to act, that it
frightened me, and made me almost sick. I had a
purpose in life and no longer felt alone. 'I am going
to be a great actress,' I would say to myself over
and over, as though words could make truth. I
memorized my lines until I could say them in my
sleep. I went to the library and did research, for
the play was set in Russia, and learned how to use
stage makeup. Was I any good on opening night? I
cannot say. Like many of the important moments in
my life, this one is shrouded.

"That year my mother told me that she and my
father were getting a divorce. Without knowing
what had gone wrong, I watched like a distant
observer as my father departed, the house and

furniture were sold, and my two cats were taken away to be put to sleep. I loved animals more than people in those days (and still do) so that the loss of the cats was worse than the loss of my father. On the day they were taken away, I crawled into a little space under the house, near the furnace room, and wept.

"The next thing I remember is my mother and me on a train heading East—sitting in a small compartment playing gin rummy. My father's relatives, to whom she was still close, lived in New York City. We would start over there.

"My mother and I set up housekeeping in a hotel near the Broadway theatre district, and the first thing I did in New York was to go out and buy a ticket to a play. I had never heard of the playwright or the star, but when the matinee was over, I sat in my seat paralyzed by emotion. Ushers were picking up discarded programs, the work-light on stage had gone on, but I could not move. Finally, an usher led me from the theatre and deposited me on the sidewalk outside. The play was *The Glass Menagerie* by Tennessee Williams, and the star was Laurette Taylor.

"I forgot about movie stars and concentrated my attention upon Broadway actresses. Lynn Fontanne, Katharine Cornell, Eva Le Gallienne. I sat in the last row of theatre balconies, holding a small flashlight and writing in a notebook, and watched these women act. I was in love with all of them, but one, Eva Le Gallienne, captured my heart with her steady pursuit of excellence in the theatre—classics, repertory. Thirty years later I would write a play for Eva Le Gallienne called *The Dream Watcher*.

"For me, having come out of a small California town, New York was a revelation. There were museums, and opera and ballet, and more book stores than I knew existed in the world. From nine to three each day I went to private school, but after three o'clock the city was mine. By age fifteen, I was taking acting classes at the Neighborhood Playhouse. By sixteen, I was studying dance with Martha Graham.

"I look back on these days with a kind of sadness, for I, on my way to becoming an actress, did not like to act. What I really liked was being alone, reading and writing, and collecting books. A loner from birth, I felt uneasy in the social atmosphere of the theatre, and suffered from stagefright so severely that I once went to a hypnotist to be cured. Every spare moment I had was spent writing stories and poems, but I did not take this seriously.

She was outlined in the burning window. (From *The Crystal Child* by Barbara Wersba. Illustrated by Donna Diamond.)

My writing seemed terrible to me, awkward, imitative, trite.

"I was now disguised to myself as an adolescent, and did all of the things that young girls in the late 1940s did. Wore blazers and bobby socks, stuck new pennies in my loafers, swooned over Frank Sinatra, sat by the phone waiting for boys to call. I wore taffeta formals to proms and received gardenia corsages, fought with my mother over curfews, wore pale lipstick and nylons, went away on my first overnight date to West Point. But the person who did these things was not real to herself. It was as though I felt an obligation to be a 'teenager' for a certain number of years. After prep school, this obligation was over.

"My father insisted that I go to college, his choice being Vassar. Instead, I boarded a train one day and traveled up the Hudson to apply at a small liberal-arts college called Bard. To my surprise, my entrance exam was an audition on stage. I did a scene from Shaw's *Saint Joan* and was accepted. My father was furious when he found out, via the mails, but I persisted, and at the age of eighteen packed my trunks and went off to school. Save for brief vacations, I never returned home.

"If each life has a pattern, and if the meshing of inner and outer events—synchronicity—does exist, then I was fated to go to Bard College. From my first day there until my last, I was happy and fulfilled. I acted in all the plays and took all the English courses. I played the piano far into the night in a little glass observatory on a hill. I kept stray cats in my room, ran a donuts and coffee enterprise that traveled from dorm to dorm, made friends, got crushes on professors, fell in love. Applying for a Fulbright Scholarship to England, to study acting, I suddenly developed cold feet and wrote a letter to Eva Le Gallienne, asking her advice. Amazingly, she wrote back—suggesting that I study in my own country rather than abroad. I took her advice and did not go.

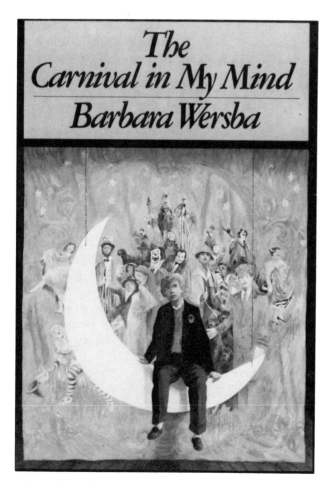

Ronald Himler's jacket illustration for the Harper & Row hardcover edition.

"Bard College was small in those days, just three hundred students, and the teachers taught on a one-to-one basis....In the summers, I went off to act in small summer stock companies. In the winter field periods, I worked at off-Broadway theatres in New York. My friends were actors, my mentors were actors—but I did not like to act. Rehearsals over, homework done, I would hole up in my dormitory room around midnight and write stories. I could not stop writing, and yet my writing caused me anguish. It wasn't any good. I never finished anything.

"I graduated from college one June, and a week later was in rehearsal in Princeton, New Jersey. The stock company was a good one, and it was said that producers and directors from New York would be coming down to see the plays. I had the lead in everyone of these plays—long, difficult parts. I was exhausted from the last year of college. And my stagefright was now chronic. The first production was *Camino Real* by Tennessee Williams. I played Marguerite Gautier, the legendary 'Camille,' and on opening night, after the curtain had come down, a famous director came backstage and said that he had a part for me on Broadway. After he left the dressing room, my fellow actors crowded round me, but where my happiness should have been was an empty space. I knew that I would never call the man, but did not know why. As far as my acting career was concerned, the journey downward had begun.

"That autumn, independent for the first time in my life, I took a coldwater flat in the East Village, got a series of part-time jobs, and began to make what in those days were called 'the rounds.' These rounds consisted of going to numerous theatrical offices, trying to see someone important, never being allowed to see someone important, and departing in anger—leaving behind a photo and resume that always ended up in the wastebasket. The tenement building I lived in on Ninth Street was crowded with young actresses, and since among us there was only one good coat—a fur—we would take turns wearing it....I worked in book shops and department stores, ran a projector for a film company, typed in offices....My worst job was waiting tables at Schrafft's, where I dropped a poached egg into a woman's bodice and was promptly fired. My best job was as the head of the correspondence department in a government housing agency. A secret acting student, I worked there by day, getting more and more promotions, while I went to acting school at night.

THE COUNTRY OF
THE HEART

Barbara Wersba

THE COUNTRY OF THE HEART

Atheneum

BARBARA WERSBA

Jerry Pinkney's jacket illustration for the Atheneum hardcover edition.

"The house on East Ninth Street has figured in several of my books, most recently in *The Carnival in My Mind,* because the building and its inhabitants were themselves like a character in a novel. In the basement lived Dennis, who was five feet tall and wanted to be an opera singer. On the top floor lived Samantha, who was a harpist, but whose room was too small for her harp. She kept the harp in the hallway. Next door to my apartment, on the second floor, was Beryl, a shady type who had a stream of gentlemen callers. In the winters all of us froze in our rooms—in the summers we roasted. Rats and roaches were common, but what I remember most from those days was the sunlight on my windowsill and the straw chair in which I would sit reading. I had painted the floors brick red, had built bookcases from floor to ceiling, and played Bach and Mozart on a dilapidated phonograph. The bathtub resided in the tiny kitchen—which meant that it was possible to bathe and cook at the same time.

"After college I had attended acting school for three years, under the guidance of a brilliant, temperamental teacher. His insistence that his students provide themselves with employment by forming their own companies was so strong, and so believable, that upon graduating seven of us did just that. Putting together a staged reading of famous stories about childhood, we hired a booking agent and went on the road. It was my job to adapt the stories into acting form, as well as act in them, and though I did not know it at the time, this work was my first real work as a writer. The stories were wonderful—by people like Dylan Thomas and Virginia Woolf—and as I shaped and cut them, and turned narrative into dialogue, I knew the first pleasure in working at a typewriter that I had ever known. The program was called *When I Was a Child,* and one day in winter, in a rented Volkswagen bus, the seven of us headed West.

"...Stuffed into the little bus with our suitcases and guitars, stage lights and costumes, we spent three wild months traveling across America, playing in college auditoriums and sleeping in run-down motels. By the time we returned, all of us worse for wear, plans were afoot to put the show on Broadway. But I had fallen ill.

"The diagnosis was hepatitis—and so, leaving the company behind, I went to a friend's house on Martha's Vineyard to recuperate. Lying there in bed day after day, staring at the ocean, free of responsibility for the first time in years, I knew that I would never return to the theatre. Something had broken in me that could no longer be repaired, and I was glad....I did not know where I was going, but after fifteen years of struggle I was free. It was then that my hostess said, 'Barbara, why don't you write something?'

"I asked her what she thought I could possibly write, and by way of answering she brought a pad of paper and a pen to my room and left me alone. I looked at the pad of paper, and then I looked at the sea and began to write. A few weeks later I had completed a story called *The Boy Who Loved the Sea.* I didn't know it was a children's story because I knew nothing about children's literature. All I knew was that this was the first piece I had ever been able to finish. It was a fantasy about a child who goes to live in the sea, and I was rather proud of it. Beyond that, I thought nothing.

"A few nights later, the chief copy editor of a New York publishing house came to dinner, and without telling me, my friend and hostess put my manuscript into the editor's purse. The editor read the

Dust jacket illustration by Beth Peck for the Harper & Row hardcover edition.

manuscript, and took it to the children's book editor at the firm where she worked....

"Suddenly I was about to have a book published, and it gave me pause for thought. What was life all about, when fifteen years in the theatre bore no fruit, but one small manuscript did? What was fate trying to tell me? I was not a good writer, but something told me that I had the temperament of a writer, that I could teach myself to write, and have more joy in doing so than I had ever had acting. Thus, at the age of twenty-six, I began a new career.

"The second book, a fantasy about ballooning in the eighteenth century, was harder to do, but I stuck at it....It was clear to me that the form in which I wanted to work was the children's book, and so I began to read children's books by the dozens, trying to understand the difference between picture books and story books and novels. I worked as hard as I had ever worked in my life, sat at the typewriter for eight hours a day, and produced a third book—this time a fantasy about mythical animals.

"I moved to Rockland County in New York, and rented a small house. The fourth book appeared, and then the fifth, as I worked steadily to improve what I was doing, to clarify what I wanted to say. I knew so little about story-telling, and yet in some ways story-telling had been the basis of my life. Reading and writing and collecting books had been my occupations since childhood.

"In 1967, I was working on an historical novel set in eighteenth-century London when a voice came into my head. This voice, that of a young boy, was so strong and insistent that I put the historical novel away, sat down at the typewriter, and did not get up again for seven months. The voice which would not stop speaking belonged to a boy named Albert Scully, and the book in which he told the story of his life was *The Dream Watcher.* On the day that I finished this book I burst into tears, for I knew it to be a milestone in my life. Little did I realize, however, the paths down which Albert Scully and I would walk.

"*The Dream Watcher,* published by Atheneum, was the first of my books to have any length and develop any real characters. Told in the first person, it is the story of a fourteen-year-old boy, a misfit and a loner, who meets a beautiful old woman who tells him that she has been a famous actress. Taking him into her home and her life, Mrs. Orpha Woodfin develops such a sense of integrity in Albert that by the time she dies, he has come into his own. No matter that she lied to him about having been an actress. What she has given him is himself.

"From the day it was published, *The Dream Watcher* changed my life. To begin with, the book sold well and received fine reviews. People all over the country began to write me about their identification with the characters, about an older person who had changed their direction in life. And it was only then that I realized that this theme of older person helping younger person had been the underlying theme of my own life. Unable to relate to my parents, I had sought parent substitutes everywhere. . . .In friends who were always older than I, and who gave of themselves generously.

"During the next few years I wrote several picture books, became a book reviewer for the *New York Times,* and began to write articles for magazines. I taught fiction writing at New York University. But *The Dream Watcher* would not go away. People connected with the movies came to see me, to inquire if the book couldn't be turned into a film. Others suggested that I do a sequel. I was well into my second novel for young people, a story set in the drug culture of the sixties called *Run Softly, Go Fast*—but *The Dream Watcher* persisted.

"The book went into paperback and kept bringing in mail. Again and again I was told that the story should be turned into a play or a film, but those possibilities seemed remote. What I wanted was to move on, to leave the book behind me and do something different.

"It was not to be—for in the early 1970s a friend of mine gave *The Dream Watcher* to Eva Le Gallienne to read, and one evening this friend called to say that Miss Le Gallienne wanted to play the part of the old woman. Although I was only forty, I felt that my life had come full circle.

"The next five years were a kind of detour, as Eva Le Gallienne and I struggled to make *The Dream Watcher* a reality. I had been so moved by meeting this actress that I had been rather mute, but when she turned to me in front of the fireplace of her Connecticut home, an old woman now, not the actress I remembered, but the personality I remembered—the vibrancy, the vitality, the beautiful voice—when she turned to me and said, 'Why don't you write me a play?' I was done for. All plans for children's books and children's novels were swept from my mind as by a great invisible broom. 'I don't know how to write a play,' I said to her. 'Learn,' she advised.

Deborah Healy's jacket illustration for Wersba's 1987 novel.

"For the next eight months I read two plays in the morning and two in the evening—to learn this difficult form—and in between I struggled to dramatize my book. As each act was completed, I would take it over to Miss LeG's house, she would give criticism, and then I would head back to my typewriter in Rockland County. . . .

"Within a year I had turned *The Dream Watcher* into a play. I had also become friends with one of the great stars of the twenties and thirties. To my surprise the glamorous woman I had admired in my childhood was herself a loner—a person who fed animals from the woods every night from her kitchen door, whose main interest in life was her garden, and whose library was the finest I'd ever seen. . . .

"We opened at the White Barn Theatre in Connecticut in 1975, and that night I had a sudden understanding of why people write plays, of why in the midst of so much difficulty and pain, playwrights persist. For at the evening's end, as the curtain calls began, and as Miss LeG was led onto the stage by the young actor who played opposite her, a kind of thunderstorm broke. People cheered, and wept, and applauded, and stamped their feet, as she took curtain call after curtain call. As the applause continued, I ran into the lobby where refreshments were being served, grabbed a glass of champagne, and, without spilling a drop, ran up the back stairs of the theatre and handed the glass to Miss LeG when she came offstage. It was one of the happiest moments of my life.

"The production at the White Barn Theatre had been a summer tryout, a preparation for what we hoped would be a Broadway production. And in the summer of 1977 that production materialized. The play was re-cast, re-designed, and a large group of us flew out to Seattle, where the play would be produced in partnership with the Seattle Repertory Theatre....But just as the White Barn production had been destined to succeed, so this new version was destined to fail. A boy who was much too old had been cast in the part of Albert. An insecure young director had been hired. Ornate, revolving sets had been designed—sets that almost swallowed up the play—and I had been asked to do countless rewrites, none of which I believed in. Opening night was a disaster, and the following day Miss LeG gathered the cast together in the theatre's green room. 'We have failed,' she told them. 'Our butterfly has been cloaked in iron.'

"I came home to Rockland County, went to bed with my two cats, and slept. For some years home had been a nineteenth-century country store, with stained glass windows, marble counters, and gas lamps—and so I walked through the house for days, staring at the books in my library and watching the sunset turn the stained glass into something evangelical. In the early 1960s, a partner and I had bought this building and restored it to its former beauty. And since it had always been a country store, we decided to operate it as one again—selling penny candy and tobacco, Vermont cheese, homebaked goods, jams and jellies, housewares, toys. It was a marvelous store, and though it never earned a penny, it received constant publicity....Theatrical people from New York drove out to sample its wares—Noel Coward, Katharine Cornell, Mary Martin, Ginger Rogers. During the seven years that we ran the store, I was a writer in the mornings and a storekeeper in the afternoons. It was a good combination.

"In order to do something after Seattle, in order to heal myself, I took a step that surprised me—I opened a school. A small school. Ten students. All women. I called it The Women's Writing Workshop, held the classes in my home, and found a new door opening....There is an old saying to the effect that the only way to learn something is to teach it—so that now, after many years of writing, I was beginning to understand writing for the first time. Guiding the students away from any need to prove themselves, to be good, to shine, I also guided myself away from these goals—and soon I was doing the assignments with them, learning to write naturally, from feeling rather than expectation....

"From the day I began writing professionally, I have worked at the same desk—a large craftsman's table that I bought for ten dollars. And after ruining dozens of typewriters with my pounding, I now type on a solid, indestructible IBM. I begin work around five in the morning, when I know it will be quiet, work for six hours, and return to work in the afternoon if I am deep in a book. For every manuscript that succeeds there are five that fail, but I can never bring myself to throw the failures away, and they are all kept in a trunk labeled *In Progress*. I have had my share of rejections and disappointments, and a certain number of calamities—like the play—but the impulse to write persists. What keeps it alive is simple curiosity. There is no literary form that cannot be explored more deeply, whether it be novel, short story, or poem, and this is what interests me.

"The first thing that comes when I am about to write a book is the title. Indeed, titles often appear far in advance of the book itself, so that I write the title on a piece of paper, paste it up over my desk, and wait. One of my favorite titles, *Let Me Fall Before I Fly*, arrived so many months before the actual story that I found myself repeating the words over and over, as though they were a mantra or a prayer. Let me fall before I fly, let me fall before I fly....Then, suddenly, I knew what the words meant and began to write a story about a little boy who owns an imaginary circus. Of all the books, this one is my favorite. It says what I believe, and it reflects my life.

"I have been blessed with many things. With awards and honors, with books published abroad, and, since 1980, with the friendship of my fine editor Charlotte Zolotow. I have spent the last twenty-five years doing what I like to do, leading the kind of life I think is right for me—and for these things, I am grateful. My career has allowed me to meet people whose talents have influenced me profoundly. Eva Le Gallienne, Janet Flanner, Irwin Shaw, Carson McCullers....

From the Seattle Repertory Theatre production of "The Dream Watcher," starring Eva Le Gallienne, 1977-1978.

"I look back on my life and ask myself questions. When have I been the happiest? Walking in the Swiss Alps, all worldly cares left behind, all values altered by the enormity of nature. When have I been the most sad? During those moments when human cruelty has been apparent to me, especially if the cruelty is directed towards animals. What do I hope for now? In a conventional sense, very little.

"I have loved being on this earth and feel grief at the thought of leaving it some day. I have been moved to the depths by the natural world, by the passionate desire of plants and animals to reproduce themselves and carry their genes into the future. A flock of Canada geese passing over my house, their honking almost like the barking of dogs, a lone male bird leading the formation—this sight can reduce me to tears. And only yesterday a great swan flew over my head on a passage unknown, its wings making a humming sound on the winter air.

"The journey continues."[1]

Footnote Sources:

[1] Adele Sarkissian, editor, *Something about the Author Autobiography Series*, Gale, 1986.

■ For More Informations See

Library Journal, September, 1968, February 15, 1973 (p. 620).

Horn Book, December, 1971.

Martha E. Ward and Dorothy A. Marquardt, *Authors of Books for Young People*, 2nd edition, Scarecrow Press, 1971.

Doris de Montreville and Donna Hill, editors, *Third Book of Junior Authors*, H. W. Wilson, 1972.

Barbara Wersba, "Barbara Wersba—As a Writer," *Top of the News*, June 1975 (p. 427).

Paul Janeczko, "An Interview with Barbara Wersba," *English Journal*, November, 1976 (p. 20).

D. L. Kirkpatrick, *Twentieth-Century Children's Writers*, St. Martin's Press, 1978.

Bulletin of the Center for Children's Books, July-August, 1982.

Washington Post Book World, August 8, 1982, September 12, 1982.

Best Sellers, October, 1982.

Paul Zindel

Born May 15, 1936, in Staten Island, N.Y.; son of Paul (a policeman) and Betty (a practical nurse; maiden name, Frank) Zindel; married Bonnie Hildebrand (a novelist), October 25, 1973; children: David Jack, Elizabeth Claire. *Education:* Wagner College, B.S., 1958, M.Sc., 1959. *Agent:* Curtis Brown, Ltd., 10 Astor Pl., New York, N.Y. 10003. *Office:* c/o Harper & Row, 10 East 53rd St., New York, N. Y. 10022.

■ Career

Allied Chemical, New York, N. Y., technical writer, 1958-59; Tottenville High School, Staten Island, N.Y., chemistry teacher, 1959-69; playwright and author of children's books, 1969—. Playwright-in-residence, Alley Theatre, Houston, Tex., 1967. *Member:* Actors Studio.

■ Awards, Honors

Ford Foundation Grant, 1967, for drama; *The Pigman* was selected one of Child Study Association of America's Children's Books of the Year, 1968, and received the *Boston Globe-Horn Book Award* for Text, 1969; *My Darling, My Hamburger* was selected one of *New York Times* Outstanding Children's Book of the Year, 1969, *I Never Loved Your Mind*, 1970, *Pardon Me, You're Stepping on My Eyeball*, 1976, *The Undertaker's Gone Bananas*, 1978, and *The Pigman's Legacy*, 1980; Obie Award for the Best American Play from the *Village Voice*, 1970, Vernon Rice Drama Desk Award from the New York Drama Critics, for the Most Promising Playwright, and New York Drama Critics Circle Award for Best American Play of the Year, all 1970, and Pulitzer Prize in Drama, New York Critics Award, 1971, all for *The Effect of Gamma Rays on Man-in-the-Moon Marigolds;* Honorary Doctorate of Humanities from Wagner College, 1971; *The Effect of Gamma Rays on Man-in-the-Moon Marigolds* was chosen one of American Library Association's Best Young Adult Books, 1971, *Pigman*, 1975, *Pardon Me, You're Stepping on My Eyeball!*, 1976, *Confessions of a Teenage Baboon*, 1977, *The Pigman's Legacy*, 1980, and *To Take a Dare*, 1982; *Media & Methods* Maxi Award, 1973, for *The Pigman; Confessions of a Teenage Baboon* was chosen one of New York Public Library's Books for the Teen Age, 1980, *The Effect of Gamma Rays on Man-in-the-Moon Marigolds*, 1980, 1981, and 1982, *A Star for the Latecomer*, 1981, and *The Pigman's Legacy*, 1981, and 1982.

■ Writings

Young Adult, Except As Noted:

The Pigman (ALA Notable Book; *Horn Book* honor list), Harper, 1968.
My Darling, My Hamburger, Harper, 1969.
I Never Loved Your Mind, Harper, 1970.

I Love My Mother (juvenile; illustrated by John Melo), Harper, 1975.

Pardon Me, You're Stepping on My Eyeball!, Harper, 1976.

Confessions of a Teenage Baboon, Harper, 1977.

The Undertaker's Gone Bananas, Harper, 1978.

(With wife, Bonnie Zindel) *A Star for the Latecomer*, Harper, 1980.

The Pigman's Legacy, Harper, 1980.

The Girl Who Wanted a Boy, Harper, 1981.

(With Crescent Dragonwagon) *To Take a Dare*, Harper, 1982.

Harry and Hortense at Hormone High, Harper, 1984.

The Amazing and Death-Defying Diary of Eugene Dingman, Harper, 1987.

A Begonia for Miss Applebaum, Harper, 1989.

Adult:

When Darkness Falls, Bantam, 1984.

Plays:

"Dimensions of Peacocks," first produced in New York, 1959.

"Euthanasia and the Endless Hearts," first produced in New York at Take 3, 1960.

"A Dream of Swallows," first produced Off-Broadway, April, 1962.

The Effect of Gamma Rays on Man-in-the-Moon Marigolds (first produced in Houston, Tex. at Alley Theatre, May, 1964; produced Off-Broadway at Mercer-O'Casey Theatre, April 7, 1970; ALA Notable Book; illustrated by Dong Kingman), Harper, 1971.

And Miss Reardon Drinks a Little (first produced in Los Angeles at Mark Taper Forum, 1967, produced on Broadway at Morosco Theatre, February 25, 1971), Dramatists Play Service, 1971.

The Secret Affairs of Mildred Wild (first produced in New York City at Ambassador Theatre, November 14, 1972), Dramatists Play Service, 1973.

Let Me Hear You Whisper [and] The Ladies Should Be in Bed ("Let Me Hear You Whisper" was televised on NET-TV, 1966; "The Ladies Should Be in Bed" was first produced in New York, 1978), Dramatists Play Service, 1973, *Let Me Hear You Whisper* (published separately; illustrated by Stephen Gammell), Harper, 1974.

Ladies at the Alamo (first produced at Actors Studio, May 29, 1975, produced on Broadway at Martin Beck Theatre, April 7, 1977, produced as "Ladies on the Midnight Planet," in Hollywood at Marilyn Monroe Theatre, 1982), Dramatists Play Service, 1977.

"A Destiny on Half Moon Street," first produced in Florida at Coconut Grove, 1985.

"Amulets against the Dragon Forces," Circle Repertory Company (N.Y.), 1989.

Screen And Television Plays:

"The Effect of Gamma Rays on Man-in-the-Moon Marigolds" (television), National Educational Television (NET), October 3, 1966.

"Let Me Hear You Whisper," NET, 1966.

"Up the Sandbox" (based on Anne Roiphe's novel), National, 1972.

"Mame" (based on Patrick Dennis' novel *Auntie Mame*), Warner Bros., 1974.

"Maria's Lovers," Cannon Films, 1984.

"Alice in Wonderland," CBS-TV, December 9, 1985.

(With Djordje Milicevic and Edward Bunker) "Runaway Train" (based on a screenplay by Akira Kurosawa), starring Jon Voight, Eric Roberts and Rebecca De Mornay, Cannon Films, 1985.

(With Leslie Briscusse) "Babes in Toyland," NBC-TV, 1986.

Also author of "The Pigman" (adapted from his novel). Contributor of articles to newspapers and periodicals.

■ Adaptations

"The Pigman" (cassette; filmstrip with cassette), Miller-Brody/Random House, 1978.

"My Darling, My Hamburger" (cassette; filmstrip with cassette), Current Affairs and Mark Twain Media, 1978.

■ Sidelights

May 15, 1936. Born in Staten Island, New York. Coming from a broken home, Zindel never knew his father very well. "Mother was a girl in her twenties when my father left. She used to have to fight to get the allowance from him and tried to keep us together, moving from apartment to apartment...."[1]

"My sister and I would see my father just about every other Christmas. Mother would take us to the Staten Island terminal and put us on the ferry, and when we got to the other side, my father would be waiting. Once or twice, he wasn't there. You could hardly blame him. It must be pretty traumatic when a man hasn't seen his kids in two years, so he takes a drink. . . .

"Once, I had a whole week together with my father, up at Star Lake. My mother would never give my father a divorce, you see, so he simply lived with a woman without benefit of clergy, and they had a marvelous life together. So this one time, my father took me up to where the woman's family lived at Star Lake. I was ten, and oh, God, what a jackass I was! On the train going up, we had lobster, and believe me, there was ample to eat for any normal boy. But my father liked to be flashy—he even took me to Toots Shor's one time—so he asked me if I wouldn't like another lobster, and in my childish ignorance I said yes, I would like another lobster. So there I sat in that dining car, eating $20 worth of lobster.

Stephen Gammell's dust jacket illustration for the hardcover edition.

Hardbound cover from Zindel's first novel.

"Then, when we got to Star Lake, I made the faux pas of all faux pas. It was Thanksgiving, and these very intelligent, very refined people had prepared a lovely dinner. . .a turkey, homemade this, home-grown that, and the woman's mother had baked a marvelous pumpkin pie. While everyone was savoring this culinary creation, I—being a perfect gentleman—said, 'Gee, this pie tastes good. It tastes just like the kind my mother makes with Flako pie crust mix.'"[2]

". . .I found out there was another world beyond that mother and sister of mine. A world where I learned there were fresh vegetables, and that you raised the seat up to urinate. Because, boy, was I pistol-whipped when I was a boy. So when my aunt says: 'You were *really* a good boy,' I know 'good' means I really was kept under control."[3]

It was a struggle for Zindel's mother to raise the children and make a living to support the family. "She worked at everything, nursing, real estate, a hot dog stand and inventions, but we usually lived in a shambles."[1]

From the Broadway production of "And Miss Reardon Drinks a Little," starring Estelle Parsons, Julie Harris and Nancy Marchand. Opened at the Morosco Theatre, February 25, 1971.

"...She and my father had had a lovely home in Oakwood on Staten Island and when their marriage broke up, she couldn't afford to keep it. But Mother just wasn't meant for apartment living. She couldn't stand anyone telling her what to do. One landlady told her how to hang her wash and plant her rosebushes, and the crowning touch that made us depart from that residence was when the landlady planted sunflowers beneath our window. They grew and they grew until they were right outside our window, and Mother felt she was being watched.

"We did manage to get a house once, in Travis. We lived there for four years—my crucial years, my adolescence. Mother got the house for five dollars down, a phenomenal maneuver on her part. We lived next door to a black family—the only one in town—and we became friends. It was just our two families against that whole Polish town. But our house was a shambles. I had a teacher who suddenly needed an exhibit for a science fair and when she heard that I had made a terrarium, she said, 'We've got to have a look at it immediately.' She drove me home and we went out into the back yard to look at the terrarium, complete with black widow spider. The next day in school—and I'll never forget this—she said to the class, 'I have been teaching in this school for twenty years and I never realized until yesterday what poverty there is in this town.'

"Mother always had a load of animals. At one time, we had twenty-six collies. Breeding dogs was one sure way to make money, Mother decided. 'Lassie' was very popular then and she was convinced that collies would sell like hot cakes. But things got out of hand. Little collies kept falling out of big collies, and eventually everyone in town got a free collie. We built a kennel for them outside, but Mother couldn't bear to leave them out over night, so finally we gave them one whole room inside the house.

"Mother used to kill a lot of them. I'd come home from school and find that one of the dogs was missing. It would turn out that he had bitten somebody and Mother was afraid that they'd come and take the dog away, so, she'd have it 'put to sleep,' as she phrased it. Then she would cry for days."[2]

"Our home was a house of fear. Mother never trusted anybody, and ours wasn't the kind of house someone could get into by knocking on the front

From the Pulitzer Prize-winning stage production "The Effect of Gamma Rays on Man-in-the-Moon Marigolds." Starring Sada Thompson (center), Amy Levitt and Pamela Payton-Wright, it opened April 7, 1970 at the Mercer-O'Casey Theatre.

door. A knock at the door would send mother, sister and me running to a window to peak out."[1]

"She instilled in me the thought that the world was out to get me...."[4]

"...I felt worthless as a kid, and dared to speak and act my true feelings only in fantasy and secret. That's probably what made me a writer."[5]

"When I write, I hear the voices of my mother and sister. I'm writing from their voices in a metaphor I know about."[1]

Zindel was provided with few resources at home to challenge his young mind. "I came from a home that never read books. We had no books in the house. We had no desire to have books in the house, and I find that kids are very much a product of their homes. That old-fashioned saying is quite true, and so we had no politics. We had no books, no theatre. We had none of those things."[6]

Staten Island became his playground and entree into other cultures. "...South Beach was Sicily; Stapleton was Killarney; Silver Lake was Alexandria; Tottenville was The Congo. I have not the least doubt I would have emerged staggeringly

polylingual if that Woman Scorned [his mother] had been a mixer.

"And each town offered a lush new backdrop: St. George—a buzzing city, hordes rushing on and off the five-cent ferry; Oakwood—a wooded backyard, pheasant families parading beneath hanging fat apples; Travis—a mad tiny airport, weekend pilots in Piper Cubs who circled above their lovers' homes and tossed bottles of Chanel No. 5 affixed to midget parachutes. And a mulberry tree. It was a time when Kilbasi, pepperoni and knockwurst were the relentless culinary dividers of this little island in New York Bay.

"By the time I was ten I had gone nowhere but had seen the world."[7]

With an active imagination, Zindel managed to keep himself entertained. "...I remember a love of marionettes—nautical, laughing, demoniacal. Some I fashioned myself. One—a grotesque sailor—was given to me for my second birthday. I recall cardboard boxes housing cycloramas, crepe-paper palm trees back-lighted by flashlight batteries with bulbs attached by twisted paper clips. The aquariums—two gallons, five gallons, twenty gallons. I sat for hours looking in at guppies hunting their young through forests of elodea. An insectarium, incredible centipedes, plump red ants—a sinister black spider unearthed in the backyard of the Travis home where I lived for my fifth Easter. I remember [that] terrarium, green silent stalks as magical to me as any bug, fish or puppet. Then there was the crippled boy who cried 'Shazaam' to become Captain Marvel—and Wonder Woman with her transparent lasso and magic girdle. And there was the terrifying world at the Empire Theater where Batman and friend were nearly murdered each Saturday morning.

"What a great love I had of microcosms, of peering at other worlds framed and separate from me."[7]

1947. Landed his first role in a play. "One day I tired of eavesdropping on the world and decided to enter it.

"At last, a part!

"I was eleven years old and selected to be one of the comic characters to make up the entourage for a 'Tom Thumb Wedding' to be held at the Dickinson Methodist Church. For those who have never heard of a 'Tom Thumb Wedding,' it is an esoteric celebration in which children who do not know what they are doing march down an aisle in a mock ceremony while their parents stand in pews and grin a lot. I believe only Sigmund Freud would know what the hell they are grinning at. Anyway, some woman with a heightened sense of character assassination designated me to portray B. O. Plenty and carry a Sparkle doll. This was my first clue that as a child I physically resembled a rather tall chicken with a thyroid condition. I was so hurt and angry at the casting I silently prayed during the wedding for the cute little boy and girl playing Tom and his bride to mature into dwarfs. I waited two years to be offered another part. Finally, it came. I was Santa Claus in the seventh-grade Christmas extravaganza at P.S. 26. Needless to say, I did not receive plaudits for my performance as a *bewhiskered* chicken with a thyroid condition.

"In the eighth grade I considered that perhaps I was trying in the wrong way to enter into the real world, so I launched my career as a vocalist. I sang 'Till the End of Time' and 'I'm Looking Over a Four Leaf Clover,' a capella for my eighth-grade shop class. I am afraid both the location and the selections were ill-chosen, and if the teacher had not been in the room, chisels and hacksaws would have gone flying through the air. And I suppose my final gesture toward being an active participant in this world was when I volunteered at the Ritz

Theater to be swung around at 180 rpms by a roller-skating acrobat who supplemented the flick."[7]

Zindel wrote his first play in high school. "I decided that even if I could not succeed in the real world, perhaps my appointed role in life was to help other people succeed. I do not quite know how, but some of my classmates got the impression I had a strange sense of humor: *macabre*, I believe, was the summoned term. A group of the student officers asked me to help create a hilarious assembly sketch which would help sell G.O. cards. I gave them a version of 'The Monkey's Paw,' which has a final moment when a corpse, having been buried for six months, returns home. This is not especially the meat from which comedies are carved. My only other script contribution was an idea for a Senior Day sketch in which, as Dean Martin sang, 'When the Moon Hits Your Eye Like a Big Pizza Pie,' some mozzarella masochist got it in the face."[7]

1951. Contracted tuberculosis. "...I...was whisked off to a sanitorium at Lake Kushaqua, New York, where once again the world became something I could look at only through a frame.

"Big deal, Paul Zindel—fifteen years old, tubercular, drab, loveless and desperate."[7]

Zindel's first original play was inspired by his time at the sanatorium. "A year and a half of feeding hummingbirds from vials of sugar water goes by and I return, cured and shy, to my high school and there write a play for a contest sponsored by the American Cancer Society. The plot: a pianist recovers from a dread disease and goes on to win tumultuous applause at Carnegie Hall for pounding out 'The Warsaw Concerto.' For this literary achievement I was awarded a Parker pen."[7]

By the time Zindel finished school, he had attended four different high schools. "I went to PS 8 and I went to PS 19 and I went to PS 26 and I went to Port Richmond High School. See, even though we moved, we did a lot of lying to make believe we stayed in the district."[3]

Majored in chemistry at Wagner College in Staten Island. Zindel found a mentor when he took a creative writing course taught by Edward Albee. "He was one of my primary inspirations in writing plays. I felt very grateful because he took time."[3]

During his last year in college, Zindel wrote his second original play: "'Dimensions of Peacocks,' the title being my subtle way of expressing a fascination with the psychiatric term dementia praecox—which has nothing to do with the theme.

It is the story of a misunderstood youth whose mother is a visiting nurse with a penchant for stealing monogrammed linen napkins from her patients by stuffing them down her bra.'"[7]

A few years later when Edward Albee's play "Who's Afraid of Virginia Woolf" was in previews, he and Zindel had a disagreement which ended their acquaintanceship permanently. "When you're young and someone famous comes your way, you want to hear him and be with him all of the time. But the parting of ways must come."[8]

"Now we smile politely when we pass each other in elevators on the way to a Dramatist Guild meeting."[8]

Zindel's father died in 1957. "...He had just retired and went up to a log cabin, a fishing shack, in Star Lake, N.Y., and he just keeled over. And he was with that woman he was with...many, many years."[3]

1958. Received B.S. in chemistry, and a year later his M.Sc.

Though he had already written two original plays, Zindel did not see a professionally produced play until he was twenty-three. "Lillian Hellman theatrically baptizes me with my first real play, 'Toys in the Attic,' in 1959. I behold for the first time Maureen Stapleton, unbelievably incandescent, a priestess of human laughter and pain. I remember thinking I had at last found what would be my religion, my cathedral.

"And at this point I cannot stop my typewriter from spilling out the experience which exploded my consciousness in a way that protects me from being a *dumb* playwright. It was early one summer evening about ten years ago. I was walking through Greenwich Village with a friend I had reason to believe possessed psychic powers. He has since gone mad. But on that evening he made me pause at an alley between two apartment houses. He told me he felt something strange was going to happen in that spot, although he did not know what or when. I did not pay much attention to his remark and we went on our way to see 'The American Dream' at the Cherry Lane Theater. It was two hours later that we were back out on the street when suddenly my friend began to run. He cried out:

"'Something's going on in the alley!'

"The alley was several blocks away but I ran with him anyway, thinking it was just a lot of nonsense. When we reached the alley, we saw twenty or more people hanging out their windows yelling, throwing money—coins and dollar bills—down to an old woman hovering over a row of garbage pails. She was stuffing the garbage into her mouth and ignoring the money as it fell around her. That incident haunted me. Shortly after I met Edward Albee and told him about it and how much it disturbed me. I could not understand why the woman had not picked up the money to buy food.

"'She was doing penance,' he told me quietly, simply."[7]

Ignited by his first theatrical experience, Zindel became an avid Tennessee Williams fan. "...I never missed an opening night of a Tennessee Williams play, except the revival of 'The Glass Menagerie,' which I've *never* seen. Of course, I've read the play many times. I used to run into Williams at least once a year. One time it would be in a Greenwich Village bar, another time at the theater. At the premiere of 'Night of the Iguana,' I cornered him in the lobby during intermission, only to have him whisked away by two men. Every time I would see him, I would say, 'Mr. Williams, I admire your plays so very much.'"[2]

1959-1969. Taught chemistry and physics at Tottenville High School on Staten Island. During his ten years of teaching, Zindel continued to write plays. His first real success came in 1964 when *The Effect of Gamma Rays on Man-in-the-Moon Marigolds* had its premiere at Houston's Alley Theatre. *Marigolds* is the story of a young girl, Tillie, who lives with her epileptic sister and her abusive mother, Beatrice. When Tillie receives recognition at school for her science project, it is clear that she will be able to break free from her mad family and find fulfillment. "*Marigolds* was written when I was twenty-five-years-old. One morning I awoke and discovered the manuscript next to my typewriter. I suspect it is autobiographical, because whenever I see a production of it I laugh and cry harder than anyone else in the audience. I laugh because the play always reminds me of still another charmingly frantic scheme of my mother's to get rich quick—a profusion of schemes all of which couldn't possibly appear in the play....I remember an endless series of preposterous undertakings—hatcheck girl, PT boat riveter, and unlicensed real estate broker."[9]

"*Marigolds* is the kind of story that just sort of pops right out of you, because you've *lived* it. My mother *was*...Beatrice. I've exaggerated, of course. It's true that Mother did a lot of the mean things that Beatrice does, but she was also capable of enormous compassion. She had been a practical

From the Broadway stage production of "Ladies at the Alamo," starring Estelle Parsons and Eileen Heckert. Opened at the Martin Beck Theatre, April 7, 1977.

Maureen Stapleton starred in the Ambassador Theatre stage production of "The Secret Affairs of Mildred Wild." Opened on Broadway, November 14, 1972.

nurse, and people were always calling her when they got sick, and she'd be on the phone half the night dispensing medical advice. Mother was never as isolated as Beatrice; she would occasionally get out and mix with people. She even had a great capacity for laughter. But she was always glad to get home, to shut the door on everything. She was afraid people were commenting on her appearance, making fun of her clothes. To tell you the truth, Mother was a beautiful example of paranoia. Only, in her case, it was *right* to be paranoiac.

"I'm very bad on dates, but I think it was in 1963 that my agent sent *Marigolds* to Nina Vance at the Alley Theater in Houston. She told me later that she probably would never have read it, except that it had a gold cover and it looked so nice that she took it home with her. It was first produced at the Alley Theater in May, 1964...."[2]

1966. Television version of *Marigolds* produced by National Educational Television. Charlotte Zolotow, editor for Harper & Row saw the production. "...Charlotte Zolotow...tracked me down and got me to write my first novel, *The Pigman*. She brought me into an area that I never explored before, my own confused, funny, aching teenage days."[5]

"I was flattered that someone would call me up and tell me they thought I had talent and offer me an advance."[10]

The Pigman was instrumental in establishing the realistic teenage novel as a distinct genre. In this story, two teenagers, John and Lorraine, two high school sophomores, befriend an elderly man they call "The Pigman" because his name is Pignati and he collects china pigs. Mr. Pignati, who is senile, becomes a substitute parent neither has ever known. He brings joy into their lonely lives until, inadvertently, John and Lorraine cause the Pigman's death. Only upon his death, do they realize their responsibility to others. Diane Farrell, in her *Horn Book* review (1969) stated: "Few books that have been written for young people are as cruelly truthful about the human condition. Fewer still accord the elderly such serious consideration or perceive that what we term senility may be a symbolic return to youthful honesty and idealism."[11]

A London *Times* reviewer added: "...an unpleasant book in some ways, but the issues are starkly real."[12]

Twentieth Century-Fox's film "The Effect of Gamma Rays on Man-in-the-Moon Marigolds," starred Joanne Woodward (right). Based on Zindel's play, it was released in 1972.

1967. Zindel took a leave of absence from teaching and went to Houston on a Ford Foundation Grant as playwright-in-residence for the Alley Theater.

1968. Before seeing the semi-autobiographical *Marigolds* on stage, Zindel's mother passed away. "...I returned to my mother's house knowing she had only a few months to live; she was unaware of the fact that she was dying. We had long before made that peace between parent and son which Nature insists not happen until the teen years have passed. During that privileged time just before she died, we enjoyed each other as friends. If she felt strong on a particular day she'd ask to go for a car ride. She loved burnt-almond ice cream, shrimp in lobster sauce, and flowers in bloom. On one of our trips we discovered a grove with a family of pheasants, a floor of lilies of the valley, and a ceiling of wisteria. Always we talked of the past— of her father, of his vegetable wagon in old Stapleton, of a man who rented a room in her father's house in which to store thousands of Christmas toys. There was always the unusual, the hilarity, the sadness. In her own way she told me of her secret dreams and fears—so many of which somehow I had sensed, and discovered written into that manuscript next to my typewriter....'"[9]

"...Mother, *did* see *Marigolds* on television and she *loved* it. She always said that it was going to be a great big hit one day."[2]

1969. Feeling that he could be of more assistance to teenagers by writing for them, Zindel quit teaching high school for good. "...I took an informal survey to find out what books young people were reading, and I discovered that there weren't many writers who were getting through to them. There was *Catcher in the Rye*, from which so much teen-age literature stems, but I discovered that many teen-agers didn't really understand what it was about.

"And when I started reading some teen-age books myself, what I saw in most of them had no connection to the teen-agers I knew. I thought I knew what kids would want in a book, and so I made a list and followed it."[10]

"I write for the people who don't like to read, as a rule. I found that the academic students, the ones from better homes and gardens, so to speak, were able to enjoy a whole range of material. Some were even able to enjoy Shakespeare! But as a rule, that left out an enormous body of students. I found even the subject of chemistry becoming too sophisticated and leaving behind a whole lot of kids, and

Zindel wrote the screenplay for the Warner Brothers film "Mame." Released in 1974, it starred Lucille Ball.

Barbra Streisand starred in the movie "Up the Sandbox." Screenplay by Paul Zindel, 1972.

even those from better homes and gardens weren't able to catch on to the new chemistry. And they had no need for it. They had need for other, more immediate bodies of information."[6]

Zindel's second young adult novel was published by Harper & Row. *My Darling, My Hamburger* is the story of a young girl with abusive parents who gets pregnant in high school and turns to an illegal abortionist.

Marilyn R. Singer, in a 1969 *School Library Journal* review, had mixed reactions to this second story: "[*My Darling, My Hamburger* is a] skillfully written story of four high school seniors. . .that has tremendous appeal on the entertainment level, but that totally cops out on the issues raised: sex, contraception, abortion. . . .The teenagers here are the most realistic of any in high-school novels to date: they have appropriate feelings and relationships; smoke, drink, swear; have refreshingly normal sexual thoughts and conflicts. The dialogue and description are so natural and entertaining (and often very funny) that the author disarms his audience (anyone who writes so convincingly must be a friend) while planting mines of moralism: *pot and sex are destructive.*"[13]

John Rowe Twonsend, in his 1969 *New York Times* review of the books considered *My Darling, My Hamburger* "...to be a better novel than *The Pigman.* . . ." Although, "as a work of literary art this is more a promise than an achievement, but it's quite a big promise and it's not a negligible achievement."[14]

Ever since the appearance of his first two books, Zindel's novels have been the objects of a good deal of controversy and evaluation. On the one hand, they have been described as humorous and honest, but, on the other, they have been condemned as "hack work" and slick "con jobs." Lavinia Russ, for instance, praised Zindel in a *Publisher's Weekly* review as being "...one of the brightest stars in the children's book sky. When Paul Zindel's first book 'The Pigman' appeared, it was so astonishingly good it made your reviewer feel like some watcher of the skies when a new planet swims into his ken. When his second book arrived and topped his first, even Keats could offer no poetry to express the joy it brought, the assurance that Mr. Zindel was no one-book writer."[15]

Whereas, Josh Greenfeld in a 1970 *New York Times* book review criticized Zindel for a lack of

Zindel co-authored the screenplay for "Runaway Train." Jon Voight and Eric Roberts starred in the 1985, Golan-Globus production.

honesty: "How do you reach the young, the teenagers? In books, as in life, I do not know. But neither, I think, does Mr. Zindel. For I do know that fiction must offer truth in the guise of illusion, not illusion instead of the truth. And the one thing our Now children can sense most assuredly, as they peer across that well-known gap at their generators, is the scent of adult con."[16]

Because Zindel's young adult novels have recurring themes of abusive adults and desperate teenagers, he has met with criticism. He believes that he is confronting the reality of teenage life. "Teenagers *have* to rebel. It's part of the growing process. In effect, I try to show them they aren't alone in condemning parents and teachers as enemies or ciphers. I believe I must convince my readers that I am on their side; I know it's a continuing battle to get through the years between twelve and twenty—an abrasive time. And so I write always from their own point of view."[17]

"The way I see my world is reflected in what I write. I find the way I see the world constantly undergoes transition. This is part of a maturation process, part of the experiences that go on. But again very seriously I feel there's a type of biological clock that allows certain insights into the world and into life, and those change. The fearlessness that teenagers have about death is no longer a fearlessness that I have. When I look at most of my work I see the words 'bathos' and hyperbole ringing out, which was once diagnosed as my style of seeing things—things exaggerated. In that exaggeration I am able to see the world exaggerated as a place of home which, in a sense, can be the dream of the nonexistence of death. Through pathos and hyperbole I can see the world as one of the most hilarious and comic places that there can be to live. Then, by the use of these qualities again, I can look at another element and see the world as quite ghastly, see it through very morbid eyes and find everything threatening and dangerous. So there's a great complexity of these feelings.

"These themes have been repeated in my work. So in a sense, what I'm telling you is self-analysis which really is not as valuable as a person with a more objective viewpoint, the critic, the reader who follows my works, who can look at them and see the themes which are repeated over and over again and that in a sense tell what the author's true vision of the world is. So what I think of the world really is reflected through my books. It's in transi-

A BANTAM STARFIRE BOOK

SENIOR YEAR ISN'T THE END OF
HIGH SCHOOL — IT'S THE BEGINNING OF LIFE!

PAUL ZINDEL

AUTHOR OF THE PIGMAN

MY DARLING,
MY HAMBURGER

Cover from the paperback edition of Zindel's second novel.

tion and like the motion of being keys on a piano: I just play different ones at different times, but what I do learn now, and what I'm concerned about now, is how to maintain the most sensible level of happiness and fulfillment for myself, while at the same time trying to satisfy the demands of society which are to bring innovation to civilization, to institutions, to make contributions which make the world a better place to live. So that really I try to satisfy both. I see the world as a problem solving situation, and the solution of those problems through fiction seems to be the adventure that I've chosen for myself."[6]

Zindel's mother's prediction came to pass when on April 7, 1970, *Marigolds* opened Off-Broadway at the Mercer-O'Casey Theatre to rave reviews. He received the Drama Critic's Circle Award, the Obie for the best American play, and the Drama

Desk Award for the most promising play. *Marigolds* was then moved to Broadway to the New Theatre. Zindel became the second Off-Broadway playwright to win the Pulitzer Prize for Drama. "I was watching 'King Kong' on TV when the news came about the Pulitzer Prize. All I knew was that whatever this prize was, it was going to make me have more friends and maybe bring love into my life because I was a very unhappy person. I was immediately whisked off to Hollywood. It was all very preposterous and exciting and corrupt and fun and damning and useful. The prize brings with it many curses and many blessings."[5]

The play's success brought financial rewards. "The first thing you do when you are handed a lot of money, you have the power to be whoever you were inside all along. Everybody says, 'Oh, he's so ugly now that he's become famous.' They're always complaining about people who suddenly become mean. You're mean all along; it's just when you have the money you have a chance to test that meanness. You also find out all the things you thought were a god, or all the things that limited you are no longer a proper excuse. The first thing you should do is crack up. It's like all the stops are pulled out. It's very easy, like I used to do, to go off on tremendous benders to Mexico and team up with lots of young kids, and try to keep up with their water glasses of stingers as they down them and rush down the coast and go swimming with pearl divers. You're on a path to really crack up."[18]

February 25, 1971. Zindel's next play *And Miss Reardon Drinks a Little* opened on Broadway at New York's Morosco Theatre. The story involves the three Reardon sisters who have been permanently scarred by a neurotic, tyrannical mother, now deceased. "I now know how much of the family is in the play. I have felt faint and even had to leave the theater because seeing the scenes played was such an overwhelming experience. I'm just beginning to understand the role of the emotions in our lives."[19]

With the emotional exhaustion of reworking the play (originally written in 1966), and the disappointment of mixed reviews, Zindel entered psychoanalysis. "The pattern is set when you're born. Children come into the world in good shape, usually. But they don't own the world. They are ruled. And parents are cruel in ways they don't recognize, really hard on kids. Even good, caring, loving parents. That situation makes for masochism in the child, any child, because nobody can measure up to expectations. Then the kids go to school where they learn the formal way of pretending to behave according to acceptable values. But they're still warped children, suppressing deep feelings that have to come out some way. That's when the masochism becomes hostility....Most grow up to release hostility in humor, but usually it's hurtful humor. All the pain felt and inflicted comes from feeling inferior inside.

"To linger in that state and really sink to the depths of self-pity is worthless. It can lead to suicide, at worst, or lasting misery. The thing, then, is to pull yourself out of masochism, hostility, and up to the next stage: setting goals. But this can cause more trouble, the exaggeration of creative plans, getting into unreality, larger-than-life dreams of glory."[20]

"...I began having heart attacks. They weren't real. I was down in Mexico, and starting in August I had violent heart spasms, which they said was angina. From there it went to brain tumors. From there it went to potassium deficiency.

"I had a checkup, two weeks in the hospital, and started to go to a psychoanalyst. Oh, well, yes—I'd had fifty sessions of therapy when I was fifteen and out of a TB sanitorium, with a man that never said *one word* to me.

"So now I'm driving, I'm on the road to Virginia, and I have a seizure: palpitations, malaise. I had a six o'clock appointment I wanted to keep, and I'm lying there in the motel in the position good for heart patients, saying: 'Jesus, they told me this was imaginary.' And then I remembered Freud, and remembered having passed some sign on the road.

"I couldn't remember exactly, but I did remember Freud writing about a certain gate and graveyard in Vienna that whenever he looked up at it, something written on it, he passed out. I knew if I could think of that sign I passed just before the attack....

"I had to think about it for about half an hour. I was even going to drive back and look at it. Now this is what the sign said: MARYLAND. This is my mother...buried in...WOODLAND. The moment I realized that, the whole illness just fell right off me and I was stark raving healthy."[3]

October 25, 1973. Married Bonnie Hildebrand. "...She was publicity director at the Cleveland Playhouse when they were doing *Marigolds.* She's a girl from New York who had a Gypsy Rose Lee type of mother who trained Bonnie to tap-dance on toe. She died when Bonnie was sixteen, leaving her with the major talent of tap-dancing on toe, which was going out of fashion.

"When I met Bonnie she was married to a psychologist who was running suicide clinics. She divorced him about a year later and we started living together. At that time I was going to a psychoanalyst six days a week, and this psychoanalyst made me pay $360 a week whether I was in town or not.

"I decided not to let him get away with that, so if I was out of New York I would call him and take the hour on the phone, which he resented. Eventually I got smart and decided to let Bonnie take over a few of those hours when I was away...."[20]

1974. Son, David, born; two years later daughter, Elizabeth Claire. "Fatherhood? I really wanted it. You see, I really think I had one enormous teenage from thirteen to around thirty-seven...."[20]

Struggling to overcome many old fears, Zindel made an effort to break down personal barriers, but was unable to entirely avoid a mid-life crisis. "I was afraid of flying for fifteen years, but last May [1975], I booked eleven flights in a row, including Leningrad and Moscow. Luckily we took the baby along, a great icebreaker. People would come

Jacket from the 1984 novel.

running up and we'd have these baby parties in front of the Museum of Religion and Atheism.

"But in Paris, after two months of traveling, I got ill, had a breakdown of the mental processes. Because you can only take so many images without your brain going kaput. I heard Candy Bergen on the tube say the same thing happened to her in China. But what it was, I was turning forty."[20]

1977. Zindel's third play, *Ladies at the Alamo*, opened on Broadway. In it Zindel continued his exploration of women with five strong females who are involved in a power struggle for control of an important theater complex in Texas. "This play was a complete departure for me. Until now, I've written mainly very personal psychological dramas like *Marigolds*. With *Ladies* I've relied more on my imagination and technique and less on my memories."[21]

Zindel and his family moved to California. "I think I was headed very much to becoming a first class hack in this town. I think it was because I had bought the whole California dream.

"I married a wife who had many aspirations as a princess. We have children who go to the best schools. We're wedged in between Walter Matthau and Angie Dickinson with Roger Moore across the road. I felt suddenly I was maybe ten steps ahead on some kind of game where I didn't belong.

"I also found it was a major corruption to my writing and I also kind of knew what I was doing 'cause I did pull a novel out of it."[10]

By 1981, he was ready to return to New York and to Broadway. "I'm excited to be coming back, I'm going to do my best to get to the top of the heap. I'm not cynical about Broadway, it's terrific. It's the platform for our best writers, and the marketplace of our dreams."[22]

"No human being particularly loves the microcosm to which he is born. His life is a wandering from one sphere to another, each equally filled with imperfection. But it is a part of the human spirit for man to stalk a perfect world, a world he can control. In that is the primordial thrust which demands that Theater exist. The uniqueness of the Theater is that it is the ultimate companion of reality. If one can cause a moment to happen on the stage, it is quite possible that one can make it happen in reality. The Theater is the least illusionary phenomenon in the world. Other mediums can cut, fade, lip-sync, overlap, dissolve, but a moment must be truer, more real on the stage.

"Because Theater demands greater honesty, people now wonder if it is dying. It just happens that little honesty can emerge at this particular time of chaos in our world because nobody knows what the hell is going on. No wonder no one's writing anything terribly honest. Frauds succeed right and left in television and the movies because there are more guiles, more hiding places for their dishonesty. Unhappily, at this moment even our theaters are laced with transient fakers—special effects personnel who are determined to lure the public by being cruder, lewder and nuder...."[7]

"I think the theater is becoming a director's world. Technique, special effects, a lot of theatrical tools. I love the tools, I love the nudity, the pigments opening up, but as far as *content*—there is no content.

"I feel that the playwrights are failing. They seize on the most obvious problems and present them in a scientific, journalistic manner, gleaning from the surface. They are titillated by the obvious and they fail to articulate the atomic age. Arthur Kopit failed to accomplish anything for the poor Indians or for anyone else in 'Indians.' Sam Shepard merely mentions obvious problems in 'Operation Sidewinder,' without adding any understanding, any new insight."[2]

"Sometimes the audience overtakes certain aspects of its Theater. At the moment, the lives of the audiences are often far more theatrical and dramatic than what is available to them on the stage. The public has stolen the greasepaint and raped the wardrobe mistress. Histrionics have taken to the streets—braying, battling and bludgeoning. Our country has taken on the accoutrements of theater. But no one can kill Theater. It can become dormant for a period of time, but Theater is so inextricably a voice, a device for survival, that man will rediscover it within himself time and time again. Thank God, the theatrical drought cannot ever last for too long a time. Man eventually tires of dishonesty and crawls off alone, perhaps in a dark place, to commune with his instinct once more. His dream is of a brilliant world, a universe too colossal and golden for him alone to create in totality, and so he marks out a space in the sand. Into it he places actors, and to those actors he gives words. Move for me. Dance for me, he whispers. Here in this place I will glimpse what paradise can be."[7]

Footnote sources:

[1] "Zindel Having Problems and Lots of Fun Too," *Morning Telegraph*, July 30, 1970.

[2] Guy Flatley, "And Gamma Rays Did It!," *New York Times*, April 19, 1970.

[3] Jerry Tallmer, "Hearts and Marigolds," *New York Post*, May 8, 1971.

[4] Stephen M. Silverman, "How 'Moon's' Zindel Stays Happy in His Work," *New York Post*, March 6, 1978.

[5] Sidney Fields, "Author Has Chemistry for Kids," *Daily News*, March 9, 1978.

[6] Paul Janeczko, "In Their Own Words, an Interview with Paul Zindel," *English Journal*, October, 1977.

[7] Paul Zindel, "The Theatre Is Born within Us," *New York Times*, July 26, 1970.

[8] Laurie Winer, "A Talk with Paul Zindel," *Other Stages*, May 20, 1982.

[9] P. Zindel, *The Effect of Gamma Rays on Man-in-the-Moon Marigolds*, Bantam, 1971.

[10] Sean Mitchell, "Grown-up Author's Insight into Adolescent Struggles," *Dallas Times Herald*, June 27, 1979.

[11] Diane Farrell, "The Pigman," *Horn Book*, February, 1969.

[12] Peter Fanning, "Nasties in the Woodshed," *The Times Educational Supplement* (London), November 21, 1980.

[13] Marilyn R. Singer, "My Darling, My Hamburger," *School Library Journal*, Movember, 1969.

[14] John R. Townsend, "It Takes More than Pot and the Pill," *New York Times Book Review*, November 9, 1969.

[15] Lavina Russ, *Publishers Weekly*, September 22, 1969.

[16] Josh Greenfeld, *The New York Times Book Review*, May 24, 1970.

[17] Jean Mercier, "Paul Zindel," *Publishers Weekly*, December 5, 1977.

[18] T. H. McCulloh, "The Effect of Planets on Paul Zindel," *Drama Logue*, July 22, 1982.

[19] *Sunday News* (New York), March 14, 1970.

[20] J. Tallmer, "Paul Zindel," *New York Post*, November 20, 1976.

[21] Patricia Bosworth, "The Effect of Five Actresses on a Play-in-Progress," *New York Times*, April 3, 1977.

[22] Rebecca Moorehouse, "Stardust and Marigolds," *Playbill*, September, 1981.

■ For More Information See

New York Times, June 27, 1965, October 4, 1966, March 8, 1971.

Horn Book, February, 1969 (p. 61), April, 1970 (p. 171), June, 1971 (p. 308), October, 1976.

Times Literary Supplement, April 3, 1969 (p. 355), April 2, 1971 (p. 385), December 10, 1976 (p. 1549), April 7, 1978 (p. 383).

School Library Journal, November, 1969 (p. 137), April, 1980 (p. 129), October, 1980 (p. 160).

Clive Barnes, "Theatre: 'Gamma Rays on Marigolds,'" *New York Times*, April 8, 1970.

Village Voice, April 16, 1970.

Guy Flatley, "...And Gamma Rays Did It!," *New York Times*, April 19, 1970.

Time, April 20, 1970.

Harold Clurman, "Theatre," *Nation*, April 20, 1970.

Scholastic Voice, April 27, 1970.

Library Journal, June 15, 1970 (p. 2317).

Tom Prideaux, "Man with a Bag of Marigold Dust," *Life*, July 4, 1970.

Paul Zindel, "The Theater Is Born within Us," *New York Times*, July 26, 1970.

"Marigolds' Author Complains: Zindel Having Problems, and Lots of Fun, Too," *New Yorker*, December 5, 1970, March 6, 1971.

Washington Post, January 27, 1971.

C. Barnes, "Theatre: Reardon Sisters Arrive," *New York Times*, February 26, 1971.

New York Sunday News, March 14, 1971.

Newsday, May 4, 1971, May 8, 1971.

"Prizewinning Marigolds," *Time*, May 17, 1971.

Martha E. Ward and Dorothy A. Marquardt, *Authors of Books for Young People*, Scarecrow, 1971.

Variety, June 17, 1972, July 28, 1982 (p. 18), August 20, 1982, April 20, 1983 (p. 188), December 18, 1985 (p. 66).

English Journal, November, 1972 (p. 1163).

B. Gill, "The Theatre," *New Yorker*, November 25, 1972.

Elementary English, October, 1974 (p. 941).

James T. Henke, "Six Characters in Search of the Family: The Novels of Paul Zindel," *Children's Literature*, 1976.

Contemporary Literary Criticism, Volume 6, Gale, 1976, Volume 26, 1983.

Patricia O'Haire, "5 for the 'Alamo,'" *Daily News* (New York), February 15, 1977 (p. 22).

C. Barnes, "The Stage: 'Ladies at the Alamo,'" *New York Times*, April 8, 1977.

Bulletin of the Center for Children's Books, May, 1978, October, 1978, December, 1984.

Stanley Hoffman, "Winning, Losing, but above All Taking Risks: A Look at the Novels of Paul Zindel," *Lion and the Unicorn*, fall, 1978.

Children's Literature Review, Volume 3, Gale, 1978.

D. L. Kirkpatrick, editor, *Twentieth-Century Children's Writers*, St. Martin's, 1978, 2nd edition, 1983.

David Rees, "Viewed from a Squashed Eyeball," in *The Marble in the Water: Essays on Contemporary Writers of Fiction for Children and Young Adults*, Horn Book, 1980.

Times Educational Supplement, November 21, 1980 (p. 32).

Voice of Youth Advocates, October, 1981 (p. 40).

"Paul Zindel's Play: Memories of People Living Half Lives," *New York Times*, October 23, 1981 (p. C2).

"A Theatregoer's Notebook," *Playbill*, October, 1981.

"Notes on People," *New York Times*, May 19, 1981.

Sally Holmes Holtze, *Fifth Book of Junior Authors and Illustrators*, H. W. Wilson, 1983.

William Goldstein, "Coming Attractions: What 13 Well-Known Authors Are (or Are Not) Working on Now," *Publishers Weekly*, January 6, 1984.

"Peoplescape," *Los Angeles*, March, 1984.

Wilson Library Bulletin, December, 1984, January, 1985.

Dictionary of Literary Biography, Volume 7, Gale, 1983, Volume 52, 1986.

Publishers Weekly, July 26, 1985.

Cumulative Index

Author/Artist Index

The following index gives the number of the volume in which an author/artist's biographical sketch appears.

Aiken, Joan 1924- 1
Alexander, Lloyd 1924- 1
Bonham, Frank 1914- 1
Carpenter, John 1948- 2
Colman, Hila 1
Ellis, Bret Easton 1964- 2
Forster, E. M. 1879-1970 2
Guisewite, Cathy 1950- 2
Hamilton, Virginia 1936- 2
Herriot, James 1916- 1
Hinton, S. E. 1950- 2
Jones, Chuck 1912- 2
Jordan, June 1936- 2

Keillor, Garrison 1942- 2
Kennedy, William 1928- 1
Kerr, M. E. 1927- 2
King, Stephen 1947- 1
Klein, Norma 1938- 2
Kundera, Milan 1929- 2
Larson, Gary 1950- 1
L'Engle, Madeleine 1918- 1
Lloyd Webber, Andrew 1948- 1
Lucas, George 1944- 1
Morrison, Toni 1931- 1
Mowat, Farley 1921- 1
Pascal, Francine 1938- 1

Paterson, Katherine 1932- 1
Paulsen, Gary 1939- 2
Peck, Richard 1934- 1
Pinkwater, Daniel Manus 1941- 1
Sachs, Marilyn 1927- 2
Sagan, Carl 1934- 2
Salinger, J. D. 1919- 2
Shepard, Sam 1943- 1
Strasser, Todd 1950- 2
Taylor, Theodore 1921- 2
Wersba, Barbara 1932- 2
Zindel, Paul 1936- 2